THE LETTERS OF BEETHOVEN

BEETHOVEN
From the oil portrait by Georg Friedrich Waldmüller (1823)
(*By courtesy of Die Piperdrucke Verlags-GmbH, Munich*)

THE LETTERS
OF
BEETHOVEN

Collected,
Translated and Edited with an Introduction,
Appendixes, Notes and Indexes

by

EMILY ANDERSON

VOLUME III

LONDON
MACMILLAN & CO LTD
NEW YORK · ST MARTIN'S PRESS
1961

MACMILLAN AND COMPANY LIMITED
London Bombay Calcutta Madras Melbourne

THE MACMILLAN COMPANY OF CANADA LIMITED
Toronto

ST MARTIN'S PRESS INC
New York

LIST OF LETTERS

Letters not in the German collected editions are marked *
Letters to which all missing passages have been restored are marked †

VOLUME III

1823

1823

1823

1823

1824

1824

1825

1825

b

1825

1826

1826

1827

LIST OF APPENDIXES

These Appendixes include fifteen letters and other documents not in the German collected editions and one letter to which the missing passages have been restored.

LIST OF ABBREVIATIONS

AMZ	= *Allgemeine Musikalische Zeitung.* Leipzig.
Breuning	= Gerhard von Breuning, *Aus dem Schwarzspanierhause.* Vienna, 1874.
DKMZ	= *Deutsche Kunst- und Musik-Zeitung.* Vienna.
DM	= *Die Musik.* Berlin and Leipzig.
FRBF	= Theodor von Frimmel, *Beethoven-Forschung.* Vienna, 1911–1928.
FRBH	= Theodor von Frimmel, *Beethoven-Handbuch.* Two volumes. Leipzig, 1926.
FRBJ	= Theodor von Frimmel, *Beethovenjahrbuch.* Two volumes. Leipzig, 1908–1909.
FRBS	= Theodor von Frimmel, *Beethoven-Studien.* Two volumes. Leipzig, 1905–1906.
FRNB	= Theodor von Frimmel, *Neue Beethoveniana.* Vienna, 1890.
GA	= *Beethovens Werke. Kritische Gesamtausgabe.* 25 volumes. Breitkopf & Härtel, Leipzig. 1866–1868, 1888.
Hanslick	= Eduard Hanslick, *Geschichte des Concertwesens in Wien.* Vienna, 1869.
Kalischer (Kal.)	= Alfred C. Kalischer, *Beethovens sämtliche Briefe.* Five volumes. Berlin, 1907–1908. Vol. I revised by Kalischer. Berlin, 1909.
KFR	= Kalischer-Frimmel. Volumes II and III of Kalischer's edition of Beethoven's letters, revised and enlarged by T. v. Frimmel. Berlin, 1910–1911.
KHV	= Georg Kinsky. *Das Werk Beethovens. Thematisch-bibliographisches Verzeichnis seiner sämtlichen vollendeten Kompositionen.* Nach dem Tode des Verfassers abgeschlossen und herausgegeben von Hans Halm. Munich, 1955. (The works not hitherto given an Opus No. are here numbered and listed as WoO, *i.e.* Werk ohne Opuszahl, ' Work without Opus No.'.)
KK	= Kastner-Kapp, *Ludwig van Beethovens sämtliche Briefe, herausgegeben von Emerich Kastner.* New edition, revised and enlarged by Dr. Julius Kapp. Leipzig, 1923.
Köchel	= *83 Originalbriefe Ludwig van Beethovens an den Erzherzog Rudolph, herausgegeben von Dr. Ludwig, Ritter von Köchel.* Vienna, 1865.

KST	= Emerich Kastner, *Ludwig van Beethovens sämtliche Briefe.* One volume. Leipzig, 1910.
Moscheles	= Ignace Moscheles, *The Life of Beethoven.* Two volumes. London, 1841. This work is a translation of the first edition of Schindler's biography of Beethoven (Münster, 1840), edited with footnotes and some additional material.
NBJ	= *Neues Beethoven-Jahrbuch*, edited by Adolf Sandberger. Augsburg and Braunschweig.
NFP	= *Neue Freie Presse.* Vienna.
NMZ	= *Neue Musik-Zeitung.* Stuttgart and Leipzig.
Nohl	= Dr. Ludwig Nohl, *Briefe Beethovens.* Volume I. Stuttgart, 1865. *Neue Briefe Beethovens.* Volume II. Stuttgart, 1867.
Nottebohm	= Gustav Nottebohm, *Beethoveniana.* Leipzig, 1872. *Zweite Beethoveniana.* Leipzig, 1887.
NV	= Gustav Nottebohm, *Ludwig van Beethoven. Thematisches Verzeichnis.* Second edition. Leipzig, 1925.
Peters	= L. v. Beethoven. *Seine an den Verlag von Hoffmeister und Kühnel, später C. F. Peters, Leipzig, gerichteten Briefe.* C. F. Peters, Leipzig. No date.
Prelinger [P.]	= Fritz Prelinger, *Ludwig van Beethovens sämtliche Briefe und Aufzeichnungen.* Five volumes. Vienna and Leipzig, 1907–1911.
Schiedermair	= Ludwig Schiedermair, *Der junge Beethoven.* Leipzig, 1925. New edition. Bonn, 1947.
Schindler	= Anton Schindler, *Ludwig van Beethoven.* Fifth edition, with an introduction and notes by Fritz Volbach. Münster, 1927.
Schmidt	= Leopold Schmidt, *Beethoven-Briefe.* Berlin, 1909.
Schöne	= Dr. Alfred Schöne, *Briefe von Beethoven an Marie Gräfin Erdödy und Magister Brauchle.* Leipzig, 1867.
Schünemann	= Georg Schünemann, *Ludwig van Beethovens Konversationshefte.* Three volumes. Berlin, 1941–1943.
Sonneck	= O. G. Sonneck, *Beethoven Letters in America.* New York, 1927.
TDR	= Alexander Wheelock Thayer, *Ludwig van Beethovens Leben.* Von Hermann Deiters neubearbeitet und von Hugo Riemann ergänzt. Five volumes. Leipzig, 1917–1923. Third edition.
	This biography, originally written in English, was translated into German by Deiters. The first three volumes were published by Schneider, Berlin, in 1866, 1872 and 1879. After Thayer's and Deiters's death the fourth and fifth volumes were completed by Riemann and published in 1907 and 1908.

LIST OF ABBREVIATIONS

TK
=A. W. Thayer, *Life of L. v. Beethoven*. Edited, revised and amended from the original English manuscript by H. E. Krehbiel. Three volumes. New York, 1921.

Unger
=Dr. Max Unger, *Ludwig van Beethoven und seine Verleger S. A. Steiner und Tobias Haslinger in Wien, Adolf Martin Schlesinger in Berlin*. Berlin and Vienna, 1921.

WRBN
=Franz Wegeler und Ferdinand Ries, *Biographische Notizen über Ludwig van Beethoven*. Coblenz, 1838. With a supplement by F. Wegeler. Coblenz, 1845. Reprint by A. C. Kalischer. Berlin and Leipzig, 1906.

Zekert
=Dr. Otto Zekert, *Apotheker Johann van Beethoven*. Vienna, 1928.

ZMW
=*Zeitschrift für Musikwissenschaft*. Leipzig.

OTHER ABBREVIATIONS

P.P.
=Praemissis Praemittendis, *i.e.* with the necessary introduction, a form of address occasionally used in business letters.

P.T.
=Pleno Titulo, or Praemissis Titulis, a formal type of address similar to P.P.

WoO
=Werke ohne Opuszahl. Cf. *KHV*.

NOTES ON MONEY VALUES

THE following notes have been compiled from information contained in Muret-Saunders's German-English Dictionary, in Professor W. H. Bruford's *Germany in the Eighteenth Century* (Cambridge, 1935), in Professor O. E. Deutsch's *Schubert: A Documentary Biography* (London, 1946) and in the letters of Beethoven, who occasionally quotes the equivalent values of coins and frequently refers to the fluctuating rates of exchange between Austria and some other countries. As in the early nineteenth century there were several standards in common use for the minting of gold and silver coins, the values here given are of necessity only approximate. Furthermore, no allowance has been made for the change in purchasing power of English money since the eighteenth century.

GERMANY AND AUSTRIA

Taking the South German kreuzer as the standard, the following equivalent values of small coins are obtained:

1 kreuzer = four pfennige, about one halfpenny.
[1 heller = about half a farthing.
1 pfennig = less than one heller, a mite.]
1 groschen = about three kreuzer, or 1½d., the value quoted in Sir George Smart's *Journals* during his visit to Vienna in 1825.
1 gulden (60 kreuzer) = about two shillings.
1 reichsthaler (90 kreuzer) = about three shillings.
1 rheinthaler (120 kreuzer) = about four shillings.

The following gold coins were in common use in Germany and Austria:

1 ducat (used all over Europe) = 4½ gulden, about nine shillings.
1 pistole (originally a Spanish coin, used all over Europe) = 7½ gulden, about fifteen shillings.
1 friedrich d'or (used chiefly in Prussia) = 8 gulden, about sixteen shillings.

1 carolin (used chiefly in South Germany) =9 gulden, about eighteen shillings.

The French louis d'or, the value of which fluctuated considerably, was worth slightly more than two ducats, about twenty shillings.

The Italian zecchino (a Venetian gold coin) was worth slightly more than one ducat, about ten shillings.

During the Napoleonic wars the Austrian State went bankrupt, and by a *Finanz-Patent* promulgated on February 20, 1811 and put into force three weeks later, an emergency currency was introduced. Redemption bonds (*Einlösungsscheine*) were substituted for bank-notes at the rate of one for five. Thus paper money was depreciated to one-fifth of its nominal value and converted into a new State paper currency, called *Wiener Währung* (i.e. Viennese currency, V.C.). Another currency which continued to be used after the introduction of the new paper currency was the old *Konventions-münze* (i.e. Assimilated coinage, A.C.). This currency had been adopted in 1753 by a treaty with Bavaria and was based on the 20-gulden rate, called *Konventionsfuss*. There were 60 kreuzer to the gulden both in the old currency and in the new. But from 1811 onwards 5 gulden V.C. were worth only about 2 gulden A.C. Hence Beethoven's income of 4000 gulden guaranteed by his three patrons in 1809 became in 1811 approximately 1600 gulden. How-ever, the original value of his income was eventually restored, because the quarterly payments were soon made in redemption bonds.

LIST OF ILLUSTRATIONS

VOLUME III

xxix

LIST OF ILLUSTRATIONS

LIST OF FACSIMILES OF LETTERS

FACSIMILE OF MUSIC

1823

1823

(1121) *To Count Moritz Dietrichstein*

[*MS not traced*] [1]

YOUR EXCELLENCY!   [VIENNA, *c. January* 1, 1823]

I hear that the post of Imperial and Royal Chamber Music Composer, which Teyber [2] held, is again to be filled, and I gladly apply for it, particularly if, as I fancy, one of the requirements is that I should occasionally provide a composition for the Imperial Court. Seeing that I have composed, and am still composing, works in all branches of music, I do not consider that I can be accused of taking too great a liberty if I recommend myself to Your Excellency's favour, the more so as you know that my position is not exactly very brilliant and that, had it not been for my poor health, I should *unfortunately* have had to leave Vienna long ago in order to lead a life free of anxiety for the future.

Your Excellency's most devoted servant
BEETHOVEN

(1122) *To Georg August von Griesinger*

[*Autograph in the Beethovenhaus, Bonn, H. C. Bodmer collection*]

SIR!   [VIENNA, *January* 7, 1823]

Since I intend to publish my grand Mass, which I finished composing some time ago, not as an engraved work but in a way which I consider more honourable and perhaps more advantageous for me, I am asking you for your advice and, if possible, for your good offices in this undertaking. I am thinking of offering the work to all the great courts.[3] As I

[1] Taken from an article by Anton Schlossar published in *DM.*, Berlin, 1910, 13, p. 46. According to Schlossar this letter, which bears no address, was certainly intended for Count Moritz Dietrichstein.

[2] Anton Teyber (1754–1822) became a cellist at the Vienna Court Opera in 1792 and eventually composer of chamber music and teacher of music to the Imperial children. He died on November 18, 1822. His post of Chamber Music Composer was never filled.

[3] King Frederick August of Saxony became a subscriber, and on November 20, 1823, Beethoven sent a copy for him to the Saxon Legation in Vienna by his nephew. See Letter 1243.

am quite inexperienced in all matters not pertaining to my
art, you would infinitely oblige me if you would communicate
your views to my brother, the bearer of this letter. I would
have called on you myself, but I am again somewhat indisposed.
Since I have always been accustomed to regard you as interested in the progress of art and in the advancement of its
disciples, I am convinced that you will condescend to further
my wishes by your sympathetic interest —

I remain, Sir, with kindest regards, your most devoted

BEETHOVEN

(1123) *To Prince Nikolas Galitzin, St. Petersburg* [1]

[*MS in the Musée Adam Mickiewicz, Paris*] [2]

VOTRE ALTESSE !   VIENNA, *January* 25, 1823

Je n'aurais point manqué de répondre plutôt à Votre
lettre du 9. Nov., si la foule de mes affaires ne m'avait empêché
de vous écrire.[3] C'est avec bien du plaisir que j'ai observé
que Votre Altesse s'approche des ouvrages de mon esprit.
Vous désirez d'avoir quelques quatuors ; comme je vois, que
vous cultivez le violoncelle, je prendrai soin de vous contenter
en ce point.   Etant contraint de vivre des produits de mon
esprit, il faut que je prenne la liberté de fixer l'honoraire de
50 ducats pour un quatuor. Si votre Altesse y consent, je la
prie de bientôt m'en avertir, et d'adresser cette somme au
banquier Hénikstein à Vienne ; je m'oblige d'achever le
1^{mier} quatuor à la fin du mois de Février, ou au plus tard à
la mi-mars.[4]

---

[1] Prince Nikolas Borissowitch Galitzin (1794–1860) was a gifted amateur
cellist and an ardent promoter of musical enterprises in St. Petersburg. His
enthusiastic letters to Beethoven, which are quoted in full in *TDR* V, App. II,
indicate that he had a profound understanding of music in general. He was
largely responsible for the first performance in its entirety of the 'Missa Solemnis'
at St. Petersburg in April, 1824.

[2] Written by Karl and signed by Beethoven.

[3] Galitzin's first letter to Beethoven, dated November 9, 1822, is quoted in
TDR IV, 324. In it he describes himself as 'aussi passionné amateur de musique
que grand admirateur de votre talent', asks Beethoven to compose one or two
quartets for a fee which the latter would fix, and adds that his instrument is the
cello.

[4] This quartet, Op. 127, was not sent to Galitzin until March, 1825.

En vous témoignant mon vrai intérêt de votre talent de musique, je remercie votre Altesse des égards qu'elle a bien voulu me marquer, en me choisissant pour augmenter, s'il est possible, votre amour pour la musique. J'ai l'hoñeur d'être
de votre Altesse
le très-humble serviteur
LOUIS VAN BEETHOVEN [1]

(1124) *To Anton Felix Schindler*

[*Autograph in the Deutsche Staatsbibliothek, Berlin*]

[VIENNA, *January*, 1823]

Please come to me as soon as possible about that Swedish story,[2] for I must go out afterwards. Breakfast will be ready —

(1125) *To Anton Felix Schindler*

[*Autograph in the Deutsche Staatsbibliothek, Berlin*]

[VIENNA, *January*, 1823]

MOST EXCELLENT OPTIMUS OPTIME !

I am sending you herewith the calendar. The paper markings indicate all the legations in Vienna. If you could just extract from it quickly a list of the courts, we could then expedite the task in hand.[3] By the way, as soon as my brother butts in, please — *co-operate with him.* For, if you don't, we may well experience *sorrow* instead of *joy* —

Do try to get hold of some philanthropist who will lend me money on the security of a bank share, so that, in the first place, I may not put the generosity of my exceptional friends, the B[rentanos], too severely to the test, and so that I myself may not be financially embarrassed owing to the holding up of this money, for which I have to thank the splendid arrangements and precautionary measures of my *dear* and worthy brother —

[1] For Galitzin's reply, dated February 23, 1823, see *TDR* V, 552-553.
[2] Schindler has written on the autograph 'about the Swedish diploma'. On December 22, 1822, Beethoven had been made an honorary member of the Royal Academy of Arts and Sciences, Stockholm. Cf. Letter 1117, p. 983, n. 2.
[3] I.e. of making a list of possible subscribers to the 'Missa Solemnis' and sending them a circular letter.

It would be pleasant if you were to turn up at Mariahilf¹ at about half past three this afternoon or perhaps in the morning—
Other people must not notice that we should like to have the *money* ² —

(1126) *To Anton Felix Schindler*

[Autograph in the Deutsche Staatsbibliothek, Berlin]

[VIENNA, *January*, 1823]

EXTRAORDINARILY EXCELLENT FELLOW!!
Don't forget to produce the bank share as surety —
Please fetch *Karl* at Blöchlinger's at about one o'clock and drive him to my rooms. You can then take a carriage and fetch Bach who will most certainly come. Or just take a carriage with Karl from the Josephstadt and drive straight to me and then from me to Bach —
All good wishes, excellent fellow, yours
BEET ³ —

(1127) *To Anton Felix Schindler*

[Autograph in the Deutsche Staatsbibliothek, Berlin]

DEAR S[CHINDLER], [VIENNA, *January*, 1823]
Don't forget about the b[ank] s[hare].⁴ It is extremely necessary to see to this. I should not like to have legal action taken against me for absolutely nothing at all. My brother's behaviour in this affair is quite typical of him — The tailor has been ordered for today. Meanwhile I trust that by using kindness I can put him off for today —
In great haste, yours ⁵

¹ Mariahilf was, and still is, a suburb of Vienna. Beethoven is evidently referring to some coffee house where he and Schindler frequently met.
² Schindler adds the remark 'because we sorely need it'.
³ The remainder of the signature has been torn off.
⁴ Schindler noted on the verso of the autograph: 'In 1823 Steiner and Haslinger threatened to summons Beethoven in connexion with the 800 gulden V.C. which he owed the firm; and this was before he had received any payment for the copies of the "Missa Solemnis". So he was obliged to sell a bank share in order to satisfy these creditors.' See also Schindler, II, 41-43, where this letter is quoted.
⁵ This letter is not signed.

NB. I am not going out at all, for I am not feeling well. If you would like to come *to dinner*, then do so.[1]
Vous êtes invité de diner chez moi.[2]

(1128) *To Joseph Uibel* [3]

[Autograph in the Beethovenhaus, Bonn, H. C. Bodmer collection]

SIR !   [VIENNA, *January*, 1823]
It was not at all necessary for H[err] L[ind] to arrange for legal action to be taken against me. For I never denied the justice of his demands. It is true that my brother did consider his bill to be rather excessive in several particulars, even though formerly the cost of living was much higher. Nevertheless Herr Lind *finally* accepted *my invitation* to send his agent to my brother; and all this time I have been waiting for him to do so. But now as I see that he, H[err] L[ind], wants to revenge himself on me *who am innocent*, therefore, since it was previously my wish that this affair should be wound up, I will settle the bill tomorrow without delay —
With kindest regards I remain, Sir, your most devoted
                                                                  BEETHOVEN

(1129) *To Joseph Lind*

[Autograph in the Deutsche Staatsbibliothek, Berlin]

DEAR LIND !   [VIENNA, *January*, 1823]
I am coming to you on Wednesday, at about four o'clock in the afternoon at the latest, and shall then settle up everything —
                              Your most devoted
                                                                  BEETHOVEN

[1] The NB. is written on the left side of the recto.
[2] This sentence is written on the verso beside the address.
[3] Joseph Uibel was a lawyer, whose address in 1825 was in the Inner City Renngasse 153, near the hotel 'Zum Römischen Kaiser'.

(1130) *To Anton Felix Schindler*

[Autograph in the Deutsche Staatsbibliothek, Berlin]

[VIENNA, *January*, 1823]

There is nothing else to be done but to agree to the arrangement about the two sh[ares] as well, although I find it quite disproportionate.[1] Therefore be so kind as to make whatever arrangement you consider suitable. Come to me as soon as you have come to terms with yourself —

Your friend
BEETHOVEN

(1131) *To Anton Felix Schindler*

[Autograph in the Deutsche Staatsbibliothek, Berlin]

[VIENNA, *January*, 1823]

I see from my notebook [2] that you have doubts about that business with Diab[elli] concerning the Mass. So I beg you to come soon. In that case we will not give him the var[iations] either, for my brother knows someone who will take both works —

So we can discuss the matter with him —

Amicus
BEETHOVEN

(1132) *To Anton Felix Schindler* [3]

[Autograph in the Deutsche Staatsbibliothek, Berlin]

MOST EXCELLENT FELLOW!!   [VIENNA, *January*, 1823] [4]

In accordance with the following hattisherif [5] you are to appear at the Mariahilf coffee house at half past three this afternoon so that we may hear your statements about several

---

[1] See Schünemann, II, 347 ff, where the advisability of selling two bank shares is discussed with Schindler.

[2] Beethoven uses the word 'Büchel', referring possibly to one of his Conversation Books.

[3] Beethoven addressed this note: 'A Monsieur de Schindler, premier membre engage et attachè aux Faubourg de J[oseph]stadt'.

[4] Schindler dated this note: 1823, in the winter months.

[5] A Turkish government edict made irrevocable by the Sultan's mark.

punishable actions — Should this h[atti]s[herif] not reach you today, it is your bounden duty to be at my rooms at half past one tomorrow; and when you have partaken of bread and water you will be under arrest for 24 hours —

L.V.!! ≡ BTHVN

(1133) *To Ferdinand Ries, London*

[*Autograph in the Beethovenhaus, Bonn, H. C. Bodmer collection*]

MY DEAR, KIND RIES!   [VIENNA], *February* 5, 1823

So far I have received no further news about the symphony.[1]   Meanwhile you can certainly rely on receiving it, for I have made the acquaintance here of a very amiable and cultured man who has an appointment at our Imperial Embassy in London.[2]   He will undertake to assist me later in forwarding the symphony from Vienna to you in London, *so that it will soon be there.*   If I were not so poor as to have to live by my pen, I would not accept anything from the P[hilharmonic] Soc[iety]. As things are, however, I am obliged to wait until the fee for the symphony has been forwarded to Vienna.— But in order to give some proof of my affection for and confidence in that Society, I have already given to the aforementioned gentleman at the Imperial Embassy the overture I mentioned in my last letter.[3]   As he is leaving Vienna in a few days, he himself will hand it to you, my dear fellow, in London.   I suppose that *Messrs. Goldschmidt & Co.*[4] *will have your address.   If not, do give it to them* so that this man, who is so very obliging, may not spend a long time looking for you — I am leaving it to the Society to make the necessary arrangements about the overture.   The Society may keep it and the symphony too for 18 months.   For I would only publish it after that time. Now I have one more request.   My brother here, who can afford to keep a carriage and pair, has nevertheless tried to

[1] The ninth symphony, which Beethoven composed for the Philharmonic Society, London, but dedicated to King Friedrich Wilhelm III of Prussia. The score of the symphony was published by Schott in August, 1826, as Op. 125.
[2] This was Bauer, who was a secretary at the Austrian Embassy in London.
[3] Op. 124.   The letter referred to has not been traced.
[4] A London banking firm, to whom Beethoven usually addressed his letters for Ries.

make money out of me as well; and so, without asking me, he offered this very overture to a London publisher called Boosey. Do make Boosey understand that for the time being no decision can be taken about his being given the overture; and tell him that I will write about this myself — In this matter everything depends on the Philharmonic Society.[1] Just be so kind as to say that my brother made a mistake about the *overture* — In regard to other works about which my brother has written to Boosey, the latter, I fancy, could have them. I now realize that he *bought* them from me in order to make *money* out of them — O frater![2] Returning to the subject of the overture, I particularly request you to write to me as soon as you have received it and to let me know whether the P[hilharmonic] Soc[iety] will take it, for, if not, I would publish it soon — I have received *nothing* of the symphony you have dedicated to me. If I did not regard this dedication as a kind of challenge which I must take up, I would long ago have dedicated some work to you. But, *as things are*, I still think that I must first see your *work*; and how gladly would I express my thanks to you by means of some present. Indeed I am deeply in your debt for so much affection and for so many kindnesses you have shown me. If my health improves as the result of a cure at a watering-place which I am to take next summer, then I shall kiss your wife in London in 1824 —

Wholly your

BEETHOVEN

[1] The two sentences from 'Do' to 'Society' are added at the top of the third page.
[2] The whole passage from 'In regard' to 'frater' is added at the foot of the third page.

(1134) *To the Grand Duke Ludwig I of Hesse, Darmstadt* [1]

[*MS in the Hessisches Staatsarchiv, Darmstadt*] [2]

YOUR ROYAL HIGHNESS !   VIENNA, *February* 5, 1823

The undersigned has just finished his latest work which he considers to be the most excellent product of his mind. It is a grand solemn Mass for four solo voices, with choruses and a full grand orchestra; and it can also be performed as a grand oratorio.

He therefore cherishes the desire most humbly to send a copy of this Mass in score to Your Royal Highness and thus begs with all submission that Your Royal Highness would most graciously condescend to grant him the supreme permission to do so. Since, however, the copying of the score necessitates considerable expenses, the undersigned ventures most humbly to inform Your Royal Highness that for this great work he has fixed the moderate fee of 50 ducats; and he flatters himself that he will enjoy the exceptional honour of being allowed to count Your Royal Highness among the number of his distinguished subscribers —

Your Royal Highness's
most obedient
LUDWIG VAN BEETHOVEN

[1] Ludwig I (1753–1830) became Grand Duke of Hesse when the Electorate was made a Grand Duchy in 1806.

[2] This letter offering a manuscript copy of the 'Missa Solemnis' for 50 ducats was sent to several courts, embassies and legations and to a few influential persons. As the differences in the wording of these letters are quite immaterial, only one copy of the letter has been included in this edition. In the end there were only ten subscribers. For this list see Letter 1452 and *KHV.* 363.

The letter was written by Schindler and signed by Beethoven. A reply was sent from Darmstadt on February 26th, ordering a copy of the Mass.

(1135) *To Karl Friedrich Zelter, Berlin*

[*Autograph in the Beethovenhaus, Bonn, H. C. Bodmer collection*]

MY VALIANT FELLOW-ARTIST!   VIENNA, *February* 8, 1823 [1]
The reason why I am writing to you is that I have a request to make. Although we are now so far apart and cannot talk to one another, yet unfortunately even writing can be only a rare event for me — I have composed a grand Mass which could also be performed as an oratorio (for the benefit of the poor — an excellent practice that has now been introduced). I have decided, however, not to have it engraved and published in the usual way, but to send it only to the principal courts. The fee amounts to 50 ducats. Apart from those copies which have been subscribed for, no others will be published, so that the Mass will be virtually only in manuscript — But there will have to be a fair number of manuscript copies if the composer is to make any profit — I have handed to the Royal Prussian Legation in Vienna a petition that His Majesty the King of Prussia should condescend to take a copy ; and I have also written to Prince Radziwill requesting him to take up the matter [2] — I do beseech you to do what *you* can in this respect. A work of this kind might be useful to the Singakademie as well, for with slight alterations it could even be performed by voices alone. Still the more the voices are doubled and multiplied and supported by the instruments, the more powerful should be the effect — It would also be suitable as an oratorio, seeing that the societies for poor relief require works of this kind — As I have been constantly in poor health for several years and, therefore, not exactly in the most flourishing circumstances, I have had recourse to this expedient. I have written many works indeed — but have *gained by writing* [3] — practically nothing [4] — I am more accus-

[1] The autograph is endorsed: 'Received February 15, 1823'. Zelter replied on February 22nd.
[2] Prince Anton Heinrich Radziwill (1755–1833), who since 1815 had been Stadtholder of the Grand Duchy of Posen, was a composer of some merit. Beethoven dedicated to him two works, Op. 108 published in 1822, and Op. 115 published in 1825. Both the King of Prussia and Prince Radziwill in fact subscribed to the 'Missa Solemnis'.
[3] Beethoven here plays on the words 'geschrieben' (written) and 'erschrieben' (gained by writing).   [4] In the autograph there is just the digit 0 (zero).

tomed to direct my gaze upwards [1] — Yet for his own sake and for the sake of others a man is compelled to come down to earth. And no doubt this too is part of the destiny of man — With sincere regard I embrace you, my dear fellow-artist.

Your friend

BEETHOVEN [2]

(1136) *To Johann Wolfgang von Goethe, Weimar*

[Autograph in the Goethearchiv, Weimar]

YOUR EXCELLENCY!   VIENNA, *February* 8, 1823

Still ever living, as I have lived since my youth, in your immortal and ever youthful works, and never forgetting the happy hours spent in your company, I am now faced with the fact that I too must remind you of my existence — I trust that you received the dedication to Your Excellency of '*Meeresstille und Glückliche Fahrt*' which I have set to music.[3] By reason of their contrasting moods these two poems seemed to me very suitable for the expression of this contrast in music. It would afford me much pleasure to know whether I had united my harmony with yours in appropriate fashion. Indeed your criticism, which might almost be regarded as the very essence of truth, would be extremely welcome to me. For I love truth more than anything; and in my case it will never be: veritas odium parit.[4] — Soon perhaps several of your ever unique poems which I have set to music ought to be appearing and these will include '*Rastlose Liebe*'.[5] How highly would I value a general comment from you on the composing of music or on setting your poems to music! — Well, I have a request to make of Your Excellency. I have composed a grand Mass, which, however, I do not want to publish yet, but merely intend to send to the most eminent courts. The fee is only

---

[1] Many of Beethoven's contemporaries who knew him have recorded his 'Blick nach oben', i.e. his tendency to look upwards.

[2] Nohl I, p. 224, note, gives in full Zelter's favourable reply to Beethoven's request. It is warm-hearted and sympathetic.

[3] Op. 112, published in score by Steiner in February, 1822, was dedicated to Goethe. On May 21, 1822, Goethe noted in his diary 'Received a score from Beethoven'.

[4] 'Truth produces hatred.' Cf. Letter 969, p. 841, n. 2.

[5] Beethoven sketched a melody for this poem but his setting was never completed.

50 ducats. With this in view I have applied to the Legation of the Grand Duchy of Weimar which has accepted my petition to His Excellency the Grand Duke and has promised to forward it to him. The Mass can also be performed as an oratorio; and, as everyone knows, the societies for poor relief do need works of that kind nowadays! My petition is that Your Excellency would draw the attention of His Excellency the Grand Duke to my work so that that illustrious personage too may become a subscriber. The Legation of the Grand Duchy of Weimar hinted to me that it would be a great advantage if the Grand Duke's favourable opinion could be secured in advance — I have composed so many works, yet *gained from them* — practically nothing. Yet now I am no longer alone. For more than six years I have been a father to my deceased brother's son,[1] a promising youth of nearly sixteen, absolutely devoted to learning and already quite at home in the prolific writings of ancient Greece. But in this country that kind of education costs a good deal; and in the case of young students we must think not only of the present but also of the future; and however much my thoughts have been directed solely to things above, yet my attention must now be turned also to *things on earth* — My income is *worth practically nothing* — For several years my poor health has not allowed me to undertake professional tours or, I might say, to avail myself of all the means by which a *livelihood* is made! If, however, I recover my health completely, I shall certainly be entitled to expect many more and greater windfalls — But Your Excellency must not think that I dedicated to you 'Meeresstille' and 'Glückliche Fahrt' because I was going to ask you to use your influence on my behalf. Those works were dedicated to you as long ago as May, 1822; and at that time I had not thought of publishing the Mass in this way — the idea occurred to me only a few weeks ago. — The admiration, the love and the esteem which already in my youth I cherished for the one and only immortal Goethe have persisted. Feelings like these are not easily expressed in words, particularly by such an uncouth fellow *as myself*, for my one aim has been to master the art of music. But a strange feeling is constantly prompting me to say all this to you, seeing that I live in your

[1] I.e. since November, 1815.

writings — I know that you will not fail to use your influence on this particular occasion on behalf of an artist who feels only too keenly to what an extent *mere gain* detaches him from *his art.* Yet *need* compels him to act and to work *on behalf of others and for others* — We can always see clearly what is good; and thus I know that Your Excellency will not reject my petition — A few words to me from you would fill me with happiness —

I remain, Your Excellency, with

my most profound and infinite regard,

BEETHOVEN [1]

(1137) *To Carl Friedrich Peters, Leipzig*

[*Autograph in the Beethovenhaus, Bonn, H. C. Bodmer collection*]

MY DEAR GOOD FELLOW!   VIENNA, *February* 15, [1823] [2]

I am distressed to hear of your family loss and I deeply sympathize with you in your sorrow. May time assuage it — I am informing you of what concerns you and me, namely, that last Saturday the three songs,[3] six bagatelles [4] and a tattoo (Turkish music), instead of a march, were dispatched to you. I feel sure that you will forgive the delay. I am convinced that if you look into my heart *you will not accuse me of a deliberately blameworthy action.* I also sent to the post today the two tattoos, which were still missing, and the fourth grand march. I thought it would be better to let you have, instead of four marches, three tattoos and a march, seeing that the former can also be used as marches.[5] The regimental Kapellmeisters are the best judges of how to use music of that kind. Let me add that pianoforte arrangements of these works could also be made.— You will see from the songs how I proceed

---

[1] So far as is known, Goethe, who was then in rather poor health, did not answer this letter. The Grand Duke of Weimar did not become a subscriber to the 'Missa Solemnis'.

[2] According to the endorsement this letter was received on February 20th and answered on February 24th.

[3] Op. 121b, 'Opferlied', a setting of a poem by F. Matthisson for soprano solo with choral and orchestral accompaniment; Op. 122, 'Bundeslied', a setting of a poem by Goethe for voices with wind-instrument accompaniment; Op. 128, 'Der Kuss', a setting of a poem by C. F. Weisse as an arietta with pianoforte accompaniment. These three songs were published by Schott in 1825.

[4] Op. 119.

[5] These are listed in *KHV.* as WoO 18-20 and WoO 24.

as an artist. One song has an accompaniment for two clarinets, one horn, violas and cellos — and can be sung either without pianoforte accompaniment and only with these instruments, or with the pianoforte and without these instruments.[1] The second song has an accompaniment for two clarinets, two horns and two bassoons and can also be sung with these instruments only or with pianoforte accompaniment alone.[2] Both songs have choruses; and the third song is a rather elaborate arietta with pianoforte accompaniment only [3] — I hope that you will now be satisfied. I should be very sorry if these delays were ascribed solely to my fault or to any deliberate intention.

Time is flying and running off with the post. I shall let you have more information next Wednesday both about the piano quartet and the violin quartet — Further, I will send you a written statement about the *Mass*, for the decision, of which you will hear, is about to be taken.—

As for the two and even more bagatelles you have received, please send the draft for 16 ducats to me, as you did before, so that I may then forward them to Herr Meissel.[4] For I am really extremely busy and still not yet in the best of health — More news on Wednesday [5] — May Heaven help you to bear your sorrow. Who is there who has not suffered *some similar loss*, and who is there who willingly *bewails* a bereavement of that kind?

With all my heart I embrace you.

Your most devoted

BEETHOVEN

[1] Op. 121b.   [2] Op. 122.   [3] Op. 128.
[4] See Letter 1141, p. 1004, n. 1.
[5] Beethoven was writing on Saturday, February 15th. The next extant letter to Peters is dated Wednesday, February 26th.

(1138) *To Anton Felix Schindler*

[*Autograph in the Deutsche Staatsbibliothek, Berlin*]

[VIENNA, *c. February* 15, 1823]

EXTRAORDINARILY EXCELLENT FELLOW!

Tomorrow first of all to G[allenberg].[1]   You must first look up what I have written to him —

All good wishes till we meet at *noon.*

Your
B — N

(1139) *To Friedrich Duncker, Berlin* [2]

[*Autograph in the Beethovenhaus, Bonn, H. C. Bodmer collection*]

MY ESTEEMED FRIEND!   VIENNA, *February* 18, 1823

How often am I with you in spirit!   Indeed there ought to be a special kind of telegraphy for friends; and if there were, what a great and rapid mental communication there might be between kindred spirits.   As it is, the field of really intimate relations between *human souls*, how fallow must it often lie!!   It is a very long time since I heard from you. But no doubt you are busily engaged in *furthering the interests of a great many people.*   Well, though there is rarely an occasion or an impelling reason for us to talk to one another and though we may even feel that by so doing we are inconveniencing one another, yet we must welcome that necessity which compels us again to draw very near to those to whom we know that we shall be most welcome whenever they can exercise the noble

[1] On a separate leaf attached to this autograph Schindler wrote the following note: 'This was about the score of 'Fidelio' which Beethoven wanted to have a look at in connexion with a request from Dresden.   In 1823 Count Gallenberg was in charge of the musical archives of the Kärntnertor Theatre.   On this occasion Beethoven took the opportunity of telling me about Count and Countess Gallenberg, for the latter, Giulia Guicciardi, had been formerly his love.'   See Schünemann II, 357.

[2] Johann Friedrich Leopold Duncker, who was Secretary to the Privy Council of Prussia, had accompanied King Friedrich Wilhelm III to the Congress of Vienna in 1814–1815.   During his stay in Vienna Duncker lived with Giannatasio del Rio's family and through them made the acquaintance of Beethoven.   He had written a tragedy, 'Leonore Prohaska', which he hoped to have performed in Vienna and for which Beethoven composed some incidental music, listed in *KHV.* as WoO 96.   Duncker died in 1842.

virtues of humanity for our benefit — For the last three
years I have been constantly ailing; and two years ago when
your friend came to Vienna I had hardly recovered more or
less from attacks of rheumatism; then immediately after his
departure I was taken ill with jaundice; and last winter I
suffered from a chest complaint. So far as the latter illness
is concerned, my condition has certainly improved; but I
am not yet fully recovered and perhaps I shall not do so until
the summer, when I can complete my convalescence at some
watering-places — In the meantime, however, I have composed
several works including a grand solemn Mass. Although a
man may find his greatest happiness in constantly looking
upwards, yet in the end he too is obliged to pay attention to his
immediate necessities. My indifferent health and my care for
my adopted son Karl (now a promising youth of sixteen and
already quite at home in the splendid intellectual treasures of
the ancient Romans and Greeks; yet here too the present
already makes many demands on my purse and provision
must also be made for the future), both these considerations
compel me to collect a fair amount of what people call the
good things of life; and thus one has to do a great many things
which one would not otherwise bother about. Well, I am
now returning to the grand solemn Mass, which I mentioned
above and which could also be performed as an oratorio. I
have invited all the most eminent courts to subscribe to it, for
it is to appear only in manuscript. With this in view I have
also applied here to Prince Hatzfeld,[1] who has promised to
forward to His Majesty the King of Prussia my petition concerning the Mass.[2] The fee is 50 ducats. A small number of
subscribers will not be of much use, as the outlay for having
it copied is heavy. Perhaps in this case you will exert your
influence so that the King will subscribe. I have written
to Prince Radziwill[3] too about this, and perhaps the *Prince*
himself would subscribe. I know that whenever you can you
gladly perform good deeds for others and, not least, for me —
My beloved friend, let me say in closing that my desire is that
we might meet again and let *our souls* feast upon each other.

[1] For a note on Prince Hatzfeld see Letter 1508, p. 1300, n. 2.
[2] The King of Prussia was the first subscriber to the 'Missa Solemnis'.
[3] Cf. Letter 1135, p. 996, n. 2.

Yet even though we are deprived of this enjoyment, I shall ever preserve the memory of your love and friendship; and your other splendid intellectual achievements are also very often in my remembrance.—

Ever with love and admiration your most devoted

BEETHOVEN

(I have written to Zelter too about this.) [1]

(1140) *To Moritz Schlesinger, Paris*

[*MS not traced*] [2]

MY DEAR SCHLESINGER!   VIENNA, *February* 18, 1823

I believe that what you were looking for in that parcel, what was missing or not, was noted — Do look for it!

Of the works which I recently offered you the overture is for a large orchestra and was performed for the first time on October 3rd at the opening of the new theatre in the Josephstadt.[3]

Please send me the works of Méhul which you mentioned.[4] Further, I require a few copies of the Scottish songs from your worthy [father?] in Berlin [5] . . . I require a few copies with a gilt binding. Please reply.

The dedication of the C minor sonata is to Antonia Brentano, née von Birkenstock.[6]

Reply quickly, quickly, quickly to your [friend]

BEETHOVEN

---

[1] This remark is written in brackets at the side of page 4 of the autograph. Cf. Letter 1135, p. 996.

[2] Taken from *TDR* IV, 387-388. According to *TDR* IV, 387, n. 4, the copy found in Thayer's papers was apparently written in another hand and was rather illegible. The bracketed words have been supplied by the editor.

[3] Op. 124.

[4] See Letter 1267, p. 1111.

[5] Op. 108. The German edition had been published by A. M. Schlesinger, Berlin, in July, 1822.

[6] Op. 111. This sonata was intended for Antonia Brentano, as was also Op. 110, but in the end it was dedicated to the Archduke Rudolph. Nevertheless the London edition published by Clementi & Co. (1823?) included the dedication to Antonia Brentano.

(1141) *To Herr von Meissl* [1]

[Autograph in the Gesellschaft der Musikfreunde, Vienna]

SIR!   [VIENNA, *c. February* 19, 1823]

Most respectfully do I request you to have the parcel of music sent to Herr Peters today for certain. This is really an urgent matter, as he is in a hurry to have it. I am not well and at the moment I happen to have no one with me whom I could trust to see to this — So you will forgive the trouble I am giving you. What consoles me is that I know how very much attached you are to Herr Peters —

With kindest regards I remain, Sir, your devoted

BEETHOVEN

(1142) *To King George IV of England, London*

[Autograph in the Deutsche Staatsbibliothek, Berlin] [2]

VIENNA, *February* 24, 1823

I now venture most submissively to put forward to Your Majesty my most humble petition. At the same time I make bold to add another one.

As long ago as 1813 the undersigned, complying with many requests put forward by several Englishmen residing in Vienna, took the liberty of sending to Your Majesty his work entitled 'Wellingtons Schlacht und Sieg bei Vittoria', because nobody in England yet possessed a copy. Prince von Razumovsky,[3] who was then Russian Ambassador to the Imperial Court and happened to be in Vienna, undertook to forward this work to Your Majesty by a courier.

For many years the undersigned cherished the agreeable hope that Your Majesty would most graciously have him in-

---

[1] The Meisl (not Meissl) brothers were wholesale merchants who had their office in the Rauhensteingasse and occasionally forwarded Beethoven's parcels to Leipzig and Berlin. On this occasion they were probably sending to Peters at Leipzig the music mentioned in Letter 1137. See also Letter 1145, p. 1008.

[2] This is the draft of a letter which was presumably sent to the King of England. In the Royal Archives at Windsor, however, there are no letters from Beethoven. See Schünemann II, 370.

[3] Count Razumovsky was created a Prince in 1815.

formed of the safe arrival of his work.   But as yet he has not been able to boast of this happiness and has had to content himself merely with the brief announcement of Herr Ries, his worthy pupil, who duly informed him that Your Majesty had most graciously condescended to give the above-mentioned work to Herr Salomon, then Director of Music, and to Herr Smart, who were to have it performed in public at the Drury Lane Theatre.[1]   The English papers announced this too and even added, as Herr Ries did also, that this work had been received with extraordinary applause both in London and everywhere else.

Your Majesty will forgive, no doubt, the sensitivity of the undersigned for whom it has been very mortifying to have to hear all this through indirect channels.   And Your Majesty will most graciously allow him to mention that he spared neither time nor expense when presenting this work to Your Most Excellent Majesty in the most proper manner in order therewith to afford you the greatest pleasure.

From all these circumstances the undersigned draws the conclusion that the work may have been presented to Your Majesty in some unsuitable way;   and as his most humble petition, which he again puts forward, affords him the opportunity of approaching Your Majesty, he now ventures most submissively to send to Your Majesty an engraved copy of the score of the Schlacht bei Vittoria.   This copy has been lying ready for this purpose ever since the year 1815 and has been kept back so long only on account of the uncertain position in which the undersigned was placed about the whole affair.

As he is convinced of the great wisdom and favour with which Your Majesty has always known how to value and to bring happiness to art and to the artist, the undersigned flatters himself that Your Majesty will most kindly consider, and most graciously comply with, his most humble petition.[2]

---

[1] The work was first performed in London at the Drury Lane Theatre in February, 1814.

[2] Beethoven's draft has this addition written in another hand : 'Convaincu de la haute Sagesse dont Votre Majesté a toujours su apprecier l'art ainsi que de la haute faveur qu'elle accorde à l'artiste le soussigné se flatte que Votre Majesté prendra l'un et l'autre en consideration et vaudra en grace condescendre a sa tres-humble demande.'

à Vienne le 24 fevrier.

(1143) *To Ferdinand Ries, London*

[*Autograph in the Beethovenhaus, Bonn, H. C. Bodmer collection*]

My dear, beloved Ries!   Vienna, *February* 25, 1823
I am taking this opportunity of writing to you through Herr von Bauer, Imperial and Royal Secretary of Embassy. I don't know what to do about the symphony.[1] But I am hoping for a further communication from you. It would be necessary, of course, to have the draft made out and enclosed. Well, this Herr von Bauer, who is as intelligent as he is kind-hearted, has already promised to arrange for the symphony to be forwarded to London as quickly as possible; and I have only to hand it in at Prince Esterházy's residence.[2] — You are also receiving herewith the promised overture.[3] If the Philharmonic Society desires to keep this too for 18 months, the overture is at its disposal. Nobody has yet received it, and nobody will have it until I receive an answer *from you* about it. If the Philharmonic Society is as poor as I am, then it need not give me anything. But if it is better off, as I have good reason to believe and cordially hope and desire that it is, then I leave it entirely to the Society to treat me, in regard to the overture, exactly as it likes — You are also receiving six bagatelles or *trifles, and again another five*, which belong together, in two parts. Dispose of them as favourably as you can.[4] I hope that you have *received the two sonatas*; and again I beg you to drive *a hard bargain* for these.[5] For indeed I need the money. The winter and several factors have again reduced my resources; and it is not easy to have to live almost entirely by my *pen*. In the spring of 1824 I shall be going to London in order to kiss your wife. We shall still have plenty of time to write to one another about my journey. If I had only received your dedication, I would have dedicated this overture to you at once, provided that it would win applause

---

[1] The ninth symphony, Op. 125.
[2] Prince Paul Esterházy was Austrian Ambassador in London.
[3] Op. 124.
[4] Op. 119, eleven bagatelles for pianoforte solo, was published by Clementi & Co. This edition and Schlesinger's Paris edition appeared at the end of 1823, before the Vienna edition, which was not published until April, 1824.
[5] Op. 110 and 111.

in London — Now all good wishes, my dear friend, make haste with the symphony; and whatever sum you can obtain for the sonatas and the bagatelles, any money in fact, should be sent to Vienna soon. For it will be welcome — Heaven bless you and give me an opportunity of rendering you some kindness —

With the most friendly thoughts, your

BEETHOVEN

(1144) *To Charles Neate, London*

[Autograph in the Beethovenhaus, Bonn, H. C. Bodmer collection]

MY DEAR AND VALUED FRIEND! VIENNA, *February* 25, 1823

As Ries has written to tell me that you would like to have three quartets from me, I am writing to ask you to be so kind as to let me know when you would like to receive them. I am satisfied with the fee of 100 guineas which you offer. But, as soon as you hear from me that the quartets are ready, please send a draft for the 100 g[uineas] to a Viennese banking house *where I shall also deliver* the quartets and at the same time receive the 100 guin[eas].— I trust that you are leading a pleasant and happy life in the bosom of your small family.[1] But why are you not in Vienna so that I might have the pleasure of witnessing your happiness? — I have sent Ries a new overture for the Philharmonic Society;[2] and I am only waiting for the arrival of the draft to dispatch immediately the new symphony[3] from Vienna and, what is more, by an opportunity provided by our Imperial and Royal Embassy. The bearer of this letter is Herr von Bauer, who is as intelligent as he is amiable and who can tell you a good deal about me — If my health, which has been very poor for the last three years, should improve, I hope to go to London in 1824. Let me know what compositions the Philharmonic Society would like to have, for I would gladly compose for it. I should like to visit

---

[1] Charles Neate's small family consisted of his wife, an only daughter Catherine, born in 1819, who died of consumption in 1841, and an only son Charles, born in 1821, who became an engineer, worked in Brazil from 1852 to 1867, then returned to London, where he set up a consulting practice in Westminster, and died unmarried in 1911.

[2] Op. 124.   [3] Op. 125.

England and meet all the splendid artists there. Such a visit would benefit me materially too, for I shall *never* be able to achieve anything in Germany — You need only write my *name* on a letter to me and I shall certainly receive it — That all good and beautiful things may be your portion is the wish of your sincere friend

BEETHOVEN

(1145) *To Carl Friedrich Peters, Leipzig*

[*Autograph in the possession of Alfred Cortot*]

SIR !   VIENNA, *February* 26, 1823

It was always my custom to send to the post on Saturday everything intended for the North. But in the meantime I have moved into rooms at least three quarters of an hour from the post. So I have sent the parcel for you to the Gebrüder *Meissel*,[1] whose custom in this respect is a different one, inasmuch as they send their parcels to the mail coach on *Friday*. I really cannot say which is the better arrangement. But I consider it necessary *as a man of honour* to assure you that by last *Friday* [2] *all the missing sheets* were duly delivered to M[eissel] for you.

Now for a few more points. In one of the bagatelles or trifles there is this passage : [3]

When the notes are written out they should all appear thus :

But the passage should be printed as it is at the mark ⊠ and similarly wherever this passage occurs. —

In regard to the Mass, I have only just seen when going through my correspondence that you wrote to me that of

---

[1] Cf. Letter 1141, p. 1004.
[2] Beethoven first wrote 'Saturday', deleted it and wrote 'Friday' above it.
[3] Op. 119, no. 3.

BEETHOVEN
From the lithograph by Engelmann after the drawing by Stephan Decker (1824)
(*Emily Anderson, London*)

course you would take it — Whichever one of the two or three
Masses you receive, you need not worry, for in music you will
never find me anything but a true artist — My very best
wishes. Spring will soon be here and will provide the sufferer
with a fair field in which to lament in silence! [1]

Your

BEETHO [2]

(1146) *To the Archduke Rudolph*

[*Autograph in the Gesellschaft der Musikfreunde, Vienna*]

YOUR IMPERIAL HIGHNESS! [VIENNA], *February* 27, [1823]
I have already been to the Castle this morning, not, I
admit (for I was not yet suitably attired), in order to visit
Y.I.H., but merely to ask Zips [3] to inform you that I had
called and that I was extremely delighted to hear of your return
to Vienna. But I failed to find Y.I.H. at his usual residence;
and when I knocked at a place where I thought that Y.I.H.
might be, it seemed that my attire was far from suitable.
So I quickly made myself scarce, and I am merely sending you
before the end of the day a written assurance that I have
called. Tomorrow I will call again and wait upon you and
at the same time learn whether the usual *musical intellectual
exercises* are to be resumed, and when? On the surface it
may seem disgraceful that all this while I have not written to
Y.I.H., but I wanted to wait until I had sent you the Mass.
But as there were really a horrible lot of mistakes in it, so much
so that *each part* had to be checked, my writing to you was
delayed by very many other tasks which could not be postponed. In addition there were some other circumstances
which prevented me from writing, just as a man, when he
least expects it, is confronted with very many things to do.
But that Y.I.H. has always been in my thoughts is proved by
the accompanying copies of a few new pieces,[4] which for several
months now have been lying in readiness for Y.I.H. I did

---

[1] Cf. the beginning of Letter 1137, p. 999.
[2] Here a corner of the sheet is torn.
[3] Franz Joseph Zips was a minor official in the service of the Archduke. See
FRBH II, 473 and Schünemann I, 306.
[4] These works were probably the Gratulations menuett in E♭ for orchestra
(WoO 3), the overture in C 'Die Weihe des Hauses' (Op. 124) and the additional
chorus with soprano solo and orchestral accompaniment for 'Die Weihe des

not want to send them to you, however, before I could let you have the Mass. *The latter* is just being bound and will then be handed by me to Y.I.H. with all due homage [1] — While expressing my extreme delight at being able to wait upon Y.I.H. again in person, I remain with all due reverence

Your Imperial Highness's

faithful and most obedient servant

BEETHOVEN

(1147) *To the Archduke Rudolph*

[*Autograph in the Gesellschaft der Musikfreunde, Vienna*]

Postscript [2]   [VIENNA, *February*, 1823]

The Mass in its complete form will soon be in Y.I.H.'s hands. It should and would have been there long, long ago, but — but — but — after becoming more closely acquainted with my circumstances Y.I.H. will even wonder how, as it is, I have yet contrived to finish this work —

(1148) *To Anton Felix Schindler*

[*Autograph in the Beethovenhaus, Bonn, H. C. Bodmer collection*]

MOST EXCELLENT FELLOW!   [VIENNA, *February*, 1823] [3]

I am still in bed and I do beg you to come to me this morning — The question of the Mass is urgent — Please dine with me next Sunday. My excursions to the Castle [4] now hardly leave me time to eat — Therefore please come to me

---

Hauses' (WoO 98). Copies of these three works with remarks in Beethoven's hand, which were sent to the Archduke, were presented after the latter's death to the Gesellschaft der Musikfreunde, Vienna, in 1834. See Nottebohm, *Zweite Beethoveniana* (Leipzig, 1887), p. 396, note.

[1] See *KHV.* 362. The copy, now in the Gesellschaft der Musikfreunde, Vienna, is entered in the Archduke's list of musical works with the remark: 'This beautifully copied MS was delivered by the composer in person on March 19, 1823'.

[2] This postscript does not appear to belong to the previous letter, no. 1146.

[3] Schindler noted on the autograph 'January or February, 1823'.

[4] Beethoven is referring to his visits and lessons to the Archduke Rudolph.

for certain this morning so that all the questions relating to the Mass may be settled at top speed —

Your friend

BEETHOVEN

(1149) *To the Royal Academy of Music, Stockholm*

[MS in the Kungl. Musikaliska Akademiens Bibliotek, Stockholm] [1]

VIENNA, March 1, 1823

C'est avec bien du plaisir, mais pourtant pas sans embarras, que je recoit l'hommage que l'Accademie royale suédoise de Musique rend à mes médiocres mérites.[2] Je serais au comble de mes vœux, s'il se presentoit une occasion pour moi, de lui être utile par rapport de la musique ; ce qui ne serviroit que pour déclarer, que la culture des arts et des sciences ont toujours été, et seront toujours la plus beau lien des peup[les] plus eloignés. Je souhaite bien que l'Accademie Roya[le] de musique prenne toujours plus succès dans cet art si illustre et si salutaire pour le bonheur de peuples. Plût à Dieu que mes vœux fussent acceptés aussi sincèrement que je suis prêt à les réaliser.

Finalement je profite de cette occasion honorable pour faire souvenir Sa Majesté le Roi de moi, et je supplie Monsieur le Secrétaire de l'Accademie, auquel j'ai l'honneur de me recommander, de remettre cette lettre à Sa Majesté.[3]

Je suis avec les plus grande éstime de l'Accademie royale très humble serviteur.

LOUIS VAN BEETHOVEN

[1] Written in another hand and signed by Beethoven.
[2] On December 22, 1822, Beethoven had been made an honorary member of the Swedish Academy of Arts and Sciences, founded on September 8, 1771. He had now been made a member of the Royal Academy of Music at Stockholm.
[3] Letter 1150.

(1150) *To King Karl XIV Johann of Sweden, Stockholm* [1]

[*MS in Bernadotteska Familjearkivet, Stockholm*] [2]

SIRE!   VIENNA, *March* 1, 1823

L'Academie royale de musique m'ayant fait l'honneur de me présenter une place au nombre de ses membres extérieure, je prends la liberté de me rapprocher de Votre Majesté. La présence de Votre Majesté à Vienne, et l'intérêt qu'elle prit avec quelques Seigneurs de la suite à mes médiocres talents, s'est profondement gravé dans mon coeur. Les exploits qui avec tant de justesse élevèrent Votre Majesté au thrône de Suède, excitoient l'admiration général, particulièrement de ceux qui avoient le bonheur de connôitre personellement Votre Majesté. Il en fut de même chez moi. Le temps, où Votre Majesté montoit sur le thrône, sera toujours considéré come Epoque de grande importance; et come je suis pas moins homme qu'Artiste, et sachant, comme premier, de remplir mes devoirs le plus exactement possible, j'ai souvent admiré avec le plus vif intérêt, les actions et les soins que Votre Majesté prend des arts; ce qui me determine à ajouter à cette lettre une invitation particulière, afin que Votre Majesté daignât souscrire pour l'œuvre qui y est annoncé. Conduit par une cause particulière, je souhaite que les chefs de l'Europe seulement aient parte à cet œuvre.

Aussi ai-je appris, que l'auguste fils de Votre Majesté, le prince héréditaire, a beaucoup de talent pour la musique.[3] Peut-être pourrai-je augmenter son goût, et principalement élever ses talents. Pour pouvoir réaliser ce souhait, quelques détails sur sa culture musicale me feroient bien du plaisir, aussi voudrois-je avec le plus grand empressement composer un œuvre, et le dédier au Prince héréditaire cependant il faudroit que je susse par avance, par quel genre de musique

---

[1] The famous Jean Baptiste Jules Bernadotte (1763–1844) was first a zealous supporter of Napoleon who in 1804 appointed him Marshal of France. In 1810 Bernadotte commanded in the Netherlands and was offered the crown of Sweden as Karl XIII, later Karl XIV. He took part in the last German campaign against Napoleon. Before his death he succeeded in bringing about the union of Norway and Sweden. He did not subscribe to the 'Missa Solemnis'.

[2] Written in another hand and signed by Beethoven.

[3] The only son of Karl XIV Johann was Oscar I (1799–1859), who succeeded his father in 1844.

je serais en était de répondre aux souhaits de Votre Majesté et à ceux du Prince Royale.

Votre Majesté est un objet d'amour, d'admiration et d'intérêt à tous ceux qui savent éstimer les rois ; les sentiments de vénération que j'ai pour Votre Majesté, ne peuvent guère être augmentés.

Qui Votre Majesté daigne accepter l'hommage sincére du plus respectueux de ses serviteurs

LOUIS VAN BEETHOVEN

(1151) *To Johann Baptist Bach*

[*Autograph not traced*] [1]

DEAR AND HONOURED FRIEND !   VIENNA, *March* 6, 1823

Death can come without any previous warning ; and at the moment there is no time to make a legal will. I inform you, therefore, in this letter written in my own hand that I nominate my beloved nephew Karl van Beethoven heir to my entire property and that I declare that after my death every-thing, without exception, *which can be described as being in my possession shall belong to him as the sole owner* — I appoint you his curator ; and, should this will not be superseded by another one, you are entitled and requested to find for my beloved nephew K[arl] v. Beethoven a guardian, who must not be, however, my brother Johann van Beethoven,[2] and to entrust my nephew to this guardian in accordance with the traditional laws.

I declare this written document to be valid for all time, just as if it were my last will and testament before my death — I embrace you with all my heart — Your sincere admirer and friend,

LUDWIG VAN BEETHOVEN

NB.[3] The capital amounts to seven bank shares ; and whatever additional cash may be available will, like the bank shares, become my nephew's property.

---

[1] From a photostat in the Beethovenarchiv, Bonn.
[2] The words from 'who' to 'Beethoven' are added at the foot of the third page.
[3] The NB. is added on the first page.

(1152) *To Franz Brentano, Frankfurt am Main*

[*Autograph not traced*] [1]

NOBLE FRIEND!   VIENNA, *March* 10, 1823

You have heard nothing from me for a very long while. Meanwhile I trust that some time ago you received through *Geymüller* the 300 gulden which you lent me in such a noble way. It is easier to feel and sense certain kindnesses and benefits bestowed upon us than to find at once the suitable expressions for these feelings. Command me to undertake whatever task you choose, provided it be within my power to perform it, and I will make every effort to prove to you my regard, my affection and my gratitude — Please forward this letter to Simrock.[2] You will see from it what is the present position in regard to the Mass.[3] Thank God, my health is better. But baths which I must take during the summer still have to restore it completely — I am very hopeful because my nature is that of a polyp. Moreover good health is extremely necessary for my work and in its turn improves with the help of my work — I send you my best regards. My most ardent wish is to be able to show you how much I honour and love you —

May the Lord send to your family also everything that is good and beautiful —

And may He long preserve *your dear ones for you* —

Your friend and servant

BEETHOVEN

(1153) *To Nikolaus Simrock, Bonn*

[*Autograph in the Beethovenhaus, Bonn, H. C. Bodmer collection*]

DEAR SIMROCK!   VIENNA, *March* 10, 1823

I can well imagine how strange I must seem to you. But never before have my circumstances so played havoc with my

---

[1] Taken from Kal. IV, no. 880. Kalischer transcribed the autograph then in private ownership.   [2] Letter 1153.
[3] Kal. IV, pp. 206-207, quotes two informative letters from Nikolaus Simrock to Brentano about his negotiations with Beethoven for the publication of the 'Missa Solemnis'.

time as they have been doing lately for a good while. You will most certainly receive a Mass from me. But I have written another Mass and am still hesitating which one I should give to you.[1] That is what is holding me up at the moment. Do be patient a little longer until after Easter when I will let you know immediately on what date I shall be sending off one of these Masses to Herr von Brentano and will inform you at once of its dispatch — I am now going to compose another Mass for our Emperor, and that very soon — I can't offer you any other works because I am really being pressed on all sides. But *perhaps* I could give you a new overture which I composed for the opening of the new Josephstadt Theatre.[2] The fee would be 50 ducats. The overture is composed in the grand style.[3] By the way, you might let me know some time whether you could make use of any works of the following kind, for instance, the 'Ruinen von Athen' an epilogue by Kotzebue with choruses, aria and duet,[4] and, further, a prologue by the same author 'König Stephan, Ungarns Wohltäter' also with choruses, and treated almost entirely as a melodrama.[5] Well, whatever you may do about that, you will most certainly receive one of the two grand Masses which have already been composed. But you must just be patient until after Easter when I shall have decided which one I am going to send you — No doubt you are feeling very much inclined to laugh at my *seemingly* unmethodical behaviour. But only recently have I been allowed to hope for a recovery of my health. And then I have been pestered on all sides. If only you were here, you would soon have a clear picture of everything — All good wishes. My heartfelt greetings to all your family and to all to whom you think that my greetings would give pleasure —

Ever your friend
BEETHOVEN

You could also have from me songs, bagatelles or trifles for the pianoforte and so forth.

[1] Cf. Letter 1106, p. 976, n. 3.
[2] The words from 'which' to 'Theatre' are added at the foot of the page.
[3] Op. 124.   [4] Op. 113.   [5] Op. 117.

(1154) *To Luigi Cherubini, Paris* [1]

[Autograph in the Deutsche Staatsbibliothek, Berlin] [2]

[VIENNA, *shortly before March* 15, 1823]

MOST HIGHLY ESTEEMED SIR!

I am greatly delighted to take this opportunity of approaching you in writing. Quite often I am beside you in spirit, for I value your works more highly than all other compositions for the theatre. But the world of fine arts must lament that for some time, in our Germany at any rate, no new great theatrical work of yours has appeared. However highly your other compositions may be valued by true connoisseurs, yet it is a real loss to art *not yet* to possess some new product of your intellect composed for the theatre. True art is immortal; and the true artist finds deep satisfaction and pleasure in the true and great creations of genius. So I too am enchanted whenever I hear of a new work composed by you, and I take as much interest in it as I do in my own works — In short, I honour and love you — Were it not for my persistent ill health I might look forward to meeting you in Paris; and with what extraordinary pleasure should I then be able to discuss artistic questions with you ? ! — And here I must add that to every artist and lover of art I always talk about you with enthusiasm. Otherwise perhaps you might think that because I have a request to make of you, this is merely the introduction to it. But I hope that you do not credit me with such petty sentiments. —

My request is as follows : I have just finished a grand solemn Mass and my intention is to send it to the European courts, because at present I do not wish to publish it in engraved form. Therefore through the French Embassy in Vienna I have had an invitation forwarded to His Majesty the King of

---

[1] Luigi Cherubini (1760–1842), born at Florence, settled permanently in Paris in 1788 as a composer of operas. Early in July, 1805, he visited Vienna and made the acquaintance of Beethoven, who esteemed Cherubini above all living writers of dramatic music.

[2] This is a draft in Beethoven's handwriting of the letter which, according to his calendar, was dated March 15, 1823, and seems to have been sent to M. Schlesinger in Paris for delivery. See Letter 1176, p. 1033. But according to a passage in the diary of Schindler, who visited Cherubini in Paris in 1841, the latter did not receive Beethoven's letter. See Dr. Marta Becker, *Anton Schindler, der Freund Beethovens* (Frankfurt am Main, 1939), p. 42.

France to subscribe to this work, and I am convinced that on your recommendation the King will certainly take it.[1] Ma situation critique demande que je ne fixe pas seulement comme ordinaire mes pensées au ciel, au contraire il faut les fixer en bas pour les nécessités de la vie; whatever may be the result of my request to you I shall always love and admire you, et vous resteres toujours celui de mes contemporains, que je l'estime le plus si vous voulez me faire une extrème plaisir, c'etait si m'ecrireres quelques lignes, ce que me soulagera bien — l'art unie tout le monde, how much more then true artists, et peut êtres vous me dignes aussi, de me mettre, to count me too among that number.

Avec la plus haute estime

votre ami e serviteur

BEETH.

(1155) *To Anton Felix Schindler*

[Autograph in the Deutsche Staatsbibliothek, Berlin] [2]

DEAR SCHINDLER,   [VIENNA, *shortly before March* 15, 1823]

I don't know whether the other copy has been corrected. So I am sending this one — Please be sure to say nothing about N. in S.[3] Bl[öchlinger] is already uneasy about this.

In great haste, your friend

BEETHOVEN

(1156) *To Anton Felix Schindler*

[Autograph in the Deutsche Staatsbibliothek, Berlin]

[VIENNA, *March*, 1823]

I am now going *to the coffee house* where you could join me — There are only two methods of dealing with the Mass,

[1] The passage from 'I have just finished' to 'certainly take it' is not in the original draft but is added in Schindler's version in II, 352. Louis XVIII became a subscriber and sent Beethoven in addition a gold medal which is now in the Gesellschaft der Musikfreunde, Vienna.

[2] This note is written on the fourth and last page of Beethoven's draft letter to Cherubini. Cf. Letter 1154.

[3] Beethoven is referring to Johann Niederstätter, Professor of Latin Literature and Greek Philology at Salzburg. See Schünemann III, 56, n. 1.

that is to say, the publisher shall refrain from publishing it before a certain date or, if not, we shall refuse to accept any subscription —

I request you to taste this heavenly soup which my house-k[eeper] has prepared.

(1157) *To Anton Felix Schindler*

[Autograph in the Deutsche Staatsbibliothek, Berlin]

MOST EXCELLENT FELLOW —   [VIENNA, *March*, 1823] [1]
I need not be at court [2] until about half past four — So you may come to me after dinner —

I pay not the slightest attention to your opinion of the soup. *The soup is bad —*

(1158) *To Carl Friedrich Peters, Leipzig*

[Autograph in a private collection]

SIR !   VIENNA, *March* 20, 1823
The other three marches are only going off to you today.[3] A week ago today we missed the post. However slovenly my arrangements have been with you this time, you would surely not think this extraordinary, if only you were here and saw my predicament. Well, to describe it would be too long for you and for me — I find that I have something else to add about the works *which have already been dispatched.* For the performance of the grand march no. 4,[4] several regimental wind-instrument players might combine, and if this were not practicable, suppose, for instance, that one regimental band were not powerful enough to fill all the parts, well then, a bandmaster of this kind could easily produce it by leaving out a few parts — In Leipzig too you will find somebody who will show you how this march can be played with fewer instruments, although indeed I should be sorry if the march were not to be engraved exactly as it is — Now for this Turkish music, which should be numbered as follows :

[1] Schindler has dated this note 'February or March, 1823'.
[2] I.e. with the Archduke.   [3] Probably WoO 18-20.   [4] WoO 24.

tattoo in F  *etc.* No.1 [1]

The tattoo in C which you have already received is No. 2.[2] You will easily get the hang of all this from the other two, as well as from No. 1 which I have quoted above.[3] The other verses of Goethe's Bundeslied will follow.[4] If possible, they should all be written in under the voice part. Remember that everything is to follow in strict order; and finally the musical addition of the last verse 'Auf ewig so gesellt'[5] — Note that in the pianoforte part of Matthisson's Opferlied the melody is added in above, and that the various words, voce and ritornello, are then omitted, since, as the pianoforte part could not be written in score, they have only been added for the sake of clearness *while the engraving is being done*[6] —

I ought to mention that the two songs with instrumental accompaniment can be performed either alone with instrumental accompaniment or alone with pianoforte accompaniment. If I were you I would publish both of them in score *with the pianoforte arrangement* and mention on the first music sheet what I have indicated above —

So many songs have been composed with pianoforte accompaniment that for this reason I have made a change for once — The tenor clef, alto clef and even the bass clef could be transposed to the treble clef —

You must forgive the numerous corrections in the works you have received. My old copyist is blind[7] and the younger one must first be trained.[8] But at any rate there are *no mistakes* — Now to your other remarks. But first of all I do urge you to publish these works very soon —

I can let you have many more trifles of the same kind if you want to continue the series[9] — It is impossible to send you a violin quartet and a piano quartet at once. But if you

[1] WoO 18.   [2] WoO 20. Peters did not publish any of these marches.
[3] After this sentence a fairly long passage apparently about his bagatelles has been obliterated by Beethoven and is illegible.   [4] Op. 122.
[5] This is the last line of the last verse of Goethe's poem 'Bundeslied'.
[6] Op. 121b.
[7] Schlemmer, who had copied for Beethoven for 30 years, died a few months later.
[8] Either Rampel or Gläser. See Letter 1335, p. 1158, n. 4, and Letter 1252, p. 1097, n. 1.   [9] I.e. of bagatelles.

let me know in good time *when* you would like to have both these works, I will make every effort to please you. I must add, however, that the lowest fee I accept for a violin quartet is 50 ducats and for a piano quartet 70 ducats, because otherwise I should be a loser. Why, for violin quartets I have been offered much more than 50 ducats apiece. But I never like to ask too much; and therefore in your case I will definitely keep to 50 ducats, which is now really the usual price. The other offer was in truth an exceptional one, and of course I am accepting it too. I must ask you, however, to let me know soon when you would like to have these works. If you don't, although I would gladly give you the preference, it would be almost impossible to do so. You are well aware, for I told you this some time ago, how quartets and sonatas in particular have soared in price, so that when it comes to *a great work* even the composer is bound to feel *ashamed*. At the same time my situation demands that my actions be determined by what is likely to be more or less of advantage to me. Quite different considerations operate, of course, in the case of the work itself. There, thank God, I never think of the advantage to be reaped but only of *how I am composing.* —

As to the Mass, I will also send you a written document which I request you to sign. For in any case the time is approaching when you will receive the one or the other. Apart from yourself two other persons have come forward, each of whom would like to have a Mass. So I intend to compose three at least. The first is quite finished, the second is *not yet finished*, the third I have not yet begun.[1] In regard to this third Mass, however, I must have some certainty so that I may be safeguarded in any contingency. You can have that Mass provided you pay me 1000 gulden A.C., as we arranged, that is to say, as soon as I inform you that the work can be dispatched from Vienna.[2] About the publication of my collected works I will send you a written statement too. Indeed it is high time to do so — Our Steiner is lurking in the background — but more of this some other time. In

---

[1] The first is, of course, the 'Missa Solemnis': the second is a Mass in C sharp minor, for which sketches exist: nothing is known about the third Mass. Beethoven frequently referred to the existence of works which were not even in an embryonic state and which he merely intended to compose.

[2] The words from 'that is to say' to 'Vienna' are added at the foot of the page.

general, never send a draft for the fee until you have heard from me that the work is ready to be dispatched —

I must close. I hope that your grief is now a little less intense at any rate —

Your friend
BEETHOVEN

(1159) *To Ferdinand Ries, London*

[Autograph in the possession of Mrs. E. Korner]

DEAR RIES!   [VIENNA], *March* 22, 1823

I gave the overture [1] to Captain v[on] Bauer who has an appointment at our Imperial Embassy.[2] If you have not yet received it, just enquire about it there —

The symphony is not yet finished.[3] But it will only take me a fortnight to finish it, and then I will immediately deliver it to H[err] v[on] Kirchhoffer —

As I had heard nothing more from you since your last letter, I did not know how I stood. That is the reason why the symphony is not yet finished — and you know — what my circumstances are — Well, have you not received two sonatas, one in A♭ major and one in C minor?[4]

Captain Bauer has also taken with him some short pieces — for the pianoforte —

In haste. With affection and friendship I remain your

BEETHOVEN

(1160) *To the* [*Schleiermachersche Kabinettsregistratur*],[5] *Darmstadt*

[Autograph in the Hessisches Staatsarchiv, Darmstadt]

MOST HONOURABLE SIR,   VIENNA, *March* 24, 1823

I am greatly delighted to receive from you the news that His Royal Highness the Grand Duke deigns to accept my Mass

---

[1] Op. 124.
[2] Bauer had left Vienna at the end of February. Cf. Letter 1133, p. 993, n. 2.
[3] The ninth symphony, Op. 125.
[4] Op. 110 and 111.
[5] For a note on E. C. Schleiermacher, who was Secretary to the Grand Ducal Cabinet of Hesse, see Letter 1225, p. 1076, n. 4.

which I have offered him.[1]   But I am particularly gratified
that His Royal Highness has expressed to me his pleasure
through you.   This reassures me that my petition to H.R.H.
the Grand Duke about the Mass was not regarded as *importu-
nate* —

I request you, most honourable Sir, to convey to H.R.H.
my respectful thanks for the favour of being allowed to number
H.R.H. among my subscribers.   This too will bring me the
greatest honour, since H.R.H. is regarded as a connoisseur
and patron of all that is good and beautiful.   I send you,
most honourable Sir, my best compliments, and with my most
humble regards I remain your

BEETHOVEN

(1161) *To Karl Friedrich Zelter, Berlin*

[Autograph in the Musée de Mariemont]

SIR !   VIENNA, *March* 25, 1823
I am availing myself of this opportunity to send you my
very best wishes — The bearer of this letter has asked me to
recommend her most strongly *to you*.   Her name is Cornega.[2]
She has a fine mezzo soprano voice and is altogether an artistic
singer who has also appeared in several operas with success —

I have again considered very carefully your proposal for
your Singakademie.   If the work should ever be engraved and
published I will send you a copy without accepting any remuneration.[3]   Certainly a large portion of it could be performed
almost entirely *a la cappella*.   But the whole work would have
to be revised; and perhaps you would have the patience to
do this — Besides there is in any case one number in this
work which is performed entirely *a la cappella*.   And indeed
I should like to describe this style as preferably the only true
Church style — Thanks for your willingness to help, but from

---

[1] The Grand Duke Ludwig in reply to Beethoven's application of February 5,
1823 informed him on February 26th that he wished to subscribe to the Mass.
See an article by Adolf Schmidt in *DM*, III, 12 (1904).   Cf. Letter 1134,
p. 995, n. 1.

[2] Nina Cornega, born in 1795, an Italian mezzo-soprano who was a pupil of
Salieri, was leaving for St. Petersburg and intended to stay for a while in Berlin.
She became later a famous teacher of singing.

[3] Beethoven is referring, of course, to his 'Missa Solemnis'.

an artist *such as you are and, moreover, covered with honours,* I would never accept anything — I honour you and only long for an opportunity to prove my regard for you in some tangible way. With the greatest respect your friend and servant

BEETHOVEN

(1162) *To Anton Felix Schindler*

[Autograph in the Deutsche Staatsbibliothek, Berlin]

S[COUN]D[RE]L !   [VIENNA, *Spring*, 1823]

Nothing whatever is being altered in the Diab[elli] instrument [1] beyond leaving unspecified *the time* when these people are to receive the Mass from me [2] —

In any case *you* must rely on my desire to be considerate to others — I should only require the manuscript of the var[iations] [3] for a few hours in the evening or whenever it would be most convenient for Di[abelli]. For even if D[iabelli] is ready in three weeks, Engl[and] will have time enough to engrave them, since a copy can't get over there so quickly; and that will be to my advantage. For indeed, in spite of all I still need to have much more money before I can live in reasonable comfort — Don't be a Papageno.

Don't forget about the carpenter, S[coun]d[re]l-in-chief.

(1163) *To the Archduke Rudolph*

[Autograph in the Gesellschaft der Musikfreunde, Vienna]

YOUR IMPERIAL HIGHNESS !   [VIENNA, *Spring*, 1823]

I shall not be able to wait upon you again for a few days more, because the dispatch of the works, about which I have already informed Y.I.H., is a matter of great urgency. For if something like this is not attended to punctually, all can easily be lost. Y.I.H. can readily conceive how much time is taken up with arranging for the copies to be made and with checking each part; really it would be difficult to find a

---

[1] I.e. contract for publication.
[2] The words from 'when' to 'we' are added at the foot of the page.
[3] Op. 120.

more tiresome occupation [1] — Y.I.H. will spare me, I dare say, the enumeration of all the circumstances which bring about such a contingency. Only necessity has driven me to undertake the work; and in any case I have spoken about it *so frankly* because I consider that Y.I.H. must not be led to misjudge me. For unfortunately I know only too well how eagerly some people are striving to prejudice Your Highness *against me*. But time will yet show that in every respect I have acted as loyally and dutifully as was humanly possible. If only my situation were as perfect as my zeal to serve Y.I.H., a happier man than myself could not be found —

      Your Imperial Highness's
            faithful and most obedient servant
                            BEETHOVEN

(1164) *To Johann van Beethoven*

[Autograph not traced] [2]

[VIENNA, *Spring*, 1823]

I received yesterday a very interesting letter which would enable you to make an advantageous deal, and one which would certainly be to your profit. You see that I am always the same. But I refuse to be treated inconsiderately, in the way Herr S. [3] and his colleagues are inclined to do —

Hence I request you to come over very soon, [4] as I must go out later on and must also know today whether you want to undertake this business. I should like you to do so, at any rate for your own sake.

                    Ever your true brother —

The housekeeper has just gone off to enquire about rooms at Hetzendorf. [5]

    [1] I.e. manuscript copies of the Mass for the subscribers.
    [2] Taken from Nohl II, no. 238. Nohl transcribed the autograph which was then in private ownership.
    [3] Possibly Steiner or Schlesinger, with whom Beethoven was still negotiating about the publication of his 'Missa Solemnis'.
    [4] Beethoven and his brother were then living in adjoining houses, Kothgasse 60 and 61.
    [5] According to Nohl this remark is added in pencil at the top of the first page. Beethoven moved to Hetzendorf on May 17th.

IGNAZ SCHUPPANZIGH (1776–1830)
From the oil portrait by Joseph Danhauser
(*Oesterreichische Galerie, Vienna*)

(1165) *To Anton Felix Schindler*

[*Autograph in the Deutsche Staatsbibliothek, Berlin*]

[VIENNA, *Spring,* 1823]

What is the name of the gentleman who is now reporting on the Swedish diploma, and what kind of office does he hold? I must have this information because I want to write to him myself in order to apologize for not coming in person, and because in any case a letter from me will always produce a good effect —

(1166) *To Antonio Pacini, Paris* [1]

[*Autograph in the Bibliothèque du Conservatoire de Paris*]

MONSIEUR!   VIENNA, *April* 5, 1823

C'est mon Frère, qui me disait, que vous souhaities de posseder quelques-unes de mes compositions. quant au Trio, je l'ai cédé à un amateur pour dix mois, ce temps écoulé, vous pouves l'avoir.[2] Tout ce que je suis en état de vous offrir pour le coup ce sont 33 variations sur le thème d'une valse pour le piano grand œuvre.[3] 6 Bagatelles pour le piano.[4] deux chansons (de göthe et mathisson) avec l'accompagnement de piano seul, ou avec l'accompagnement de plusieurs instruments.[5] j'en ai fixé l'honoraire de 400 francs — Je vous pris de me repondre sans délai, plusieurs d'autres Editeurs désiront d'avoir de mes œuvres.

Votre très humble serviteur

LOUIS VAN BEETHOVEN [6]

---

[1] Antonio Francesco Gaetano Pacini (1778–1866), a native of Naples, settled in 1804 in Paris where he produced operas and taught singing. About 1806 he founded a music publishing firm, more especially for Italian operas, which in 1846 was taken over by Bonoldi Frères.

[2] The trio Beethoven is offering is probably WoO 28.

[3] Op. 120.

[4] Probably the first six bagatelles of Op. 119.

[5] Op. 122 and 121b.

[6] Beethoven's address noted on his letter in another hand is Kothgasse 60.

(1167) *To Ferdinand Ries, London*

[*First portion of the autograph not traced,* [1]
second portion of the autograph in the Universitätsbibliothek, Bonn]

DEAR RIES!   VIENNA, *April* 25, 1823

The Cardinal's stay in Vienna for about four weeks, during which period I had to give him every day a lesson lasting two and a half, and sometimes three, hours, has robbed me of a great deal of time. For after such lessons one is hardly able on the following day to think and, still less, to compose.

Yet my persistently distressing situation demands that for the time being I should compose whatever can bring me in money to spend for my immediate needs. What a sad discovery you are making!! And now owing to the many worries I have been enduring I am not well and even my eyes are troubling me! At the same time you must not be anxious about me. You will soon receive the symphony.[2] Only this miserable state of affairs is really the reason why you have not received it sooner — In a few weeks too you will receive a new set of 33 variations on a theme, a work which I have dedicated to your wife.[3]

Bauer has the score of the Schlacht von Vittoria, dedicated to the then Prince Regent,[4] for which I have yet to receive the cost of having it copied — All I ask is that you should interest yourself in this matter, dear friend! I [5] shall be satisfied with whatever you can get for it. But do see that the C minor sonata is engraved immediately.[6] I promise the publisher that it will not appear anywhere else first. And, if necessary, I will also send him the copyright for England. But it must be engraved at once — As the other one in A♭, even though it may already have arrived in London, has been engraved

---

[1] The first portion of this letter has been taken from *WRBN.*, pp. 185-186.

[2] Op. 125.

[3] Op. 120, the 33 pianoforte variations on a waltz theme by Diabelli, was published in June, 1823, by Cappi & Diabelli with a dedication to Antonia Brentano.   [4] Since 1820 George IV of England.

[5] From this point the remainder of the autograph is in the Universitäts-bibliothek, Bonn.

[6] Op. 111 was engraved by Clementi & Co. (1823?) with a dedication to Antonia Brentano.

inaccurately, well then, the English publisher if he engraves it too, can announce his edition as the correct one.[1] I am inclined to think that a matter of that kind merits the grateful recognition of an English publisher (in clinking coins, I mean) — After all we both know what sort of people those worthy publishers are. They are the most barefaced blackguards. Well now, all good wishes, my dear R[ies]. May Heaven bless you. With all my heart I embrace you. Give my greetings to all those who would like to have them — As for the tender subject of your marriage, *you yourself* will always find a sort of *opposition* from me, I mean, an opposition to *you* and a proposition *for your wife*.

Ever your friend

BEETHOVEN

(1168) *To Ignaz Schuppanzigh* [2]

[Autograph in the Geigy-Hagenbach collection]

[VIENNA], *April* 26, 1823

---

[1] Op. 110 was engraved by Clementi & Co. (1823 ?).

[2] Ignaz Schuppanzigh (1776–1830), son of a Viennese schoolmaster, became one of the most eminent violinists of his day, particularly as a quartet player. He was first a member of Prince Lichnowsky's private quartet and in 1808 he became first violin in the famous quartet of Count Razumovsky which existed until 1816. After the disbanding of this quartet, due chiefly to the fire which destroyed the Razumovsky Palace in 1815, Schuppanzigh settled for some years in St. Petersburg. He returned to Vienna in April, 1823 (Beethoven's welcome took the form of the above canon), and soon afterwards reformed his quartet and gave performances. Schuppanzigh was excessively stout and like Boldrini was fair game for Beethoven's jibes. Sir George Smart, who visited Beethoven in September, 1825, remarks in his diary (see *Leaves from the Journals of Sir George Smart,* edited by H. B. and C. L. E. Cox, London, 1907, p. 114) : 'He calls Schuppanzigh Sir John Falstaff, not a bad name considering the figure of this excellent violin player.' See *FRBH* II, 161-164.

[3] In *KHV.* this five-part canon is listed as WoO 184. The words are: Falstafferel Falstaff lass dich sehen (Little Falstaff, let us see you).

staff erel ———:——— Fa - lstaf   Falstaf   Falstaff lass dich

sehen   Falstafferel Falstafferel ———:——— Fa - lstaf

Falstaf   Falstaf lass dich sehen   Fal stafferel ———:——— Fa-

- lstaf   Fallstaf   Falstaff lass dich sehen

Falstafferel   Falstaf   Falstaf   Falstaf lass dich sehen

amici

amicus

BEETHOVEN

To the highly born
   I. von Schuppanzig
      sprung from
   the old English noble family
   of Milord Fallstaf.

See Shakespeare's biography of
   Mylord Fallstaf.[1]

(1169) *To [Franz Grillparzer]*[2]

[*Autograph in the Beethovenhaus, Bonn, H. C. Bodmer collection*]

SIR !   [VIENNA, *late April*, 1823]
   I am the innocent cause of your having been pestered
and besieged.   But the only commission I gave was to ascertain

---

[1] Both these sentences are written in Beethoven's hand on the verso.

[2] The autograph of this undated letter bears no address.   But on internal and circumstantial evidence the letter was undoubtedly written to Grillparzer and probably in the spring of 1823.   Franz Grillparzer (1791–1872), the famous Austrian dramatic poet, had met Beethoven in 1805 at the house of his uncle Joseph Sonnleithner.   Their first discussion about their operatic plan took place

the truth of the report that you had written an opera libretto in verse for me. How grateful I should be to you for your great kindness in having this beautiful poem sent to me in order to convince me that you have really considered it worth while to offer a sacrifice to your sublime Muse on my behalf — I hope that your health will soon improve. I too am in poor health. A country life is the only condition that gives me some relief. During the next few days I am to go into the country ; and then I hope to see you at my place where we can discuss all the necessary points — Partly because I am excessively overwhelmed with work and partly because, as I have already mentioned, I am in poor health, I am prevented at the moment from calling on you in person and expressing to you more vividly than I can do in writing, the great pleasure which you have given me with your glorious poem. I might almost say that I am prouder of this event than of any one of the greatest distinctions which could be conferred upon me.

> With kindest regards, your most devoted
> BEETHOVEN

(1170) *To Count Moritz Dietrichstein*

[MS not traced] [1]

YOUR EXCELLENCY !   [VIENNA, *c. April*, 1823]
I was very sorry to miss you. But I look forward to the pleasure of calling on you again on some future occasion. I will also discuss with Your Excellency as soon as possible the graduale and the offertory in order to learn whether you approve of my ideas about them and of the way in which these ideas should be carried out.[2] In regard to the Agnus Dei and the Dona nobis pacem I entirely agree with you, and I have almost followed the same method more or less in another Mass. But I will comply with Your Excellency's proposal

at Beethoven's rooms in Vienna on May 17, 1823. For an excellent account of Grillparzer's and Beethoven's association and collaboration on their projected opera 'Melusine' see *FRBH* I, 181-187.
    [1] Taken from Schlossar. *DM.*, Berlin, 1910, No. 13, p. 39.
    [2] Count Dietrichstein had suggested to Beethoven that he should compose a Mass for the Emperor. There are extant sketches for a Mass in C♯ minor. See Nottebohm, *Zweite Beethoveniana* (Leipzig, 1887), pp. 152, 541, 543.

even more closely. For it is high time to *break away from* the humdrum methods which have been established, above all when it is a question of true Divine worship.

I remain, Y[our] E[xcellency], with my most heartfelt and kindest regards your

BEETHOVEN

(1171) *To Anton Felix Schindler*

[Autograph in the Deutsche Staatsbibliothek, Berlin]

[VIENNA, *April*, 1823]

Show the enclosed to Baron Müller ¹ — If necessary, you may say that that rascal L[ichnowsky] also did not pay more than 400 gulden —

Kindly write me a few lines to say whether you found Baron Müller yesterday evening.

In any case give the enclosed to Baron M[üller] as quickly as possible.

(1172) *To Antonio Diabelli*

[Autograph in the Royal College of Music] ²

MY DEAR DIABELLI!   [VIENNA, *April*, 1823] ³

In my opinion the copying could be done in the following way, which would be best for you and for me. My manu-

¹ A Hungarian nobleman, Sigismund Count von Pronay Tót-Próna und zu Blathnitza, alias Baron Müller, offered his beautiful villa (Villa Pronay) at Hetzendorf to Beethoven as a summer retreat in 1823, an offer which Beethoven accepted. He remained at Hetzendorf for three months.

² The autographs of this letter and of Letter 575 were found in November, 1956, in a brown paper parcel in a safe in the Royal College of Music. The parcel contained not only letters to Sir George Grove, the first Director of the College, who died in 1900, but also autograph letters of Mendelssohn, Spontini, etc. This discovery was discussed by the music critic of *The Times* in an article published on December 7, 1956. A facsimile of the above letter, apparently hitherto inedited, was included in an article on 'Beethoven letters in the R.C.M.' by the present editor, published in the *R.C.M. Magazine* for July, 1958.

³ This short letter was probably written in the spring of 1823 when Beethoven, after considerable hesitation, had decided to allow the firm of Cappi & Diabelli to publish his 33 pianoforte variations on a waltz composed by the latter, and before going off to the country was arranging with Schindler for the copying and proof-reading.

script is written on sheets. You could give Schindler all the sheets you have copied and your *copy* as well. You would always have *your copy* returned to you on the day I received it. In this way we should *both* press on quickly with the work —

In the greatest haste, your friend

BEETHOV[EN]

(1173) *To Anton Felix Schindler*

[*Autograph in the Deutsche Staatsbibliothek, Berlin*]

[VIENNA, *April*, 1823]

Most respectfully do I request you to tell me why this Hetzendorf business could not be settled by yesterday? — And for what reason that gentleman, Bar[on] Müller, wants to come to me at eight or twelve o'clock today? Further, I request you to let me have the address of Baron Müller and the Countess.[1]

BEETHOVEN

This is not a question of *conferring favours*. On the contrary, what is *lawful* and *right* will decide here without respect of persons.

(1174) *To the Archduke Rudolph*

[*Autograph in the Gesellschaft der Musikfreunde, Vienna*]

YOUR IMPERIAL HIGHNESS!　　　　　[VIENNA, *April*, 1823]

I felt very ill yesterday and the day before; and unfortunately I had no one whom I could send to inform Y.I.H. As I felt better yesterday evening I went into town in order to ask Schlemmer to correct the sonata.[2] He was not at home and I left a message asking him to come here today. I am

---

[1] Possibly the pianist Frau von Jenny mentioned by Beethoven in his letter to Neate of April 19, 1817 (Letter 778, p. 681, n. 1). Therese and Susanna von Jenny were members of the Gesellschaft der Musikfreunde, Vienna. See O. E. Deutsch, *Schubert, A Documentary Biography* (London, 1946), pp. 60-61.

[2] Op. 111. Beethoven is referring to the corrections to the Paris edition published by Schlesinger in 1822. These were for the Vienna edition published in 1823 by Cappi & Diabelli.

sending you the sonata by him and I shall be with you before
four o'clock today in order to wait upon Y.I.H.

Your Imperial Highness's

most obedient servant

L. v. BEETHOVEN

(1175) *To Ferdinand Ries, London*

[*Autograph in the Beethovenhaus, Bonn, H. C. Bodmer collection*] [1]

[VIENNA, *April*, 1823]

. . . as well as coping with my cruel predicament I still
have many debts to discharge. Hence I shall be delighted to
hear whether you have come to an agreement about the Mass
and can let me have the fee as well. By that time the Mass
will have already been copied for dispatch to London. As
to the few sovereigns who have received copies of it one need
have no scruples about them. If a Viennese publisher raised
no objection to that, still less should a London publisher
bother his head about it, seeing that, in addition, I am giving
a written undertaking that in any event not a single note of it
shall be published either in engraved form or in any other
form — and, what is more, the statement guarantees all this
in full.[2] Press forward urgently with all these arrangements
for your poor friend; moreover I am awaiting your plan for
my journey. Things have become too difficult. I am being
shorn by the Cardinal more closely than I used to be. If I
don't go to him, my absence is regarded as a crimen legis
majestatis.[3] The additional payment I receive consists in my
having, moreover, to draw my miserable earnings by means
of a *stamped form* — Since you, it seems, would like to have a
dedication from me, how gladly will I gratify your desire,
much more gladly, entre nous, than the desires of the *greatest
bigwigs*. The devil knows how one is to avoid being man-
handled by them. The dedication of the new symphony will
be *to you* — I hope that I shall eventually be the recipient of
a *dedication* from you —

[1] A portion of this fragmentary letter is in Schindler's hand. The passage is
indicated below.

[2] There was no English edition of the 'Missa Solemnis' in Beethoven's lifetime.

[3] A violation of the sovereign's law, i.e. *lèse-majesté*.

Bauer is receiving herewith a fresh communication to the King in which, however, mention is made only of the Schlacht bei Vittoria, which he took with him in engraved form. There is no reference to the Mass. Please be so kind as to tell Herr Bauer to open the former in order to see what the communication contains. Herr Bauer was not given the Mass. It amounts to this, in fact : Bauer is to open the letter which he took from here to the King and in it he will see what has been written to the King about the Schlacht von Vittoria.[1] *The communication to him which now follows is substantially the same,* but no further mention is made of the Mass. Well, our amiable friend Bauer should see whether he cannot obtain for it at any rate a butcher's knife or a tortoise. It is understood, of course, that the engraved copy of the score will also be presented to the King — Bauer is *returning to Vienna at the end of May.* So please *be so kind* as to acquaint him *immediately* with what concerns him — Today's letter will cost you a lot of money. Just deduct the amount from what you are going to send me. How sorry I am to have to trouble you — God be with you — Give my best greetings to your wife until I arrive in London. Take care. You think that I am *old,* but I am a *youthful old man* —

Ever your
BEETHOVEN

(1176) *To Louis Schlösser* [2]

[Autograph in the Beethovenhaus, Bonn, H. C. Bodmer collection]

[VIENNA, *May* 6, 1823] [3]

I am sending you, my dear Schlösser, a letter for Cherubini and one for the publisher Schlesinger.[4] You will have to

[1] The whole passage from the beginning of the paragraph to 'Vittoria' is in Schindler's hand.

[2] Louis Schlösser (1800–1886), a musician and composer who after being trained in Vienna by Seyfried, Mayseder and Salieri, became Kapellmeister at Darmstadt, his native town. In his *Erinnerungen an Beethoven,* first published in 1880, Schlösser gives a graphic and moving description of his meeting with Beethoven. Before Schlösser's departure for Paris Beethoven gave him, on May 6th, a copy of his canon on the opening words of Goethe's poem 'Edel sei der Mensch', listed in *KHV.* as WoO 185.

[3] The date is noted in another hand.

[4] Moritz Schlesinger who had started his own publishing house in Paris in 1821.

enquire *about the latter's address* at Steiner's *house* in the little Paternostergasse. Just say that *I* have sent you with an introduction to Herr von Haslinger — Give all kinds of amiable messages to Cherubini and tell him that my most ardent longing is that we should soon have another opera composed by him, that, moreover, of all our contemporaries I have the highest regard for him and that I trust that he has received my letter and that I most earnestly desire to have a few lines from him — Enquire also from Schlesinger whether he received the letter to Cherubini and delivered it [1] and what is the reason why I have not yet received any copies of the C minor sonata — which I ought to have received.[2] I most urgently request you to be so very kind as to write to me from Paris about these two matters, i.e. Cherubini and Schlesinger. In the Paris post, where the letters are just thrown into a chest, one must take care not to forget to add the postage fee, because, if not, the letters are left lying there and one can only recover them by writing to Paris about them.

May Heaven grant you everything that is good. I shall always be glad to take an interest in you —

Your devoted

BEETHOVEN

(1177) *To Carl Lissner, St. Petersburg* [3]

[*Autograph in the Nationalbibliothek, Vienna*]

MY WORTHY HERR LISSNER!   [VIENNA, *May* 7, 1823] [4]

Herr von Schuppanzigh, who is now in Vienna,[5] has assured me that you ardently desire to purchase some of my

---

[1] Evidently Beethoven's letter dated March 15, which Cherubini never received. Cf. Letter 1154, p. 1016, n. 2.

[2] Op. 111.

[3] Carl Lissner (Karl Ivanovich Lisner), born in Czechoslovakia, was a music dealer and publisher who in 1795 opened his firm in St. Petersburg. He published the *Giornale Musicale del Teatro Italiano*, edited by Bernhard Theodor Breitkopf (1745–1820), which appeared from 1795 to 1798. According to the Russian Directories Lissner was still doing business in 1824.

[4] The autograph is endorsed in another hand : 'In Petersburg. Vienna, May 7, 1823.'

[5] After the disbanding of the Razumovsky quartet owing to the destruction by fire of Count Razumovsky's palace on December 31, 1815, Schuppanzigh went on tour and finally settled in St. Petersburg. He returned to Vienna in April, 1823. Cf. Letter 1168, p. 1027, n. 2.

intellectual products for your firm — Perhaps you would like to have the following works, namely :

Six bagatelles or trifles for pianoforte solo, the fee 20 gold ducats [1]

33 variations on a popular theme for pianoforte solo, which form one work, 30 gold ducats.[2]

Two grand songs with choruses, settings of poems by Goethe and Matthisson, which can be sung either with a suitable instrumental accompaniment or with a pianoforte accompaniment, 12 gold ducats — [3]

I request you to let me have a reply as quickly as possible, for other publishers too would like to have some of my works [4] —

I am, Sir,

Your most devoted

LUDWIG VAN BEETHOVEN

(1178) *To Anton Felix Schindler*

[*Autograph in the Deutsche Staatsbibliothek, Berlin*]

[VIENNA, *May*, 1823]

The question is whether it is better that the postman who is nearest to Hetzendorf should fetch the letters from here or whether the letters should lie here at the Post Office.[5]   In that case, however, the mail coach dispatch office would have to be informed and, what is more, at the place where letters are given out in exchange for receipts —

[1] Op. 119.   [2] Op. 120.   [3] Op. 122 and 121b.
[4] So far as is known, Lissner did not publish any work composed by Beethoven.
[5] Beethoven moved to Hetzendorf on May 17th.   He remained there until August 13th, when he went to Baden.

(1179) *To Anton Felix Schindler, Vienna*

[*Autograph in the Deutsche Staatsbibliothek, Berlin*]

[HETZENDORF, *shortly after May* 17, 1823] [1]

BEGINNING

Papageno, say nothing about what I said about Prussia.[2] No attention should be paid to my remark; it can only be compared to Martin Luther's Table Talk. I am asking my brother [3] too not to take off his padlock [4] and not to divulge anything below and above the Selchwurstgasse [5] — The var[iations] were left behind.[6] Send them out by the house-keeper. And send me also those intended for London — Don't act in accordance with your self-conceit, for, as it is, everything is going wrong.

CONTINUATION

I request you kindly to let me know where the diploma was put the last time before it had to be sent to the Government, and how long ago it was dispatched. What is that wretched story again about Prince E[sterházy]? [7]

END

Find out from that arch-clown Diabelli when the French copy of the C minor sonata is to be printed so that I may obtain it for proof-reading.[8] At the same time I have made the condition that I shall receive four copies of it, including one on fine paper for the Cardinal. If on this occasion too Diabelli behaves in his usual boorish way, I will sing him a

[1] Schindler noted '1824' on the autograph, which on internal evidence is impossible. One paragraph and two sentences have been obliterated by Beethoven.
[2] I.e. about the King of Prussia's delay in replying to the invitation to subscribe to the Mass. In the end the King did so.
[3] In the autograph the word 'Papageno', which follows, is obliterated.
[4] In Mozart's opera 'Die Zauberflöte', Act I, sc. 3 and 5, Papageno's mouth is padlocked as a punishment for telling lies.
[5] Probably Kothgasse, where Beethoven and his brother had been living in adjoining houses.
[6] Op. 120.
[7] Esterházy did not subscribe to the 'Missa Solemnis'.
[8] Op. 111.

bass aria in person in his shop, so that both the shop and the Graben may resound with it [1] —

Your most humble servant

BEETHOVEN

(1180) *To Anton Felix Schindler, Vienna*

[Autograph in the Deutsche Staatsbibliothek, Berlin]

[HETZENDORF, shortly after May 17, 1823*]*

SAMOTHRACIAN S[COUNDRE]L,[2]

What has happened to the trombone part? [3] It is quite certain that the fellow still has it — seeing that he did not put it in when he delivered the Gloria and that we failed to notice how bad his copying was and therefore did not think of taking the trombone part from him. If necessary, I shall go into Vienna to see the police about this — I am sending herewith for Rampel,[4] first of all, the theme of the variations, which he should just copy on a separate single sheet — and then he still has to copy the remainder until the 13th variation or, rather, to the end of the 12th variation.[5] That finishes this business —

You will have to extract from Schlemmer what is still missing in the Kyrie —

Show him my postscript; and now satis — I will have nothing more to do with such arrant s[coundre]ls —

My best wishes, but do attend to everything — I have to bandage my eyes at night and must spare them a good deal, for, *if I don't,* as Smetana [6] writes, I shall write very few more notes.

My very best regards to Wocher,[7] whom I shall visit in

---

[1] On the autograph Schindler has noted: 'Diabelli, who was quite unmoved by Beethoven's abusive language in connexion with Op. 111, wrote to the composer that he would take down the threatened bass aria, have it engraved and even pay him for it. After this Beethoven showed a little more forbearance.'
[2] According to Schindler Beethoven is alluding to the mysteries of musical art, and chiefly of his own compositions. Samothrace, a small island in the Aegean Sea, was formerly celebrated for its religious mysteries, into which the votaries had to be initiated.
[3] I.e. of the 'Missa Solemnis'. See *KHV.* 361.
[4] See Letter 1335, p. 1158, n. 4.   [5] Of Op. 120.   [6] Cf. Letter 657, p. 599, n. 2.
[7] Anton Wocher was courier to Prince Paul Esterházy, who was then Austrian Ambassador in London.

1037

person as soon as I go into town; and let me know whether
the var[iations] have been sent off already?

All good wishes [1]

Postscript

Diabelli is receiving herewith the old material and a fair
amount of new material.[2]

My eyes, which are rather worse than better, allow me to
see to everything only very slowly.

As soon as Diabelli has finished this work, send it out to
me and then he will receive everything else at once — That
the owner must have the manuscript in order to prove that
he really is the owner is a regulation which is new to me, and
I never heard of such a thing; what goes to prove the contrary
is the collection of MSS which I still possess; engraved copies
were made of several of them and they were then returned
to me —

I admit that occasionally I have been asked for a written
statement about the ownership of a work; and D[iabelli] too
can have this —

D[iabelli] could have claimed a copy. But you know what
that copy turned out to be, the more so as it was desirable
to hand over the var[iations] to D[iabelli] as quickly as was
humanly possible.

(1181) *To Anton Felix Schindler, Vienna*

[Autograph in the Deutsche Staatsbibliothek, Berlin]

DEAR S[CHINDLER]! —   [HETZENDORF, *after May* 17, 1823]

I hope that this business which is so tiresome for you may
turn out exceedingly well.[3] In any case I was *unfortunately*
not quite *wrong* not to trust Diab[elli] entirely —

All that I have to ask you today is to collect several patterns
of flannel at the big shops. It would please me well if before
you go to my brother?! you would bring me the patterns

---

[1] The autograph is not signed.
[2] Beethoven means more variations than the original nine.
[3] In his note on the autograph Schindler states that Beethoven is referring to
the dispute between himself (Schindler) and Diabelli about the 'Missa Solemnis'.

with their prices. For I can no longer stand this accursed flannel which I am wearing at present —

Yours,

BEETHOVEN

(1182) *To Antonio Diabelli, Vienna*

[*Autograph in the Beethovenhaus, Bonn, H. C. Bodmer collection*] [1]

DEAR DIABELLI!   [HETZENDORF, *late May*, 1823]
You should do the engraving exactly from the Paris copy [2], for the other one has some additional mistakes.[3] Just send me the proofs here and I will return them at once. *Make haste.* It serves them *both* right, for they deserve it, although indeed I am no advocate of such treatment — Please let me have four copies for myself, one of which should be on fine paper for His Eminence — Well, there is one more favour for which I shall perhaps beg you in a fortnight and *only for the period of a fortnight*, which is, to lend me *then* 300 gulden V.C. The reason for this request is my poor health which has been even more impaired by my horrible rooms. Why, quite recently for a whole three weeks I had in addition *sore eyes* (and by the doctor's orders I was forbidden to write or to read). Today at last is the first day I have been using my eyes again, and even so very carefully and very sparingly — *Perhaps it may not be at all necessary*, but be so kind as to let me have a letter to say whether, if I should need it, I could certainly count on being able to borrow this sum from you for a fortnight. Well, I have merely to complete a work which will immediately bring me in some money. Hence you need only expect this request from me if I have not completely finished this work by a definite date — Perhaps, as we cannot do so immediately, we might come to some arrangement about it for the future — From all this you will gather in what difficulties these business transactions connected with the Mass have landed me. A merchant must have money *in advance*, but where is it to come from? In short, things are all very

---

[1] This autograph letter, presented to Schumann in 1845, was kept in his album together with a lock of Beethoven's hair.
[2] Moritz Schlesinger's edition of Op. 111. See *KHV.* 319-320.
[3] Probably the printed edition of Sauer & Leidesdorf. See *KHV.* 320.

badly arranged, and more to my loss than to my advantage. Judging by what the circumstances still appear to be, I consider that it is too late for me to retreat [1] — In all matters which concern me you must trust neither my worthy brother nor Herr Schindler. *Each is true to his type, but in a different way —*

Should you have anything to discuss with me, whatever it may be, do apply to *me alone.* Bitter experiences have also taught me this —

Your friend
BEETHOVEN

Please let me have a reply about that one point —

(1183) *To Anton Felix Schindler, Vienna*

[Autograph in the Deutsche Staatsbibliothek, Berlin]

MOST EXCELLENT FELLOW!   [HETZENDORF, *May,* 1823]
Please let me know about Esterházy and also about the post. At any rate a postman *from the Mauer* [2] has been here. I do hope that the matter has been settled satisfactorily —

No news yet from *Dresden* [3] — In a few days I will invite you to dinner, but indeed I still have a bad eye. Today at last it seems to be recovering, but I must not use it, or at least hardly at all —

Your friend
BEETHOVEN

(1184) *To Tobias Haslinger, Vienna*

[Autograph in the Beethovenhaus, Bonn, H. C. Bodmer collection]

MOST EXCELLENT A[DJUTAN]T!   [HETZENDORF, *May,* 1823]
Please let me have a copy of the trio in B♭, of the violin sonata in G, of the solo sonata in E and of the solo sonata in A.[4] Please put in also the arrangement for pianoforte duet

---

[1] This sentence is added at the foot of the page.
[2] Mauer, popularly called 'Die Mauer', is a village not far from Mödling.
[3] The King of Saxony sent his acceptance in July, 1823.
[4] Op. 97, 96, 109 and 101.

of the sixth symphony.[1] About the last-mentioned work I am writing today or on Saturday to Breitkopf & Härtel, since this will have to be done in any case — For the arrangement is to be made at their expense —

Lastly, please add the pianoforte arrangement of the symphony in A,[2] and the pianoforte arrangement of the symphony in F.[3] —

For all these works I am in your debt, just as you are in mine. Ever your et et et

L. v. BTHVN [4]

(1185) *To Anton Felix Schindler, Vienna*

[Autograph in the Deutsche Staatsbibliothek, Berlin]

[HETZENDORF, May, 1823]

The arrangement was that you should provide the necessary bedclothes for yourself, just as I too did formerly in other similar cases, and because such a thing is a foregone conclusion — Well, the housekeeper will now procure them for you and I will pay for them [5] — Don't go to Schlemmer again. *Karl* is going there himself tomorrow morning. Please let me have the subscription form *for Prince Esterházy*, although it has been closed — I have another and a better idea about that. I want to write to him myself. But as I am not satisfied with the invitation, I want to alter it myself [6] — When you write to me, just write in exactly the same way as I do to you, that is to say, without giving me a title, without addressing

---

[1] For particulars of this arrangement of Op. 68 for pianoforte duet by Friedrich Mockwitz see *KHV*. 163. It had been published by Breitkopf & Härtel in December, 1822.

[2] For particulars of the pianoforte arrangement of Op. 92 made by A. Diabelli and published by Steiner see *KHV*. 260.

[3] The pianoforte arrangement of Op. 93 made by Haslinger and corrected by Czerny was published by Steiner.

[4] The address on the verso in Beethoven's hand is:

An Herrn von Tobias, Edler v. Hass—
Lin—
Ger—

[5] In the autograph, which is not signed, this paragraph is obliterated but can be deciphered.

[6] In the autograph the passage from 'for Prince Esterházy' to 'myself' is added at the foot of the page. Schindler has noted on the autograph that after mature deliberation Beethoven did not write to the Prince. See Letter 1188, p. 1043, n. 4.

me, without signing your name. Vita brevis, ars longa. And you need not use figures of speech,[1] but just say precisely what is necessary —

(1186) *To Anton Felix Schindler, Vienna*

[*Autograph in the Public State Library, Leningrad*]

[HETZENDORF, *May*, 1823][2]

Many compliments to the Director of Police and to Herr von Ungermann. The six gulden will follow. But they should not be given to him[3] until he has taken down the placard and delivered the receipt for the house-rent to the worshipful police[4] and has also undertaken to behave in future like a civilized person —

In haste, your
BEETHOVEN

NB. The worshipful police are most politely requested to settle the matter today with the landlord as quickly as possible, seeing that a much more important affair will demand their attention immediately afterwards[5] —

(1187) *To Anton Felix Schindler, Vienna*

[*Autograph in the Deutsche Staatsbibliothek, Berlin*]

[HETZENDORF, *late May*, 1823]

There are a great many mistakes in Diabelli's engraving of the variations.[6] Kindly collect the variations again at Dia-

---

[1] In the original the word used is 'figürlich'.
[2] Noted by Schindler who also transcribed this letter on the verso of the autograph.
[3] In his transcript Schindler adds 'to the landlord'.
[4] The words from 'But they' to ' police' are added at the foot of the page.
[5] This NB. appears at the top of the page above the letter proper. Schindler, who deleted the NB., noted on the verso of the autograph: 'This "much more important affair" was connected with the sordid marriage of his brother Johann. Beethoven wanted to report this dishonourable woman, who was no better than the widow of his late brother Carl, to the police, who incidentally were not authorized to deal with such matters. From that time forward Beethoven continued to urge his brother to divorce his wife and to appoint their nephew Karl heir to his property.'   [6] Op. 120.

belli's tomorrow. But the corrected copy must be sent along
with them —

As to the mistakes in the sonata — well, *you* must see from
the engraved copy the places where it is being sold *here*.[1]   I
think that it would only cost a small sum to have the errata
engraved or printed here. But do everything immediately
and then inform the publishers, that is to say, tell them how
many copies you have; make haste with everything, make
great haste. We are dealing with the mistakes we marked
and which Schlemmer copied.

If Schlemmer is satisfied with five gulden, he might earn
these too, provided there are as many sheets as copies. But
here too you must keep a watchful eye — See that everything
is done quickly, i.e. in the quickest way — [2]

(1188) *To Anton Felix Schindler, Vienna*

[*Autograph in the Deutsche Staatsbibliothek, Berlin*]

[HETZENDORF], *June* 1, 1823

Please be so kind as to look up Rampel,[3] or if you have
already received his work to send it out to me along with the
other material. Diabelli too will have finished his work by
now; and you can send that as well — Kindly give Schlemmer
the trombone parts on really good paper, since in that way
they are easier to copy.— I have written to Wocher myself;
and to save time I have sent by Karl, who happened to be
driving back to town, the invitation to Prince E[sterházy] —
We made only trifling alterations in the letter — such as *eure*
instead of *euere* and so forth, Nicolas instead of Nicola, alterations necessitated by the fact that you are really not a conscientious speller —

Well, you may now be so kind as to enquire from Herr
W[ocher] about the result of my application. I am doubtful
about its being favourable, for I suspect that he is not at all
well disposed to me, at any rate judging by his attitude on
previous occasions.[4] I am inclined to think that things of that

---

[1] Op. 111, first engraved in 1822 by Moritz Schlesinger in Paris.
[2] The autograph is not signed.   [3] See Letter 1335, p. 1158, n. 4.
[4] Prince Nikolaus Esterházy did not subscribe to the Mass.

kind can only be got out of him through women [1] — Thanks
to your kind efforts we now know at least how we can send a
letter to that worthy Scholz [2] — The bad weather and in
general the worse air in town are preventing me from going
into Vienna.[3]   Meanwhile my best wishes for your welfare
until I see you —

Your amicus
BEETHOVEN

PS.

It will certainly be all right to use the post, for in addition
I have made arrangements in town to ensure that no mistake
shall be made in that respect—

In Dresden we have drawn — blanks — Schlemmer has
just turned up and is again pressing me for money.   I have
now advanced him 70 gulden.   Business men, but not poor
devils like myself, can indulge in speculations — So far all I
have gained from that wretched speculation is an increase
in my debts [4] — I presume that you have seen that the Gloria
is finished ? ! — If only my eyes were cured, so that I could
write again, I could then carry on —

Have the var[iations] now been sent off to London ? [5]

NB.   So far as I remember, no mention is made in the
invitation to Prince Esterházy of the fact that the Mass is to be
distributed in manuscript only.   What mischief can be caused
by this omission !   I presume that Herr Artaria offered to
supply the Prince with a free copy of the Mass etc., so that
H[err] A[rtaria] might steal a work of mine for the third time.[6]
Wocher's attention must be drawn to this.

[1] This sentence is added at the foot of the page.
[2] Benedikt Scholz, Director of Music at Warmbrunn in Silesia, had on his own initiative written a German text for the Mass in C, Op. 86, which Beethoven received from him on April 26, 1823.   Beethoven was so delighted with his version that he wanted Scholz to provide a German text for the 'Missa Solemnis'.   Unfortunately Scholz died during the following year.   The autograph of the vocal parts of Op. 86 with Scholz's German text is in the Beethovenhaus, Bonn.
[3] According to Schindler's note on the autograph Beethoven is referring to the Countess Schafgotsch of Warmbrunn, who was then in Vienna.
[4] A reference to the small number of subscribers to the Mass.   In the end there were only ten.
[5] This remark and all the following ones are written upside down on the cover of the letter.   The variations are the Diabelli variations, Op. 120.
[6] The first time was in connexion with the string quintet, Op. 29, published in December, 1802, by Breitkopf & Härtel.   Cf. Letter 68, p. 78, n. 1.

It is understood that in such a transaction Papageno's good offices are not required.[1]

(1189) *To Anton Felix Schindler, Vienna*

[*Autograph in the Deutsche Staatsbibliothek, Berlin*]

SAMOTHRACIAN![2]   HETZENDORF, *on the 2nd of* [*June,* 1823]

Don't trouble to come here until, let us say, a hattisherif[3] has been issued. Meanwhile you have no reason to fear the *golden* rope — My swiftly sailing frigate, the highly and nobly born Fr[au] Schnaps,[4] will usually enquire after your health every two or three days —

All good wishes.

B[EETHOVE]N

And don't bring anyone.
All good wishes.

(1190) *To Moritz Schlesinger, Paris*

[*Autograph in the Beethovenhaus, Bonn, H. C. Bodmer collection*] [5]

VIENNA, *June* 3, 1823

Errata which I most humbly request you to have corrected immediately both for your sake and for mine [6] —

Page 2, bars 2 and 3 instead of  the

lower slur must be removed and marked thus ⌒⌒ over the 5 quavers.

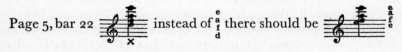 Page 5, bar 22 instead of there should be

---

[1] This remark is added in pencil at the side of the page.
[2] Cf. Letter 1180, p. 1037, n. 2.
[3] Cf. Letter 1132, p. 992, n. 5.
[4] Beethoven's housekeeper in 1823.
[5] One of the two leaves of the autograph is missing. Hence this list of corrections is not complete.
[6] Mistakes in the Paris edition of Op. 111.

Page 8, bar 9 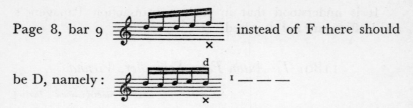 instead of F there should

be D, namely :  ¹ — — —

— — return the copies ; and although I was in a hurry I wrote what was correct, as it is here, and twice over. Nevertheless, incredible though it may seem, the first six notes were quite wrong, although they were correct in the first copy which was sent to me. But here the seventh note $_c^e$ was not right —

Page 22, bar 6 in the bass, instead of

there should be

In the same bar in the treble instead of a note

there should be only a dot after the F, namely :

As a striking incident, someone has sent me two copies in order to show me, strange though it be, how far one can succeed in imitating. One copy was engraved by you in Paris, the other by Leidesdorf in Vienna and so identical in every respect that neither can be distinguished from the other. The prices too are identical.² Apparently you know how to choose your friends. I understand that Diabelli too is now engraving it ³ — Although I have not received a copy from

¹ The first page ends here. The next two pages are missing. The fourth page then begins with Beethoven's remarks.
² This sentence is added at the foot of the page.
³ For further corrections of mistakes in the Berlin and Paris editions of Op. 111 see Letter 1190a.

you, yet I have considered it my duty to inform you of the new mistakes and the old ones which are still there ; and I request you to have them carefully corrected —

BEETHOVEN

(1190a) *To [Antonio Diabelli, Vienna]* [1]

[Autograph in the Beethovenhaus, Bonn, H. C. Bodmer collection]

[HETZENDORF, *June*, 1823]

Mistakes discovered as having been made by the two beach pedlars and rag-and-bone Jews called Schlesinger, between the Seine, the Thames, the Spree and the Danube. All whom they may concern are requested to examine them and to protect themselves from loss —

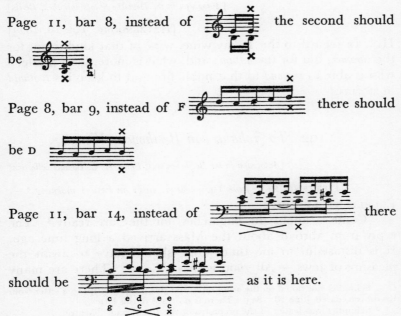

Page 11, bar 8, instead of   the second should be

Page 8, bar 9, instead of F   there should be D

Page 11, bar 14, instead of   there should be   as it is here.

[1] The present editor is indebted to Dr. Dagmar Weise for informing me of her acceptance of the theory put forward by Herr Hubert Unverricht that this list of corrections to Op. 111 was sent, not to A. M. Schlesinger, as suggested in the *Beethoven-Jahrbuch* 1953/54, pp. 50-51, but to Diabelli for the Vienna edition of this sonata. Cf. Letter 1190, p. 1045, n. 6.

Page 2, bar 2, instead of  there should

be . The lower slur should be removed.

Page 5, bar 22, instead of 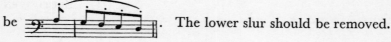 the second chord should

be

(1191) *To Anton Felix Schindler, Vienna*

[Autograph in the Deutsche Staatsbibliothek, Berlin]

[HETZENDORF, *June* 18, 1823]

II.[1] In regard to the Tokay wine, wine of that kind is not for the *summer*, but for the *autumn* and, what is more, for a fiddler [2] who is able to *respond* to that noble fire and to keep his *foothold* in storms [3] —

(1192) *To Johann van Beethoven, Vienna*

[Autograph in the Beethovenhaus, Bonn, H. C. Bodmer collection]

[HETZENDORF], *June* 19, [1823], *early on Friday morning* [4] —
EXCELLENT FELLOW!

Come — about the bagatelles, for they are ready.[5] The reply from abroad about the Mass arrived a long time ago. It is distasteful to me that — one should have to await the pleasure of Jews — All good wishes. Come. There are many

---

[1] Schindler has noted on the autograph that this is a postscript to a letter from Beethoven, dated June 18, 1823. There is no trace of this letter.

[2] Schindler was leader of the orchestra of the Josephstadt Theatre.

[3] In his biography of Beethoven (II, p. 298) Schindler elucidates the incident of Beethoven's present to him of six bottles of Tokay wine which he had received from an admirer.

[4] In 1823 June 19th fell on a Thursday. Beethoven had evidently kept the letter until the following morning.

[5] Op. 119.

things to discuss and you have good sense — in your pocket—
All good wishes, my worthy brother ? ? ! ! ! !

Yours and your faithful brother ¹

LUDWIG

Venes d'abord il y a des affaire d'une grande importance.²

(1193) *To Franz Schoberlechner, Vienna* ³

[Autograph in the Deutsche Staatsbibliothek, Berlin]

[HETZENDORF, June 26, 1823]

A capable fellow requires no other recommendations than
those from some respectable houses to others.

(1194) *To Anton Felix Schindler, Vienna* ⁴

[Autograph in the Deutsche Staatsbibliothek, Berlin]

[HETZENDORF, end of June, 1823]

Surely it must have been clear to you that I would have
nothing to do with this matter ⁵ — As for the question of
'being noble',⁶ I think I have given sufficient proof to you
that I am so on principle.   Indeed I fancy that you must have

¹ Beethoven spells the German 'Bruder' 'Brudere'.
² This remark is added outside on the fold beside the seal. Whenever Beethoven wished to add remarks on letters already sealed and to be delivered by hand, as this one obviously was, he usually did so in French so that the bearer could not understand them.
³ Franz Schoberlechner (1797–1843) was a young Viennese pianist who had been an *enfant prodige*. In 1823 Schoberlechner, who had held the post of Director of Music at the court of the Duchess of Lucca, travelled to Russia after giving concerts in Germany. From 1831 until about 1840 he lived and worked in Florence. See Hanslick, p. 223, n. 1. On June 25, 1823, Schoberlechner, then in Vienna, wrote to Beethoven asking him for letters of introduction to patrons in Leipzig, Dresden, Berlin, Moscow, Warsaw, etc. Beethoven did not reply but scrawled the above remark beside the address of the applicant's letter. For Schoberlechner's letter see Kal. IV, p. 271.
⁴ Beethoven addressed this letter: 'Pour Monsieur Papageno L[umpen] K[e]rl de Schindler'.
⁵ I.e. with Schoberlechner's request for letters of introduction. In his letter the applicant stated that Schindler had encouraged him to apply to Beethoven. Schindler in a remark written on Schoberlechner's letter denies this.
⁶ In his letter Schoberlechner hinted that persons of noble character were always glad to help young people to improve themselves.

noticed that even in the matter of my principles I have in no wise exceeded *the limits I had set myself* —
Sapienti sat on that subject [1]

(1195) *To Anton Felix Schindler, Vienna*

[*Autograph in the Deutsche Staatsbibliothek, Berlin*]

[HETZENDORF, *June*, 1823] [2]

Here are the copies of the Gloria.   The ternions [3] are quite new instruments to me.

Don't forget the reply about the diploma, for I want to attend to that myself.   I am coming tomorrow to hand out the Credo in person —

O very wise one!   I kiss the hem of your coat.

NB.   Schlemmer is to have the tiny sheet.   Stay at home a little longer tomorrow morning.[4]

(1196) *To Anton Felix Schindler, Vienna*

[*Autograph in the Deutsche Staatsbibliothek, Berlin*]

[HETZENDORF, *June*, 1823]

I am replying to the essential points as promptly as possible —

Schlemmer has been to see me.   *He always comes out here to me* so that the work may proceed in an orderly way, *such as it now demands.*

Hence you need no longer gallop up the four flights of stairs — And do not pay any more calls at the Embassies *which have subscribed* [5] —

When writing to all the heads I myself shall manage to put the affair in its proper light and I shall explain the delay —

---

[1] This letter is not signed.

[2] In a note on the autograph Schindler states that this letter was written at Baden in the summer of 1823.   This is impossible because Schlemmer died before Beethoven left Hetzendorf on August 13th.

[3] A ternion is a quire of three sheets, each folded in two.   An ordinary quire is made up of four sheets.   Beethoven is evidently attempting a joke.

[4] The NB. is added at the top of the page with a line drawn underneath.

[5] Here two and a half lines have been obliterated and are indecipherable.

Please leave the variations in your room ¹ so that the house-keeper may take them with her. Perhaps I shall have another opportunity of sending them to London — As soon as the rain *really* begins to pour in, the w[inter] windows can be fixed, but not until then — Chuck out that house churl at once and shut the door on him.

I cannot accept those delightful invitations just yet.² I am busy working as much as my bad eye allows me to ; and if the weather is fine I go out. I will express my thanks, of course, in person to those two lovely women for their kindness — Not a word from Dresden — I shall wait until the end of this month and then I will instruct a lawyer at Dresden — ³

I will let you know about Schob[erlechner] tomorrow —

Vale.

(1197) *To Antonio Diabelli, Vienna*

[Autograph in the Museum of Musical Culture, Bucharest]

[HETZENDORF, June, 1823]

I advise you to have another look yourself at the C minor sonata, for the engraver is not sufficiently musical.⁴ And, of course, the speed with which the work was done is another reason, I admit — I am again sending you my manuscript for the purpose of checking the work — My eyes must still be spared —

Your friend
BEETHOVEN

It will be time enough if I have the other copies of the sonata on Monday afternoon. Thank you for the six copies ; and I shall be equally delighted to reiterate my thanks for another six.

¹ Here one and a half lines have been obliterated and are indecipherable.
² Beethoven is referring to invitations from the singers Henriette Sontag and Karoline Unger. For a note on the former see Letter 1289, p. 1125, n. 2.
³ The King of Saxony sent his acceptance in July, 1823.
⁴ Op. 111 had been engraved by Moritz Schlesinger (Paris) in 1822. Cappi & Diabelli's edition appeared in 1823.

(1198) *To Anton Felix Schindler, Vienna*

[Autograph in the Deutsche Staatsbibliothek, Berlin]

[HETZENDORF, *June*, 1823]

If the last proofs of the variations [1] are ready, as I presume they are and as I shall see today when you have received some proof-sheets, then I will request Herr Diabelli to let me have as soon as possible the eight copies on fine paper which he has *very kindly* promised me — The weather is bad. But even if I am alone, I am never *lonely* —

God be with you.

(1199) *To Anton Felix Schindler, Vienna*

[Autograph in the Deutsche Staatsbibliothek, Berlin]

[HETZENDORF, *June*, 1823]

What has been done about Schlemmer?

Tell my brother that if he requires anything from me, he has only to have a letter sent to me through you and that you will let him have my letter of reply — I have thought out something in connexion with that diplomat,[2] something that is going to be presented to that fellow like a resounding pistol shot —

As for the carpenter tell him that I am not well, but that I shall come in immediately about the chest.

I shall find a way of raising some money.[3]

(1200) *To Anton Felix Schindler, Vienna*

[Autograph in the Deutsche Staatsbibliothek, Berlin]

[HETZENDORF, *June*, 1823]

Please be sure *not to forget about Smetana*. We are expecting you to dinner tomorrow, and shall wait for you until about

---

[1] The words 'of the variations' are added at the foot of the page. The variations are, of course, Op. 120.

[2] I.e. that schemer. Beethoven constantly accused Johann of intriguing against him.   [3] Letters 1198-1200 are not signed.

one o'clock — It is just too unfortunate about the house churl —
It is difficult to arrange everything from here —

All good wishes until tomorrow when we shall be delighted
to see you.

I have been into Vienna but not on account of that idiotic
landl[ord], etc.

(1201) *To Antonio Diabelli, Vienna*

[Autograph not traced] [1]

[HETZENDORF, *June*, 1823]

I absentmindedly sent you my manuscript yesterday instead of the French edition of the C minor sonata.[2] Please return
it.   If you would like to have the French edition returned
to you, I will send it to you immediately, although I should
be glad to be allowed to keep it.   The text of the corrected
proofs of the variations will surely be finished; and please be
so kind as to send it to me for my further approval.[3] As for
the promised eight copies, I have come to the conclusion that
your first offer to let me have the eight copies on fine paper
would be, after all, very welcome, since I could put a few of
my friends under an obligation to me by presents of that kind.

The metronome will be attended to, though this will have
to be postponed for a little, because I am now too hard pressed
for time.   Your friend

BEETHOVEN

(1202) *To Antonio Diabelli, Vienna*

[Autograph not traced] [4]

[HETZENDORF, *June*, 1823]

As soon as the corrections to the sonata have been finished,
return them to me together with the French c[opy] [5] — I

---

[1] The autograph of this letter was stuck into the cover of a Beethoven sketch-
book of 1825, which belonged to Cecilio de Roda, who published it in *Un quaderno
di autografi di Beethoven del 1825* (Torino, 1907).

[2] Op. 111.

[3] Op. 120.

[4] From a facsimile in Sonneck, p. 16. The autograph was then in private
ownership in America.

[5] Op. 111.

shall let you know soon about the metronome — Kindly do a bit of checking yourself, for my eyes can scarcely stand any more checking without injury — Your friend

BEETHOVEN

And please send also the corrections to the variations.[1]

(1203) *To the Archduke Rudolph, Vienna*

[Autograph in the Gesellschaft der Musikfreunde, Vienna]

YOUR IMPERIAL HIGHNESS!   HETZENDORF, *July* 1, 1823 [2]

Since Y.I.H.'s departure I have been ailing almost the whole time; and latterly I have been having bad pain in my eyes. This has subsided, however, but only to the extent that during the last week I have been able to use my eyes again, though sparingly. From the accompanying receipt dated June 27th Y.I.H. will see that I have sent you some music. As Y.I.H. seemed to enjoy hearing the C minor sonata, I thought that I should not be too presumptuous if I gave you the surprise of dedicating it to Your Highness.[3] The variations were copied certainly five or even six weeks ago. But in the meantime the condition of my eyes did not allow me to check them all; and I hoped in vain for a complete recovery. So in the end I let Schlemmer check them; and although they may not look very tidy, yet they should be correct.[4] The C minor sonata was engraved in Paris, and very inaccurately; and as it was engraved again here, I made certain so far as possible that it would be correct —

I shall soon send you a finely engraved copy of the variations.[5] With regard to the Mass which Y.I.H. would like to see more generally available, the condition of my health, which had then been rather poor for several years, demanded that I should think out a way of improving my situation to some extent, the more so as on its account I had incurred heavy debts and had to refuse, for the same reason also, invitations to

---

[1] Op. 120.
[2] The autograph is dated June 1st in Beethoven's hand. But on internal evidence this must be a mistake for July 1st.   [3] Op. 111.
[4] Evidently a manuscript copy of Op. 120 made specially for the Archduke Rudolph.
[5] Op. 120 was published in Vienna by Cappi & Diabelli.

go to England. The Mass seemed to be the very thing. I was advised to offer this work to several courts. However difficult I found it to do this, yet I was convinced that if I failed to take this step I should only have myself to blame. I sent therefore to several courts an invitation to subscribe to this Mass. I fixed the fee at 50 ducats, because the general opinion was that this was not an excessive sum and that if there were several subscribers some profit would be made. So far the list of subscribers has brought me honour, it is true, for their Royal Majesties of France and Prussia have subscribed. Moreover I received a few days ago from Petersburg a letter from my friend Prince Nikolaus Galitzin in which that truly amiable Prince informs me that His Imperial Russian Majesty has also become a subscriber and that I shall soon have more details about this from the Imperial Russian Embassy in Vienna.[1] At the same time, although a few others have subscribed, I have not yet received as much as the amount of a publisher's fee for this Mass. On the other hand there is for me the advantage that the work is still *mine*. The expense of having the work copied is also very great and will be even greater, because I am adding three new movements, which when I have finished composing them, I shall immediately send to Y.I.H. — Perhaps Y.I.H. would not find it troublesome to use your influence on behalf of the Mass with the Grand Duke of Tuscany so that His Highness too might order a copy. An invitation to the Grand Duke of Tuscany was already sent off, it is true, a long time ago by von Odelgha, his agent in Vienna ;[2] and Odelgha solemnly assures me that the invitation will certainly be accepted. But I am rather doubtful, for several months have now elapsed and I have heard nothing more.[3] Since this business has now been set going, it is only natural that I should do my utmost to achieve the purpose I have in view.— I have found this undertaking most difficult ; and I have found it even more difficult to tell Y.I.H. about it or to express my feelings about it, but '*Necessity knows no law*' — I am only too grateful to Him who rules the stars in the firmament, that I can now begin to use my eyes again. At the moment I am

---

[1] Prince Galitzin's letter, dated June 2nd, is quoted in full in *TDR* IV, 554.
[2] Carlo di Odelgha was the envoy of the Grand Duke of Tuscany.
[3] The Grand Duke of Tuscany did become a subscriber.

composing a new symphony for England, i.e. for the Phil-harmonic Society, and I hope to finish it in less than a fortnight.[1] As yet I cannot put any strain on my eyes for long. So I beg Y.I.H. to be patient a little longer about Your Highness's variations.[2] I think them charming; but all the same they require a more thorough examination than I have been able to give them. Y.I.H. must now continue, in particular, your exercises in composition and when sitting at the pianoforte you should jot down your ideas in the form of sketches. For this purpose you should have a small table beside the piano-forte. In this way not only is one's imagination stimulated but one learns also to pin down immediately the most remote ideas. You should also compose without a pianoforte; and you should sometimes work out a simple melody, for instance, a chorale with simple and again with different harmonies according to the laws of counterpoint and even neglecting the latter. This will certainly not give Y.I.H. a headache; nay, rather, it will afford you real enjoyment when you thus find yourself in the very swim of artistic production.— Gradually there comes to us the power to express just what we desire and feel; and to the nobler type of human being this is such an essential need — My eyes bid me stop writing.— I wish Y.I.H. all that is beautiful and good; and in sending you my compliments I describe myself with the deepest reverence as

Your Imperial Highness's
most faithful servant
L. v. BEETHOVEN

(1204) *To the Archduke Rudolph, Vienna*

[*Autograph in the Gesellschaft der Musikfreunde, Vienna*]

Postscript [3]   [HETZENDORF, *July* 1, 1823]

Should Your Imperial Highness desire to give me the pleasure of a letter, please be so kind as to have it addressed

---

[1] According to Schindler II, 56, the score of the ninth symphony (Op. 125) was finished in February, 1824.

[2] Evidently Beethoven had given the Archduke Rudolph another theme on which to compose variations. This second theme has not been identified. See *KHV.* 592-593.

[3] This postscript is almost certainly an addition to the preceding letter.

'To L. v. Beethoven in Vienna', for even when I am at Hetzendorf I receive all my letters quite safely.— I wonder whether Y.I.H. would be so gracious, that is to say, if you do not find it inconvenient, as to recommend the Mass to Prince Anton at Dresden, so that His Royal Majesty of Saxony might become a subscriber, which he would certainly do if Y.I.H. were in some way to express your appreciation.[1] As soon as I am informed that you have shown me this favour, I will immediately apply to the Director General of the Royal Theatre and of Music at Dresden,[2] the person who is responsible for making such arrangements, and I will send him the invitation to the King of Saxony to become a subscriber. But I should not like to do this without an introduction from Y.I.H.— Moreover *my opera Fidelio* was performed with great applause during the festivities in honour of the visit to Dresden of the King of Bavaria; and all their Majesties attended the performance. I heard this from the above-mentioned Director General, who asked me through Weber [3] for the score and sent me afterwards a really handsome present.[4]— I know that Y.I.H. will forgive me for troubling you with this request. Y.I.H. will, of course, be aware how little I am given to importuning you. Should there be anything offensive in my request, however, anything which may displease you, then, of course, it is clearly understood that I am none the less convinced of your noble-mindedness and graciousness. My petition is prompted neither by greed nor by a desire to profiteer, for I have always shunned such low motives. But necessity compels me to make every effort to extricate myself from my present predicament. In order to forestall any harsh criticism, it is certainly best to be frank — Owing to my persistent ill health which has prevented me from composing as much as I used to, I am burdened with a debt of 2300 gulden A.C., and only by making extraordinary efforts shall I be able to discharge

---

[1] Prince Anton, brother of the King of Saxony, was the Archduke Rudolph's brother-in-law. The King became a subscriber to the 'Missa Solemnis'. His letter of acceptance, dated September 12, 1823, is quoted in Kal. V, p. 338.

[2] Geheimrat von Könneritz. See Letter 1210, p. 1065, n. 2.

[3] It is known that during the first six months of 1823 Beethoven wrote at least three letters to Carl Maria von Weber, who visited him at Baden on October 5, 1823. All Beethoven's letters to Weber have disappeared.

[4] Geheimrat von Könneritz had sent Beethoven a present of 40 ducats. See Letter 1210, p. 1065, n. 4.

it. If only the number of subscribers can be increased, this will be some help; and if my health improves, for which there are good grounds for hope, then by means of my compositions I shall again be able to stand firmly on my own feet — Meanwhile I trust that Y.I.H. will not treat my frank confession ungraciously. If I were not liable to be accused of not being as *active* as I used to be, then I would have kept silence, as I always do. In regard to the recommendations, I am quite convinced that Y.I.H. is glad to do good *wherever you can* and that in this respect you will make no exception *in my case.* —

With the deepest reverence I remain Your Imperial Highness's

most faithful servant

L. v. BEETHOVEN

(1205) *To Anton Felix Schindler, Vienna*

[*Autograph in the Deutsche Staatsbibliothek, Berlin*]

HETZENDORF, *July* 2, 1823

MOST EXCELLENT HERR VON SCHINDLER!

The landlord's brutality which has persisted from the very beginning of my stay in that house until now, demands the help of the Imperial and Royal Police.[1] Just apply to them. As for the winter windows, the housekeeper had been ordered to see to them, especially after the very heavy rain, and to find out whether it was necessary to fit them owing to the possibility of rain pouring into the rooms. But she did not find that rain had poured in nor was then pouring in at all. So acting on this conviction I had the bolt padlocked in order that that particularly brutal fellow should not open my rooms during my absence, as he had threatened to do — Tell the police how he behaved later on when you were there and how he displayed the card without my having given him notice, which in any case I need not do until July 25th —

He is acting quite as unfairly in refusing to let me have the receipt for the quarter from April 24th to July 25th, as this notice shows, seeing that I am to pay for lighting, a thing I had never heard of; and those horrible rooms without *stove*

[1] Beethoven is referring to his rooms at Kothgasse 60.

heating and with the most wretched *general heating* cost me at least 250 gulden V.C. as an extra expense apart from the rent,[1] merely in order to keep body and soul together during the winter I spent there —

It was deliberate swindling on his part, seeing that I was never allowed to see the rooms on the first floor but only those on the second, so that I should know nothing of the many drawbacks of the former. I really cannot understand how it is possible *for the Government to tolerate such a disgraceful method of heating which is so injurious to human health.* You remember what the walls in your room looked like with the smoke and how much it cost even to lessen, let alone entirely to remove, that nuisance. Meanwhile the main thing is that he should be ordered to take down the notice card and let me have my receipt for the rent which I have paid. In no circumstances will I pay for that wretched lighting, seeing that, in any case, I was faced with excessive expenses merely in order to keep alive in those rooms. — The condition of my eyes does not yet allow me to stand town air; otherwise I would go to the Imperial Police myself —

Your most devoted

L. v. BEETHOVEN

(1206) *To Anton Felix Schindler, Vienna*

[*Autograph in the Deutsche Staatsbibliothek, Berlin*]

[HETZENDORF, *shortly after July* 9, 1823]

Here is the letter to Herr von Obreskow.[2] So now take it to him and say that as far as the money is concerned, only a receipt need be sent to me, for which, as soon as I send it there, the money can be given to whoever hands in the receipt— As soon as I receive this money, you will immediately get 50 gulden V.C. for your pains. Don't say anything more than is necessary, for people only get annoyed with you. Similarly don't say anything about the Mass not being finished, for that is not true; the new numbers are really additions — Don't bother me with anything else —

---

[1] The words from 'as an' to 'rent' are added at the foot of the page.

[2] Von Obreskow was chargé d'affaires at the Russian Embassy in Vienna. He had returned to his post on July 9th. Beethoven's letter has not been traced.

Papageno's master sends you all good wishes.

I have given your address.[1] But without adding any remarks mention, if necessary, the place, explaining exactly how it was that France too sent the money to you.

And always remember that people of that rank represent royalty itself.

(1207) *To Franz Stockhausen, Paris* [2]

[Autograph in the possession of Frau Julia Wirth-Stockhausen]

HETZENDORF, *July* 12, 1823
In the country.

SIR !

You have honoured me with a letter; and I must say that your letter indicates your goodwill to me. I only wish that I could really deserve all the pleasant things you believe you are entitled to say about me — I am delighted to hear of Cherubini's kind welcome to S[chlösser]. I only wish that I could always show Cherub[ini] my esteem as much as it is possible for me to esteem anyone, but — vita brevis, ars longa — an excessive amount of things to be done — frequently prevent me from doing the things I would most like to do — As to my Mass, I was advised to start a subscription list for this work, and so far it is being circulated in manuscript only; and in this way the King of France, the Emperor of Russia, etc. and a few other sovereigns have subscribed. It will be a long time before this work is published in engraved form. I have sent you a subscription form. Should a few more subscribers come forward I should be well pleased, but I don't want any publishers, for of course they would only make havoc of this work,[3] inasmuch as partly on account of my circumstances also I have started a subscription of this kind. For my income in Vienna is *without substance*; [4] and I

---

[1] This and the following sentences are added on the verso of the autograph.

[2] Franz Stockhausen (1792–1868), born at Cologne, was a harpist and composer and the father of the famous baritone singer Julius Stockhausen (1826–1906). He settled in Paris where in 1822 he founded an Académie de Chant. He married the soprano singer, Margarete Schmuck. See Julia Wirth-Stockhausen, *Julius Stockhausen, der Sänger des Deutschen Liedes* (Frankfurt, 1927).

[3] The words from 'but I' to 'this work' are added at the top of the second page.

[4] Beethoven's favourite play on the word 'Gehalt', i.e. 'income' and 'substance'.

myself have been constantly ailing for three and a half years. Moreover, for the last three and a half months I have been suffering from *a disease of the eyes* — Please make enquiries or even have a notice inserted in the petites affiches [1] asking whether there is not an ardent lover of music in Paris who is also a dentiste (a dentist). Last summer I received from this man a letter written, I must say, with a profound knowledge of the subject and a genuine love of the art. An unhappy event during the present quarter deprived me of a rather large portion of my papers, among which there was also the letter from this Paris dentist (dentiste). Unfortunately his name has entirely slipped my memory and therefore I am not even in a position to reply to that very cordial and wellmeaning letter. Perhaps you will be able to trace the writer; and I trust to your kindness of heart to inform me if you do. This dentist fellow seems to be fonder of instrumental than of vocal music [2] — As to the sonata in A, that would be tantamount to transforming a miniature into a fresco painting.[3] However, just send it to me by mail coach and I shall soon see what can be achieved by means of such a metamorphosis — I send my best compliments to *your* female singer of 'Adelaide' [4] and to *all my worthy brothers* [5] — I thank you for the quite undeserved affection you are showing me, and with all my heart I remain your most devoted servant

BEETHOVEN

All letters to me need only be addressed 'To L. v. Beethoven in Vienna', with which address I always receive them safely.

Postscript

I can well believe that the price is too high to attract subscribers or, let us say, advance purchasers — But you would oblige me if you would inform me whether you could easily find a publisher in Paris who would produce the Mass in score after a year and a half for a fee of 1000 gulden A.C. (I don't

---

[1] The present editor is indebted to Mr. E. Lockspeiser for the suggestion that if Beethoven was not merely referring to the personal column of a Paris newspaper he may have had in mind the journal *Annonces, affiches et avis divers* also called *Petites affiches*, which was superseded in 1814 by the *Journal Général de France*.

[2] This sentence is added at the top of the third page.

[3] Possibly Franz Stockhausen had suggested, or had made, an arrangement for chamber or orchestral performance of Beethoven's pianoforte sonata Op. 101.

[4] Op. 46.   [5] I.e. brothers in the art of music.

know how much that is in French money). That was the sum offered to me previously, before I opened the subscription list in Germany. Or if one were to start a subscription for a score to be engraved, would one be likely to find subscribers in Paris ? It is clearly understood that in that case an absolutely different and much lower price would be fixed. Perhaps both schemes might be combined, that is to say, possibly for a certain number of subscribers one could obtain from the publisher a certain number of copies at a very much lower price than it would be necessary for the subscribers to pay individually — Speculations of that kind are indeed a great nuisance to me. But my small income and my poor health compel me to make strenuous efforts to better my position. Moreover I don't live selfishly for myself alone, for I am providing for the orphan my brother has left me. Education in Vienna is very expensive ; and, what is more, it is hampered by complicated arrangements. And since my dear adopted son is absolutely devoted to the pursuit of knowledge he will need to be supported even after my death ; and for this maintenance arrangements have to be made as well — Don't tell Herr Schlösser anything about these projects. It is better to be silent about many things. For what one discloses no longer belongs to one — But give my greetings to Herr S[chlösser] — On the whole, circumspection is necessary in all matters so far as I am concerned, seeing that I am so very much the object of envy and persecution.[1]

(1208) *To the Archduke Rudolph, Vienna*

[*Autograph in the Gesellschaft der Musikfreunde, Vienna*]

YOUR IMPERIAL HIGHNESS !   HETZENDORF, *July* 15, 1823

I hope that you are in excellent health. As for my eyes, they are improving, it is true, but very slowly. I think, however, that in six or, at most, seven days I shall be able to have the pleasure of waiting upon Y.I.H. If only I did not have to wear glasses, the trouble would clear up more quickly. It is an unfortunate business and it has put me back in every

---

[1] A separate sheet contains in Beethoven's handwriting Stockhausen's address in Paris and the following remark : ' I will write to Schlösser soon.'

way.   What consoles me is that I feel certain that Y.I.H. is convinced that I am always willingly and joyfully at your service. — I have another request to make of Y.I.H. which I trust that you will graciously grant, namely, that I beg Y.I.H. to be so very kind as to let me have a testimonial on the following lines, that is to say: *that I have composed the grand Mass for Y.I.H., that it has been in your possession now for a considerable time and that you have given your most gracious permission for it to be made available to the public.*   In any case *that* was the original intention; and that is more or less the truth.   And on that account I may all the more hope for such a favour.   A testimonial of this kind will be extremely useful to me.   For how could it ever have occurred to me that my slight talents would expose me so greatly to envy, persecutions and defamatory statements?   Moreover, my first intention was to ask Y.I.H. for permission to publish the Mass.   But the pressure of circumstances and, in general, my awkwardness in dealing with worldly matters and my poor health have been responsible for this muddle. — If the Mass can be engraved and published some time later on, then I hope that I shall be allowed to dedicate the engraved edition to Y.I.H.   The dedication could then be followed by the list of the small number of illustrious subscribers.[1]   I shall always revere Y.I.H. as my most noble patron and, wherever possible, make this known to the world at large.

Finally, I again entreat you not to deny me this favour, i.e. the testimonial I have requested.   It will cost Y.I.H. only a few lines, which, however, will have the most favourable consequences for me.

I shall bring Y.I.H.'s variations with me.[2]   Not many alterations will be necessary; and then it will be a most delightful and pleasant composition for those who enjoy music. — I must seem to you to be a very insistent suppliant. I request you to be so kind as to let me have the testimonial as soon as possible, for I need it —

With the deepest reverence I remain Y.I.H.'s
most obedient servant
L. v. BEETHOVEN

[1] See Letter 1451.   [2] Cf. Letter 1203, p. 1056, n. 2.

(1209) *To Ferdinand Ries, London*

[*MS not traced*] ¹

MY DEAR RIES!   HETZENDORF, *July* 16, 1823

I was greatly delighted at receiving your letter the day
before yesterday. — — — Presumably the variations will have
reached London by now — — I could not draft the dedication to your wife myself because I do not know her name.²
So write it out on behalf of your and your wife's friend.³
Give your wife a surprise with this, for the fair sex likes to have
surprises — Between ourselves the best thing of all is a combina-
tion of the surprising and the beautiful! — As for the Allegri
di Bravura I must have a look at yours ⁴ — — To be candid,
I must confess that I am not partial to this type of composition,
for it only encourages mechanical playing to an undue extent;
I am referring, of course, to the Allegri I have come across.
I have not yet seen yours, but I will ask for them at —,⁵ with
whom I beg you to be wary in your dealings. Would it not
be possible for me to undertake some commissions for you
here? These publishers, who in order to deserve their name
should be in a perpetual state of embarrassment,⁶ are pirating
your works and you are not making any profit out of them.
Perhaps some other arrangement might yet be devised — Of
course I will send you a few choruses and, if necessary, will
compose a few new ones. That is what I really prefer — — —
    Thanks for the fee for the *bagatelles*.⁷ I am quite satisfied —
Don't give anything to the King of England — Take whatever
you can get for the variations, for I shall be satisfied with
anything.⁸ But I must stipulate that the only reward I shall
accept for the dedication to your wife is a kiss which I am to
receive from her in London. You sometimes mention guineas
and I receive only pounds sterling. Yet I understand that

¹ Taken from *WRBN.* pp. 186-187.
² Beethoven intended to dedicate his Diabelli variations, Op. 120, to Ries's
wife. But in the end he dedicated this work to Antonia Brentano.
³ Beethoven means, of course, himself.
⁴ C. F. Peters had published 'Due Allegri di Bravura' for pianoforte solo,
composed by Ries.   ⁵ A word is omitted here.
⁶ Beethoven's usual pun on 'Verleger' (publisher) and 'verlegen' (embarrassed).   ⁷ Op. 119.   ⁸ Op. 120.

there is a difference. Don't be annoyed with a pauvre musicien autrichien about this. I assure you that my situation is still difficult — I am also composing a new string quartet.¹ Would it be possible to offer it to the musical or unmusical Jews in London? — En vrai juif! —

I embrace you most cordially. Your old friend

BEETHOVEN

(1210) *To Geheimrat von Könneritz, Dresden* ²

[Autograph not traced] ³

SIR! HETZENDORF, *July* 17, 1823

My signature to the receipt and my thanks are arriving rather late.⁴ But I have been very busy, the more so as the condition of my health is now improving and God knows how long that will last. So I hope you will forgive the delay — Relying on the description sent to me by my dear friend *Maria Weber* ⁵ of your excellent and noble disposition, I thought I might venture to approach you, Sir, about something else, namely, a grand *Mass* which I am circulating only in manuscript. Although my first application was rejected, yet I consider that, since my revered Cardinal, His Imperial Highness the Archduke Rudolph, has written to His Royal Highness Prince Anton, urging him to recommend the Mass to His Majesty the King of Saxony, a further attempt might at least be made. For it would certainly redound to my honour to be able to include as a connoisseur of music His Majesty the King of Saxony, and to give him a prominent place among my illustrious subscribers, such as, for instance, the King of Prussia, His Majesty the Russian Emperor, His Royal Majesty

¹ Op. 127.
² Little is known about Hans Wilhelm Traugott von Könneritz, born in 1753, who from 1819 to 1824 was Kapellmeister and Director of the Court Theatre at Dresden.
³ Taken from Nohl I, no. 275.
⁴ Von Könneritz had sent Beethoven a fee of 40 ducats for a performance of 'Fidelio' under C. M. von Weber's direction on April 29, 1823, in the Royal Opera House at Dresden. The famous singer Wilhelmine Schröder-Devrient made her début in the part of Fidelio and the whole performance was received with acclamation. The first version of 'Fidelio', i.e. Leonore I, had already been produced at Dresden on April 12, 1815. ⁵ Cf. Letter 1204, p. 1057, n. 3.

the King of France and so forth — Having supplied you with these particulars I leave it to you, Sir, to decide how and where you can best exert your influence; today I find it impossible to do so, but next post-day I shall have the honour of sending you an invitation for His Royal Majesty of Saxony to subscribe to my Mass. At any rate I know that you are not likely to think that I am one of those who *compose* merely out of an ignoble love of gain; but indeed there are circumstances which sometimes compel a man to act in opposition to his inclination and principles!! — My Cardinal is the most kind-hearted Prince, but — he has no money. I trust you will forgive me my seeming importunity. If I can perhaps serve you in some way with my mediocre talents, that would afford me infinite pleasure —

I remain, Sir, with kindest regards, your devoted servant

BEETHOVEN

(1211) *To Carl Friedrich Peters, Leipzig*

[Autograph in the Beethovenhaus, Bonn, H. C. Bodmer collection]

SIR!   [HETZENDORF], *July* 17, 1823

As soon as the work intended for you or your customers is finished, I will deliver it at once to the Gebrüder Meissl. If the fee has to be raised, you will be informed of this too — Spare me any more letters, since you *never* know *what you want* — Not a word about your — behaviour to me — But this lapse of yours I really must condemn, i.e. that you reproach me for having accepted money in advance. It is clear from your letters that you urged me to take it; and certainly I never asked you for it.[1] For you say 'that you always make money advances to some composers' — I was accosted in the street here and told to go and collect the money. My circumstances at that time demanded the greatest secrecy. Hence in order to avoid giving rise to gossip I took the money, and our dealings have now been brought to a standstill. Who is to blame for this but yourself?! Let me add that quite different sums of money are lying ready for me to collect. And people

---

[1] The words from 'and certainly' to 'it' are added at the foot of the page.

are willing to wait, because they take into consideration my art and my health, which is again impaired — You may be sure that I have found you out in a moral or, rather, a commercial and *musical* sense. Nevertheless I will bear in mind your money which is waiting for me. For I am in full possession of my faculties and do not need to attach any *honours* to my name.

BEETHOVEN

(1212) *To Geheimrat von Könneritz, Dresden*

[*Autograph not traced*] [1]

SIR !   VIENNA, *July* 25, 1823

Forgive my importunity in sending you this enclosure. It contains a letter from me to His Royal Highness Prince Anton of Saxony, to which is added the invitation to His Royal Majesty of Saxony to subscribe to the Mass.[2] In a recent letter to you I mentioned that my most gracious Lord the Cardinal Archduke Rudolph had written to His Royal Highness Prince Anton urging him to persuade His Royal Majesty of Saxony to take the Mass. I beg you to exert your influence to the utmost. But I leave it entirely to you, Sir, to do exactly as you like and in a manner befitting the taste and outlook of your country. Although I am inclined to think that my Cardinal's recommendation will carry some weight, yet the most important and, in fact, the supreme decisions must always be zealously promoted by the advocates of what is good and beautiful. So far, in spite of all the outward glory I have gained, I have scarcely made in money what I should have received for this work from the publisher, chiefly because the copying expenses have been very heavy. My friends conceived this idea of circulating the Mass, for I, thank God, am quite ignorant of all business matters. Meanwhile there is no member of our Austrian state who would not have been a loser; and so was I. Were it not for my ill health which has persisted for years, a foreign country would have provided me with a carefree existence, a life, I mean,

---

[1] Taken from Nohl I, no. 276.
[2] These enclosures have not been traced.

without concern save for my art. Do judge me kindly and not to my disadvantage. I live entirely for my art and for the purpose of fulfilling my duties as a man. But unfortunately this too cannot always be done without the help of the *powers of the underworld* — While I warmly recommend my work to your consideration, I also trust that your love of art and your philanthropic disposition in general will prompt you kindly to inform me in a few words as soon as there is any tangible result.

I am, Sir, with the deepest regard your most devoted

BEETHOVEN

(1213) *To Louis Spohr, Cassel* [1]

[*Autograph in the Stadt- und Universitätsbibliothek, Frankfurt am Main*]

MY DEAR AND HONOURED SPOHR !   VIENNA, *July* 27, 1823

A short time ago I had a visit from a singer who belongs to the Electoral Theatre of Hesse.[2] I have forgotten his name, but he brought me letters of introduction from you and Professor Grosheim.[3] I was delighted to hear about you and to learn too that your merits have won the recognition they deserve. As I know that you are one of those noble artists who gladly exert themselves on behalf of others as well, it has occurred to me that I ought to tell you about a grand Mass which I am circulating only in manuscript and by subscription or advance purchase. So far the Emperor of Russia, the King of France, the King of Prussia and a few other heads of state have subscribed. I sent an invitation also to His Excellency the Elector of Hesse through the Legation in Vienna but have not yet received a reply informing me of his

[1] Louis Spohr (1784–1859), born at Braunschweig, rapidly made his mark as a violinist and composer. From 1805 to 1812 he was leader of the orchestra at Gotha. He then came to Vienna to be leader at the Theater an der Wien for three years. In 1822 he was appointed Kapellmeister at Cassel where he remained for the rest of his life. He published in 1831 his famous work on violin playing. Since 1921 Cassel has had a Spohr Museum.

[2] This was Franz Hauser (1794–1870), a renowned operatic bass singer, who was then attached to the Court Opera at Cassel. Later he settled in Vienna as a teacher of singing.

[3] Georg Christoph Grosheim (1764–1841), born at Cassel, was for 51 years a teacher of music in his native town. He also composed and wrote numerous treatises on the theory of music.

decision. Perhaps you would be the best person to take charge of this affair. The fee has been fixed at 50 gold ducats, because it is a big work and the copying of it is very expensive. As I have been constantly in poor health now for several years I really must direct my gaze to *earthly matters,* although I would *much rather direct it to things above.* I am convinced that, just as I am willing to act in the interest of yourself and of every noble artist, you will gladly act on my behalf if you consider it suitable and within your powers to do so — Do ensure that the result of your application, and, if possible, a favourable one, shall reach the Electoral Legation in Vienna — Kindly remember me to Professor G. C. Grosheim, to whom I owe a reply and very many thanks. Tell him that I shall soon work off all my arrears; and ask him to be good enough not to judge me by appearances, that is to say, unfavourably —

I have little news to send you from here, save to tell you that we are having a rich harvest in raisins (i.e. dried or pressed grapes) ¹ —

With most cordial remembrances and kindest regards to yourself, from your friend and servant

BEETHOVEN

I hope to
have a few lines
from you in reply.

(1214) *To the Archduke Rudolph, Baden*

[Autograph in the Gesellschaft der Muskifreunde, Vienna]

YOUR IMPERIAL HIGHNESS!   [HETZENDORF, *late July,* 1823]

I had just been taking a short walk and stammering out a canon 'Grossen Dank!' ² — — — But when I came home and was about to write it down for Y.I.H. I found a petitioner waiting for me. He is under the strange delusion that a petition presented through me would be more acceptable to

---

¹ Beethoven is playing on the word 'Rosinen' (grapes) as a reference to the contemporary craze in Vienna for Rossini's operas. He had a very poor opinion of Rossini as a composer.

² See Nottebohm II, p. 177, note. This footnote to sketches for the second movement of the ninth symphony quotes a two-part canon on the words: 'Grossen Dank für solche Gnade' (Many thanks for such a favour). There is no trace of a copy of this canon for the Archduke Rudolph.

Y.I.H. What is one to do? A good deed cannot be performed too quickly, and one must defer to such strange delusions now and then — The bearer of this letter is Herr Drechsler, Kapellmeister of the theatres in the Josephstadt and at Baden.[1] He would like to obtain the vacant appointment of second court organist. He has a good knowledge of thorough-bass, is also a competent organist and, moreover, has a favourable reputation as a composer; and all these qualifications recommend him for this post. He believes, *and rightly so*, that the best recommendation, and one which would certainly procure this post for him, would be a recommendation from Y.I.H., since Y.I.H., who is a fine connoisseur and performer, knows best how to value true merit. And His Imperial Majesty would certainly prefer such a testimonial to all others. Hence I add my entreaties, rather diffidently, I admit, to those of Herr Drechsler. Yet convinced as I am of Y.I.H.'s charitable and gracious disposition I am inclined to hope that the eminent patron and protector of all that is good will gladly use his influence on this occasion too so far as he can —

Tomorrow you will receive my canon together with the confession of my conscious and unconscious sins for which I shall entreat your most gracious absolution. Unfortunately my eyes still prevent me today from expressing in person to Y.I.H. my wishes for all that is beneficial to yourself.

Your Imperial Highness's
most faithful and most obedient servant
BEETHOVEN

Postscript

Moreover, the fact that for ten solid years Herr Drechsler has been an unpaid Professor of thorough-bass at St. Anna's [2] deserves to be taken into account.

[1] Joseph Drechsler (1782–1852), a prolific composer of church music, light operas and incidental music for plays, had been attached to various churches in Vienna. He did not obtain the post for which Beethoven recommended him. But he conducted at the Leopoldstadt Theatre from 1822 to 1830 and in 1844 was Kapellmeister at St. Stephen's.

[2] A small church in the Annagasse, off the Kärntnerstrasse, built in the 15th century.

(1215) *To the Archduke Rudolph, Baden*

[*Autograph in the Gesellschaft der Musikfreunde, Vienna*]

Your Imperial Highness!   [Hetzendorf, *late July*, 1823]
I have just been told here that Y.I.H. is to be in Vienna
tomorrow. If I cannot yet follow the promptings of my heart,
please ascribe this to the condition of my eyes. I am much
better, but for several days more I dare not face town air,
which continues to have a bad effect on my eyes. My sole
desire is that the next time you come in from Baden Y.I.H.
would be so gracious as to send me word and also be so kind
as to let me know at what time I should call. Indeed I am again
looking forward to the pleasure of seeing my most gracious lord.
But since, of course, Y.I.H. will not remain in Vienna for
long, it is surely necessary that we should use this short period
to make arrangements for our artistic studies and exercises —
I myself will bring you 'Grossen Dank' ÷ ÷ ÷ or, if not,
the thanks will be sent to Baden ¹ — Herr Drechsler thanked
me today for the *liberty* I had taken in recommending him to
Y.I.H. He added that Y.I.H. received him very graciously,
and for this I too express my profound thanks. May it please
Y.I.H., moreover, not to allow your resolve to be shaken. For
I understand that the Abbé Stadler ² is trying to obtain this
post for somebody else. It would also be a great help to
Drechsler if Y.I.H. would be so kind as to mention the matter
to Count Dietrichstein — Once more, please be so gracious
as to have me informed when you return from Baden so that
I may immediately hasten into town to wait upon the only
lord and master I have in this world — Y.I.H.'s health seems
to be good. Thanks are being rendered to Heaven by so many
who desire this, among whose number I too must be counted.

Your Imperial Highness's
most faithful and most obedient servant
BEETHOVEN

¹ For the Archduke Rudolph's reply from Vienna to Beethoven's application
on behalf of Drechsler see Kal. IV, pp. 300-301. It is dated July 31, 1823, and
in it he urges Beethoven to write down his canon.
² For a note on the Abbé Stadler see Letter 1468, p. 1275, n. 2.

(1216) *To Anton Felix Schindler, Vienna*

[Autograph in the Deutsche Staatsbibliothek, Berlin]

[HETZENDORF, *July*, 1823]

MOST EXCELLENT S[COUN]D[RE]L OF EPIRUS and not less of Brundusium and so forth !

Give this letter to the Beobachter.[1] But you must write his name on it — Ask him also whether his daughter has made good progress with the pianof[orte] and whether I might present her some time with a copy of my compositions ? — I wrote down '*honorary member*'. But I don't know whether that is the correct term, or whether perhaps it should be merely '*as a foreign member*'. *I am ignorant about and never* pay attention to such matters.

Moreover you have something about this story to deliver to Bernardum non Sanctum.[2] Do ask Bernard for information about that villain Rupprecht. Tell him all about that chit-chat and find out how one could punish those slanderers.

Enquire from both those philosophical journalists[3] whether *this appointment is an honourable or a dishonourable one*? —

I am dining at home today. If you want to come, do so —

Please ask Herr Beobachter to excuse the muddled appearance of my letter — I have far too much to do.[4]

Find out too whether one can procure a copy of the Beobachter.[5]

(1217) *To Joseph Anton von Pilat, Vienna*[6]

[Autograph in the Deutsche Staatsbibliothek, Berlin]

SIR !   [HETZENDORF, *July*, 1823]

I should consider it an honour if you would be kind enough to mention in your so generally esteemed paper my

[1] Beethoven means 'to the editor of the *Beobachter*', who was then Joseph Anton von Pilat. See Letter 1217.
[2] Since 1819 J. K. Bernard had been chief editor of the *Wiener Zeitung*.
[3] I.e. Pilat and Bernard.   [4] Written on the left side of the page.
[5] Written on the right side of the page.
[6] Joseph Anton von Pilat (1782–1865) in 1811 took over the editorship of the *Oesterreichischer Beobachter* from Friedrich von Schlegel. See *FRBH* II, 19.

election as foreign [1] member of the Royal Swedish Academy of Music. Though I am far from being vain and ambitious, yet it would assuredly be advisable not to ignore my election completely, seeing that in practical life one must also live and work for others, who no doubt may frequently benefit by a designation of this kind — Forgive me for troubling you; and please be so kind as to let me know how I can serve you. I shall then be delighted to comply with your wishes —

I remain, Sir, with the deepest respect, your most devoted

BEETHOVEN

(1218) *To Joseph Karl Bernard, Vienna* [2]

[Autograph not traced] [3]

DOMINUS BERNARDUS
NON SANCTUS! [HETZENDORF, *July*, 1823]

We request you to set down on paper in a suitable form this conferring of membership by foreign countries, such as Scandinavia and so forth, to give it to the printers and to back it up, make it known, have it exhibited in public, and so forth and so on. We are most horribly immersed in notes and needs. Hence we too have not been able to see you, amice optime. But doubtless Heaven will again ordain that we may soon do so. In this hope I remain

amicus optimus BEETHOVEN Bonnensis

(1219) *To Anton Felix Schindler, Vienna*

[Autograph in the Deutsche Staatsbibliothek, Berlin]

[HETZENDORF, *July*, 1823]

I am feeling very ill and have violent diarrhœa today. Anything may happen to me amongst these veritable Hottentots. I am taking medicine to help my poor stomach which

---

[1] 'Foreign' is inserted over 'honorary' deleted.
[2] On the verso there is the following address in Beethoven's handwriting: 'To Herr von Bernard, Director of all the Press institutes, leading operatic librettist in Europe'.
[3] From a photograph in the Stadtbibliothek, Vienna.

is completely ruined — Meanwhile I expect you to come to-morrow as early as possible. As it is very hot, it is best to come very early. If you can be here at any rate at five o'clock, I will order the carriage for half past five — Schlemmer is mortally ill, he is dying, do go to him. Perhaps he will mention the bill. It has been made out for 165 gulden, but I think I owe him 25 gulden more — Please come in good time tomorrow. In a few days you will have your 50 — but you must make an application in a certain quarter [1] —

(1220) *To Anton Felix Schindler, Vienna*

[Autograph in the Deutsche Staatsbibliothek, Berlin]

[HETZENDORF, *July*, 1823]

Please give an order today for certain to your cobbler to go to the boarding school at about 12 o'clock tomorrow and to measure Karl for overshoes —

I trust that everything has gone off well —

(1221) *To Joseph Karl Bernard, Vienna*

[Autograph in the Beethovenhaus, Bonn, H. C. Bodmer collection]

[HETZENDORF, *Summer*, 1823]

This letter was written a long time ago. Do nothing, however, until *Schindler comes to you*. And please say nothing whatever about *Rupprecht*.[2] For we might wrong him over this, seeing that he promised to keep quiet about the affair. Everything will soon be cleared up —

---

[1] Schindler noted on the autograph: 'All the same, I never received the 50 gulden so often promised to me for my efforts in connexion with the subscriptions to the "Missa Solemnis"'.

[2] Cf. Letter 1216, p. 1072.

(1222) *To Anton Felix Schindler, Vienna* ¹

[*Autograph in the Deutsche Staatsbibliothek, Berlin*]

[HETZENDORF, *Summer*, 1823]

MOST EXCELLENT H[ERR] S[CHINDLER] —

As we have not seen you today, we beg you to wait for our housekeeper tomorrow morning. You can then tell her whether you are driving out here with her or later, for it is an extremely urgent matter —

Your poor downtrodden

B[EETHOVE]N

(1223) *To Anton Felix Schindler, Vienna*

[*Autograph in the Deutsche Staatsbibliothek, Berlin*]

[HETZENDORF, *Summer*, 1823] ²

S[COUN]D[RE]L OF S[AMOTHRACI]A!

Why, you were sent word yesterday that you were to betake yourself to the South Pole, while we were to go off to the North Pole, although indeed Capt[ain] Parry has already smoothed out the slight difference.³ But there was no potato purée there — I request Bach, to whom I send my best regards and very many thanks for his efforts on my behalf, to inform me to what price the rooms at Baden may possibly soar. And moreover we should have to see how we could arrange to bring Karl out there every fortnight (and cheaply, Heaven help us over poverty and cheapness!). You could make that your business, for you have admirers and friends amongst the bosses and country coachmen ⁴ —

If this letter reaches you in time, it would be well for you to go to Bach today, so that I may have the reply tomorrow morning. For if you don't, it will be almost too late —

¹ The address on the verso in Beethoven's handwriting is: 'Per il Signore Povero Papageno'.
² Noted by Schindler on the autograph. The letter was probably written in July, for Beethoven moved to Baden on August 13th.
³ Sir William Edward Parry (1790–1855), a naval officer and explorer, rendered good service in preparing the way for the eventual discovery of the North Pole.
⁴ Schindler has noted on the autograph that Beethoven is alluding to patrons.

Tomorrow too you could pounce on that rascal of a copyist from whom I do not expect anything good. He has had those variations now for a whole week.[1]

Your amicus

BEETHOVEN

(1224) *To Anton Felix Schindler, Vienna*

[*MS not traced*] [2]

[HETZENDORF, *Summer*, 1823]

Mr. High-flyer who never arrives, Mr. Rock-bottom who cannot be fathomed — everything was ready yesterday — so now *you* — may go to *Gläser*.[3] I shall expect you to dinner at Hetzendorf at half past two — If you turn up later, something will have been kept for you —

(1225) *To Ernst Christian Schleiermacher, Darmstadt* [4]

[*Autograph in the Hessisches Staatsarchiv, Darmstadt*]

MOST HONOURABLE SIR! VIENNA, *August* 2, 1823

I have the honour to inform you that the Mass can be delivered very soon to the Grand Ducal Legation in Vienna. I know that H.R.H. the Grand Duke will not take it unkindly if I request H.R.H. graciously to arrange for the fee of 50 ducats to be sent here to the Grand Ducal Legation. The copying expenses have, in fact, proved to be heavier than I myself thought they would be. An abominable rumour which is being circulated by my enemies that this Mass is not yet finished will be disproved by means of a testimonial from my most gracious patron His Imperial Highness the Archduke

---

[1] Rampel was probably making a copy of the Diabelli variations to be sent to London. This work, Op. 120, had been published by Cappi & Diabelli in June, 1823. For a note on Rampel see Letter 1335, p. 1158, n. 4.

[2] Taken from Nohl I, no. 269.

[3] See Letter 1252, p. 1097, n. 1.

[4] Ernst Christian Schleiermacher (1755–1844) was a Privy Councillor and also Private Secretary to the Grand Duke of Hesse. He is particularly noted in German biography for his strong support of the scientist Liebig.

Rudolph to the Grand Ducal Legation. For this Mass was in fact finished in 1822 — Herr Schlösser, who is in the service of H.R.H. the Grand Duke, will not fail to inform you in what a cordial and friendly manner I received him as a young and talented artist. Unfortunately I had to treat Herr André, the Kapellmeister and Hofrat, very differently.[1] For his behaviour was so *brutal* that I wrote to tell him not to call on me *again*. Only later did I learn that this gentleman was in H.R. Highness's service. Had I known this at the time, out of consideration for H.R.H. I would have tolerated his behaviour without rebuking him — Forgive me, Sir, for troubling you with matters of this kind. But who is there who does not like to appear at least *as good* as he is *in reality*? And who knows how an incident of this kind may be represented, seeing that not seldom is the *veritas odium parit* [2] very much in evidence?

I beg you to recommend me very specially to the favour of H.R.H. the Grand Duke and to assure H.R.H. that I return my most sincere thanks for granting me the honour of being allowed to number H.R.H. among my very distinguished subscribers, such as the Emperor of Russia, the King of Prussia, the King of France and so forth. No doubt another opportunity will present itself which will enable me to show that I am not quite unworthy of this favour. I beg you, Sir, to accept my infinitely great respect for you —

> I remain, Sir,
> Your most devoted servant,
> LUDWIG VAN BEETHOVEN

(1226) *To Franz Brentano, Frankfurt am Main*

[Autograph in the Beethovenhaus, Bonn]

SIR!   HETZENDORF, *August* 2, 1823

I ought to have replied to your friendly communication a long time ago. But I was prevented by an excessive amount of work and also by an eye complaint which I have had for two and a half months and which is not yet completely cured.

---

[1] Johann Anton André (1775–1842), son of Johann André (1741–1799), the founder of the music publishing house at Offenbach.
[2] Truth begets hatred. Cf. Letter 969, p. 841, n. 2.

However loth I am to avail myself again of the kindness you have shown me, yet I should very much like to send a heavy parcel of music intended for London by mail coach to Frankfurt, thence by water or by land (it would probably be too slow by water) to Holland, and from there by sea to London. The parcel is too heavy to be carried by a courier. I hear that you have a son in London and therefore I think that the parcel could be dispatched thither most easily through your kind intervention and with the help of your information. I shall be delighted to refund all the expenses incurred.[1] But please send me a reply about this as quickly as possible, for the matter is very urgent. You said in your letter that your little boy's health is improving. I am extremely glad about this. I hope that your wife too is well and also all your children and brothers and sisters. For all your family are always very dear to me — I only wish that I were in a position to express my thanks to you in the manner you would most desire —

I remain, Sir, with my kindest regards, yours sincerely,

BEETHOVEN

(1227) *To Karl Friedrich Müller, Berlin* [2]

[*Autograph in the possession of Dr. M. J. Mannheim*]

SIR !   VIENNA, *August* 8, [1823]

I will gladly and willingly serve you, as I would serve every true artist. So far as possible I shall justify your confidence in me, provided that you yourself are not mistaken about what you believe you will find in me —

Assuring you of my heartfelt desire to help you,

I am, Sir, your most devoted

BEETHOVEN

[1] This sentence is added at the foot of the page.
[2] The address on the verso in Beethoven's handwriting is: 'An seine
    Wohlgebohrn K. F. Müller
    Gesang und Klavierlehrer
    in Berlin
    abzugeben Grosse Friedrichstrasse No. 203.'
Karl Friedrich Müller (1796–1845), born in Holland, first became a pianist and eventually settled in Berlin as a music teacher. He composed songs and pianoforte music and also wrote books on the theory of music.

(1228) *To the Archduke Rudolph, Vienna*

[*Autograph in the Gesellschaft der Musikfreunde, Vienna*]

YOUR IMPERIAL HIGHNESS !   [HETZENDORF, *early August*, 1823]
I am indeed feeling very ill and not only on account of my eye complaint. I am hoping to drag myself to Baden tomorrow to engage some rooms and shall then have to go there for good in a few days' time.¹ The town air has a bad effect on my whole constitution; and I have impaired my health just because I went twice into town to see my doctors. It will be easier to visit Y.I.H. from Baden. I am inconsolable, both on account of Y.I.H. and on my own account, for my activities are so greatly restricted — I have marked one or two passages in the variations; when we meet I shall explain my remarks more fully ² —
Your Imperial Highness's
ever constant and most faithful servant
BEETHOVEN

(1229) *To Anton Felix Schindler, Vienna*

[*Autograph in the Deutsche Staatsbibliothek, Ber in*]

[HETZENDORF, *c. August* 13, 1823]
SAMOTHRACIAN S[COU]ND[RE]L !
Make haste, the weather is just right. But it is better to be too early than too late, presto, prestissimo, we are driving off from here.³

¹ According to Letter 1232, p. 1082, Beethoven settled at Baden on August 13th.
² Probably another set of variations which the Archduke Rudolph was composing. Cf. Letter 1203, p. 1056, n. 2.
³ Beethoven was moving from Hetzendorf to Baden.

(1230) *To Karl van Beethoven, Vienna* [1]

[Autograph in the Beethovenhaus, Bonn, H. C. Bodmer collection]

DEAR BOY!   BADEN, *August* 16, 1823

I did not want to say anything to you until I should feel better *here*, which so far is not entirely the case.[2] I came here with catarrh and a cold in my head, both serious complaints for me, seeing that, as it is, the fundamental condition is still catarrh; and I fear that this trouble will soon cut the thread of my life or, worse still, will *gradually* gnaw it through — Moreover my abdomen, which is thoroughly upset, must still be restored to health by medicines and dieting; and for this we have to thank our *loyal servants*! You can imagine how much I am running about, for only today did I begin again *properly* (*improperly*, as you know, is an involuntary attitude of mine) to serve my muses.— I *must serve them*, but that must not be noticeable; and, after all, the baths are more inviting, at any rate to me, and tempt me to enjoy the beauties of nature. At the same time nous sommes trop pauvres, et il faut écrire ou de n'avoir pas de quoi — Work hard now so that all the preparations may be made for your competitive examination; and be modest, so that you may prove to be superior to and better than what people think you are —

Just send your laundry straight to Baden. You can *wear* your grey trousers *at home* at any rate, for, dear son, you are again becoming very *dear*! [3] The address is 'at the coppersmith's' etc. Let me know at once whether you have received this letter. I will send you a few lines for Schindler — that contemptible object — chiefly because I do not care to have any direct association with that miserable fellow — If only I could write as quickly as I think and feel, I should certainly be able to tell you some rather remarkable things — But for today all I wish is that a certain Karl should be absolutely worthy of my love and of my very great care for him and

[1] The letter is addressed to Blöchlinger's boarding school in Vienna.
[2] Beethoven had been at Baden since August 13th. See Letter 1232, p. 1082.
[3] Beethoven is playing on the two meanings of the German 'teuer' which, like the English 'dear', can mean 'precious' and 'expensive'.

should know how to value all this. Although, as you know, I make no great demands, yet there are many ways in which one can display the nobler and better side of one's nature and in a manner that others can recognize and feel — With all my heart I embrace you.

Your faithful and sincere father.

(1231) *To Johann van Beethoven, Gneixendorf*

[Autograph in the Beethovenhaus, Bonn, H. C. Bodmer collection]

DEAR BROTHER!   BADEN, *August* 19, [1823] [1]
    I am delighted to hear that you are in better health. As for me, my eyes are not yet quite cured ; and I came here with a ruined stomach and a horrible cold, the former thanks to that arch-swine, my housekeeper, the latter handed on to me by a beast of a kitchen-maid whom I had already chucked out once and then taken on again — You should not have taken up the matter with *Steiner*. I will see what can be done. It may be difficult to arrange for the songs *in puris*, as the text is in German. It would probably be easier to do this with the overture.—

    I received your letter of August 10th through that miserable rascal *Schindler*. Remember that you need only send your letters straight to the post where I shall certainly receive them all. For I avoid as far as possible that low-minded, contemptible fellow — Karl can't join me until the 29th when he will write to you.[2] But you will not be entirely neglected,[3] and you will receive letters from Karl and from me through him. For, however little you may deserve it so far as I am concerned, yet I shall never forget that you are my brother ; and in due course a good spirit will imbue your heart and soul.[4]

---

    [1] On the verso of the autograph another hand has noted 'written in the late summer of 1824'. But on internal evidence the year must be 1823.
    [2] At the end of August, 1823, Karl left Blöchlinger's boarding school for good. He was then just 17.
    [3] The following passage, deleted by another hand, is still legible: 'whatever those two *canailles*, that loutish fat woman and her bastard, may do to you '.
    [4] The following passage, deleted by another hand, is still legible: 'a good spirit which will separate you from those two *canailles*, that former and still active whore, with whom her fellow miscreant slept no less than three times during your illness and who, moreover, has full control of your money, oh, abominable shame, is there no spark of manhood in you ? ! ! ! '

Now for something else. You have my own manuscript of some numbers of the 'Ruinen von Athen'. I really need it because the copies were made from the Josephstadt score from which a good many passages were omitted which are only to be found in my manuscript scores. As I happen to be composing something else of this kind I badly need my manuscripts. So let me know in writing where I can get hold of them. I earnestly beg you to do this. I will let you know some other time about coming to stay with you. Am I to become so degraded as to mix in such low [1] company? But perhaps this could be avoided and we might still spend a few days with you?! I will write some other time about the remaining points in your letter. All good wishes. I hover over you unseen and influence you through others so that the scum of the earth [2] may not strangle you —

Ever your faithful
brother.

You should address your letters direct to me in Vienna [3] —

(1232) *To the Archduke Rudolph, Vienna*

[Autograph in the Gesellschaft der Musikfreunde, Vienna]

YOUR IMPERIAL HIGHNESS!   BADEN, *August* 22, 1823

From what you said in your very gracious letter to me I thought that Your Highness would again come here to Baden. I arrived here on August 13th in a very poor state of health, but I am now feeling better. I was again afflicted with my catarrhal trouble which had in fact improved. Furthermore, my abdomen was in the most wretched condition and, moreover, I was suffering from this eye complaint. In short, my constitution was completely undermined. I just had to try to get here without even being able to see Y.I.H. Thank God, my eyes have improved so much that now I can again use them a certain amount by daylight. My other complaints are also disappearing; one cannot expect much more in so

---

[1] This adjective has been deleted by another hand.
[2] The previous four words have been deleted by another hand.
[3] This reminder is added at the top of the first page to the left of the date.

short a time.   How dearly I should love to have Y.I.H. here
so that in a few days we could make up for all that lost time.
Perhaps I shall be so fortunate as to be able to wait upon
Y.I.H. here at Baden and prove to Your Highness my most
fervent zeal in your service — For this reason how sadly do I
regret my wretched state of health!   However much I desire
a complete recovery, yet I greatly fear that this will [never] be;
and therefore I trust that Y.I.H. will be indulgent.[1]   At any
rate I can still show how happy I am to serve Y.I.H.; and
my greatest desire is that you would be so gracious as to make
use of my services.   And in this hope I remain Your Imperial
Highness's faithful and most obedient servant

L. v. BEETHOVEN

(1233) *To Karl van Beethoven, Vienna*

[Autograph in the Stadtbibliothek, Vienna]

BADEN, *August* 23, 1823

Goodbye,[2] little rascal . . . . most excellent little rascal . . .
Dear boy, I received today your letter of yesterday.   You
mention 31 gulden.   But I did send you as well the six gulden
you asked for.   Perhaps you didn't find them owing to their
having been mixed up with other papers — S[chindler]s receipt
should run as follows:

The Baron's housekeeping	10 gulden
My housekeeper	9 gulden
enclosed	31 gulden
Total	50 gulden

which I, the undersigned, have duly received.

S[CHIN]DLER

He spent only one day with me here in order, as you know, to
engage rooms.   He slept at Hetzendorf and on the following
morning, from what he told me, he returned to the Josephstadt.
By the way, don't indulge in gossip at his expense, for it
might injure him.   Indeed he is sufficiently punished by being
what he is.   But I must tell him the truth bluntly, since his

---

[1] The bracketed word 'never' has been added by the present editor.
[2] Beethoven uses the familiar form 'Ade'.

evil character, which is addicted to intriguing, demands that he be treated seriously. — If it is not absolutely essential to send the laundry, leave it until I come in on the 29th.[1]   For as you are only sending it now, it would hardly be possible for you to have it back on the 28th, the day of your examination.   So it would be better to give the servant, if necessary, a pair of breeches which could easily be washed in your neighbourhood — I remember the notice sent by Petiscus.[2]   If he is worth the money, well, we must have him. *What is useful* should *not* be a subject for calculation.   God will not forsake us.   Admittedly the expenses are heavy at the moment.   I am now expecting Blöchlinger's bill also.   If there is anything else to mention, don't forget it, so that we may not be delayed on the 29th.   As for the servant, we must still keep him for a while, until we are together again.   For all this household arrangement with the old woman must come to an end; she no longer smells or sees or *tastes* — My poor stomach is in constant danger.   The former housekeeper of the Josephstadt has now offered her services again.   She would be more suitable, if we had a manservant as well.   But *this old woman* requires service and help.   The kitchen-maid I got rid of before is a horrid pig.   For the moment the manservant has certainly a decent lodging.   He will go far before he can find *one like it*.   But whether he stays or leaves, he must keep us informed of his whereabouts; and when we meet we can discuss the arrangement.   Just think, a kitchen-maid now costs, including her bread money, 10 gulden, 44 kreuzer a month, i.e. 128 gulden, 48 kreuzer a year; the manservant 20 gulden a month, and boot money and clothes; and with the *old woman* we should have to have another woman as well.   My health is better, but I am not as well as I used to be — Now all good wishes.   The daily round exhausts me — I wish you all the best, my dear son.   Czerny, your former teacher, is here and is dining with me tomorrow.   You will find several people here who will interest you —

Your affectionate father.

[1] The day Karl was leaving his boarding school for good.
[2] Not identified.   He was probably Karl's crammer.

(1234) *To* ?

[*MS not traced*] 1

BADEN, *August* 31, 1823

The work itself can be delivered in a few weeks.

(1235) *To Anton Felix Schindler, Vienna*

[*Autograph in the Deutsche Staatsbibliothek, Berlin*]

[BADEN, *end of August*, 1823]

I must have corrected and attested copies of all three documents.

I am sending herewith 45 kreuzer. How could you bring yourself to accept such a thing from that house churl, who presented it too with a threat? Where is your judgment? No doubt, where it always is! —

Tomorrow morning 2 I will send for the corrected and attested copies and the originals. It is not certain whether the woman is coming. Do be so kind as to stay at home until eight o'clock —

If you would like to come to dinner tomorrow or even today, you may do so. But you must let me know for certain, because arrangements of this kind either for the people here or in general for myself cannot be made later than half past two o'clock. The housekeeper will give you fresh information about rooms in the Landstrasse. It is high time. As soon as you hear of something on the Bastei or in the Landstrasse, you must report to me at once — And on account of the well we must know which room the landlord uses.

Vale.

---

1 Taken from KK, no. 1163. The letter, of which this is a fragment, is supposed to have been addressed to the Grand Duke of Hesse-Darmstadt with an acknowledgment of the latter's payment for his copy of the 'Missa Solemnis'.

2 The additional words 'or if one could find you now' have been obliterated.

(1236) *To Anton Felix Schindler, Vienna*

[*Autograph in the Deutsche Staatsbibliothek, Berlin*]

[BADEN, *end of August*, 1823]

Please forward the parcel today and also interview during the morning, if possible, this housekeeper who lives on the third floor in the courtyard of Glockengasse No. 318. She is a widow, knows how to cook and wants to work merely for board and lodging, an arrangement which of course one could *not* agree to or only *on certain conditions* — Things are getting beyond me with this one [1] — I can't invite you. But *in any case* I shall most certainly be grateful to you.

(1237) *To Ferdinand Ries, London*

[*Autograph in the Beethovenhaus, Bonn*] [2]

MY DEAR FRIEND!   BADEN, *September* 5, [1823]

You say that I ought to look around for someone to attend to my affairs. Well, that is the very thing I did in respect of the variat[ions], I mean, my friends and Schindler looked after them for me, but alas! how badly! The variations were to appear first of all in Vienna after they had been published in London. [3] But everything went wrong. The dedication to Brentano [4] was only to apply to Germany. I was under a great obligation to her and could publish no other work at the time. In any case only the Viennese publisher Diabelli got those variations from me. But everything went through the hands of Schindler. I have never yet met a more wretched fellow on God's earth, an arch-scoundrel whom I have sent packing — I can dedicate some other work to your wife instead. You must have received by now my last letter about the Allegri di Bravura. [5] Well, I think that I might get

---

[1] Frau Schnaps.
[2] The autograph, which bears no address, consists of one leaf written on both sides.   [3] Op. 120.
[4] Antonia Brentano. The first edition published by Cappi & Diabelli has this dedication. A manuscript copy made by Rampel and corrected by Beethoven, now in the Beethovenhaus, Bonn, H. C. Bodmer collection, was dedicated to Ries's wife. It is dated April 30, 1823, and was intended to serve for a London edition. See *KHV.* 349.   [5] Cf. Letter 1209, p. 1064, n. 4.

30 ducats a piece for them. But I should like to be able to publish them immediately in Vienna as well, a connexion which could be easily established. Why should one let those Viennese scoundrels make such a profit? The work would not be given to a publisher here until I had heard that it had arrived in London. By the way, you yourself must fix the fee, for you know best what London conditions are — The copyist finished the score of the symphony a few days ago.[1] So Kirchhoffer and I are only waiting for a good opportunity to send it off — I am here, where I arrived in a very sick condition. For my health, when all is said and done, is very shaky and, Good Heavens, instead of enjoying as others do the pleasures of bathing, my financial straits demand that I should compose every day. And as well as taking the baths I have to drink mineral waters — The Mass will be sent off in a day or two. I am waiting to hear from Kirchhoffer how it is to be dispatched, for it is too bulky to be given to a courier — In my last letter you will have read all my remarks about the Mass — I will send you choruses. Let me know soon about commissions for oratorios so that I may fix the time immediately — I am sorry for both of us — and particularly about the variations, seeing that I composed them more for London than for Vienna. It is not my fault — Reply soon, very soon, both about the conditions and about the time. My best greetings to your family from [your] true [friend]

BEE[THOVEN] [2]

(1238) *To Franz Christian Kirchhoffer, Vienna*

[*Autograph in the Beethovenhaus, Bonn, H. C. Bodmer collection*]

MY DEAR KIRCHHOFFER!   BADEN, *September* 5, 1823

You will receive the score of the symphony in a fortnight at latest [3] — All that must be done now is to dispatch the Mass as quickly as possible to Ries, who sends you friendly greetings through me. We can't make use of couriers, because the work forms too large a parcel. It would have to be split

---

[1] Op. 125.
[2] At the end of the autograph the ink has faded so badly that the bracketed words and the remainder of Beethoven's signature have been supplied by the present editor.   [3] Op. 125.

up, which would take *a long time* to do. *Arrange* for Brentano's letter to be sent, shall we say, by way of Trieste. You must decide. As you suspected, Ries has not yet taken a decisive step in this matter. But I think that he will exert himself when the work arrives in London — Choose a day to come to Baden and you will be welcomed with affection and friendship by my Karl and me.

In great haste, your

BEETHOVEN

(1239) *To Franz Christian Kirchhoffer, Vienna*

[*Autograph not traced*] [1]

[BADEN, *shortly after September* 5, 1823]

MY DEAR KIRCHHOFFER,

Would it not be possible to dispatch a parcel to London through the English Embassy? Please be so kind as to enquire. I will send for a reply about this tomorrow or whenever you consider it right and suitable. We, that is to say, my Karl and I, will certainly see you at dinner with us on *Sunday*. The weather seems to be improving again, and your company will give us both a great deal of pleasure —

Your most devoted

BEETHOVEN

(1240) *To Louis Spohr, Cassel*

[*MS in the possession of the Spohrgesellschaft, Cassel*] [2]

MY VERY DEAR FRIEND !   BADEN, *September* 17, 1823

It has afforded me much pleasure that you have honoured me with an immediate reply to my letter. In regard to the point referred to about the Mass I remember that somebody told me not to have an invitation sent to Hesse-Cassel because he was convinced that it would not be accepted. So far as I know, no invitation was sent off. In this connexion Hauser made me think differently. Having ascertained from him that my works were not quite unknown at Cassel I gathered fresh hope that perhaps after all His Excellency the Elector too might

---

[1] Taken from a facsimile in Karl Geigy-Hagenbach, *Autografenbuch* (Basel, 1925), p. 250.

[2] Written by Schindler and signed by Beethoven.

accept my invitation, seeing that even the Emperor of Russia, the King of France and the King of Prussia are among the number of my illustrious subscribers.[1] I have already made enquiries several times at the Hessian Legation, but each time there was nobody there and I was told that everyone was in the country. But as I am now at Baden for the sake of my health, it is very inconvenient to forward this invitation through the Legation. Hence I have thought it best to send it to you direct; and I venture to request Geheimrat [2] Rivalier to deliver it to His Excellency the Elector. I myself will thank the Geheimrat later on in writing for this kind action —

My health was not yet fully restored when Hauser came to see me. I was very poorly when I came here, but I now feel better than I did. My *eye complaint* too is rapidly clearing up.

As to your enquiry about *my opera* it is true that *Grillparzer* has written a libretto for me and that I too have already made a start.[3] But on account of my poor health several other works were set aside which I must now take up again. When these are finished I will set to work again at the opera and will let you know with what success.

Hauser told me that you had composed double quartets.[4] I was delighted to hear this. They will certainly be welcomed by the musical public. I am equally delighted to see from your letter that you are leading a peaceful country life with your family, to whom I send my best regards. My most ardent desire is to be able to lead that kind of life. But unfortunately my circumstances have not yet permitted it.

I send you my wishes for all that is good and to your advantage, and I trust that you will keep me in your friendly remembrance.

I remain, as always, your friend and fellow-artist

BEETHOVEN

PS.

Please ensure that I shall soon have a reply. Let me add that admittedly the undertaking appears on the

---

[1] The Elector of Hesse-Cassel did not subscribe to the Mass.

[2] The full title is 'Geheimer Cabinetsrat'. This official has not been identified. But Professor O. E. Deutsch has suggested Count Karl de la Rivalière.

[3] On Grillparzer's libretto 'Melusine'.

[4] Among many other chamber music works for unusual combinations of instruments Spohr composed four double string quartets.

surface to be very successful; but there are also certain difficulties connected with it. The copying expenses have greatly exceeded the amount I expected to have to disburse. Once more I urgently beg you for an early reply. And so that no distrust may be harboured, the copy will be delivered to the Electoral Hessian Legation on receipt of the fee. Although the number of subscribers is not large, yet it is sufficient to enable me to dispatch a copy at once. The fee is 50 ducats.

(1241) *To Anton Felix Schindler, Vienna*

[Autograph in the Deutsche Staatsbibliothek, Berlin]

SIGNORE PAPAGENO!   [BADEN, *c. September* 20, 1823]

Please be sure to look after these two parcels today with my housek[eeper], I mean the ones I have indicated — and see that they don't cost too much —

In order that your evil tongue may no longer injure unduly that poor native of Dresden, I inform you that the money arrived today with the gracious consideration which my honour demands ¹ — Gladly though I would render to you in this connexion my thanks *by word and deed*, I cannot yet put an end to this affair which is so close to my heart. I hope to be more fortunate in a few weeks' time — Isn't Count Golovkin the Russian Ambassador? ² Could you not enquire at the Russian Embassy whether there is a courier there who could take a parcel to Prince Galitzin? If not, then it will have to go by the mail coach on Tuesday —

Your absolutely very humble servant

BEETHOVEN

NB. In regard to the Russian Ambassador I must have particulars of his rank and his name in connexion with the dispatch of the *parcel* I have mentioned.

¹ Prince Anton's letter of acceptance is dated 'Dresden, September 12, 1823'.
² Count Golovkin, then Russian Envoy to the Imperial Court, had been previously Russian Envoy in Stuttgart (Würtemberg) and had attended the Congress of Vienna in 1815. The NB. about the Russian Ambassador is written on the left side of the page.

(1242) *To Franz Grillparzer*

[Autograph in the Stadtbibliothek, Vienna]

DEAR AND HONOURED SIR!   [VIENNA, *Autumn*, 1823]
    The directors would like to know your conditions for
your Melusine. Thus far they have expressed themselves of
their own accord; and that is surely preferable to our importuning them for their opinion. — For some time my household has been in great disorder or I would have looked you
up before now and invited you to visit me in return — But
for the time being send the directors your conditions in writing
or send them to me and I will then forward them myself —
As I have been overwhelmed with business it has been impossible for me to visit you; and it is so still. But I hope to do
this sometime — my no. is 323.[1]
    You will also find me in the afternoon at the coffee house
opposite the Goldene Birne.[2] If you would like to come,
please come *alone*. As you must have noticed at Hetzendorf,
this obtrusive hanger-on [3] of a Schindler has long ago become
extremely odious to me — Otium est vitium — With all my
heart I embrace you and honour you sincerely.

                            Wholly your
                                BEETH[OVEN]

(1243) *To Georg August von Griesinger*

[Autograph not traced] [4]

SIR!   [VIENNA], *Thursday, November* 20, [1823]
    I have the honour to inform you that my nephew will
deliver to you the Mass intended for His Majesty the King

    [1] In the autograph the number has been faintly pencilled in another hand.
This was Ungargasse no. 323, rooms into which Beethoven moved after his return
from Baden.
    [2] This was a small tavern, but a good one, with a dance hall.
    [3] Beethoven uses the word 'Appendix'.
    [4] Taken from La Mara, *Klassisches und Romantisches aus der Tonwelt*, 1892, p. 100.
The autograph was then in private ownership.

of Saxony and, what is more, between ten and eleven o'clock this morning. I have so many matters to deal with that I can only add that I shall give myself the pleasure of seeing you as soon as possible.

With kindest regards, your most devoted

BEETHOVEN

(1244) *To Prince Nikolas Galitzin, St. Petersburg*

[MS in the Bibliothèque Publique et Universitaire, Geneva] [1]

VIENNA, December 13, 1823

Pardonnez-moi, mon Prince honoré! Lorsque l'exemplaire de la messe vous fut envoyé, je me trouvai encore à Baden, et il y a peu de temps que par les exemplaires qui furent remis à quelques autres de mes souscripteurs, je m'aperçus, à mon grand dépit, du défaut de la premiere feuille du Gloria, que j'avais fait couper de l'original pour empêcher toute fraude ou vol de la part du copiste; c'est pourquoi je crains que cette feuille ne manque aussi à l'exemplaire que vous avez reçu. Que je suis faché de cet accident fatal, quoique arrivé sans ma faute! Ce pendant j'espere que cette feuille vous viendra encore à juste temps. En cas, que cela ne fût pas, vous pourriez peut-être vous procurer pour quelque temps l'exemplaire tout à fait complet, qui a été envoyé à S.M. L'empereur de la Russie. Au commencement du Gloria (In Gloria dei patris) le tempo a été oublié, qui doit être marqué de la manière ci-jointe.

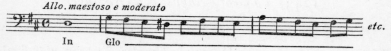

Je viens de recevoir votre lettre si aimable du 29 novembre, mais c'est avec tristesse et battement de cœur que je la recois.[2] Au premier jour de poste qui viendra, j'aurai l'honneur d'y repondre.

LOUIS VAN BEETHOVEN

[1] Written by Karl and signed by Beethoven.
[2] For Galitzin's letter see *TDR* V, 556-557. In this letter he calls Beethoven the third hero of music, succeeding Mozart and Haydn, and begs him to send more compositions.

PS.

Je ne me souviens pas, si je n'ai, de la raison marquée, aussi fait couper la dernière feuille du Gloria; pour prévenir à toute méprise, j'aurai l'honneur de vous l'envoyer presque en même temps avec la première. Mais si la fin du Gloria que vous trouverez écrite au commencement de la page suivante, ne manque pas, je supplie Votre Altesse de m'en avertir.[1]

(1245) *To Ignaz Moscheles*

[*Autograph in the possession of Dr. Georg Rosen*]

DEAR MOSCHELES!   [VIENNA, *December* 26, 1823][2]

I am delighted to serve you whenever I can — *Four horn parts* are missing. I have just noticed this; and certainly you

[1] For Galitzin's reply, dated December 30th, see *TDR* V, 557-558. In this letter he informs Beethoven that his copy of the Mass was complete.

[2] This date of receipt has been noted by Moscheles on a separate sheet with the remark that the note referred to the overture in C, Op. 115, which Beethoven had lent him for performance at his concert at the Court Theatre on December 15, 1823, for which Beethoven also lent him his Broadwood pianoforte.

did not leave them with me, for the music has been lying in exactly the same place all this time —

My best regards to Giuliani.[1]

Your friend

BEETHOVEN

(1246) *To Anton Felix Schindler*

[Autograph in the Beethovenhaus, Bonn, H. C. Bodmer collection]

[VIENNA, 1823]

I am sending you K[anne]'s book which apart from the rather dull first act is so excellently written that it would really not need a first-rate composer [2] — By that I do not mean that it would be the most suitable text *for me*. Still if I could get rid of certain commitments which I undertook some time ago, who knows what might happen — or may happen! —

In great haste, your friend

BEETHOVEN

Kindly inform me that you have received the book.

(1247) *To Anton Felix Schindler*

[Autograph in the possession of the Historical Society of Pennsylvania]

[VIENNA, 1823]

As you will see from the report to the police, yesterday's incident is certainly calculated to bring this matter to the notice of the worthy police authorities.[3] The statements of

[1] Mauro Giuliani (*c.* 1780–*c.* 1840), born at Bologna, was largely responsible for raising the guitar to the status of a serious instrument both by his masterly performances and by his very numerous compositions. He first came to Vienna in 1807 and remained there as performer and teacher until 1820 when he returned to Italy. Hanslick, p. 218, describes the year 1827 as the epoch of Moscheles, Mayseder and Giuliani, Mayseder being the violinist of the party.

[2] Friedrich August Kanne (1778–1833), poet, musician, composer and critic, came to Vienna from Saxony in 1808. He spent the rest of his life in Vienna where he edited the *Allgemeine Musikalische Zeitung* from 1821 to 1824. He was an enthusiastic admirer of Beethoven's compositions. See *FRBH* I, 247-248. Evidently Kanne had written a libretto, or found a libretto, for Beethoven.

[3] Both Nohl I, p. 253, note, and *TDR* IV, 446 connect this note with Beethoven's interference in the domestic affairs of his brother. The autograph has been dated by Schindler.

an unnamed person tally exactly with yours. In this case private individuals can no longer help. Only officials invested with authority can do so.

Your
BEETHOVEN

(1248) *To the Archduke Rudolph*

[Autograph in the Gesellschaft der Musikfreunde, Vienna]

YOUR IMPERIAL HIGHNESS! [VIENNA, 1823]

I was deeply touched at receiving yesterday your kind letter to me. To be allowed to flourish too in the shade of a flourishing tree which is bearing splendid fruit is a solace for those who are able to feel and perceive what is on a higher plane. And that is what I feel under the aegis of Y.I.H.— My doctor assured me yesterday that I really am recovering from my illness. But I must still take a whole bottle of mixture in 24 hours and, as it is a purgative, I find the treatment extremely weakening. At the same time, as Y.I.H. will see from the enclosed instructions given by my doctor, I have to take a good deal of exercise. Meanwhile there is reason to hope that soon, although I may not be completely recovered, I shall yet be able to spend a good deal of time with Y.I.H. during your stay in Vienna. Because I cherish this hope, my good health will assuredly return even more quickly than usual — May Heaven bless me through Y.I.H. and may the Lord Himself ever watch over and guard Y.I.H. There is nothing higher than to approach the Godhead more nearly than other mortals and by means of that contact to spread the rays of the Godhead through the human race. — Profoundly moved by Y.I.H.'s gracious thoughts for me I hope very soon to be able to call on you in person —

Your Imperial Highness's
most obedient and faithful servant
BEETHOVEN

(1249) *To Gustav Dollinger* [1]

[Autograph not traced] [2]

[VIENNA, 1823]

. . . You must forgive the late arrival of the letter, but for a considerable time now my health has been in an almost critical state. . . .

(1250) *To [Anton Felix Schindler ?]*

[Autograph in the British Museum] [3]

[VIENNA, 1823]

QUITE AMAZING AND MOST EXCELLENT FELLOW!

At two o'clock precisely we shall sit down to table ; and we shall expect you most certainly — since there will be something for you to eat — Note that today you can read in the Graben about the new ale-house which was opened there yesterday —

In great haste, yours

(1251) *To Franz Xaver Latzel* [4]

[Autograph not traced] [5]

[VIENNA, 1823]

As I do not know your worthy name, I am just writing to say that I will certainly take the rooms which I saw yesterday. Today it was impossible and tomorrow it will also be impossible ; but the day after tomorrow you will receive the deposit.

In haste, your most devoted

BEETHOVEN

[1] Not identified.

[2] Taken from catalogue no. xxxvi of L. Liepmannsohn. November, 1906, lot 1051.

[3] This autograph note written in ink is neither dated nor signed nor addressed.

[4] Little is known about Franz Xaver Latzel who was a Viennese musician, a performer on the double bass, and a teacher of singing. See *FRBH* I, 321-322.

[5] Taken from *FRNB.* pp. 128-129. The autograph was then in private ownership. The note was addressed to Alleegasse, no. 36, 3ter Stock, where Latzel lived from 1819 to 1823.

(1252) *To Peter Gläser* [1]

[Autograph in the Stadtbibliothek, Vienna]

DEAR HERR GLÄSER,   [VIENNA, 1823]
   Please look through and correct the parts of the Credo
from No. 1.[2] But I must have them tomorrow and, what is
more, at about eight o'clock. Further, please have the enclosed
flute part of the Agnus, which I simply cannot find, copied
today also, so that I may receive it tomorrow along with the
parts of the Credo.—

                                 Your most devoted
                                             BEETHOVEN

(1253) *To Anton Felix Schindler*

[Autograph in the Deutsche Staatsbibliothek, Berlin]

                                                  [VIENNA, 1823]
   *I am sending you those portions of the trombone parts which you
still require.* I will send someone for them tomorrow morning.
Or if you have somebody available, then it would be well,
nay, even imperative, to send them in to me copied out and
ready for the copied score, together with the original manuscript —

(1254) *To [Anton Felix Schindler ?]*

[Autograph in the Deutsche Staatsbibliothek, Berlin] [3]

You know how I am placed ! —   [VIENNA, 1823]
   I think that is the best way to proceed : I will not have
anything to do in a question of discretion with a person who
has once already broken his word to me and in such a way.—
That is the ultimatum, and I shall not alter it in any way

---

   [1] Peter Gläser was the father of Franz Joseph Gläser (1798–1861), conductor
and composer, who in 1822 became Kapellmeister at the newly rebuilt Josephstadt
Theatre. He had settled in Vienna to help with the copying of scores for this
theatre. See *FRBS.* II, pp. 11-15.
   [2] Evidently Gläser was copying portions of the 'Missa Solemnis'.
   [3] The autograph is neither dated nor signed nor addressed.

whatsoever — either the one or the other. Please come to dinner with me. By the way, there must be no postponement in this affair except on the money side — He may pay the fee in six weeks and even later.

(1255) *To Peter Gläser*

[*Autograph not traced*] [1]

[VIENNA, 1823]

You are receiving herewith the trombone parts you still required. Tomorrow morning I will send for the copies . . . and please send the original manuscript too — I think it advisable that you should now press forward as much as possible with the parts to be duplicated. Therefore please do *not* come tomorrow, for we cannot have any short rehearsals without the duplicated parts.—

[1] Taken from sale catalogue no. 264 of Stargardt, April 29, 1927, lot 591.

1824

(1256) *To Joseph Karl Bernard*

[*Autograph in the Beethovenhaus, Bonn, H. C. Bodmer collection*] [1]

DEAR FRIEND ! [VIENNA, *early January*, 1824]
Please do make enquiries today about Frau van Beethoven
and, if possible, assure her at once through her doctor that
from this month onwards she can enjoy her full pension *as
long as I live.* And I too will endeavour so far as possible to
make such provision for Karl that should I predecease her,
he will not require the half of her pension —
As a matter of fact it was always my intention to allow her
the full enjoyment of her pension immediately after Karl
left the boarding school.[2] But as she is so ill and in such
straitened circumstances, she must be helped at once. God has
never forsaken me in this difficult task ; and I shall continue
to trust in Him. If possible, please let me have news of her
today. I shall make a point of persuading my pigheaded
brother also to contribute something to help her —
With cordial greetings, your
BEETHOVEN

(1257) *To Frau Johanna van Beethoven*

[*Autograph in the Beethovenhaus, Bonn, H. C. Bodmer collection*]

[VIENNA], *January* 8, 1824
Our many occupations made it quite impossible for Karl
and me to send you our best wishes on New Year's Day. But
I know that even without this explanation you are fully assured
of both my and Karl's sincerest wishes for your welfare —
As for your need of money, I would gladly have helped you
out with a sum. But unfortunately I have too many expenses
and debts and am still waiting for certain payments, so that

---

[1] This letter is written in pencil.
[2] Karl had left Blöchlinger's boarding school on August 29, 1823. He had
been there since June 22, 1819.

I cannot prove to you at once and on the spot my readiness to help you ¹ — Meanwhile I assure you now in writing that henceforth and for good you may draw Karl's half of your pension. We shall send you the receipt every month and then you yourself can draw it. For it is no disgrace whatever to draw it in person every month (I know that several acquaintances of mine draw their pensions every month). Should I be comfortably off later on and in a position to provide you from my income with a sum large enough to improve your circumstances, I will certainly do so — Further, I undertook long ago to pay the 280 gulden, 25 kreuzer which you owe Steiner.² No doubt you have been informed of this. Moreover for a considerable time you have not had to pay any interest on that loan —

You have received from me through Schindler pension payments for two months — On the 26th of this month or a few days later you will receive the amount of the pension for this month — As for your lawsuit, I will soon discuss that matter with Dr. Bach ³ —

Both Karl and I wish you all possible happiness —

Your L. v. BEETHOVEN who is
most willing to help you.

(1258) *To Joseph Karl Bernard*

[*Autograph in the Beethovenhaus, Bonn, H. C. Bodmer collection*]

[VIENNA, *c. January* 10, 1824]

The quickest way would be to let the doctor see the letter which I wrote to *her*.⁴ Perhaps your housekeeper too might make a few enquiries about her. But she will hardly want

¹ A short fragment, the end of a letter from Beethoven to an unknown recipient, of which there is a photograph in the Beethovenarchiv, Bonn, mentions the same private difficulty : '. . . to be remitted soon, for just now, as usual, I must disburse, and I should be receiving, a good deal of money—'

² According to a note dated March 28, 1818, the autograph of which is in the Beethovenhaus, Bonn, Beethoven's sister-in-law Johanna undertook to pay Steiner by August 1, 1818 this amount of five per cent. interest on capital formerly borrowed from him and already repaid.

³ It has not been possible to discover any particulars of this lawsuit.

⁴ Obviously Beethoven's sister-in-law Johanna. The letter referred to may be Letter 1257.

to go to such a place, any more than I would.[1]

Should this sum be too small for her present requirements, then I will do more. That depends on what the doctor says.

(1259) *To Joseph Karl Bernard*

[Autograph in the Beethovenhaus, Bonn, H. C. Bodmer collection]

DEAR BERNARD !   [VIENNA, *early January*, 1824]

In view of the small amount of time at my disposal it is too inconvenient for me to write in person to the doctor, to whom, however, I send my kindest regards. Well, to be brief, what she can certainly rely on is her pension, which is 406 gulden 30 kreuzer V.C. and the yearly interest on 6700 gulden V.C., amounting to 335 gulden V.C. ; and she is supposed to receive from *Hofbauer* [2] too 480 gulden V.C. per annum. Since Hofbauer, I understand, believes that he is the father of the child, *he is probably right.* And as she has become such a strumpet I consider that after all I should make Karl realize the guilt of *her wicked behaviour.* Hence if these 480 gulden of Hofbauer's are really and truly being paid to her, I think that she ought not to be allowed to enjoy the whole remaining half of her pension. Perhaps such an eminent man as the *doctor* could clear up the matter. Let me add that I do *not* want *to have anything to do with her personally.* I am sending her herewith 11 gulden A.C. Please have it delivered to her through the *doctor* and, what is more, in such a way that she may not know where it has come from. But please obtain a written statement from her that she has received this sum — If we could be fully informed about all the circumstances, then we might see what could still be done for her ; and I am prepared to help in every way —

Your friend
BEETHOVEN

[1] This paragraph is written on one side of the sheet. The remainder is written on the verso.

[2] Cf. Letter 1045, p. 909, n. 4.

(1260) *To the Directors of the Gesellschaft der Musikfreunde*

[Autograph in the Gesellschaft der Musikfreunde, Vienna]

GENTLEMEN !   VIENNA, *January* 23, 1824

As I have been overwhelmed with work and am still suffering from an eye complaint, you must very kindly forgive my tardy reply — In regard to the oratorio I trust that veritas odium *non* parit. *It was not I* who chose H. v. B[ernard] to write the text. I was assured that the Society had commissioned him to write it — For as H. v. B[ernard] has to edit his newspaper, it is difficult to have many discussions with him.[1] Hence it would have had to be a long task, and indeed a very unpleasant one for me, seeing that H. v. B[ernard] had written for music nothing but his 'Libussa', which at that time had not yet been performed.[2] But having come across the work in 1809 and knowing too that since then it had undergone a great many alterations, I could foresee with the utmost assurance that to collaborate with him in this undertaking would certainly be difficult. Hence I was all the more compelled to insist on having the whole text; and at last I contrived to obtain the first part. But according to B[ernard]'s statements this part had to be altered again; and therefore I had to return it, so far as I remember. In the end I received the whole text at exactly the same time as it was sent to the Society.[3] Owing to other engagements into which I had entered and which by reason of my former more delicate state of health I had not been able to meet, I really had to hurry in order to fulfil my promise, the more so as you are aware that *unfortunately my sole livelihood comes from the works which I compose. Now, however, several passages, indeed I may say a great many passages,* in B[ernard]'s oratorio *will have to be altered.*

[1] Bernard had been editor-in-chief of the *Wiener Zeitung* since October, 1819.

[2] This libretto was set to music by the well-known conductor and composer Konradin Kreutzer (1780–1849) as a romantic opera which was successfully produced at the Kärntnertor Theatre on December 4, 1822.

[3] In October, 1823. In the end Beethoven did not set to music Bernard's text 'Der Sieg des Kreuzes'. Nor is there any evidence of his having made an attempt to do so.

I have in fact marked a few of them and shall soon finish marking the rest; and then I shall inform B[ernard] of them. For, although the subject is very well thought out and the poetry has some merit, yet it just cannot remain *as it is at present.* 'Christus am Ölberge' was completed by myself and the *poet* in a fortnight.[1] But the *poet* was musical and had already written several works to be set to music. And I could discuss our undertaking with him at any moment. Well, we need not enquire into *the value* of poems of this kind. We all know how to deal with them. The good lies here in the middle. But so far as I am concerned, I prefer to set to music the works of poets like Homer, Klopstock and Schiller. For at any rate, even though in their works there are difficulties to overcome, these *immortal poets* are worth this trouble — As soon as I have worked out with B[ernard] the alterations in his oratorio I shall have the honour to inform you that this has been done and also of the date when the Society can certainly count on having the work. That is all I can say about it at the moment — As for the 400 gulden V.C. which were sent to me as an *unsolicited* gift, I would have returned them long ago, had I really been able to foresee that the work on this oratorio might last much longer than I expected. It distressed me indeed not to be able to express my opinion about this. Hence in order to repay the Society the interest on this sum, for the time being at any rate, I conceived the idea of collaborating with the Society in organizing a concert. But neither Herr Schindler nor my brother was authorized to say anything about it; and I certainly did not intend that it should be done *in that way.* Please be so kind as to inform H[err] L[eopold] v[on] Sonnleithner about this too. Let me add that with all my heart I thank you for the offer of the stands and of other help in general which the Society has made to me. I will avail myself of this offer in due course — I should be delighted to hear whether later on, i.e. after my concert, the Society would like to make use of the works performed, which include a new symphony as well. For, to tell the truth, the grand Mass is more in the style of an oratorio and was really intended for the Society. I shall be particularly pleased if people discern in my action my unselfishness and at the same time my zeal to

[1] Op. 85 was composed in March, 1803, on a text by Franz Xaver Huber. Cf. p. 339.

serve the Society, in whose charitable activities in the cause of art I shall always take the greatest interest —

Be pleased to accept, Gentlemen, my great regard for you in all respects.

LUDWIG VAN BEETHOVEN

(1261) *To Johann Baptist Bach*

[*Autograph not traced*] [1]

ESTEEMED FRIEND !   [VIENNA], *January* 24, [1824] [2]

Herr von Schindler assures me that you are willing to honour and delight me with your presence at *dinner* tomorrow. Do please keep your promise, for I have also made arrangements for my Karl to share the pleasure of your company. So I most certainly expect you. It is not necessary to express to you more definitely with what affection and happiness we are looking forward to seeing you, for, as it is, you have long been convinced of our feelings.—

With cordial devotion and sincere regard,

your friend
BEETHOVEN

Schindler will fetch you.

(1262) *To Joseph Karl Bernard*

[*Autograph in the Beethovenhaus, Bonn, H. C. Bodmer collection*]

[VIENNA, *late January*, 1824]

MY DEAR AND BELOVED FRIEND !

As to your oratorio various portions of it, even in its plan, would have to be altered for me. To go into all these points at once is impossible for me on account of my urgent occupations which cannot be postponed. Moreover such alterations would take some time [3] — If you can find someone else of a different opinion, which would be quite possible, well

---

[1] From a photograph kindly supplied by Gilhofer, Vienna.

[2] In 1824 January 24th fell on a Saturday. Most probably Beethoven was giving his dinner party, fixed for 'tomorrow', on Sunday, as he frequently did.

[3] In the autograph this sentence is added at the foot of the page.

then, I cannot and must not take it amiss if you entrust your very sound work to him. This must not lead you to think that I fail to appreciate your talent and your merits. But it has always been my principle never to stand in anybody's way. As for the Society which, since it had convinced itself that this oratorio would be composed more quickly, expressed its unfavourable opinion of me, although I had neither provoked nor expected such an outburst, I will certainly see to it that it shall not suffer any loss —

You saw that I was engaged in moving into new quarters; and since arrangements of this kind usually take up some time, so it was with me also. Otherwise I should have come to see you myself. Let me beg you not to think that I am false in any way. You know well how much I love the truth —

Ever your friend
BEETHOVEN

(1263) *To Anton Felix Schindler*

[*Autograph in the Deutsche Staatsbibliothek, Berlin*]

[VIENNA, *early in* 1824] [1]

Here is the parcel for the Russian Embassy.

Please have it delivered at once —

By the way, leave a message to say that I will soon call on him in person. For I feel hurt that people are distrusting me. Thank God, I am in a position to prove that I am far from deserving such treatment. Moreover my honour will not tolerate it either! —

[1] In a note on the verso of this unsigned autograph Schindler dates this letter 'Winter, 1824' and on the recto adds the remark that Beethoven's reminder referred to the delivery of a copy of the 'Missa Solemnis' for the Russian Emperor, who had already sent his subscription.

(1264) *To* [*Tobias Haslinger*]

[*MS in the Gesellschaft der Musikfreunde, Vienna*] [1]

[VIENNA, *c. February* 3, 1824]

DEAR LORD HIGH CHANCELLORSHIP ! [2]

After mature consideration we are now handing over to you the Finance Department; and we request you to have the sum of 125 gulden sent to us from the Treasury, a sum which within 14 days at latest you can replace from our domains. As soon as you have improved your financial affairs by means of your penetrating intelligence you will then take over again the Lord High Chancellorship. Let me add that we are amazingly attached to you and that we wish you this and that, and also anything else, from which you may take the best.

Our secretarius perpetuus [3] will explain everything to you verbally in the most lucid and most circumstantial manner.

Our greetings to the Directorate of Acoustics. But the staff cannot yet be increased, because so far too little is known about the acoustics of comets [4] —

Dixi.

BEETHOVEN

(1265) *To Tobias Haslinger*

[*Autograph in the Beethovenhaus, Bonn, H. C. Bodmer collection*]

MOST EXCELLENT TO !   VIENNA, *February* 17, 1824
—   BI !
—   AS !

Be so *kind* as to give Herr Ecker,[5] who will hand you a receipt for it, the sum of 55 gulden, 32 kreuzer A.C. It has not yet been collected; and, moreover, Karl has always to

---

[1] Written by Karl and signed by Beethoven. The word 'Dixi' before the signature is also in Beethoven's hand.

[2] The letter is addressed on the verso in Karl's hand 'To the Lord High Chancellorship'. See Letter 1265, p. 1109.

[3] Karl. Cf. Letter 1087, p. 959.

[4] Probably an allusion to the possibility of Haslinger's meteoric rise to fame. In 1826 after Steiner's retirement Haslinger became head of the firm.

[5] Not identified.

undertake several fruitless errands for that purpose. Perhaps some easier method of fetching it might be devised. Until now indeed I always paid this sum at once out of my own pocket, mais — the latter is more *empty than full* — But tell Herr E[cker] that he must go to you. Once and for all I refuse to let him come to me, for his *behaviour* is such that people regard me as his debtor. In any case matters are not settled any more quickly in that way; and I should have thought that one would find few such good-natured fools as myself. Generosity should be respected. If not, I will not give anything more — My dear fellow, Karl is going to you this afternoon and will hand you the receipt. You will kindly deduct the 125 gulden V.C. and let us have the remainder without more ado. On the 25th of this month your exchequer will once more rest on the soundest foundations. My most excellent Lord High Chancellor, I send you all good wishes, all good wishes. My health is again very weak and shaky.

Karl will be with you today for certain and bring the Archduke's receipt.

Your grateful amicus
BEETHOVEN

NB. Karl will call on you this afternoon for certain in order to hand you the Archducal Episcopal Cardinal's receipt for 750 gulden V.C. (I repeat, 750 gulden in Viennese currency).[1]

(1266) *To Heinrich Albert Probst, Leipzig* [2]

[*Autograph not traced*] [3]

SIR!   VIENNA, *February* 25, 1824

As I am being continually urged to compose new works and am overwhelmed in general by a correspondence which is almost too extensive for me, I can only now reply to your letter — Since you desire to have some of my compositions,

---

[1] This NB. is written on the first page of the autograph above the text of the letter.

[2] Heinrich Albert Probst, born at Dresden in 1791, opened a music publishing house at Leipzig in 1823. Friedrich Kistner (1797–1844) was his partner and in 1831 became the head of the firm. Probst was also agent in Germany for the firm of Artaria.   [3] Taken from Unger *DM.*, October, 1923, pp. 11-12.

I am informing you for the present of a few which I could let you have at once, and also of the fees for these works. They are: Three songs with pianoforte accompaniment, two of which have also suitable accompaniments for other instruments and can be performed without a pianoforte; the third is an arietta which is not long but entirely durchgeführt.[1] The fee for all three is 24 gold ducats — Six bagatelles for pianoforte solo which, however, are longer than the ones I previously published. The fee is 30 gold ducats [2] — A grand overture for full orchestra, with which a new theatre is going to be opened in due course.[3] (It is clearly understood that you will receive the score of the overture and that you may have the pianoforte arrangement made or any other arrangements whatsoever) [4] — In the case of the overture the sole condition must be added that it shall not be published until the month of July. It is clearly understood, however, that as soon as you take it, it will be and remain for ever wholly your property —

That is what I can offer you for the moment. But as soon as I hear of your acceptance, I will offer you *greater works* — All I ask is that you should reply quickly. For other foreign publishers too have written to me about compositions. But unfortunately they are all further away than Leipzig; and I confess that corresponding with people at a very great distance is irksome to me and that I prefer to deal with people near at hand. True, Vienna is nearest of all. But I don't care to have anything more to do with Vienna — One more remark, which is, that I don't like to separate these three works — However little there may be in me of the business man or merchant, yet I really must thank Heaven which is so blessing me in my works that, though admittedly I am not rich, I have yet been enabled by means of my compositions to *live for my art*. And from that point of view I need not be ashamed of refusing to despise some gain from my intellectual labours —

I remain, Sir, your most devoted

BEETHOVEN

---

[1] An alternative expression for 'durchkomponiert'. Cf. Letter 81, p. 95, n. 7. The songs are Op. 121b, 122 and 128.

[2] Op. 126.

[3] Op. 124, performed at the opening of the newly rebuilt Josephstadt Theatre.

[4] This bracketed sentence is added at the foot of the second page.

(1267) *To Moritz Schlesinger, Paris* [1]

[*MS in the Beethovenhaus, Bonn, H. C. Bodmer collection*] [2]

SIR !   VIENNA, *February* 25, [1824]

I thank you for the score of Méhul's [work that you have sent me ?], which is so worthy of him and [is bound to make us mourn ?] his loss even more.[3]   In connexion with your proposal about compositions of mine I am offering you a grand solemn Mass with choruses, solos and full orchestra.[4]   Indeed your father wanted to take it some time ago.   But I am compelled to live entirely on the receipts from my works ; and some additional advantages were put forward to me, inasmuch as several monarchs acquire the Mass in manuscript copies.   Let me add that in this case there is not the slightest danger that any portion of it will be sold.   The fee is 1000 gulden A.C.   Furthermore, the Königstadt Theatre in Berlin has received a new overture for its opening ceremony.   This you could publish at any rate in May, 1824, when presumably the theatre will have been opened.[5]   In case of delay the publication would have to be postponed.   The overture is my property and will become yours as soon as you receive the score.   You can do what you like with it.   The fee is 50 gold ducats (Imperial and Royal ducats).   Furthermore, I am offering you the score of a perfectly new grand symphony which, however, cannot be published until 1825.[6]   It has a grand Finale with choruses and vocal solo parts, in the same manner as my choral fantasia, but on a larger scale.[7]   The fee is 600 gulden A.C.   Later on you will receive new quartets as well.   But these must first

---

[1] The original letter is not addressed.   But on internal evidence it was undoubtedly intended for Moritz Schlesinger in Paris.

[2] This letter, which is badly scorched at the centre fold, was written by Karl and signed by Beethoven, who also wrote the last ten words and the date, but not the year.   The words and phrases in square brackets have been supplied by the present editor.

In 1826 Moritz Schlesinger's firm in Paris was destroyed by fire, no doubt with the loss of many letters from Beethoven.

[3] Méhul had died of consumption in October, 1817.   Cf. Letter 1140, p. 1003.

[4] Op. 123, which in the end was published by Bernhard Schotts Söhne in 1827.

[5] Op. 124.   The theatre was not opened until August 4, 1824, when Karl Wilhelm Henning conducted the overture.   See Letter 1343, p. 1165, n. 1.

[6] The ninth symphony, Op. 125.

[7] Op. 80.

be [completed?]. My greetings to Schlösser to whom I wish all success. Only lack of time prevents me from writing to him. He can assure you of my truthfulness and testify how wrong you were to think anything else — I am writing to your father as well.[1] And now I request you to reply with all speed, because there are others too who want to have these works. The Mass can be published as soon as it is engraved. Perhaps I shall spend next [winter?] in the South of France and, if so, I want to see Paris as well. But please reply quickly. As soon as you let me know that you are taking some works, I will arrange for them to be copied and will inform you of a place where I can draw the fees on delivering the works. You too might decide which place this shall be.

In great haste and with all speed, your most devoted

BEETHOVEN

(1268) *To Friedrich Kalkbrenner* [2]

[Autograph in the possession of Richard Franko Goldman] [3]

MY VERY DEAR FRIEND !   [VIENNA, *February*, 1824]

An unforeseen circumstance obliges me to be away from home until this evening and deprives me of the pleasure of being able to see you and Herr D.[4] — As to the works which I would gladly entrust to you to take to London, the copyist will not have them ready for ten or twelve days. Unfortunately my regular copyist has gone *to his eternal rest* and and I only recently took on my present one.[5] Hence everything proceeds

[1] A. M. Schlesinger in Berlin.

[2] Friedrich Wilhelm Michael Kalkbrenner (1788–1849), son of the German composer Christian Kalkbrenner (1755–1806), became a celebrated pianist and also a teacher and a composer. He lived in Paris from 1806 to 1814 and in London from 1814 until 1824, when he returned to Paris, where he remained until his death from cholera.

[3] First published with a facsimile in the *Juilliard Review*, vol. IV, no. 1, 1956–1957, in an article by Nathan Broder, pp. 16-20.

[4] Almost certainly François Joseph Dizi (1780–1840), the Belgian harpist and composer, who spent most of his life in London and in 1830 settled in Paris. Cf. Letter 534, p. 504, n. 1. During his third visit to Vienna in 1823–1824 Kalkbrenner had given a concert with Dizi in the Kleiner Redoutensaal on January 25, 1824. But circumstances suddenly obliged Kalkbrenner and Dizi to return to London almost immediately afterwards. See Hanslick, pp. 220 and 256.

[5] Schlemmer, Beethoven's regular copyist, had died in the summer of 1823. His new copyist was probably Rampel. See Letter 1335, p. 1158, n. 4.

more slowly than formerly, the more so as the score must again be copied as a score.¹ Moreover everything must be checked by me and in addition I have been suffering for a long time now from an eye complaint — But I hope that you are going to stay in Vienna a little longer, particularly as in many quarters I hear wishes expressed that you would give another concert, an undertaking in which I take the most lively interest ; and, if you do this, you will most certainly be able to take all those works of mine to L[ondon].

    With all my heart I embrace you ; and my sole desire is to be able in some way to serve you —

                    In sincere friendship
                            your
                                BEETHOVEN

(1269) *To Heinrich Albert Probst, Leipzig*

[*Autograph in the Deutsche Staatsbibliothek, Berlin*]

[VIENNA, *March* 10, 1824]

. . . I could even publish now.² Unfortunately I must still talk about myself and tell you that it is undoubtedly the greatest work I have ever composed.³ The fee would be a thousand gulden A.C. — A new grand symphony, which has a Finale introducing voices, solo and choruses, with a setting of the words of Schiller's immortal 'Lied an die Freude' in the same way as my pianoforte fantasia with chorus, but on a far grander scale.⁴ The fee would be six hundred gulden A.C. But in the case of this symphony I must make the condition that it shall not appear until July of next year, 1825. As a compensation for this long delay, however, I would gladly undertake to make the pianoforte arrangement *for you* gratis. And in general, if we were to form a closer connexion, you would always find me willing to do you a kindness ⁵ —

¹ Probably the score of the ninth symphony, Op. 125.
² The beginning of this letter has been torn off. The letter is addressed in Beethoven's hand and endorsed by the firm.
³ The 'Missa Solemnis'.
⁴ The ninth symphony, Op. 125. The choral fantasia is Op. 80, which had been published in 1811.
⁵ The autograph is not signed.

(1270) *To Bernhard Schotts Söhne, Mainz* [1]

[Autograph in the possession of Bernhard Schott, Mainz]

SIR !   VIENNA, *March* 10, 1824

Most respectfully do I request you to convey to the E[ditoria]l B[oar]d of the C[äcili]a [2] my thanks for their kind attention. How gladly would I serve them so far as my mediocre talents in that respect would permit, if I did not feel within me a greater impulse to reveal myself to the world by means of my compositions. I have instructed someone, however, to find you a correspondent who is reliable (very difficult to discover in Vienna owing to the general partisanship). If I come across anything remarkable of mine (but Heaven knows how difficult that would be), I will gladly have it sent to you through such a correspondent; and, moreover, if you insist on having it and if my almost ceaseless occupations permit me to do so, I will send it to you myself —

In regard to my works which you would like me to send you, I offer you the following, but you must not delay too long in reaching a decision about this :— a new grand solemn Mass with solo voices and choruses and a full orchestra. Although I find it difficult to talk about myself, yet I must say that I consider this to be my greatest work.[3] The fee would be 1000 gulden A.C. : a new grand symphony which concludes with a Finale (in the style of my fantasia for piano with chorus, but on a far grander scale) with vocal solos and choruses, based on the words of Schiller's immortal and famous song 'An die Freude'.[4] The fee is 600 gulden A.C. A new quartet for two violins, viola and violoncello, for which the fee is 50 gold ducats [5] —

I am letting you have these business details merely in

[1] This famous firm of music publishers at Mainz was founded in 1773 by Bernhard Schott. After his death in 1817 his sons Andreas (1781–1840) and Johann Joseph (1782–1835) carried on the business. The firm, which still exists, published some of Beethoven's greatest works, such as Op. 123, 125 and 131.

[2] Schott published *Caecilia: eine Zeitschrift für die musikalische Welt*, edited by G. Weber and S. W. Dehn, Mainz, 1824–1848.

[3] The 'Missa Solemnis' was published by Schott early in 1827 as Op. 123.

[4] Op. 125, published by Schott in August, 1826.

[5] Op. 127, the first of Beethoven's late string quartets, was published by Schott in June, 1826.

order to comply with your wishes. When dealing with these particulars do not judge me as a business man. But although I am a true artist, I dare not despise competition. For by earning money I am enabled to work loyally for my Muses and to provide in some liberal way for very many other people— With regard to the works I have mentioned the reply would have to be sent to me very soon —

I am, Sir, your most devoted

BEETHOVEN

(1271) *To Joseph Karl Bernard*

[*Autograph in the Beethovenhaus, Bonn, H. C. Bodmer collection*]

MY DEAR BERNARD! [VIENNA, *early March*, 1824]

S[chindler] is going to show you the present from the King of France.[1] You doubtless realize that to circulate news of this kind is well worth while both for my honour and for the King's. It is clear that His Majesty did not want just to *fob me off* by paying for his copy. This action shows, to my mind, that he is a generous King and a man of refined feeling. I leave it entirely to you to decide how you are going to make this event known in your valuable periodical [2] —

We will soon discuss the question of your oratorio.[3] When we last discussed it you completely misunderstood me. Since then I have been overwhelmed with such an amount of work that it is really difficult for me always to cope with the details of everyday life. But I hope [4]

[1] The gold medal sent by Louis XVIII arrived on February 20, 1824. It is now in the Gesellschaft der Musikfreunde, Vienna.

[2] The *Wiener Zeitung*, of which Bernard had been chief editor since October, 1819.

[3] Bernard had written a text 'Der Sieg des Kreuzes' which Beethoven was to set to music for the Gesellschaft der Musikfreunde, founded in 1812.

[4] The remainder of this letter has been torn off.

(1272) *To Count Moritz Dietrichstein* [1]

[*MS in the Beethovenhaus, Bonn, H. C. Bodmer collection*] [2]

YOUR EXCELLENCY!   VIENNA, *March* 21, 1824

As I have heard that I am not to have April 7th for my concert, I most humbly beg Your Excellency to grant me the Grosser Redoutensaal for a concert on April 8th, and preferably at about noon, a time which will inconvenience neither the Theatres nor myself.[3] I am deeply obliged to Your Excellency for the ready kindness you have always shown me and, what is even more flattering, for the fact that Your Excellency is not entirely unsympathetic to my art. I hope soon to have an opportunity of demonstrating to Your Excellency my very deep respect and admiration.

Your Excellency's
most obedient
LUDWIG VAN BEETHOVEN

(1273) *To [Count Moritz Dietrichstein]*

[*Autograph not traced*] [4]

YOUR EXCELLENCY!   [VIENNA, *March*, 1824]

I have been approached from various quarters with the suggestion that I should give a grand concert. I request you, therefore, to grant me permission to give it in the Grosser Redoutensaal and on the evening of April 8th.[5] Duport is entirely in favour of it.[6] About the Mass for His Majesty I

[1] Count Moritz Dietrichstein (1774–1864), a strong supporter of Beethoven, was Director of the Burgtheater from 1821 to 1826 and in 1826 was put in charge of the Court Library. Cf. Letter 180, p. 201, n. 1.
[2] Written by Schindler and signed by Beethoven. In the Deutsche Staatsbibliothek, Berlin, there is a draft of this letter in Beethoven's hand with a note by Schindler about Prince von Trautmannsdorf. See Sonneck, p. 192 ff.
[3] In the end Beethoven's two concerts were given on Friday, May 7th, in the Kärntnertor Theatre and on Sunday, May 23rd, in the Grosser Redoutensaal.
[4] Taken from Schlossar *DM.*, No. IX/13, 1910, p. 40.
[5] This permission was evidently not granted. Beethoven did not give his two concerts, his last ones, until May 7th and 23rd.
[6] Louis Antoine Duport (1783–1853), formerly a ballet dancer, was then the authorized representative of Domenico Barbaja, who had leased the Kärntnertor Theatre from 1822 to 1825.

must still beg to be excused.[1] The next time I see you I shall enlighten you about everything concerning that work — I know that you will forgive me for not calling on Y[our] E[xcellency] in person. But I have an enormous amount to do ; and I know that that is the case with Y[our] E[xcellency] as well. And you too do not stand on ceremony.

Your Excellency's
most devoted servant
L. VAN BEETHOVEN

(1274) *To Anton Felix Schindler* [2]

[Autograph in the Deutsche Staatsbibliothek, Berlin]

[VIENNA, *Spring,* 1824]

You must address the cover 'To His Royal Majesty of Saxony'.

Let me know if you hear anything about rooms — Shall I see you perhaps one of these days ? —

(1275) *To Peter Gläser*

[Autograph in the Beethovenhaus, Bonn]

MY DEAR HERR GLÄSER ! [VIENNA, *April,* 1824]

I asked you to copy exactly what I had written.[3] But alas ! I find that *the words* are written out in the very way I did not want, just as if it had been done *on purpose.* Hence I insist once more that most particular attention be paid to the way the words are entered *under the notes.* It is not a matter of indifference if the consonants are added immediately to the vowels, which should be drawn out, as I showed you and explained to you and, what is more, told S[chindler] to remind you. I really do insist that the score be written out

---

[1] Early in 1823 Count Moritz Lichnowsky had urged Count Dietrichstein to commission Beethoven to compose a Mass for the Emperor. Cf. Letter 1170, p. 1029, n. 2.

[2] This note is addressed in Beethoven's hand to Schindler at Kothgasse, No. 60. Apparently Schindler was then occupying the rooms vacated by Beethoven.

[3] According to Unger, *NBJ.* III, 1926, p. 55, no fewer than five copyists shared the copying of the ninth symphony, i.e. Rampel, Schlemmer's son, Paul Maschek, Peter Gläser and possibly the Czech Wolanek.

exactly as it stands. *In regard to the words,* such as 'so——ft', for example, the consonant should not be added until after the *end* of the *lengthening.* It is quite clearly written; and you can see that in the *copy of the score* similar instances have always been corrected in order that the words should be written *exactly as I consider they should be,* i.e. *in accordance with my principles*; and two vowels, such as 'ei', for instance, even when the word ends with consonants, should be joined together. But the consonants must not be added until the *lengthening* is over; and this procedure should be adopted in the case of one or two consonants.

Please carry on with your copying. I don't need your copy of the score, as I have *my own,* from which Schlemmer and others, who are immensely superior to M[aschek], have copied out both scores and [parts] [1] — I am sending you the second movement too, so that the coda may be added as well. *The coda has not been altered*; it was only due to my forgetfulness that it was not added at once. Besides, in this matter I am of the same opinion as some great men such as Haydn, Mozart and Cherubini who never hesitated to delete, shorten or lengthen and so on — Sapienti pauca.[2]

I most earnestly request you not to inflict on me a third and fourth task. You will see from the enclosed parts that, once and for all, I will never abandon my method of composition in regard to *lengthened vowels*; nor can I ever deviate from it, since I am far too strongly convinced that I am right —

Your most devoted servant
BEETHOVEN

(1276) *To Anton Felix Schindler*

[Autograph in the Deutsche Staatsbibliothek, Berlin]

[VIENNA, *April,* 1824]

If there is anything to report, you may write, but do seal your letter. There are wafers and sealing wax on the table for this purpose —

---

[1] A word, probably 'parts', is missing here.
[2] Cf. Letter 953, p. 821, n. 1.

Write down where Duport is living and at what time he is usually at home, whether he can be seen alone, or whether other people will be present — and, if so, what people? — I am not feeling well. Portes vous bien — I am still considering whether I shall have a word with Duport myself or write to him, a thing which I should not do without being rather bitter —

Don't think of waiting for me to dine with you, but I hope you will enjoy your meal. I am not coming, for the bad food we had yesterday has made me sick.

A carafe of wine has been put there for you.[1]

(1277) *To Tobias Haslinger*

[*MS not traced*] [2]

DEAR TOBIAS, [VIENNA, *April*, 1824]

We need no more parts except for those of my best club members. But the plates should be corrected from the parts I am sending you. If not, another set of proofs will have to be dealt with. Piringer [3] has been instructed to select the eight best violinists, the two best viola-players, the two best cellists. . . . That is the number who are to augment the orchestra.

[1] The autograph bears no signature. The last sentence is added on the verso beside the address. On the verso Schindler has written the following comment: 'This letter was written at the time of the negotiations with the Theatrical Administrator Duport about the concerts to be held in 1824 and to include the ninth symphony and the "Missa Solemnis". The letter written at last to Duport evidently infuriated that fox. For he wrote to Beethoven asking him to write the letter over again and to address it to someone else, adding that he (Duport) would then turn it to Beethoven's advantage. Beethoven complied with Duport's request but included some extremely cutting expressions applicable to Duport as well, and then addressed the letter to me. I handed Duport this strange epistle in person. He expressed his satisfaction and even found the cuts and thrusts intended for himself highly entertaining. But the result? None whatever! This letter is in Vienna, but who owns it?'
[2] Taken from *FRBH* I, 198.
[3] See Letter 1370, p. 1194, n. 2.

(1278) *To Herr von Sartorius, Imperial and Royal Censor* [1]

[Autograph in the Deutsche Staatsbibliothek, Berlin]

SIR !   [VIENNA, *April*, 1824]

As I am told that the Imperial and Royal Censorship will raise objections to the performance of some church works at an evening concert in the Theater an der Wien, all I can do is to inform you that I have been invited to arrange this performance, that all the compositions required have already been copied, which has necessitated considerable expenditure, and that the time is too short to arrange forthwith for the production of other new works [2] —

In any case only three church works, which, moreover, are called hymns, are to be performed. [3] — I urgently request you, Sir, to interest yourself in this matter in view of the fact that, as it is, there are so many difficulties to cope with in any undertaking of this kind. Should permission for this performance not be granted, I assure you that it will not be possible to give a concert and that the entire cost of having the works copied will have been met to no purpose —

I trust that you still remember me —

I am, Sir, with kindest regards, your most devoted

BEETHOVEN

(1279) *To Ignaz Schuppanzigh*

[Autograph in the Deutsche Staatsbibliothek, Berlin]

[VIENNA, *April*, 1824]

Don't visit me any more.   I am not giving a concert.

B—VN

[1] This is the address on the verso of the letter in Beethoven's handwriting. Dr. Franz Sartori, born in 1782, was Head of the Central Book Censorship Office.

[2] Beethoven's letter of application was sent in connexion with his concert which was eventually held in the Kärntnertor Theatre on May 7th and repeated in the Grosser Redoutensaal on May 23rd.

[3] At the first concert three numbers of the 'Missa Solemnis' were sung, at the second concert only the Kyrie, the vocal trio Op. 116 and Rossini's aria 'Di tanti palpiti', transposed for a tenor voice.

HENRIETTE SONTAG (1806–1854) as Donna Anna in Mozart's 'Don Giovanni'
From a mezzotint by F. Girard after a portrait by P. Delaroche (*c.* 1828)
(*Macmillan & Co., Ltd., London*)

(1280) *To Anton Felix Schindler*

[*MS in the Deutsche Staatsbibliothek, Berlin*] [1]

[VIENNA, *April*, 1824]

I request you to come to me tomorrow morning *early*, if possible, or at about 12 o'clock, for I have an oxygen acid to tell you about. Duport said yesterday that he had written to me. But I have not received the letter. What is best of all, however, he declared that he was satisfied. At the same time he is still waiting for the chief dive which will extend far beyond the proscenium.

From bottom C$^\sharp$ to top F —

BEETHOVEN

(1281) *To Anton Felix Schindler*

[*Autograph in the Deutsche Staatsbibliothek, Berlin*]

[VIENNA, *April*, 1824]

After talks and discussions lasting for six weeks I now feel cooked, stewed and roasted. What on earth is to be the outcome of this much discussed concert, if the prices are not going to be raised? What will be left over for me after such heavy expenses, seeing that the copying alone is already costing so much? — —

(1282) *To Anton Felix Schindler*

[*Autograph in the Deutsche Staatsbibliothek, Berlin*]

[VIENNA, *April*, 1824]

I request you not to come again until I send you word to do so. There will be no concert.[2]

B———N

---

[1] Written by Karl. Beethoven has added the last sentence and his signature.
[2] This sentence is added at the foot of the page.

(1283) *To Count Moritz Lichnowsky* [1]

[Autograph in the Deutsche Staatsbibliothek, Berlin]

[VIENNA, *April*, 1824]

I despise what is false —
Don't visit me any more. There will be no concert —

B———VN

(1284) *To Ferdinand Rzehaczeck* [2]

[Autograph in the Deutsche Staatsbibliothek, Berlin] [3]

[VIENNA, *late April*, 1824]

MY DEAR HERR VON RZEHACZECK!

Schuppanzigh has assured me that you are going to be so kind as to lend me the necessary instruments for my concert. Encouraged by this assurance I ask you to let me have them; and I hope that I shall meet with no refusal if I earnestly beg you to send them —

Your most devoted servant

BEETHOVEN

(1285) *To a Copyist*

[Autograph in the Beethovenhaus, Bonn, H. C. Bodmer collection]

[VIENNA, *end of April*, 1824]

Copy everything exactly as I have indicated; and use some intelligence here and there. For, of course, if bars are copied on pages differently from those of the manuscript, the necessary connexions must be observed; and the smaller notes too ; for almost half of your notes are never exactly on or between the lines. If all the movements of the symphony are going to be copied as you have copied the first Allegro, the whole score will be useless [4] — I need the solo vocal parts

---

[1] This note is addressed on the verso in Beethoven's handwriting.
[2] Not identified. Evidently a dealer in musical instruments.
[3] Now on deposit in Tübingen University Library.
[4] Evidently a reference to the copying of the ninth symphony. Cf. Letter 1275, p. 1117, n. 3.

which have already been copied, and also the violin parts and so forth which have not yet been checked, so that instead of one mistake there may not be 24 — As for the title-pages and end-pages I need these more urgently, that is to say, today or tomorrow. It is doubtful whether the Leopoldstadt is nearer than the Ungargasse. But it is obvious that things are more difficult to arrange in the L[eopoldstadt] than at my home.[1]

BEETHOVEN

(1286) *To Karl Friedrich Hensler* [2]

[*Autograph not traced*] [3]

ESTEEMED FRIEND!   [VIENNA, *end of April*, 1824]

Please be so kind as to send me the parts of the overture which I composed for the opening of your theatre.[4] I intend to have this work performed at a concert which I am giving. As this time I have a larger orchestra and must therefore have these parts copied in duplicate, you will have them back neatly copied out instead of your present copies which were rather clumsily made at the time owing to the rapidity with which the work was done and to the great untidiness of the copyists. I am always hearing of your good health and prosperity, in which I take a great interest, even though I can see you only very seldom.

With kindest regards, your friend

BEETHOVEN

[1] Beethoven was then living in the Ungargasse.

[2] Karl Friedrich Hensler (1759–1825), born in Würtemberg, became a dramatic poet and a theatrical director. For a time he was in charge of the theatres at Baden and Pressburg. From 1803 to 1813 he was manager of the Leopoldstadt Theatre and in 1817 he was temporary manager of the Theater an der Wien. In 1821 he acquired the Josephstadt Theatre which he had rebuilt and reopened on October 3, 1822, with a performance of two festival plays by Karl Meisl (1775–1853), for the first of which Beethoven composed a new overture 'Die Weihe des Hauses', Op. 124.

[3] Taken from Frimmel, *Neue Beethoveniana* (Vienna, 1890), p. 138. The autograph was then in private ownership.

[4] Op. 124, which had been conducted by Franz Gläser (1798–1861), a composer of operettas, who conducted the music for the reopening of the Josephstadt Theatre on October 3, 1822. The performance was repeated on October 4th, 5th and 6th.

(1287) *To Anton Felix Schindler* [1]

[Autograph in the Deutsche Staatsbibliothek, Berlin]

[VIENNA, *early May*, 1824]

Now to the Birne [2] after 12 o'clock — with my bowels completely empty and feeling starved — then to the coffee house,
then back here again and then off to Penzing [3] immediately,
for, if not, I shall lose *those rooms.*

(1288) *To Anton Felix Schindler*

[Autograph in the Stadtbibliothek, Vienna]

[VIENNA, *shortly after May* 7, 1824]

I do not accuse you of having done anything wicked in
connexion with the concert.[4] But stupidity and arbitrary
behaviour have ruined many an undertaking. Moreover I
have on the whole a certain fear of you, a fear lest some day
through your action a great misfortune may befall me. Stopped-
up sluices often overflow quite suddenly; and that day in the
Prater I was convinced that in many ways you had hurt me
very deeply — In any case I would much rather try to repay
frequently with a small gift the services you render me, than
have you at my table. For I confess that your presence irritates
me in so many ways. If you see me looking not very cheerful,
you say 'Nasty day again, isn't it?' For owing to your vulgar
outlook how could you appreciate anything that is not vulgar?! In short, I love my freedom far too dearly. I will
certainly invite you occasionally. But it is impossible to
have you beside me permanently, because such an arrangement would upset my whole existence — Duport has agreed
to the concert taking place next Tuesday.[5] For he has
again refused to allow the singers to perform in the Land-

---

[1] This note is addressed on the verso in Beethoven's hand; 'For Herr v.
Schindler, Sc-dr-L'.   [2] Cf. Letter 1242, p. 1091, n. 2.
[3] Near Schönbrunn. It is now a suburb of Vienna.
[4] Beethoven's first concert held in the Kärntnertor Theatre on Friday,
May 7th.
[5] The second concert was given on Sunday, May 23rd, in the Grosser Redoutensaal.

ständischer Saal,¹ which I could have had tomorrow evening. Moreover he has again appealed to the police. So please take the notice and find out whether there is any objection to a second performance — I would never have accepted the kindnesses you have rendered me without returning them ; and I will never do so — As for friendship, well, in your case that is a difficult matter. In no circumstances would I care to entrust my welfare to you, because you never reflect but act quite arbitrarily. I have found you out once already in a way that *was unfavourable to you* ; and so have *other people too* — I must declare that the purity of my character does not permit me to reward your kindnesses to me with friendship alone, although, of course I am willing to serve you in any matter connected with your welfare —

B.

(1289) *To Henriette Sontag* ²

[*Autograph not traced*] ³

VIENNA, *May* 12, [1824]

MY LOVELY AND PRECIOUS SONTAG !

I have always been intending to call on you sometime and thank you for your fine contribution to my concert. Well, I hope to be able in a day or two to visit you and to take you and Unger ⁴ out to lunch in the Prater or the Augarten. For it is now the most beautiful season for that. I understand that the concert is to be repeated in about a week ⁵ . . . you will . . . support it, and for this I shall always be grateful

¹ The hall in the Landhaus, the assembly rooms of the Diet of Lower Austria or Landstand (county council). The building in the Herrengasse still exists. At that time this was one of the few halls in Vienna where public concerts could be held, as in the Court Theatres, the Redoutensäle and the hall of the Gesellschaft der Musikfreunde.

² Henriette Gertrude Walpurgis Sontag (1806–1854), a famous soprano, was born at Coblenz, trained at Prague and came to Vienna in 1822. She met Beethoven in September of that year (cf. Letter 1097, p. 967, n. 4). She took the soprano solo part in the ninth symphony and in portions of the 'Missa Solemnis', performed at Beethoven's concert on May 7, 1824. She married later Count Rossi.

³ Taken from *FRBH* II, 224-225. Frimmel copied in 1918 the autograph which has since disappeared. Apparently a corner of the letter was torn.

⁴ Karoline Unger (1803–1877), a contralto singer of outstanding merit, sang the solo parts at Beethoven's concerts in 1824.

⁵ The concert was repeated with a slightly different programme on May 23rd.

to you. My very best wishes to you until I have the pleasure of seeing you.

Your true friend and admirer

BEETHOVEN

(1290) *To Bernhard Schotts Söhne, Mainz*

[Autograph in the Stadtbibliothek, Mainz]

GENTLEMEN!   VIENNA, *May* 20, 1824

It was impossible to answer your letter sooner, for I have been far too busy. I have had the enclosed letter [1] written by a business man, since I am not very well up in matters of this kind. If these proposals suit you, do let me know very soon, for other publishers want to have my works, i.e. each publisher would like to have one of them. But I must confess that this correspondence with publishers at home and abroad has become very heavy and that I should like it to be curtailed. — In regard to a quartet I cannot yet give you a definite promise. But, provided that you reply as soon as possible, I can certainly let you have the two works which I have mentioned.— I have not yet received a copy of your 'Cäcilia', which must first pass our censorship ! ! ! [2]

All good wishes. The person you have recommended to me is to show me some of his compositions the day after to-morrow; and I will indicate to him in all sincerity the path which he can follow.[3] — Please let me have an answer soon about the two works, for out of consideration for other people too I must reach a decision. Since I cannot live here on my income alone, I must pay attention to such matters more than I should otherwise do —

Your most devoted

BEETHOVEN

[1] Letter 1291.

[2] There was then a severe censorship of books in Austria under Franz Sartori. Cf. Letter 1278.

[3] This was Christian Rummel (1787–1849), a pianist and violinist, who was Kapellmeister at Wiesbaden from 1815 to 1841. He composed various works for wind-instruments and also arranged Beethoven's ninth symphony and his late string quartet, Op. 127, for pianoforte duets. Schott had written to Beethoven on April 19th mentioning Rummel's forthcoming arrival in Vienna in the company of the Duke of Nassau.

(1291) *To Bernhard Schotts Söhne, Mainz*

[*MS in the Stadtbibliothek, Mainz*] [1]

SIR !   [VIENNA, *May* 20, 1824] [2]

In reply to your esteemed communication of April 27th I have the honour to inform you that I am more or less willing to let you have my grand Mass and the new symphony.[3] The price of the former is 1000 gulden A.C., and of the latter 600 gulden A.C., at the standard rate of 20 gulden. Payment can be arranged in the following way: you will send me three drafts on a reliable banking house in Vienna and this house will accept them; whereupon I shall send the works to you who will defray the cost of postage, or I shall deliver them to somebody here whom you will nominate for that purpose. The drafts can be made out for the following periods, e.g. one for 600 gulden for a month, one for 500 gulden for two months and another for 500 gulden for four months counting from the present date. If this arrangement suits you, I shall be glad if you will produce very handsome editions. Meanwhile I have the honour to remain with all due respect

your willing servant

LUDWIG VAN BEETHOVEN

(1292) *To Prince Nikolas Galitzin, St. Petersburg*

[*Autograph in the Musée Adam Mickiewicz, Paris*]

VIENNA, *May* 26, 1824

MY HONOURED AND BELOVED PRINCE !

So many of your amiable communications have remained unanswered ! — Ascribe this solely to the accumulation of my occupations, and certainly in no wise to any negligence on my part — Recently too I was invited to give a couple of concerts, at which I lost time and money; and to the disgrace of our present arrangements in Vienna I had to become the victim of an ex-dancer Duport, who is now the owner of

---

[1] Written in another hand and signed by Beethoven.
[2] Endorsed by the firm.
[3] The 'Missa Solemnis' and the ninth symphony.

the Kärntnertor Theatre ¹ — Spare me an enumeration of the
vulgar details which would enrage and disgust you also just
as much as a repetition and description of them would upset
me. But allow me to tell you that I have wasted a great deal
of time and lost a fair amount of money — I have been informed
here that at Petersburg the Mass too is going to be performed as
an oratorio on a grand scale.² Since people in Vienna are
doing nothing whatever *for me* but rather a great deal *against
me*, my present circumstances compel me to open a second
smaller subscription list for this work ; and, what is more,
exactly as Y[our] E[xcellency] once suggested in writing, to
offer an engraved copy of the score for five gold ducats.³
The score could be published and dispatched within six
months. But I cannot send you the invitation to subscribe
until I write by the next post — You will soon receive the
quartet promised to you so long ago, and perhaps the others
as well.⁴ If only the demand for great works and the encourage-
ment to compose them were not so insistent in all quarters,
the necessity of the time calls for it, *poverty* is thereby relieved
and forestalled in every way, what an incentive to promote
the composition of such works ! — Since I can well believe
that you yourself make use of works for this purpose, I will
send Y[our] E[xcellency] a new overture ⁵ and a trio, which
has been admirably performed by three Italian singers living
in Vienna.⁶ Should you like to have a new grand symphony

    ¹ Cf. Letter 429, p. 424, n. 3.
    ² The first performance of the complete work was given in St. Petersburg,
thanks largely to the enthusiastic efforts of Prince Galitzin. This event, which
took place on April 6, 1824, is described in his letter to Beethoven written two days
later. See *TDR* V, 559-560.
    ³ A second subscription list for the 'Missa Solemnis', this time for engraved
copies at a moderate price, had been suggested by Galitzin in a letter dated
August 3, 1823 (see *TDR* V, 554). It was opened in 1826 and produced 210
subscribers. For particulars of this venture see *KHV.* 363-365.
    ⁴ Despite Beethoven's promise of an early delivery, the first quartet, Op. 127,
did not reach Galitzin until April, 1825. The other two quartets, commissioned
by him and dedicated to him, Op. 132 and 130, were not completed until the
summer and autumn of that year.
    ⁵ Op. 124 was published by Schott in December, 1825, with a dedication to
Galitzin.
    ⁶ The trio is 'Tremate, empi, tremate' for soprano, tenor and bass voices with
orchestral accompaniment, Op. 116, which was performed by the Italian singers,
Dardanelli, Donzelli and Botticelli, at Beethoven's second concert on May 23rd
in the Grosser Redoutensaal. In the notices it was erroneously described as a new
composition, although the work had been performed ten years before, at a concert
on February 27, 1814. Cf. Letter 461, p. 444, n. 3.

with a Finale into which choruses and solo voices are introduced, I would have this copied too in score.¹   No special fee would be required, only a refund of the copying expenses — Perhaps it might be possible that by your efforts the Mass could be dedicated to His Majesty the Emperor of Russia ; ² and perhaps so munificent a monarch as the Emperor of Russia might even disburse a yearly pension for me, in return for which I would first send all my great works to His Majesty and would also carry out His Majesty's commissions with all speed ; and in this way material help could be given to necessitous humanity as well —

I am enclosing herewith an impression of the medal sent to me by His Majesty the King of France as a token of his satisfaction with my Mass.³   The medal weighs half a pound in gold ; and Italian verses about me ⁴ —

I remain, Your Excellency,

with all due affection and reverence,

BEETHOVEN

(1293) *To Tobias Haslinger, Vienna* ⁵

[*Autograph in the Deutsche Staatsbibliothek, Berlin*]

P. N. G. ! ⁶   BADEN, *May* 27, 1824

Please be so good as to do me the great kindness to take your hand ruler (not a Rostrum Victoriatum) ⁷ and rule for

¹ Op. 125.

² The 'Missa Solemnis' was dedicated to the Archduke Rudolph.

³ The gold medal valued at 21 louis d'or which Louis XVIII of France sent to Beethoven in February, 1824, in addition to the subscription he had already dispatched for the Mass, is now in the Gesellschaft der Musikfreunde, Vienna.

⁴ The lower edge of the third and last page of the autograph is badly torn under the seal. The fragments have been patched together to make what is left of the last sentence more or less intelligible. At Beethoven's second concert on May 23rd copies of a fulsomely laudatory poem of 20 stanzas entitled 'A Lodovico van Beethoven. Ode Alcaica' written by a young Italian admirer, Calisto Bassi, were distributed in the hall. Cf. *Mozarteums Mitteilungen*, Salzburg, November, 1920, p. 8.

⁵ The autograph, now on deposit in Tübingen University Library, bears no address. But in the letter Beethoven makes fun of Haslinger's pronunciation of the words 'Güte' and 'grosse'. Hence it was obviously intended for him.

⁶ I.e. Paternostergasse, where Steiner's publishing firm was housed.

⁷ The allusion is obscure. 'Rastrieren' means to rule lines.

me 202 music staves, approximately as I have shown here; [1] and please do so on as good paper as our running account permits. Send it all to *Karl* and by tomorrow evening, if possible, for I need it — After that you will perhaps be granted some *indulgence* —
Sent from Baden on May 27, 1824.

(1294) *To Tobias Haslinger*

[Autograph not traced] [2]

DEAR FRIEND !   [VIENNA, *May*, 1824]

You would indeed be doing me great wrong if you were to think that I sent you no tickets out of negligence.[3] I certainly thought of doing so, but like so many other things it was forgotten. I hope that some other opportunity will present itself for me to show you what I think of you — Let me add that I am in no way to blame for everything that Duport has done, and that it was he, *not I*, who made out that the trio was a new work [4] — You know very well how much I love the truth. But it is better to say nothing more about this. For not everyone knows the true state of affairs; and I, who am innocent, am being misjudged — I am not taking the slightest interest in any more offers from Duport, since in this kind of concert I have only lost time and money.
In the greatest haste, your friend
BEETHOVEN

[1] In the autograph the letter fills one page, and the remaining three pages are taken up with particulars of the music staves which Beethoven required.

[2] Taken from Nottebohm, *Ein Skizzenbuch von Beethoven* (Leipzig, 1865), p. 40. This letter is listed in a sale catalogue of G. Charavay, May, 1890, no. 11, with the following description : 'Lettre autographe signée à M. de Haslinger [fin mai 1824]. Curieuse lettre écrite au crayon et relative à un différend survenu entre Beethoven et M. Duport au sujet d'un terzetto, Op. 116, que ce dernier avait fait représenter dans un concert avec la mention "nouveau", alors que cette composition, remontant à 1801, avait déjà été interprétée en 1814. La lettre est en allemand mais la souscription dont voici le texte est en français ; Pour M. de Haslinger, général musicien et général lieutenant, etc.'

[3] Probably for Beethoven's second concert on May 23rd.

[4] Op. 116 had already been performed on February 27, 1814.

(1295) *To Adolf B. Bäuerle* [1]

[Autograph in a private collection]

Sir!   [VIENNA, *May*, 1824] [2]

In a few days I shall have the honour of discharging my
debt —

Please insert the announcement of my concert in your
esteemed paper.

Your most devoted servant

BEETHOVEN

(1296) *To Anton Felix Schindler*

[Autograph in the Deutsche Staatsbibliothek, Berlin]

[VIENNA, *May*, 1824]

Only what is absolutely necessary —

Perhaps you have everything already — Hence what you
have been promised will follow immediately this afternoon.

(1297) *To Carlo Soliva* [3]

[Autograph in the National Museum, Cracow]

[VIENNA], *June* 2, 1824

---

[1] Adolf B. Bäuerle (1786–1859) was chief editor of the *Wiener Allgemeine
Theaterzeitung.* See *FRBH* I, 28.

[2] The year 1824 is noted on the autograph in Schindler's hand.

[3] Cf. Letter 1049, p. 915, n. 1.

[4] The words of this two-part canon are taken from Metastasio's 'La Betulia
liberata' and are thus, as Dr. Hans Halm has pointed out, the only text set to
music by both Mozart and Beethoven. In *KHV.* it is listed as WoO 186.

Canone a due voci, scritto al 2do junio 1824 per il Signore
Soliva come sovvenire dal

suo amico

LUIGI VAN BEETHOVEN

(1298) *To Heinrich Albert Probst, Leipzig*

[*Autograph in the Beethovenhaus, Bonn*]

SIR!   VIENNA, *July* 3, [1824]

I have been so overwhelmed with work, to which concerts [1]
were added, that only now am I able to inform you that the
works you asked for have at last been completed and copied.
Hence they can now be delivered to Herr Loidl [2] at any
moment. So I request you to send a cheque for 100 Viennese
ducats to Herr Loidl and to inform me at the same time that
you have done so —

It is impossible for me to add anything more today.
So I am reserving that pleasure for another occasion.

With great respect,

your most devoted

BEETHOVEN

(1299) *To Bernhard Schotts Söhne, Mainz*

[*Autograph in the Stadtbibliothek, Mainz*]

VIENNA, *July* 3, [1824]

It has been impossible for me to reply sooner to your last
letter of May 27th; and even now I am writing only what is
absolutely necessary. I am willing to send you the quartet
too and, what is more, for a fee of 50 ducats, the fee I quoted
to you on a previous occasion. [3] You will most certainly
receive the quartet within six weeks; and I will let you know
when you can send me the fee —

In the case of the other two works the three time-limits
already fixed must stand. [4] But please be so good as to send
the drafts, as arranged, first of all *for the two works* to your
banker, from whom I will fetch them and to whom I will

[1] On May 7th and 23rd.   [2] Probst's agent in Vienna.   [3] Op. 127.
[4] Op. 123 and 125. Schott published Op. 125 in August, 1826.

deliver in exchange the aforesaid two works, namely, the grand Mass and the grand symphony. As for the quartet, the arrangement I have already mentioned above must stand — The cost of dispatching these works by mail coach is not so very great; and I will certainly inform the banker of the best and cheapest arrangements —

I would gladly send you much more news, but that is impossible, for I am overwhelmed with things which must be done. So I shall reserve this pleasure for another occasion — I now expect to receive your formal notice very soon [1] —

With cordial devotion, your friend

BEETHOVEN

(1300) *To Sigmund Anton Steiner*

[*Autograph in the Beethovenhaus, Bonn, H. C. Bodmer collection*]

DEAR STEINER! [VIENNA, *July* 13, 1824] [2]

To raise money is out of the question. Last year I had to pay interest on and provide security for the 600 gulden. This year I cannot manage to do that — So I request you to accept these two receipts and to give me a receipt for them. Then you will receive the remaining 150 gulden V.C. At any rate these receipts are certain; my other earnings are subject to chance. Now at last this *vexatious* debt will have been liquidated. What I earn by the products of my mind is spent largely on supporting my existence and that of my Karl. Surely *even my enemies* will allow me to value my life at least as highly as they value their own and therefore to keep body and soul together *by my pen* — Gloria in Excelsis —

You will notice that the receipt for 750 must now be written on a stamped sheet of paper. This is the only advantage which I have gained by the elevation of my most eminent patron [3] — You will soon receive too the 70 gulden V.C. for the engraving.

Your most devoted servant

BEETHOVEN

[1] I.e. the firm's acceptance or refusal.
[2] Date noted by recipient.
[3] The Archduke Rudolph, who had been created a Cardinal.

1133

(1301) *To [Antonio Diabelli]* [1]

[Autograph in the Deutsche Staatsbibliothek, Berlin]

SIR ! [VIENNA, *Summer*, 1824]

You will forgive me, I feel sure, for asking you for the score of my Mass, but I am greatly in need of it — And in any case I must remind you that no public use is to be made of it until I am in a position to tell you *how* or *when* this may be done. First of all, the Mass is to be performed under my direction and, what is more, with some new numbers composed for it; and these too I shall be delighted to let you have in due course — There are certain conventions which one cannot avoid observing, the more so as I have to depend on my foreign connexions, since Austria only provides me with vexations and gives me nothing to live on [2] —

I shall have the pleasure of calling on you soon on Karl's account —

I remain, Sir, with my kindest regards, yours sincerely

BEETHOVEN

(1302) *To Johann Baptist Bach, Vienna* [3]

[Autograph in the Koch collection]

MOST ESTEEMED FRIEND ! BADEN GUTENBRUNN, *August* 1, 1824

My heartfelt thanks to you for recommending this house, where I am really well looked after [4] — I must remind you of my will which concerns Karl. For I have an idea that some

---

[1] The autograph bears the name of this recipient in Schindler's hand.

[2] At the end of the letter after transcribing this sentence Schindler added the following remark; 'This letter with its strange contents appears to have been addressed to Diabelli who had asked for and obtained for a few days the Mass in D, which he wanted to look at. Why did Beethoven put it away? Perhaps he was ashamed of the closing sentence which he had so often written to other people and always without sufficient reason!' Evidently the letter, which is in Schindler's papers, was never sent off.

[3] The address on the verso of the autograph is in Beethoven's hand and underneath the address is this musical setting:

[4] Schloss Gutenbrunn.

day I shall have a stroke, like my very worthy grandfather whom I somewhat resemble.[1]

Karl is now and will ever be sole heir to all the property which I possess at the moment and which may be found after my death. But since one must bequeath something to relatives as well, even if one has nothing at all in common with them, my worthy *brother* [2] is to have my French pianoforte from *Paris* [3] — Karl could bring this will with him on Saturday, if that is not inconveniencing you in the slightest degree — As for Steiner he will be content if his debt is fully discharged at the end of this month and the end of September — For if something comes of the negotiations with Mainz, the delay will be just as long; and the first 600 gulden should be paid to two of the most noble persons who, when I was nearly destitute, lovingly assisted me with this sum, lending it to me without interest.[4]

My cordial wishes for your welfare. I embrace you.

With kindest regards, your friend

BEETHOVEN

(1303) *To the Archduke Rudolph, Vienna*

[Autograph in the Gesellschaft der Musikfreunde, Vienna]

YOUR IMPERIAL HIGHNESS!   BADEN, *August 23*, 1824

I am still living — but how? ! the life of a snail. For the very unfavourable weather is constantly putting me back; and it is impossible when one is taking these baths to command one's *physical strength* as usual — Well, only a few days ago I had a letter from Zürich from Nägeli, a not unimportant writer and author of books on music. He is publishing 200 poems, including some about music, and has pressed me to request Your Imperial Highness to be so gracious as to subscribe to this collection. The price is very low, i.e. 20 groschen or 1 gulden, 30 kreuzer. If Your Imperial Highness were to

[1] The Bonn Kapellmeister Ludwig van Beethoven (1712–1773).
[2] Beethoven spells this word 'Brudere', probably poking fun at some defect of speech of his brother's.
[3] The pianoforte which Sébastien Érard gave Beethoven in 1803. The latter gave it in 1825 or 1826 to his brother who later presented it to the Linz Museum.
[4] Franz and Antonia Brentano.

subscribe for six copies, *this would even create* a sensation, although I know that my most gracious lord pays no attention to anything of that kind. For the moment it will be sufficient if Your Imperial Highness will be so gracious as to let me know your intention. The money can be paid after the arrival of the copies, which will not be for a couple of months at the earliest. Well, Herr Nägeli has put forward his request; and now I myself must plead for him. Not everything can be measured with a yardstick. But Wieland says: 'How easily can a little book be valued at a few groschen'.[1] So if Your Imperial Highness by prefixing your sublime name as helping to promote this writer, will place a crown on his poems, they will certainly not be quite worthless — As I am convinced of Your Imperial Highness's interest in everything that is noble and beautiful, I am confident that my request on behalf of Nägeli will not be refused. I merely ask Your Imperial Highness to let me have your written permission to inform Nägeli that Your Imperial Highness will become a subscriber.

I assure Your Imperial Highness of my constant affection and most obedient loyalty.

BEETHOVEN

(1304) *To Antonio Diabelli, Vienna*

[Autograph not traced] [2]

DEAR DIABELLI!   BADEN, *August* 24, 1824

It was not possible for me to write to you sooner. You would like to have a grand sonata for four hands.[3] To write a work of that kind is, admittedly, not in my line, but I will gladly show you my willingness to meet your request and I agree to compose it. Perhaps I shall find time to let you have it sooner than you require it. As for the fee, I fear that it will startle you. But in view of the fact that I must postpone other works which bring me in more money and which I prefer to

---

[1] The context of this quotation has not been found. Possibly it is not a quotation from Wieland's writings.

[2] Taken from Frimmel, *Neue Beethoveniana*, 2nd edition (Vienna, 1890), pp. 143-144.

[3] In a letter dated August 7, 1824, Diabelli had asked Beethoven to write a grand pianoforte sonata for four hands in F major. And in his reply to the above letter from Beethoven Diabelli agreed to the fee of 80 gold ducats. This work was never completed. See Nottebohm II, 540-541 and *TDR* V, 141-142.

SIGMUND ANTON STEINER (1773–1838)
From a lithograph by J. E. Teltscher (1826)
(*Historisches Museum der Stadt Wien*)

compose, perhaps you will not think it excessive if I fix the fee at 80 gold ducats. You are aware that — just as a valiant knight lives by his sword — I must live by my pen. Moreover the concerts have meant a great loss to me [1] — Well, you can write to me about your commission. For if you agree to my terms, I must know this soon. As for the key in which you would like the work to be written, I will agree to your choice. All good wishes.

As always your friend and servant

BEETHOVEN

(1305) *To Heinrich Albert Probst, Leipzig*

[*Autograph not traced*] [2]

SIR !   BADEN, *August* 28, 1824

I have received your [communication] [3] of August 10th, both the letter and the cheque. Since the bad weather has prevented me from taking my baths, I must now stay on here for another week. But after that, when I return to town, I will dispatch all the works — As for Herr Peters, you will shortly receive an explanation about that transaction — You mention my new symphony. You will surely remember that I wrote to you about this symphony and also about my Mass. Well, the latter I have really disposed of already.[4] But in regard to the symphony, which is the grandest I have written so far and for which even foreign artists [5] have already made offers to me, it might be possible to arrange for you to have it. But, if so, you must make up your mind with all speed. For I have already received a portion of the fee for this symphony. At the same time I could give this man other works for the money he has paid me. Although God has specially blessed me, enabling me to help wherever I can, and although I am never at a loss for publishers, yet you are well aware

---

[1] The two concerts given on May 7th and 23rd.

[2] From a facsimile of the autograph in Tübingen University Library. A note entered on the document by its owner, Karl Viol, Amsterdam, states that the original letter was found among the papers of his grandfather, H. A. Probst, the music publisher.

[3] This word, which is missing in the autograph, has been supplied by the present editor.

[4] To Schott, who published it in 1827.

[5] No doubt Beethoven is referring to publishers.

that I like simple honesty in business dealings. Since I could give him other works, I should have no further trouble in that quarter and I could let you have the symphony. True, it could not be engraved, and published until July of next year; but if one takes into account the processes of engraving and correcting the proofs, the interval would not be excessively long — At the same time do not abuse my confidence; and do not make any use of this offer of mine in conversations with other people. My fee is 1000 gulden A.C. I would also undertake to be responsible for the two pianoforte arrangements. And the money need not be paid immediately; for instance, a draft payable in three months would do. Of course the best method would be to make it payable to a reliable firm such as Fries & Co. or Geymüller. I find money matters very tiresome. You will surely know the best and safest arrangement to make. But I do beg you to use all speed in replying to this letter, for, as I mentioned, I have already received a portion of the fee. Hence should I have to take some other decision about the symphony, it would be my duty to inform this really most honourable man immediately and to compensate him with other works.

With my best regards I remain, Sir, your most devoted

BEETHOVEN

Once more I beg you most insistently to observe the greatest secrecy about the symphony.

You are aware, I assume, that this symphony has grand choruses and solo parts in the Finale.[1]

(1306) *To Hans Georg Nägeli, Zürich*

[*Autograph in the Beethovenhaus, Bonn, H. C. Bodmer collection*]

MY VERY DEAR FRIEND!   BADEN, *September* 9, 1824 [2]

The Cardinal Archduke is in Vienna and I am here for the sake of my health. So only yesterday I received a letter

---

[1] These two sentences are written in Beethoven's hand on the verso.

[2] In the autograph an asterisk after Baden refers the recipient to a remark added at the foot of the first page of the letter; 'When addressing your letters to me, just say "in Vienna", as usual'.

from him agreeing to subscribe with pleasure to your poems, mainly on account of your services to the advancement of music, and informing me that he would take six copies. I will let you have his full title later on. Further, an unknown person, i.e. myself, is also subscribing. For, as you are doing me the honour of singing my praises, I dare not, of course, let my name appear. How gladly would I have subscribed for several copies, but my circumstances are too straitened. Since I am now the father of an adopted son, the child of my deceased brother, I must, on his account, think and act both *for the present and for the future* — I remember that you wrote to me also some time ago about subscriptions. I was then in very poor health, a condition which persisted for more than three years. But I am better now — Do send your collected lectures to the Archduke Rudolph direct and, if possible, dedicate them to him ; you will certainly receive some present, not a very handsome one, it is true, but better than nothing.[1] In your preface make a few flattering remarks about him ; for he understands music and is quite absorbed in it. He is so talented that I am sorry not to be able to take as much interest in him as I used to do.

I have sent out reminders here and there about sub-scribing to your poems and will inform you as soon as I receive any more orders —

I should like you to send me your lectures also and Sebastian Bach's five-part mass as well.[2] I will send you the amount for both from here at once. —

By the way, please do not think that my interest is involved in anything I ask. I am entirely without any petty vanity. Only in my divine art do I find the support which enables me to sacrifice the best part of my life to the heavenly Muses. Since I was a child my greatest happiness and pleasure have been to be able to do something for others. Hence you can understand how glad I am to help you in some way and to show you how highly I value your achievements. I

---

[1] Early in 1824 Nägeli had delivered in six German towns a series of lectures on music. These were published by Cotta in 1826 with a dedication to the Archduke Rudolph.

[2] Nägeli's edition of Bach's B minor mass, advertised in 1818 as about to be published, did not actually appear until 1833. Evidently Beethoven was under the impression that this edition had been published.

embrace you as one of Apollo's votaries and remain with all my heart

your
B<small>EETHOVEN</small>

Write to me soon about the Archduke and I will then prepare the ground. You need not approach him about permission for the dedication, because he will thus have a pleasant surprise, such as he ought to have ¹ —

(1307) *To Johann Andreas Streicher*

[*MS not traced*] ²

V<small>IENNA</small>, *September* 16, 1824

I gladly accede to your desire, my dear friend! to supply the various singing clubs with the vocal parts of my last grand Mass together with an organ or pianoforte arrangement, chiefly because clubs of this kind can be extraordinarily effective at public, and especially religious, celebrations, and because my chief aim when I was composing this grand Mass was to awaken and permanently instil religious feelings not only into the singers but also into the listeners.

Since, however, the copying and also the frequent checking of these parts are a very costly undertaking, I cannot ask less than 50 ducats paid in specie to cover my expenses. I am leaving it to you to make the necessary enquiries, so that I myself may devote my whole time to the task — My warmest greetings to you.

With kindest regards, your devoted

L<small>UDWIG VAN</small> B<small>EETHOVEN</small>

¹ This postscript is added at the top of the third page of the autograph.

² According to Nohl I, p. 271, note, this letter, presumably written in another hand and signed by Beethoven, was forwarded by Streicher to the committee of the Zürich Choral Society and found its way into the possession of Nägeli. Further, in the *Neue Zeitschrift für Musik* of October, 1870, Nohl published an almost identical letter addressed by Beethoven to Friedrich Wilhelm Riem (1779–1857), who had not only been organist of Bremen Cathedral since 1814 but in 1815 had also founded a choral society there. Both letters are to be found in Kal., nos. 1027 and 1028.

(1308) *To Bernhard Schotts Söhne, Mainz*

[*Autograph in the Stadtbibliothek, Mainz*]

GENTLEMEN!   BADEN, *September* 17, 1824

This is just to inform you that I never received your letter of August 19th. The reason for this I have so far failed to ascertain. In regard to your latest communication, which contained the notice to the House of Fries & Co., you may rest assured that as soon as I leave here and return to Vienna, which will be at the end of September at latest, I shall arrange to have both works copied as quickly as possible. And you will certainly receive the quartet by the middle of October.[1] As I have far too much work to cope with and as my health is poor, people must just be a little bit patient with me; I am staying at Baden on account of my health or, rather, on account of my ill health. But I am feeling better already. Apollo and the Muses are not yet going to let me be handed over to Death, for I still owe them so much; and before my departure for the Elysian fields I must leave behind me what the Eternal Spirit has infused into my soul and bids me complete. Why, I feel as if I had hardly composed more than a few notes. I wish you every success in your efforts on behalf of art. For, after all, only art and science give us intimations and hopes of a higher life — I will write again very soon and at greater length.

In haste, Sir, your most devoted

BEETHOVEN

(1309) *To Vincenz Hauschka, Vienna*

[*Autograph in the Deutsche Staatsbibliothek, Berlin*]

DEAR AND BELOVED FRIEND!   BADEN, *September* 23, 1824

I inform you that as soon as I come into town I will set Bernard's oratorio to music; and I also request you to let Herr von Bernard have the fee — All further matters, such as what we need and require, we shall discuss in town — While hailing you as the most powerful Intendant of all

[1] Op. 127.

singing and growling clubs, the Imperial and Royal Violoncello in Chief, the Imperial and Royal Inspector of all Imperial and Royal Hunts, and also the deacon of my most gracious lord, without domicile, without a roof over his head, and also without a prebend (as I am too), the most faithful servant of my most gracious lord, I wish you this and that, from which you may select the best — So that there may be no mistake, we inform you that we shall most certainly set to music Bernard's oratorio 'Der Sieg des Kreuzes' and shall finish it very soon, as attested by our signature and seal.

L. van Beethoven

Postscript No. 1 [1]
Don't let the game be devoured by cats, rats and mice. *Listen to me!* Secure for yourselves better means and more competition —

Yours in Christ and Apollo,

Beethoven

Postscript No. 2

As for the little flag
on the white tower,
well, we hope
that it will soon be flying again.

Postscript No. 3

Etc. etc. etc

(1310) *To Antonio Diabelli & Co.*

[Autograph not traced] [2]

Vienna, *September* 26, [1824]

Herr von Diabelli & Co.!

As I could not manage to fix a time, I have not been able to reply any sooner. But I now promise you that I shall be able to deliver the quintet in slightly more than six weeks [3] — I will bear in mind your wishes, without, however, restricting

---

[1] These three postscripts are added on the third page of the autograph.
[2] Taken from Frimmel, *Neue Beethoveniana*, 2nd edition (Vienna, 1890), pp. 142-143.
[3] For a discussion of this work which has been regarded as Beethoven's last musical thought, see *KHV*. 508-509, where it is listed as WoO 62. It was published in a pianoforte arrangement by Diabelli in 1838.

my freedom *as an artist* — I am satisfied with the fee of 100 gold ducats —

> With kindest regards, your most devoted
>
> BEETHOVEN

(1311) *To Johann Andreas Stumpff, Vienna* [1]

[*Autograph not traced*] [2]

MY GOOD FRIEND STUMPFF!   BADEN, *September* 29, 1824

If you don't see me, put it down to nothing else but my customary solitariness. Other contributory factors are my inclination to observe the '*Nulla dies sine linea*',[3] and the closing in of days which have now become shorter here in the mountains where one would like to strengthen one's constitution by walks and learn to meet *the coming worries* of town life by enjoying the open air and the lovely countryside. For this reason do not think less often of your friend

> BEETHOVEN

PS. I trust that your health is improving. I think that you ought to take more exercise in the form of walking.

[1] Johann Andreas Stumpff (1769–1846), a harp manufacturer born in Thuringia, settled in London in 1790. He visited Vienna in 1824 and obtained a letter of introduction from J. A. Streicher to Beethoven. For Stumpff's entertaining description of his meeting with the famous composer see *TDR* V, 122 ff. See also *FRBH* II, 271.

[2] Taken from *TDR* V, 132.

[3] No day without a line. A proverbial saying based on Pliny's anecdote of the painter Apelles in his *Natural History*, XXXV, 10, 36. The saying, which originally referred to drawing, is now commonly used of writing.

(1312) *To Tobias Haslinger, Vienna*

[*Autograph in the Koch collection*]

[BADEN, *end of September*, 1824]

Pay attention to what Karl says.

Regard yourself as a fire-brigade station, but instead of water think of money.

Send the receipt prestissimo to Prague.[2] If the money doesn't come soon, I shall have to act as an outpost.

All good wishes.

The title of Keeper of the Great Seal will shortly be conferred upon you.[3] —

B[EETHOVE]N

(1313) *To Antonio Diabelli, Vienna*

[*Autograph not traced*] [4]

DEAR DIABELLI!   [BADEN, *September*, 1824]

I do beg you to be patient for a few days longer. I myself will then call on you again and propose that you accept also the vocal numbers that go with the overture. On Monday

---

[1] This musical setting is listed in *KHV.* as WoO 205[g]. Beethoven calls Haslinger an 'alehouse musical Philistine of the Paternostergasse'.

[2] I.e. for Beethoven's half-yearly salary from the Kinsky family, payable on October 1st.

[3] Haslinger had been Steiner's partner since 1816. On the latter's resignation in July, 1826 Haslinger became sole manager of the firm.

[4] Taken from Kal., no. 1020.

I will bring you full particulars in writing of the *variations* which you will certainly *receive from me* as well as the sonatas for four hands and also the flute quintet.[1] For the overture alone I desire to be paid a fee of 50 ducats[2] — Meanwhile you may think over this proposal — Do not doubt that I shall carry out the promise I have given you —

Your friend
BEETHOVEN

(1314) *To Johann Andreas Stumpff, Vienna*

[*Autograph not traced*][3]

MY ESTEEMED FRIEND!   BADEN, *October 3, 1824*[4]

It would be very charming of you if you would call on the gentleman who lives in the Landstrasse[5] and kindly tell him exactly what ought to be done to my Broadwood instrument.

I send you my heartfelt greetings and I request you not to forget me in England and, moreover, to remember that tortoise of £600 from the King of England for my Schlacht-symphonie.

Your willing friend and so forth
LUD[WIG] VAN BEETHOVEN

(1315) *To Tobias Haslinger, Vienna*

[*Autograph in the Beethovenhaus, Bonn, H. C. Bodmer collection*]

DEAR TOBIAS!   BADEN, *in the evening of October 6*, [1824]

I do most earnestly implore you to have enquiries made immediately at the house in the Johannisgasse where we are

---

[1] Evidently Beethoven intended to compose a new set of variations. For particulars of the sonata (not sonatas) for four hands see Letter 1304. Possibly this mention of a flute quintet may be connected with the quintet referred to in Letter 1310.

[2] Op. 124 was published by Schott in December, 1825.

[3] Taken from *TDR* V, 133.

[4] See *TDR* V, 133, where it is stated that Stumpff seems to have added on this letter 'or September'.

[5] Matthäus Andreas Stein, the younger brother of Nanette Streicher. Cf. Letter 420. Stumpff added Stein's name on this letter.

going to live,¹ whether Karl slept there the night before last and last night, and, if he is at home, to have this note delivered to him at once ; and, if he is not at home, to leave it with the caretaker there to be delivered to him — He left here yesterday and has not yet returned with the housekeeper. I am alone with a person who can neither speak nor read nor write ; and at Baden I can scarcely find anything to eat unless I eat at home — On one occasion too I have had to go into Vienna to fetch Karl, for it is difficult to get him to leave a place once he has settled there. I beg you to let me know here at once what you have been able to find out. I would gladly have spent a few more days here in peace, but unfortunately I shall probably have to return to town for his sake. By the way, please do not let anybody know a word of this. God is my witness how much I have already had to suffer on Karl's account — If you can't get any information from the caretaker in the Johannisgasse, then send a messenger to the house in the Landstrasse where I used to live, to enquire from the caretaker where Frau von Niemetz ² lives, so that you may find out from her whether Karl has been to her house or is going there, in which case she should send him out here at once —

I will pay your servant for these services, of course, and also the postage for the letters — Further, please have the letter delivered to my brother Cain — and please let me know at once whether Karl is still missing or has been found.

In haste, your friend

BEETHOVEN

For God's sake reply at once.³

¹ At no. 969 in this street. The house no longer exists.
² The mother of a pupil at Blöchlinger's boarding school who was a friend of Karl's. Beethoven strongly disapproved of this friendship which is frequently referred to in the Conversation Books.
³ In the autograph this sentence is added at the left side of the fourth page.

(1316) *To Tobias Haslinger, Vienna* [1]

[*Autograph in the Beethovenhaus, Bonn, H. C. Bodmer collection*]

DEAR FELLOW! BADEN, *on the day after October* 6, 1824
Our Benjamin has now turned up here this morning, so
that I have had seventeen and a half cannon-shots fired off [2]
— Things that happened some time ago, for which he was not
to blame et sine mea culpa,[3] made me anxious. Heaven be
thanked that in spite of my agitatos everything proceeds
now and then quite well and as we should like. But it is not
surprising when one thinks of these wretched institutions that
one is anxious about a young fellow who is growing up. And
in addition there is that poisonous breath coming from
dragons! —
As for Herr Max Stumpf [4] I hear that he describes me as
his prodigal son — why prodigal?! This picture, etc. — You
will shortly receive your diploma as Keeper of the Great Seal.
But as for the doings in the little Paternostergasse club,[5]
we insist that these shall remain absolutely secret. For if not,
one would eventually apprehend that things might come to
such a pass that we might call to one another and look at one
another and say to one another: There goes one of the people
in the Paternostergasse. — As for my most gracious master,
surely he can but follow the example of Christ, i.e. suffer —
ed il maestro likewise, — but such thoughts are more or less
free. — Joy is followed by sorrow and sorrow by joy — I
hope for your sake that today you are either in joy or in

[1] The address on the verso in Beethoven's hand is:
An Seine Wohlgebohrn
Hr : Philip von Hasslinger
in Wien
abzugeben im
Paternostergässel
am Graben
in der paternostergässlerischen
Steinerschen Kunsthandlung
allda.
[2] Karl, who was born on September 4, 1806, was just eighteen.
[3] Without my fault.
[4] Probably J. A. Stumpff. Cf. Letter 1311, p. 1143, n. 1.
[5] The word used by Beethoven is 'Paternostergässlerei'.

sorrow — All good wishes, dear fellow — But surely you might come out here sometime after giving notice provisionally and getting full directions from Piringer.[1]

Your
BEETHOVEN

(1317) *To Carl Czerny, Vienna*

[*MS in the Gesellschaft der Musikfreunde, Vienna*] [2]

MY DEAR CZERNY! BADEN, *Friday, October* 8, 1824

My profound thanks for the affection you have shown me. Unfortunately my brother forgot to ask you for the pianoforte arrangements for four hands of the overture. In this case too I trust that you will comply with my request to undertake that as well.[3]

From the rapidity with which you have finished this pianoforte arrangement I see that it will give you no trouble to complete the other one also and as soon as possible.

Unfortunately thanks to my brother the matter has been considerably delayed; so that everything must now be done at breakneck speed.

I owe my brother a sum for which I have given him this overture and a few other works. That is the reason why he has been brought into this transaction. — By the way, please inform me what fee you ask for the two pianoforte arrangements. I shall be delighted to let you have it.

A long time ago I informed you of my desire to be able to serve you. So if such an occasion should arise, please do not forget me. For I am ever ready to show you my affection, gratitude and respect.

Ever your friend
BEETHOVEN

PS. Thinking that you may like to use the completed pianoforte arrangement [4] when arranging the one for four hands, I have enclosed it.

¹ See Letter 1370, p. 1194, n. 2.
² Written by Karl and signed by Beethoven.
³ Czerny's arrangement of Op. 124 for pianoforte solo was published by Schott in April, 1825, and his arrangement of the same work for four hands in July, 1825.
⁴ I.e. for pianoforte solo, which Czerny had evidently already finished.

(1318) *To Tobias Haslinger, Vienna*

[*MS in the Universitätsbibliothek, Leipzig, Kestner collection*] ¹

DEAR HASLINGER !   BADEN, *October* 10, 1824

His Excellency Count von Dietrichstein desires to have the score of the trio performed at my second concert in the Redoutensaal,² for a Court festival which is to take place during the next few days. I should be delighted to let him have it. But as my copy is in Vienna where it would have to be dug out of a pile of sheet music, I am sending the bearer of this note to you in the hope that you will not refuse to let him have it. Karl will probably go into Vienna during this week and will call on you as well.

Give it up, my good fellow, it must be done,³ my good fellow, out with it.

Your friend
BEETHOVEN

(1319) *To Hans Georg Nägeli, Zürich*

[*Autograph in the Beethovenhaus, Bonn, H. C. Bodmer collection*]

MY VERY DEAR FRIEND !   VIENNA, *November* 17, 1824

Overwhelmed with work and again indisposed, because, forgetting the late season, I did not protect myself sufficiently against the weather, I have not been able to write to you until now. In regard to your subscriptions, I have obtained only one more subscriber for two copies, Herr von Bihler, tutor to the family of His Imperial Highness the Archduke Karl — An attempt was made to secure the Archduke himself, but in vain — I have agitated in all directions, but unfortunately people here are flooded with too many appeals — This is all I can let you know in haste. I also tried to get Haslinger to do something for you — but in vain — Here in Austria we are really poor ; and owing to the hard times caused by the war,

¹ Written by Karl and signed by Beethoven, who also wrote the last sentence.
² Op. 116, performed at Beethoven's second concert on May 23rd. The parts of this work were published by Steiner in February, 1826.
³ Beethoven here uses a favourite phrase 'Es muss sein', which became the motto for the fourth movement of his string quartet, Op. 135, entitled 'Der schwer gefasste Entschluss' (the decision taken with difficulty).

which still persist, there is little left over for art and science — As for sending you the fees later on, I will undertake this faithfully. But please let me know exactly where the money should be sent? I embrace you in spirit. You may always rely on your true friend who has the highest regard for you.

BEETHOVEN

(1320) *To the Archduke Rudolph*

[Autograph in the Deutsche Staatsbibliothek, Berlin] ¹

YOUR IMPERIAL HIGHNESS!   VIENNA, *November* 18, 1824
   Being ill when I returned from Baden, I was prevented from visiting Your Imperial Highness as I desired; for I was forbidden to go out of doors. Yesterday was the first day on which I was allowed to take a walk in the fresh air — Your gracious communication was brought to me in bed just when I happened to be sweating. Since my indisposition was caused by a chill, it was impossible for me to get up. I know that Your Imperial Highness is fully convinced that I can never forget the regard I owe you — Tomorrow morning I shall have the pleasure of waiting upon you. And of course we have here at our disposal all the necessary means of fostering Your Imperial Highness's musical gifts, which cannot but contribute to the advancement of this art — my refuge — Thank God —
   Your Imperial Highness's faithful and most obedient servant

BEETHOVEN

(1321) *To Bernhard Schotts Söhne, Mainz*

[First portion of the autograph in the Stadtbibliothek, Mainz] ²

GENTLEMEN!   [VIENNA, *November*, 1824]
   I regret to inform you that it will be some time yet before the works can be sent off to you. There was not so very much more to check in the copies; but as I *did not spend the summer*

---

   ¹ Now on deposit in Tübingen University Library.
   ² The extant autograph is not complete. The remaining portion of the letter has been taken from Nohl II, no. 275, p. 253.

in Vienna, I must now give His Imperial Highness the Archduke Rudolph a lesson of two hours every day. This is so tiring that it almost unfits me for any other work. Yet I cannot live on my income; and my pen is my only other means of support. But in spite of this neither my health nor my valuable time are considered — I hope that this state of affairs will not last long. I shall then deal immediately with the small amount yet to be checked and let you have both works at once —

A few days ago I received an offer which concerns you. It runs as follows: 'that a foreign music firm would like to take from you immediately 50 copies of both works and, what is more, make a contract with you to prevent the engraved works from being pirated'. I categorically turned down the whole suggestion, for I have already had bitter experiences of such transactions (which are perhaps merely an attempt to spy on me). But if you want to do any business of this nature, I shall be delighted to make further enquiries —

Now about another offer. I have given to my brother, to whom I am indebted for many kindnesses, instead of a sum of money which I owe him, the following works, i.e. the grand overture which was performed here at my concert,[1] six bagatelles *or trifles for pianoforte solo,* several of which are rather more fully worked out and probably the best of this kind which I have composed [2] — three songs, two of which have choruses. One of them has a solo pianoforte accompaniment or an accompaniment for wind-instruments only, and the other can be accompanied by a full orchestra or by the pianoforte alone: the third song, fully ausgeführt, has only a pianoforte accompaniment ; [3] — of the overture there are already two pianoforte arrangements, one for two hands and one for four hands; and you will receive both [4] — My brother is asking a fee of 130 gold ducats for the whole lot. As he owns an estate and is wealthy, it is a matter of complete indifference to him what time-limit you desire to fix for the payment; and he leaves it to you to arrange this at your

[1] Op. 124 was performed at both concerts, on May 7th and 23rd.
[2] Op. 126 was published by Schott early in 1825.
[3] Op. 121b, 122 and 128. 'Ausgeführt' is an alternative expression for 'durch-komponiert'. Cf. Letter 81, p. 95, n. 7.
[4] Both arrangements had been undertaken by Carl Czerny. Cf. Letter 1317. They were published by Schott.

convenience.¹ But I do earnestly beg you to let me have a reply at once, for another publisher would like to have these works (this is not boasting, a thing I never indulge in).² Hence you must make haste. Thinking that perhaps you might like to possess a larger number of my works in sequence, I have asked my brother for a postponement of this transaction. Please do not be anxious about the quartet or about the other two works. Everything will be delivered during the first few days of next month. Surely you are now convinced of my sincerity. So do not suspect any cunning, double-dealing or the like. Who knows what a fine connexion may yet be established between us! —

Ever yours
BEETHOVEN

(1322) *To Bernhard Schotts Söhne, Mainz*

[Autograph in the Stadtbibliothek, Mainz]

GENTLEMEN! VIENNA, *December* 5, 1824

The works will certainly be delivered to Herren Fries & Co. this week. By the way, please do not worry if you hear perhaps of a pianoforte arrangement which I have been invited to make. This *has not been* and *will not be* undertaken. This arrangement was discussed, but only until I was quite sure *of you*. The fact is that *somebody in Vienna, whom you would hardly guess (but who is also a publisher)* advised me not to have any dealings with you. But as soon as one of my friends made enquiries at Herren Fries & Co. and found that everything was quite in order, our whole bargain was clinched; and I give you my word of honour that nothing else *has been done and that nothing else will be done.* — Somebody in Leipzig too invited me to let him have these works for performance on payment of a fee. But I sent him at once a flat refusal — I have made a point of telling you this, because I see that there are people here who are very anxious to disturb my cordial understanding with you, possibly on both sides —

I will send you contributions for your journal — But be

¹ The autograph breaks off here. The remaining portion of the letter has been taken from Nohl II, p. 253.
² Probably H. A. Probst of Leipzig.

JOHANN ANDREAS STREICHER (1761–1833)
From an oil portrait by Johann Ender (*c.* 1825)
(*Historisches Museum der Stadt Wien*)

sure not to make any mention in your journal of the lessons
I am giving to the Cardinal Archduke Rudolph.   Meanwhile
I have been making further attempts to shake off this yoke to
a certain extent.   Indeed one would like to exercise certain
authorities, *which one formerly never dreamt of doing*, but which
these modern times appear to demand.   Let us thank God for
the steam cannons which we are expecting and for the steam
shipping which we already possess.   Who knows what distant
swimmers there will be who will provide us with fresh air and
freedom ? ! — You are sure to have received the letters by now,
unless they have disappeared in the floods.   Well, you may
count most certainly on the definite dispatch of both works
before the end of the week — Heaven be with you. —
Your most devoted
BEETHOVEN

(1323) *To Johann van Beethoven, Gneixendorf*

[*Autograph in the possession of Curt Hirschfeld*]

DEAR BROTHER !   [VIENNA], *December* 10, 1824
I have heard that Mainz [1] is willing to give you 130 gold
ducats for your works.[2]   So if Herr Probst does not offer as
much, they should be given to Mainz, who will immediately
make out the bill of exchange for you as well as for me.   They
are really genuine people, and certainly not vulgar business
men.   Come soon, therefore, so that this transaction may be
turned to your advantage.
Your faithful brother
LUDWIG

[1] I.e. Bernhard Schotts Söhne.
[2] The compositions which Beethoven had given to his brother.   In a letter
to Schott, dated December 29, 1824, Johann confirmed this offer.   See Zekert,
p. 38.

(1324) *To Carl Friedrich Peters, Leipzig*

[Autograph not traced] [1]

SIR,   VIENNA, *December* 12, 1824

Streicher has written to you about something.[2] Precisely as I told him here that such a transaction would hardly be workable, so no doubt it has proved to be in reality. I am merely informing you that nothing is going to come of all these discussions about the Mass, for I have now promised it to a publisher for certain;[3] and thus it is obvious that Streicher's proposals cannot be carried out — You would have received by now a violin quartet, but I had to give it to the publisher who is getting the Mass, since he particularly asked me for it.[4] But you will certainly get another one soon or I shall make a proposal to you about a greater work, in which case the sum I have received will be deducted. Please be patient, however, a little longer, for I will certainly satisfy you — You have *wronged yourself and me*; and you are still wronging me, so I hear, by condemning, I understand, the *bad* works I am supposed to have sent you [5] — Did you yourself not ask for songs, marches and bagatelles? It occurred to you afterwards that this fee was excessive and that you could have some major work for it. That you have no judgment in an artistic sense is proved by the fact that several of these works have been, and are going to be, published, and that I have never yet had such an experience — I will discharge my debt as soon as possible; and meanwhile I remain your devoted

BEETHOVEN

I am *so situated* at the moment that I cannot do this more quickly.[6]

---

[1] Taken from Nohl II, no. 278. Nohl transcribed the autograph, then in private ownership.

[2] Evidently J. A. Streicher was corresponding with C. F. Peters about Beethoven, for on March 5, 1825 he wrote to Peters as follows : ' But what am I to say about Beethoven's behaviour to you and how can I endeavour to excuse it ? This I can only do by letting you have his own opinion of himself which he expressed in my home : "Everything I do apart from music is badly done and is stupid".'   [3] I.e. to Schott.   [4] Op. 127.

[5] Peters had rejected rather discourteously Beethoven's offer to them of Op. 119.

[6] A reference to the last sentence of the letter about discharging his debt.

(1325) *To Bernhard Schotts Söhne, Mainz*

[Autograph in the Stadtbibliothek, Mainz]

GENTLEMEN !   VIENNA, *December* 17, 1824

I inform you that I shall probably not be able to send off
the works for another week. The Archduke R[udolph] left
here only yesterday and before his departure I had to spend
a good deal of time with him. He is fond of me and marks me
out for his particular regard, but — one cannot live on that;
and although several people loudly remind him that 'whoever
owns a lamp fills it with oil',¹ he seems impervious to such
arguments. As the score must be correctly engraved, I must
still go through it several times myself; for I have no intelligent copyist. The copyist I had and upon whom I could
depend has been in his grave for eighteen months; ² but so
excellent a copyist must first be *trained* — And now I must
beg you not to have a bad opinion of me. I have *never* done
anything wicked; and to prove the truth of my statement,
when delivering the works I will send you the document
declaring your ownership — Don't you think it quite possible
that the Viennese publisher who tried to entice me away from
you, may have thought out such a method of making you
suspect me? At any rate he has already made some attempts
to prevent the establishment of other connexions, so that I
have very good reasons *for thinking so* — I received only yesterday a letter from my brother in which he *agrees* to let you have
the works I mentioned. I am glad that you are to have these
particular works. When my brother arrives, which will be
soon, I will let you have further details. The works have all
been copied and can be dispatched to you at once. And I
should like to have them engraved without delay — As for
the quartet, there is only a slight addition to be made to the
last movement; otherwise it is finished and can also be dispatched as soon as I have made this addition.³ — By the

¹ Beethoven's reference is to Plutarch, *Pericles*, 16, 7. Pericles found his former
teacher, the philosopher Anaxagoras, in distressed circumstances and starving
himself to death. The latter said : 'Pericles, people that want to use lamps pour
oil into them'.
² I.e. Schlemmer, who had died in July, 1823. Cf. Letter 973, p. 844, n. 4.
³ Op. 127.

way, my brother is quite satisfied with the method you suggested
of paying him the fee —

Ever your friend

BEETHOVEN

(1326) *To Tobias Haslinger*

[*Autograph in the Deutsche Staatsbibliothek, Berlin*]

MOST EXCELLENT FRIEND!   [VIENNA, 1824]
      Be so kind as to read this and to send it *immediately to
the authorities* —

Your servant et amicus

BEETHOVEN

Sent from home although I am not at home.

(1327) *To Anton Felix Schindler*

[*Autograph in the Deutsche Staatsbibliothek, Berlin*]

[VIENNA, 1824]

As I have something to discuss with you, please be kind
enough to come to dinner with me.   The table will be laid
for two o'clock.
      The fall of rain will not be great
      and who would mind a second baptism? [1]
When does the mail coach leave for Dresden?

(1328) *To Anton Felix Schindler*

[*Autograph in the Deutsche Staatsbibliothek, Berlin*]

[VIENNA, 1824]

You are to come to me so that you may be questioned.

Datum without giving [2]

---

[1] This verse is added at the side of the autograph which is not signed.
[2] Schindler has noted '1824' on this unsigned autograph.

(1329) *To Anton Felix Schindler*

[Autograph in the Deutsche Staatsbibliothek, Berlin]

MOST EXCELLENT FELLOW !   [VIENNA, 1824]
You may dine with me at noon. Bring your *provisions*
with you — Be ready — we are ready —

B———N

(1330) *To Anton Felix Schindler*

[Autograph in the Deutsche Staatsbibliothek, Berlin]

EXCELLENT FELLOW !   [VIENNA, 1824]
You will find us at the Goldene Birne [1] and from there we
are going to the coffee house —

(1331) *To Anton Felix Schindler*

[Autograph in the Deutsche Staatsbibliothek, Berlin]

[VIENNA, 1824]

I am now at the Birne.
Do join me here.

B.

(1332) *To Anton Felix Schindler*

[Autograph in the Deutsche Staatsbibliothek, Berlin]

[VIENNA, 1824]

To the Goldene Birne, my good fellow !

(1333) *To Anton Felix Schindler*

[Autograph in the Deutsche Staatsbibliothek, Berlin]

[VIENNA, 1824]

Most politely do I request you to let me have the testimonials, both originals and copies — As we have several

---

[1] Cf. Letter 1242, p. 1091, n. 2.

matters to discuss, least time would be lost if you would come to a meal with me some day. But it must be a definite arrangement. For to invite yourself and not to turn up is characteristic and so forth of the sort of person you are on the whole and certainly ought not to be ! —

DIXI [1]

(1334) *To Anton Felix Schindler*

[*Autograph in the Deutsche Staatsbibliothek, Berlin*]

[VIENNA, 1824]

Frau S[chnap]s is disbursing the necessary sum for our sustenance. So be here about two o'clock today for the midday meal —

I have some good news too, but we must keep this to ourselves, lest the brain-eater [2] should hear anything about it.

BEETHO [3]

(1335) *To Herr Rampel* [4]

[*Autograph in the Romain Rolland collection*]

MOST EXCELLENT LITTLE RAMPEL,   [VIENNA, 1824]

Do come tomorrow morning — But go to the devil with your 'gracious Sir'. *Only God can be called gracious* —

I have now engaged the maid, but do impress upon her to be honest and devoted to me and also to be methodical and punctual in the small services she will have to render.

Your devoted

BEETHOVEN

[1] After transcribing this unsigned autograph note which he dates 1824 (and which may have been written at Hetzendorf) Schindler adds the following comment : 'The orchestral rehearsals at the Josephstadt Theatre often lasted until 2 o'clock and sometimes even longer. From there to Hetzendorf it is a quick walk of over an hour. If one bears in mind the summer heat at this time of the day and also the fact that frequently I had to take my place in the theatre again at 7 o'clock, it was quite impossible always to keep my promise. But Beethoven rarely considered such impediments or in general any official engagements of other people. Hence the countless wrangles — and even quarrels.'

[2] Beethoven's brother Johann.

[3] The signature on the autograph is not completed.

[4] This is the only known autograph letter from Beethoven to Rampel, who after Schlemmer's death copied some portions of the ninth symphony and the late quartets. See *FRBH* II, 49.

(1336) *To Anton Felix Schindler*

[Autograph in the Deutsche Staatsbibliothek, Berlin]

[VIENNA, 1824]

I am dining at the Birne and from there I shall go to the coffee house —

I will order for you at the *Birne* —

But if you don't find me there, come on to the coffee house; for I am not sure whether you are coming —

(1337) *To Tobias Haslinger* [1]

[Autograph in the Stadtbibliothek, Vienna]

[VIENNA, 1824]

CONCERT NOTICE —

(What news have you of the Tyrolese I asked for?)

(1338) *To Peter Gläser*

[Autograph not traced] [2]

[VIENNA, 1824]

By Wednesday of next week I should like to have everything you have finished of the score of the Finale . . . . and particularly the quartet of the Finale which I urgently require. . . . It is now necessary to make haste with all speed, since I have not received anything for the last two days [3] —

---

[1] The address on the verso in Beethoven's hand is:
An des Hr:
Adjutantle
Wohlgebohrn
Pleni Gratia
bei d. G———T.

[2] Taken from sale catalogue of J. A. Stargardt, April, 1927, no. 264, lot 462.

[3] A reference, no doubt, to the copying of the ninth symphony, Op. 125.

(1339) *To the Archduke Rudolph*

[*Autograph in the Stadtbibliothek, Vienna*]

YOUR IMPERIAL HIGHNESS!   [VIENNA, 1824]
    Schlemmer's widow is bringing you the copy of the trifles composed by me.¹ The cost is 3 gulden, 30 kreuzer V.C. — It would cheer the poor woman very much if Y.I.H. would see that something is added to this sum, for she really needs help —
                        Y. I. Highness's
                            most obedient servant
                                    BEETHOVEN

(1340) *To Tobias Haslinger*

[*Autograph in the Deutsche Staatsbibliothek, Berlin*]

                                    [VIENNA, 1824]
    Be so kind as to send me my shoes together with the sword — You may have Eglantine for six days, but you must make out a receipt for it ² — Take care of yourself.
                                    Yours
                                    BEETHOVEN

(1341) *To Anton Felix Schindler*

[*Autograph in the Deutsche Staatsbibliothek, Berlin*]

                                    [VIENNA, 1824]
    I shall expect you at the Mariahilf coffee h[ouse] at about three o'clock —
                                    Your friend
                                    BEETVN

¹ I.e. Bagatelles. Probably a copy of Op. 119, published late in 1823 by Moritz Schlesinger, Paris.

² According to Unger, no. 83, n., this was the pianoforte arrangement of C. M. von Weber's opera 'Euryanthe', which was produced in Vienna on October 25, 1823. Eglantine is the name of a sinister character in this opera.

(1342) *To Tobias Haslinger*

[*Autograph in the Library of Congress*]

MOST EXCELLENT TOBIAS   [VIENNA, 1824]
in secula seculorum ! [1]

Please send to Tendler & Manstein the letter addressed to Bäuerle, as I don't know where he lives —

Please send also the letter addressed to Stainer von Felsburg to the bank for me. One can't use house wenches [2] for errands of that kind.

We shall meet this afternoon.

Your amicus
BEETHOVEN

Kindly let me know in writing
that you have received this note.

[1] To all eternity.
[2] The word used in the original is 'Stubenmenscher', 'das Mensch' meaning 'hussy, wench' or the like.

1825

(1343) To Karl Wilhelm Henning, Berlin [1]

[*MS in the Deutsche Staatsbibliothek, Berlin*] [2]

VIENNA, *January* 1, 1825

I was greatly surprised at receiving today the information that a work of mine, entitled 'Festouvertüre', engraved by Herr Trautwein, is being circulated in a pianoforte arrangement for four hands made by you from the original score which has not yet been printed.[3] For Herr Bethmann and I agreed that this overture was certainly not to be the property of the Königstadt Theatre in Berlin. Only the whole score of the 'Ruinen von Athen' with all the numbers, but not the overture, has been handed over to that theatre as its exclusive property. And some time ago I gave that very overture to an honourable publisher. It is to appear in a fortnight or a month at latest.[4] You see that in this case I am just about to suffer an infringement of my honour. For after signing a written agreement with Herr Bethmann I should never have dreamt of such a thing! Since some damage has already been done, please make every effort to prevent the circulation of that pianoforte arrangement for four hands until I write to you. I give you my word of honour that I will do this; and I shall not be long about it in case my statement has to be used. I will endeavour to make this unpleasant incident as harmless as possible, both for *you* and for *me*. You know that I have to live entirely on the products of my mind.

[1] Karl Wilhelm Henning (1784–1867), Musical Director of the Königstadt Theatre in Berlin, had opened the theatre on August 4, 1824, with a performance of Beethoven's overture 'Die Weihe des Hauses', Op. 124. During the visit of Henning and Heinrich Bethmann, the Theatrical Director, to Vienna in October, 1823, Beethoven sold to them for 56 louis d'or the score of 'Die Ruinen von Athen', Op. 114. See *KHV*. 370 and *FRBH* I, 207.

[2] MS not available. Taken from Kal., no. 1081. Written in another hand and signed by Beethoven.

[3] The pianoforte arrangement of Op. 124 had been published in December, 1824, by Traugott Trautwein, a Berlin music publisher, who had founded his firm in 1820.

[4] The score of Op. 124 was published in December, 1825 by Schott, who also issued, in April and July, 1825 respectively, arrangements for pianoforte solo and pianoforte duet, both made by Czerny.

Just imagine how detrimental such an incident can be to me. Convinced that you will show me affection rather than a callous behaviour, I remain, with kindest regards, your most devoted servant

LUDWIG VAN BEETHOVEN [1]

(1344) *To Charles Neate, London*

[*MS in the Beethovenhaus, Bonn, H. C. Bodmer collection*] [2]

MONSIEUR !   VIENNA, *January* 15, 1825

Ce fut avec le plus grand plaisir que je reçus votre lettre du — [3] par laquelle vous avez eu la bonté de m'avertir que la Société Philharmonique distinguée d'artistes m'invite à venir à Londres.

Je suis bien content des conditions que me fait la Société, seulement je désire de lui proposer de m'envoyer, outre les 300 guinées qu'elle me promet, encore 100 guinées pour faire les dépenses du voyage ; car il faudra acheter une voiture ; aussi dois-je être accompagné de quelqu'un. Vous voyez bien que cela est nécessaire ; d'ailleurs je vous prie de m'indiquer l'auberge où je pourrai descendre à Londres. Je prendrai un nouveau Quatuor avec moi.

Quant au bruit dont vous m'écrivez, qu'il existe un exemplaire de la 9ieme Symphonie à Paris, il n'est point fondé. Il est vrai que cette Symphonie sera publiée en Allemagne, mais point avant que l'an soit écoulé, pendant lequel la Société en jouira. Sur ce point il faut encore vous avertir de ne faire que de petites preuves de cette composition, en Quatuor par exemple ; car c'est la seule manière d'étudier bien une telle œuvre ; les chœurs avant tout doivent être exercés. Il y a encore quelques erreurs dont je vous enverrai le catalogue par la poste prochaine. —

Il me semble avoir été oublié dans la 2de partie de la

[1] Henning replied in a letter dated January 13, 1825, in which he maintained that the overture, Op. 124, was included in the contract for the purchase of Op. 114 and that he was fully entitled to have the pianoforte arrangement made of the former work and to publish it. See Appendix H (15).

[2] Written by Karl and signed by Beethoven.

[3] In the original letter this space is not filled in. But it should be December 20, 1824, the date of Neate's letter to Beethoven, informing him that the new symphony had arrived in London and would have its first rehearsal on January 17th. See *KHV*. 376. See also Letter 1348.

Symphonie, qu'à la répétition du minore après le Presto il faut commencer de nouveau du signe [1] et continuer sans répétition jusqu'à la ferma ; alors on prend aussitot la Code.

Je vous prie de me répondre au plus vite possible, car on demande de moi une grande composition nouvelle, que je ne commencerai cependant pas, sans avoir votre réponse. — Il faut que j'ecrive toujours, pas pour me faire des richesses, — seulement pour pourvoir à mes besoins.

Or je dois avoir de la certitude sur ce point. — Je serai bien charmé de vous voir, et de connaître la noble nation Anglaise.

Je suis avec la plus haute considération Monsieur votre sincère ami

LOUIS VAN BEETHOVEN

(1345) *To Bernhard Schotts Söhne, Mainz*

[Autograph in the Stadtbibliothek, Mainz]

GENTLEMEN,   VIENNA, *January* 22, 1825
Both works were delivered to Fries on January 16th. In my next letter I shall let you have any supplementary remarks. Both works are bound ; and Fries, whose people appear to take a real interest in them, will certainly see that they are safely dispatched and delivered. I don't think it possible that the Mass has been engraved. Such a rumour (and I certainly hope that it is only a rumour) may have been spread by a certain Stockhausen [2] who is founding a singing club. In a letter to me he said many flattering things about the Mass, adding that the Court placed *their confidence* in him and had allowed him to make a copy of it for his club (but that I need not think that this privilege would be abused).[3] The intermediary was probably the Duc de Blacas [4] who frequently went to his musical parties, as he wrote, parceque les grands sont le plus faibles — I did not feel easy about this at the time. But I hope that there is nothing in the rumour. Moreover Schlesinger is not to be trusted, for he filches wherever he can.[5]

[1] In the original letter there is a mark here in the form of an asterisk.
[2] Cf. Letter 1207, p. 1060, n. 2.   [3] This letter has not been traced.
[4] Pierre, Duc de Blacas (1771–1839), was minister under Louis XVIII and Charles X. He signed the letter to Beethoven, enclosing Louis XVIII's gold medal.
[5] Moritz Schlesinger, the music publisher in Paris.

Both of them, père et fils, have bombarded me to give them the Mass and other works. I did not condescend to reply to either of them, because after sampling them I had long ago thrown them over — It would afford me much pleasure if you yourself would send me something to sign, some document in which I would assure you that you are the sole owner of these editions, which are the only correct ones. I may as well draft the documents now —

I, the undersigned, declare by virtue of my signature that Bernhard Schotts Söhne at Mainz are the sole rightful publishers of my grand solemn Mass and also of my grand symphony in D minor. Further, I accept only these editions as the *rightful and correct ones.*

Vienna, January   , 1825 [1]

LUDWIG VAN BEETHOVEN

Furthermore, Schlesinger wanted to publish *all* my quartets and take on each time a new composition of mine at certain stated periods ; and he was prepared to pay what I wanted. But as such an arrangement might be detrimental to my plan for an edition of my collected works to be prepared by myself, this application too I did not answer. And in view of what I have just stated you might reflect upon my suggestion that it would be better to have the edition done now *by me* rather than after my death. I have already had offers for the edition, and plans for it are being sent to me too. But so far all the arrangements proposed have not seemed to me suitable for such a big undertaking. I am inclined to have more confidence in you ; and on the whole I should much prefer to be paid for it with a lump sum. I would indicate the usual minor unimportant alterations ; and for each type of work, such as, for example, sonatas, variations and so forth, I would compose a new work of the same type — Here are a couple of canons for your journal [2] — and three more are to follow [3] — as a

[1] In the autograph the day is omitted.

[2] Beethoven's canons, 'Hoffmann, sei ja kein Hofmann' on the Berlin writer and musician E. T. A. Hoffmann, and 'Schwenke dich ohne Schwänke' on the Hamburg musician Carl Schwenke (1797–*c.* 1870), were published in Schott's music review *Caecilia* for April, 1825, I, 206. In *KHV.* 684 and 690 these canons are listed as WoO 180 and WoO 187.

[3] There is no evidence that Beethoven sent three more canons to Schott. But he may have intended to send the three which are listed in *KHV.* 685 as WoO 181.

1168

NIKOLAUS ZMESKALL VON DOMANOVECZ (1759–1833)
From a silhouette in an album of the Littrow-Bischoff family
(*Historisches Museum der Stadt Wien*)

ANTON FELIX SCHINDLER (1796–1864)
From an undated photograph
(*Formerly in the possession of Isabella Egloff, Mannheim*)

supplement to a romantic biography of Tobias Haslinger of Vienna, consisting of three parts. Part 1 — Tobias appears as the apprentice of the famous Kapellmeister Fux, who is firm in his saddle — and he is holding the ladder to the latter's Gradus ad Parnassum.[1] Then, as he feels inclined to indulge in practical jokes, Tobias by rattling and shaking the ladder makes many a person who has already climbed rather high up, suddenly break his neck and so forth. He then says good-bye to this earth of ours but again comes to light in Albrechtsberger's time.[2] Part 2. Fux's Nota cambiata [3] which has now appeared is soon discussed with A[lbrechtsberger], the appoggiaturas are meticulously analysed, the art of creating musical skeletons is dealt with exhaustively and so forth. Tobias then envelops himself like a caterpillar, undergoes another evolution and reappears in this world for the third time. Part 3. The scarcely grown wings now enable him to fly to the little Paternostergasse and he becomes the Kapellmeister of the little Paternostergasse. Having passed through the school of appoggiaturas all that he retains is the *bills of exchange*.[4] Thus he firmly establishes the friend of his youth and finally becomes a member of several home-made *learned* [5] societies and so forth. If you ask him, no doubt he will permit you to publish this biography. —

In great haste and with all speed, yours,

BEETHOVEN

[1] Johann Joseph Fux (1660–1741) was an eminent Viennese composer and Kapellmeister, whose famous theoretical work on music *Gradus ad Parnassum* appeared in Latin in 1725 and was translated into German, Italian, French and English. It is still used and consulted today.

[2] Johann Georg Albrechtsberger (1736–1809) was a Viennese composer, an eminent teacher of musical theory and a famous contrapuntist whose instruction was eagerly sought. Beethoven took lessons from him in 1794. Albrechtsberger was appointed Court organist in 1772 and Kapellmeister to St. Stephen's Cathedral in 1792.

[3] I.e. changed note. This is an idiomatic melodic figure common in contrapuntal writing from the early days of polyphony and used particularly by 16th century polyphonists.

[4] Beethoven is playing on the word 'Wechsel' which appears in 'Wechselnote' (appoggiatura) and 'Wechsel' (bill of exchange).

[5] In the autograph this word appears as 'geleert' (emptied) instead of 'gelehrt' (learned), a favourite pun of Beethoven's.

(1346) *To Bernhard Schotts Söhne, Mainz*

[Autograph in the Stadtbibliothek, Mainz]

GENTLEMEN!   VIENNA, *January* 26, 1825

Just a few quick reminders — The Mass will be engraved
in the best and clearest way if an interval is left between the
wind-instruments and the brass and the drums as well; then
there should follow the two violin and viola parts and the four
solo voice parts, the four choral parts, cello part, double bass
part and, last of all, the organ part. That is how the score was
divided up by my deceased copyist.[1] In the case of the organ
part a different procedure might even be adopted, such as,
for instance, one which you may prefer to choose. The old
score was too messy to send to you. The new one has been
checked most carefully, no small task, in truth, for a copyist
who hardly understands what he is copying —

It would have been too long for you to wait to have the
whole symphony copied; and, to tell the truth, I have not
yet been able to find a copyist who has some understanding
of what he is copying. Hence I have had fresh leaves inserted
for those portions which were copied most carelessly — Sometimes the dots after notes are to be found not beside the note
but somewhere else, i.e. instead of ≝·≝ you will perhaps
have ≝·≝ and so forth. Kindly instruct the engraver
to pay attention to this and to place dots of this kind everywhere beside the notes and between the same lines —

Where this passage for the two violins occurs in the first
Allegro, in the first part, i.e.

non legato should be indicated above it — and similarly in the
second part — Furthermore, you must look up and see whether

---

[1] Schlemmer, who had died in July, 1823.

in the Dona Nobis in the Allegro Assai in this passage for the first violin the ♭ in front of D has not been forgotten, i.e.

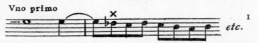

Furthermore, perhaps the tempo of the Benedictus, which should be Andante molto cantabile e non troppo mosso, has also not been indicated — In the case of the canons which I sent you and which I copied myself, and when I do so I invariably make mistakes, the third and fourth bars should run *as follows* :

Be sure to write at once *about Paris. I too could send you immediately from here a statement written in French. But whatever you decide to do in this matter I will most assuredly endorse.* — My brother has not yet received the draft. Make haste with this transaction, for he is rather thirsty for money, the more so as the draft for it was made out for Vienna and as I had a great deal of trouble with the other publisher ; besides I am not boasting when I tell you that another firm in a distant country has asked for these works — The quartet will be delivered in eight days at latest ; but indeed I am very hard pressed and busy composing another work. — With the warmest greetings and regards, your friend   BEETHOVEN [2]

In the Dona Nobis instead of the quaver appoggiaturas 𝄽𝅘𝅥𝅯 there should always be only semiquaver appoggiaturas, i.e. 𝄽𝅘𝅥𝅯 and, what is more, in the bars indicated here.

---

[1] In the autograph this passage is added at the foot of the page.

[2] The letter ends here. Beethoven's corrections and remarks are on a separate sheet of paper, dated in his handwriting 'Vienna, January 26th'.

Dona nobis { Vno 1mo   Allegretto Vivace
            { — 2do   ♪♪♪   Bars 5 6 7 8 9 10 11
            { Viola

In the parts where in these bars quaver appoggiaturas appear, all these should be altered to semiquaver appoggiaturas. NB. In the Violino 2do part these quaver appoggiaturas do not appear until the sixth bar.

After the Allegro assai, Tempo primo ⁶₈ in the Vno 2do part, bars 7 8 9 10 11 12 13 14 15 16 17 18 19 20 21 22, and in the viola part from bars 10 to 22 there should be similarly semiquaver ♪ appoggiaturas instead of quaver ♪ appoggiaturas. Likewise after the Presto, Tempo primo ⁶₈ in the Oboe 1ma bars 9, 10, 11 and Flauto 1mo bars 10 and 11 there should be semiquaver ♪ appoggiaturas instead of quaver ♪ appoggiaturas — Similarly in the same movement in the Vno 1mo and Viola parts, bars 14 15 16 17 18 19 20 there should be semiquaver ♪ appoggiaturas instead of quaver ♪ appoggiaturas — Now you can see what sort of copyists I have at the moment. The fellow is a typical Bohemian, a pandour who can't grasp what you tell him.[1] First of all he put crotchets in the appoggiaturas, then finally quavers ; and as I didn't go on checking his work I happened to notice the above when I was hurriedly packing the proofs —

(1347) *To Heinrich Albert Probst, Leipzig*

[*Autograph in the possession of Alfred Cortot*]

MY ESTEEMED HERR PROBST !   VIENNA, *January* 26, 1825

Indeed I am very sorry that this first arrangement has somehow or other come to grief. Now listen to the candid words of an equally candid man — All these works belonged to my brother who, because my circumstances were, to put it mildly, not very brilliant, advanced me a sum on their security and thus really became their owner — The difficulties you yourself created, the remarks which Herr Loidl[2] made here

[1] Ferdinand Wolanek, who copied the 'Dona nobis pacem' of Beethoven's 'Missa Solemnis'. See *KHV.* 365. See also Letter 1463, p. 1269, n. 3.
[2] Cf. Letter 1298, p. 1132, n. 2.

against him or, rather, to him *against me*, declaring that you wanted to have all the works tried out before you would pay for them, enraged my brother, who is so blindly and enthusiastically prejudiced in my favour, to such an extent that he positively refused to hand over the works, no matter what arguments I advanced; even my appeal 'Nunc dimitte illis, quia nesciunt quid faciant' [1] was of no avail. Really I did my utmost to persuade him. But as he was living on his country estate at a considerable distance from me, I trusted that in the end I should be able to arrange everything with him after his and my return to town. On his arrival in Vienna, however, he told me that he had now received much more advantageous offers from other publishers; and as he himself is a business man, he persisted in maintaining that these works of mine were priced too low; and to that argument it was difficult to find a reply. Hence he declared that you would *never grant him the amount which he could get elsewhere.* Whereupon he promised me to write to *you* himself. I then told him that I really didn't know how to settle this matter as I wished. So I asked him to let you know in writing that I would very soon offer you other works instead, works which you might perhaps prefer to have — That is a true account of this whole affair — At the moment I am composing new violin quartets. I will write to you as soon as I have finished two, or even one.[2] *I usually get* 50 gold ducats, and sometimes even more, for a quartet; and the cost of copying, which, however, is not very heavy, is also refunded to me — Well, if you would like to have two quartets, let me know; and as soon as they are finished I will write to you and, when I receive the fee, etc., the works will be delivered. — I quite thought that a letter from my brother would have enlightened you about everything; and he most certainly assured me that he had given Herr Loidl a full statement of his views. I was so overwhelmed with work that I could hardly find a moment to discuss the matter with them any further [3] — I am very

---

[1] 'Now forgive them, for they know not what they do', a variant of Luke 23, v. 34.
[2] Beethoven did not finish the first of his late quartets until February, 1825. He had been working at it since the spring of 1822. This quartet in E♭, dedicated to Prince Galitzin, was published as Op. 127 by Schott in 1826, the parts in March and the score in June.   [3] This sentence is added at the foot of the page.

sorry that you yourself are rather to blame that my good intentions in regard to you have come to nothing. Nevertheless I am grateful to you for the friendly disposition you have shown me. If I visit Leipzig, I will certainly call on you; and you will see in me a man who has been trained and disciplined in the school of misfortune —

With kindest regards, your most devoted

BEETHOVEN

(1348) *To Charles Neate, London*

[*MS in the Beethovenhaus, Bonn, H. C. Bodmer collection*] [1]

MON TRÈS CHER AMI!   [VIENNA], *January* 27, 1825

Je vous avertis, par la présente lettre, des fautes qui, je crois, se trouveront encore dans la Partition de la Symphonie en D mineur.

J'espère que vous aurez déjà ma réponse faite a votre lettre du 20 passé; [2] je suis prêt d'entrer dans toutes les conditions que me fait la Société; seulement je prétends encore 100 Guinées pour mon voyage à Londres; il serait superflu de dire, que sans cette Somme je ne pourrais guère y aller. Je vous prie de me répondre bientôt sur ce point, afin que je puisse prendre mes mesures. Je commencerais aussitôt la Symphonie; quant au Concertant, je souhaite savoir quels en seraient les Instruments — J'attends avec un désir ardent la Réponse de mon très cher et très estimé Neate —

Je suis avec la plus haute considération Votre sincère ami

LOUIS VAN BEETHOVEN

P.S. Il est possible, que les fautes, dont je vous expédie l'avertiment, ne se trouvent point dans la Partition que Vous avez reçue; mais n'en étant pas sûr, je préférai cette manière de me persuader que votre Partition est correcte.

---

[1] Written in another hand and signed by Beethoven. This letter was first published in the *Beethoven-Jahrbuch*, 1953/54, p. 45.

[2] Cf. Letter 1344.

(1349) *To Bernhard Schotts Söhne, Mainz*

[*Autograph in the Stadtbibliothek, Mainz*]

GENTLEMEN!   VIENNA, *February* 5, 1825

You will have all the works very soon — I certify by my signature that your firm is the sole owner of the Josephstadt overture and of the pianoforte arrangements of this work,[1] and also of my six bagatelles or trifles [2] and of three songs, two of which have wind-instrument or pianoforte solo accompaniment; the third song is an arietta with pianoforte accompaniment;[3] and that your editions of these works are the only correct and authentic ones and have been prepared by the composer himself.

LUDWIG VAN BEETHOVEN [4]

You do well to publish the pianoforte arrangements of the overture immediately. I see that you have already heard about Herr Henning's gross misconduct. Indeed I was just going to inform you of it. The Königstadt Theatre obtained the overture *solely for performance, and not to engrave or publish*; that was the written arrangement made here with *Bethmann.* But you are well aware that *we quarrelled with him.* So Henning thought that he had every right *not to* adhere to the contracts we had made with him. — I was immediately informed of this by one of my acquaintances in Berlin and I wrote at once to *Henning.*[5] He too replied at once saying that *admittedly that had been done with the pianoforte arrangement for four hands* and that it was now impossible to withdraw it, but that certainly nothing further would be done and that I could rely quite definitely on this assurance — I am sending you the letter, but it will not be at all necessary to take any action — Just publish

[1] Cf. Letter 1343, p. 1165, n. 4.
[2] Op. 126, published by Schott at Easter, 1825.
[3] Op. 121b, 122 and 128. Op. 128 was published by Schott in the spring of 1825, the other two songs in July of the same year.
[4] When sending the works to Schott Beethoven's brother included a covering letter in which he suggested that in order to save time the firm should commission Gottfried Weber (see Letter 1407, p. 1229, n. 2) to correct the proofs. The latter, however, returned a flat refusal, declaring that he had no desire to be Herr Beethoven's proof-reader and abusing Schott for his presumption in suggesting it.
[5] Cf. Letter 1343.

the pianoforte arrangements at once under my name or under that of Carl Czerny *who made them*; I should be glad to know that the overture too has been given to the musical public; and the Josephstadt title must remain. The dedication is to His Excellency Prince Nikolaus von Galitzin, but, of course, his name should appear only on the score.[1] — Now it would be a good thing if you were to announce these works everywhere, in Paris too and so forth. I am bestowing upon you full powers to further your own interest in the best possible way. I agree to everything you consider necessary in this respect. — I have sent you a few canons for your *Caecilia*.[2] But should you prefer to have something else, then write to me — As for Brockhausen [3] in Paris set your mind at rest, I will soon write to him — Just for a joke, *ask Tobias for my romantic biography of him*; that is more or less the way to deal with people of his type, those heartless *Viennese*. In fact he is the person *who advised me to have nothing to do with you*.

Silentium. There is nothing else to be done. Steiner, head of the firm in the *Paternostergasse* here, is an *out and out miser* and *a rogue of a fellow*; that *Tobias* is inclined to be *weak* and *accommodating*, yet I *need* him for *several things* — you may say what you like. In my association with you all that should be a matter of indifference to you — As soon as you make up your mind to undertake a complete edition of my collected works, then it should be done soon. For here and there you can expect a good deal. In each type of composition, for instance, there is a new work, *though not always a great one*. Yet it would give a good fillip to the undertaking — You may mention too in the announcements that the future editions (I refer to the new works which you have now taken, and I must ask you to remember that the Mass which has appeared in Paris is a reprint of an earlier Mass of mine [4]) are all being prepared under my supervision —

I have not received either the fourth or the fifth issue of *Caecilia* —

---

[1] Op. 124.
[2] WoO 180 and 187, which were published in this review in April, 1825.
[3] Beethoven is referring to Franz Stockhausen. Cf. Letter 1345, p. 1167, n. 2.
[4] This bracketed sentence is added at the foot of the page. Beethoven's Mass in C, Op. 86. A pirated edition of this work had been published in 1824 by Castil-Blaze, Paris. See *KHV*. 241.

Well, I send you my good wishes and ask you to let me have some friendly words from you soon.

With sincere regards, your

BEETHOVEN

(1350) *To Ignaz Schuppanzigh* [1]

[Autograph in the Beethovenhaus, Bonn, H. C. Bodmer collection]

MOST EXCELLENT MYLORD!   [VIENNA, *February*, 1825]

You may perform the quartet from today until the second Sunday.[2] It was impossible to let you have it before, because I have been far too busy with other work which *only one copyist* can manage; and altogether my not very prosperous circumstances, which compel me to undertake only what is most necessary, are partly to blame — Meanwhile the quartet will not be published for a long time, and thus remains *your sole property here in loco.* You have not sent me word about the concerts, *so we shall not hear anything* — All good wishes. I shall let you know as soon as that machine of mine is ready which will enable you to be lifted up quite comfortably to me on the fourth floor.[3] — Yours

BEETHOVEN

(1351) *To Ferdinand Ries, Bonn*

[MS in the Beethovenhaus, Bonn, H. C. Bodmer collection] [4]

DEAR RIES!   [VIENNA, *February*, 1825]

You press me so much for a reply that at the moment I can only let you have the most necessary information. I had already heard from Kirchhoffer that you had left London.[5] My extremely difficult circumstances scarcely allowed me time to write even a very short letter to you. K[irchhoffer] took

---

[1] The address on the verso of the autograph runs as follows:—Al Signore Milord stimatissimo nominato Sciuppanzig grand' uomo della Città di Vienna.

[2] Op. 127 was first performed by Schuppanzigh's quartet on Sunday, March 6, 1825.

[3] Possibly Beethoven is referring to Falstaff's appeal in Shakespeare's *Henry IV*, Part I., Act II., sc. 2, where he says; 'Have you any levers to lift me up again, being down?'

[4] Written by Karl and signed by Beethoven.

[5] Ries had returned to Germany in the autumn of 1824.

charge of the symphony which most certainly cannot appear before the end of the summer.¹ The present arrangements are merely preliminaries. The time-limit for which the London Philharmonic Society has stipulated will be observed most carefully. Bremen *never* got the symphony. Nor did Paris, as somebody wrote to me from London. How much must one endure, if one has the misfortune to become famous !

Well now, let me deal with what you want to have ! ² I shall be delighted to send you the metronome markings for Christus am Ölberge, however uncertain this tempo indication may be.³ — In regard to the symphony, I am now making you a proposal on more general lines. My situation obliges me to endeavour by means of my *notes* to extricate myself from my *needs*.⁴ Would it not be possible for you to arrange the matter *in the following way* ? I would send *you* the symphony in my score or in a careful copy of it, and also the Mass in score and the overture which I had copied for the Phil[harmonic] Society.⁵ Further, I could also let you have several trifles for orchestra and for choirs as well. In this way a club of that type would be enabled to give two or three concerts instead of one. Perhaps a fee of 40 carolins would not be too much for the club — I leave the whole matter to you. The idea of such an arrangement is not *mine* but has been put forward by those who would gladly extricate me from my *needs* by means of my *notes* — I am extremely interested in your property at Godesberg.⁶ Nobody could rejoice at this with greater envy than I whose deepest desires would be satisfied by such a possession. It seems, however, that my destiny is not going to be quite what I should like it to be. Give my

¹ The ninth symphony, Op. 125, was published by Schott in August, 1826. It was not published in England in Beethoven's lifetime.

² Ries had been asked to organize a music festival at Aix-la-Chapelle to be held at Whitsuntide, and to obtain, if possible, Beethoven's ninth symphony. See *TDR* V, 165-166.

³ Op. 85.

⁴ One of Beethoven's favourite puns, on the plural forms of 'Not' and 'Note'.

⁵ The 'Missa Solemnis', Op. 123, and probably the overture, Op. 124.

⁶ This letter is addressed in Karl's hand to :

'Herrn Ferdinand Ries,
berühmten Compositeur in Bonn.'

Evidently Ries had not yet moved to Godesberg where he had bought an estate. He was living there, however, in November, 1825, for Smart, according to his journal, dined there with Ries and his family during that month.

heartfelt greetings to your old father.[1]   I am extremely delighted to hear of his happiness.   With all my heart I embrace
you and I hope soon to be able to write to you more fully.

As always your true friend

BEETHOVEN

Do write soon to me too.[2]

(1352) *To Charles Neate, London*

[*MS not traced*] [3]

MON TRÈS CHER AMI!   VIENNA, *March* 19, 1825
    Je ne pourrai guère venir à Londres durant le printemps,[4]
mais qui sait quel accident m'y conduit peut-être en automne.
J'espére que vous vous trouvez bien dans votre famille et en
bonne santé.   Quant aux Quatuors dont vous m'écrivez dans
vos lettres, j'en ai achevé le premier et je suis à présent
à composer le second, qui, comme le troisième sera achevé
dans peu de temps.   Vous m'offrez 100 guinées pour 3 Quatuors,
je trouve cette proposition bien généreuse.[5]   Il se demande
seulement s'il m'est permis de publier ces Quatuors après un
an et demie, ou deux ans.   C'est ce qui serait très avantageux
pour mes finances.   En ce qui concerne la manière de simplifier
l'envoiement des Quatuors, et de l'argent de votre part, je
vous propose de remettre les œuvres à Messrs Fries et Co., qui
témoigneront à vous même ou à quelque banquier de Londres,
d'être possesseurs des Quatuors, et qui vous les remettront
aussitôt après l'arrivée de l'argent.
    Voici une affaire, par laquelle vous pouvez me prouver
votre amitié.   Je vous prie seulement de me répondre au
plus-tôt possible.   Je me fie toujours à votre amitié pour moi
et vous assure que vous pouvez faire de même à moi.   Je suis,
avec la plus grande considération, votre ami,

BEETHOVEN

1 Franz Anton Ries, born November 10, 1755, was then 69.
2 This remark is in Beethoven's handwriting.
3 Taken from Moscheles, *Life of Beethoven*, II, pp. 269-270.
4 Neate had written to Beethoven on February 1st, saying that the latter's
arrival in London was being awaited with impatience.
5 Of the Galitzin quartets, Op. 127, 132 and 130, only the parts of the first one,
Op. 127, were published in England by Clementi & Co. in [1827 ?].

(1353) *To Ferdinand Ries, Bonn*

[*MS in the Beethovenhaus, Bonn, H. C. Bodmer collection*] [1]

MY DEAR FRIEND!   [VIENNA], *March* 19, 1825

Just a week ago today and immediately after receiving your communication, I sent off the symphony by the first mail coach which was leaving.[2] Three movements of the symphony were copied out in score and all the parts of the Finale were copied out. I possess only *my own* score. Hence I could send you only the parts of the Finale. But by the mail coach which leaves this day week you will receive the Finale in score also, as well as other works which I am sending you. With the symphony I sent you an overture and an Opferlied with chorus;[3] but probably there are numerous mistakes in the latter. However, I will send you from here a list of the mistakes. Further, a double bassoon part for the Finale of the symphony will be despatched to you.

This is all I can tell you today, dear friend; for I am too busy. I will thank you myself in writing for your delightful proposals. I cannot do so today as I have burnt my hand. My warmest greetings to your father and to your wife. In any case you will be satisfied with me.

Ever your true friend

BEETHOVEN

(1354) *To Bernhard Schotts Söhne, Mainz*

[*MS in the Stadtbibliothek, Mainz*] [4]

GENTLEMEN!   VIENNA, *March* 19, 1825

First of all, I am sending you a notice which I have had inserted in some papers.[5] Do make haste with the pianoforte arrangements, for the one for pianoforte duet is here, exactly as it is described in the notice. The violin quartet will be delivered during the next few days.[6] Favourable offers for this work have been made to me here. But I am keeping

---

[1] Written and addressed by Karl, and signed by Beethoven.
[2] Op. 125.   [3] Probably Op. 124 and Op. 121b.
[4] Written and addressed in another hand and signed by Beethoven.
[5] For this notice see Appendix H (15).   [6] Op. 127.

my promise to you, so I pay no heed to these offers — Among my papers I still have a few trifles of which I will soon send you a list. The violin quartets are still being composed. The second one is almost finished.[1] I will send you a plan about the publication of my collected works — The canons will follow gradually. Several were written merely *stante pede* [2] and I myself have to try to remember them, as I can't find the sheets on which they were written. Since the third issue I have had no more copies of Caecilia — You will receive very soon the Opus numbers of the works I have sent you [3] — That is all I have to say in reply to your last letter — Don't forget that the symphony must not appear before the end of July or the beginning of August. Rest assured that your cordial behaviour is very agreeable and gratifying to me. I shall endeavour to reciprocate it as far as possible with sincere friendship.

Your friend
BEETHOVEN

PS. In regard to my two canons which you have received, the titles must stand as they are, that is to say, the title of the one is : *Auf einen welcher Hofmann geheissen* ; [4] and of the other : *Auf einen welcher Schwenke geheissen.*[5]

(1355) *To Bernhard Schotts Söhne, Mainz*

[Autograph in the possession of the Earl Spencer]

GENTLEMEN !   VIENNA, [*c. March* 24], 1825 [6]
The numbers of the works are as follows : —

Three songs	No. 121 [7]
Mass	No. 123
overture	No. 124
symphony	No. 125
bagatelles	No. 126
quartet	No. 127

[1] The A minor quartet, Op. 132, the second one dedicated to Prince Galitzin, was not finished until the end of July, 1825. It was not published by Schott, but by Moritz Schlesinger, Paris, and not until September, 1827.

[2] I.e. extempore.   [3] See Letter 1355.   [4] WoO 180.   [5] WoO 187.

[6] The date of arrival, April 1, 1825, has been noted twice on the autograph, i.e. on the verso and on top of the first page. The letter is also dated in Beethoven's hand: 'Vienna, March, 1825'.

[7] In the end the three songs were given the Opus numbers, 121b, 122 and 128.

I will shortly send you the tempi based on metronome markings.[1] My metronome is sick and will have to recover its *equable, regular* pulse with the help of the watchmaker —
You know that the symphony must not appear before the end of July [2] —
Furthermore, I should very much like the quartet, which is ready, not to be made *public* for some time yet. People insist on rating this quartet very high. In fact, it is the greatest and most beautiful work *ut dicunt* [3] which I have composed. The most eminent virtuosi in Vienna vie in playing it —
That is all — for today —
Would it not be possible to invent a method of multiplying copies of one's works oneself by stereotype without *being forced* to employ this scourge of copyists? —
pensés   More news soon —
With love and best regards, your most devoted
BEETHOVEN

(1356) *To Ignaz Schuppanzigh, Franz Weiss,*[4] *Joseph Linke and Karl Holz*

[*MS in the Deutsche Staatsbibliothek, Berlin*] [5]

MOST EXCELLENT FELLOWS!   [VIENNA, *March*, 1825]
Each of you is receiving herewith his part.[6] And each of you undertakes to do his duty and, what is more, pledges himself on his word of honour to acquit himself as well as possible, to distinguish himself and to vie in excellence with the others.

[1] Schott published all these works and also the C sharp minor string quartet, Op. 131.
[2] The ninth symphony was not published until the end of August, 1826.
[3] So they say.
[4] Franz Weiss (1778–1830), born in Silesia, became a famous viola player in Vienna. He first belonged to the Schuppanzigh quartet and later to the Razumovsky quartet until the latter was disbanded in 1815. After Schuppanzigh's departure for Russia Weiss remained in Vienna; and after the former's return to Vienna in April, 1823, the quartet was formed again and gave its first performance on June 14th.
[5] Written by Schindler and signed by Beethoven. The four players who formed the Schuppanzigh quartet signed their names in pencil.
[6] Probably, as Schindler has noted on the autograph, a reference to rehearsals of the E$^\flat$ quartet, Op. 127, the first but unsuccessful performance of which was given on March 6, 1825.

Each of you who is participating in the said undertaking must sign this paper.

BEETHOVEN

Schuppanzigh,   Schindler secretarius
  Weiss,
  Linke,
the accursed cello of the great master.
  Holz,[1]
the last of all, but only when signing this paper.

(1357) *To Bernhard Schotts Söhne, Mainz*

[Autograph in the Stadtbibliothek, Mainz]

GENTLEMEN!   [VIENNA, *March*, 1825]
This is just to say that the works will certainly be delivered next week — You will easily understand the reason for this delay when I tell you that owing to the unreliable copying I have had to check each part separately — For, like so many other things in Vienna, this side of the work has greatly deteriorated; the heavier the taxes the greater the difficulties. Everywhere — there is a poverty of spirit — and a poverty of purse —
I have not yet received your Caecilia.
The overture you received from my brother was performed here during the last few days.[2] I was given much praise and so forth for it. But what is that compared with the great composer above — above — above — and rightfully called the All-Highest, seeing that here below composing is only ridiculed, *the dwarfs being the all-highest* [3] ! ! ! ? ? ? — —— You will receive the quartet at once together with the other works.[4] You are indeed frank and ingenuous, qualities which so far I have not found in publishers. I am glad of it and shake hands with

---

[1] For a note on Karl Holz see Letter 1409, p. 1230, n. 2.
[2] Op. 124, together with Czerny's two pianoforte arrangements, had been sent to Mainz by Johann on February 4, 1825. See *KHV*. 370.
[3] The last five words are added at the foot of the page.
[4] Op. 127, the first of Beethoven's late quartets, was not published by Schott until the following year. It was the only one published in the composer's lifetime.

you on that account. And who knows whether I shall not do so soon in person?!

It would please me if you would now send the fee for the quartet as well to Fries in Vienna. For at the moment I need a good deal of money, since everything has to come from abroad; and here and there I have to face a delay; — partly through my own fault — My brother is adding the necessary particulars about the works offered to you and which you have accepted —

I send you cordial greetings. I see from your periodical that *Junker* is still alive.[1] He was one of the first who *noticed* me 'when I was very young and innocent'.[2] Give him my kind regards. — In great haste and with all speed, and yet this is not such a very short letter.

Your

BEETHOVEN

(1358) *To Ferdinand Ries, Bonn*

[Autograph in the Beethovenhaus, Bonn]

DEAR AND BELOVED RIES!   VIENNA, *April* 9, 1825

In haste I am letting you know only what is most necessary — In the score of the symphony [3] which was sent to you there is, so far as I remember, a mistake in the first oboe part in the first Allegro, and, what is more, in the 242nd bar, where there is

 instead of . I have checked all the instrumental parts (except those of the brass which I have checked only in part). So I think that the score will be more or less correct. I would gladly have sent you my own

---

[1] Karl Ludwig Junker, born in 1740, had died in 1797. He had a church living at Rupertshoven near Kirchberg and composed and wrote about music. In 1791 he contributed to Bossler's *Musikalische Korrespondenz* articles on Beethoven and music at Bonn. Evidently Beethoven had not heard of his death.

[2] A quotation from the poem *Phidile* by Matthias Claudius (1740–1815). It is the second line of the first verse. Beethoven's eight songs with pianoforte accompaniment, Op. 52, published in June, 1805, by the Bureau des Arts et d'Industrie, include one setting of a poem by Claudius. It is No. 1, which, according to Wegeler, was one of his earliest compositions. See *WRBN.* 21.

[3] The ninth symphony, Op. 125.

score, but I have to prepare for another concert, and the manuscript is the only copy of the score which I possess. In any case I can only hope that my health will allow me to arrange this concert, for I must soon go off to the country, the only place where I can feel well at this time of the year — You will have received by now a second copy of the Opferlied.[1] *Mark it* at once as corrected by me, so that it may not be used along with the copy you have already. Here you have a sample of the work of the wretched copyists I have had to put up with since Schlemmer's death. One can scarcely rely on a single note — Since you have already received all the written-out parts of the Finale of the symphony, I have sent you the part of the choirmaster as well. You can easily put it together from the parts in the score before the singing begins; and where the singing begins it is quite easy by taking a little thought to have the instrumental parts fitted above to the vocal parts. It was not possible to have all this copied at once; and since it was done in a hurry, you would have received only *mistakes* from this copyist. I have sent you an overture in C in $\frac{6}{8}$ time which has not yet been published.[2] On the next post-day you will receive also the engraved parts. A Kyrie and a Gloria, two of my most excellent compositions, and an Italian vocal duet are also on their way to you.[3] You will also receive another grand march with chorus, which is very suitable for grand concerts.[4] I have also another grand overture as yet unknown outside Austria.[5] But I think that you will have enough with the above works —

I await your assurance that you are making certain that nothing else is falling into other hands. If you meet the *Schotts at Mainz*, tell them that I let them have the *symphony* purely out of consideration and affection for their firm — I wish you well in that country of the Rhineland which will

[1] Op. 121b.
[2] Op. 115 was published by Steiner in April, 1825. It was dedicated to Prince Anton Radziwill.
[3] The 'Kyrie' and the 'Gloria' are portions of the 'Missa Solemnis'. But the Italian vocal duet raises a problem. Either Beethoven is referring to the Italian vocal duet 'Nei giorni tuoi felici', WoO 93, an early work composed in 1802–1803 and not published during his lifetime; or he meant to say 'Singterzett', vocal trio, which in that case would be 'Tremate, empi, tremate', Op. 116. Cf. Letter 1292, p. 1128, n. 6.
[4] Op. 114. This work was published in score by Steiner in April, 1826.
[5] Op. 124.

ever be dear to me. To you I wish all possible enjoyment of life, and to your wife and to your father all that is good and beautiful.

Your friend

BEETHOVEN

(1359) *To Dr. Anton Braunhofer* [1]

[Autograph in the Beethovenhaus, Bonn, H. C. Bodmer collection]

MY ESTEEMED FRIEND,   [VIENNA, *April* 18, 1825] [2]
    I am not feeling well and I hope that you will not refuse to come to my help, for I am in great pain. If you can possibly visit me today, I do most earnestly beg you to come —
    In constant gratitude and with my best regards, your

BEETHOVEN

(1360) *To Hofrat Karl Peters*

[Autograph in the Beethovenhaus, Bonn, H. C. Bodmer collection]

HONOURED FRIEND!   [VIENNA, *April*, 1825]
    I am convinced that K[arl] took these steps solely out of *false modesty*. Sound him thoroughly. If he wants to continue his studies I am prepared to do everything in my power to enable him to feel less acutely what he has experienced.[3] He could be sent to the Gymnasium in Vienna or to some place at a considerable distance from Vienna, for instance, to Graz or somewhere else. At any rate he ought to continue his study of philosophy for the next two years, for he could then take up any career he chooses — That is all I have to say on

---

    [1] Dr. Anton Braunhofer, Professor of Natural History at the University of Vienna, was Beethoven's medical attendant during the years 1820 to 1826, but not during his last illness. See *FRBH* I, 60. Beethoven dedicated to Braunhofer his song 'Abendlied unterm gestirnten Himmel' (WoO 150), written down on March 4, 1820, and he composed for him the two canons WoO 189 and WoO 190. For the former dated May 11, 1825, see Letter 1371, p. 1196. For the latter dated June 4, 1825, see Letter 1385, p. 1205.
    [2] On the autograph the date has been noted by the recipient, and Beethoven's address is added in Karl's hand. It is 'Johannisgasse No. 969 im 4ten Stock, rechts die Tür'.
    [3] Since the autumn of 1823 Karl had been studying literature and philology at Vienna University. But according to a conversation quoted in *TDR* V, 510, he was endeavouring to convince Beethoven that he had no talent for these studies.

that subject. But if he absolutely *refuses* to study any longer or, rather, if he thinks that he is unable to overcome the difficulties of his studies (although, as I have already said, I consider that false modesty and *dread* of the examinations are the chief reasons for his behaviour) well then, I am willing to fall in with *that*, namely, with *his adopting a business career*, to which, I admit, I have always been opposed. In that case he can enter the Polytechnic Institute [1] — I shall agree to whatever you consider to be for the best —

With kindest regards, your friend

BEETHOVEN

(1361) *To Joseph Böhm* [2]

[Autograph not traced] [3]

[VIENNA, *Spring*, 1825]

Do come to me this morning or, what would be the best arrangement, come and dine with me at about two o'clock.

Your friend

BEETHOVEN

[1] In the spring of 1825 as a preparation for a business career Karl entered the Polytechnic Institute of which Dr. Reisser, who greatly admired Beethoven, was Deputy Director. See Letter 1369, p. 1193, n. 5.

[2] Joseph Michael Böhm (1795–1876), born at Pest, became an eminent violinist. After studying with Rode he came to Vienna in 1815 and a few years later was appointed Professor at the Conservatoire of the recently established Gesellschaft der Musikfreunde and also became a member of the orchestra of the Hofkapelle. His string quartet gave the first really successful performance of Beethoven's Op. 127 on March 23, 1825.

[3] Taken from Frimmel, *Beethovenforschung*, vol. I, no. 2, July, 1911, p. 60.

(1362) *To Karl van Beethoven*

[*Autograph in the Beethovenhaus, Bonn, H. C. Bodmer collection*] [1]

[VIENNA, *Spring*, 1825]

You will find me at the Michaeler Haus at about one o'clock.

Your faithful

Bring the tailor's address with you.   father

(1363) *To Anton Felix Schindler* [2]

[*Autograph in the Deutsche Staatsbibliothek, Berlin*]

[VIENNA, *Spring*, 1825]

I have waited until half past one. But as the caput confusum [3] has gone ahead and as I know nothing about what is going to happen and as Karl has gone on from the University to the Prater, I have had to go off, so that Karl, who must leave early, may have something to eat. You will find me *at the Wilder Mann.*[4]

(1364) *To [Karl Holz?]* [5]

[*Autograph in the possession of Alfred Cortot*]

[VIENNA, *Spring*, 1825]

In haste I beg you, if you repeat anything of what I told you about changing money, at least not to mention any name — I *must* now bear many, many trials, but they are all the outcome of *the good deeds* which I have partly performed and still wish to perform —

Ever your friend

BEETHOVEN

---

[1] First published in the *Beethoven-Jahrbuch*, 1953/54, p. 23.
[2] The address on the verso of this unsigned note, written in Beethoven's hand, is: 'For Herr von Schindler, Moravian skull'. Schindler was the son of a National School teacher at Meedl in Moravia.
[3] Beethoven frequently accused Schindler of being muddle-headed.
[4] An inn in the Prater.   [5] See Letter 1409, p. 1230, n. 2.

(1365) *To Tobias Haslinger* [1]

[Autograph in the Koch collection]

MOST EXCELLENT FELLOW! [VIENNA, *Spring*, 1825]

To bi —— as To bi —— as

Fill up the interval. But if you are so shameless as to praise yourself, then I will disclose the full truth. Enclosed are the proofs. When you have corrected the mistakes, please let me have [the parts [3]] by tomorrow.[4] Please do not forget always to put after cresc. some little double dashes like these

= = =

Look after yourself.

Your etc., etc., etc.

BEETHOVEN

[1] The address on the fourth page of the autograph runs as follows:
An des Herrn
Tobias Hass u.
Die Herren Lin
wie auch Ger
wohl u. übel gebohren
allhier.

[2] This musical setting is listed in *KHV*. as WoO 205[h].

[3] The words in brackets have been supplied by the present editor.

[4] Probably the overture, Op. 115, published by Steiner in April, 1825.

(1366) *To Heinrich Friedrich Ludwig Rellstab* [1]

[Autograph in a private collection] [2]

[VIENNA, *April*, 1825]

I am [convalescent?][3], but I still feel extremely weak. So you must content yourself with this slight token of remembrance [4] from your friend.

B.

(1366a) *To Heinrich Friedrich Ludwig Rellstab* [5]

[Autograph in a private collection]

[VIENNA, *April*, 1825]

I am feeling worse than before, but I hope that in a few days I shall be better and shall then have the great pleasure of seeing you at my home.

Your

BEETHOVEN

(1366b) *To Heinrich Friedrich Ludwig Rellstab*

[Autograph not traced] [6]

[VIENNA], *May* 3, 1825

As I am about to go into the country,[7] I had to make some preparations yesterday myself; and unfortunately you

[1] Heinrich Friedrich Ludwig Rellstab (1799–1860), a gifted writer and poet living in Berlin, where his father owned a music publishing firm, visited Beethoven during a stay in Vienna in April and May, 1825. Ludwig Nohl in his *Beethoven nach den Schilderungen seiner Zeitgenossen* (1877) freely uses Rellstab's reminiscences of his talks with Beethoven published in his *Garten und Wald* (1854) and *Aus meinem Leben* (1861). See also *TDR* V, 196-210.

[2] This note is faintly pencilled on the empty page of an undated letter from Rellstab to Beethoven enclosing his libretto 'Orest', in the hope that the latter would compose another opera. On the same page is a short list in Johann's handwriting of books suitable for operatic texts, including Scott's *Kenilworth*.

[3] In the autograph there is only a capital R., but in the first sentence of his letter to Schott of May 7, 1825 (Letter 1368) Beethoven uses exactly the same phrase, giving the word 'Reconvalescenz' in full.

[4] The autograph does not contain the canon referred to and inserted in all the German editions. It is listed in *KHV* as WoO 203 and is quoted in this edition in Letter 1366b.

[5] This pencilled note is not addressed, but as it is attached to the documents described in Letter 1366, n. 2, it was almost certainly intended for Rellstab.

[6] Taken from L. Rellstab, *Garten und Wald* (Leipzig, 1854), IV, p. 109.

[7] Beethoven went to Baden on Saturday, May 7th. Rellstab left Vienna on Wednesday, May 4th.

happened to call without seeing me. Forgive me, but I am still in very poor health. Since it is possible that I may not see you again, I wish you all the success that can be conceived. Think of me when writing your poems.

Your friend
BEETHOVEN

Give my love and regards to *Zelter*, that valiant promoter of true art!

Das Schö - ne zu dem Gu - ten. Das

(1367) *To [Anton Felix Schindler, Vienna ?]* [2]

[Autograph not traced] [3]

BADEN, *May* 6, 1825 [4]

In no circumstances are you to leave the bell and the bell-ropes and so forth in my former rooms. No suggestion was made to those people that they should *take over anything* from me. The locksmith never came to remove the bell when I was there, and my ill health has prevented me from sending somebody from here into town. Surely those people could have had the bell taken down, seeing that they have *no right* to keep it — Well, whatever happens, I absolutely refuse to leave the bell there. I need one here and can make use of this one. For a bell would cost me twice as much here as in Vienna, since *bell-ropes are the most expensive articles* to buy from locksmiths — If necessary, go at once to the Imperial and Royal Police — The window in my room was exactly like that when I moved in. But you may pay for it and also for

[1] The words of this canon are from Matthisson's *Opferlied*, the final setting of which by Beethoven, Op. 121b, was composed in the summer of 1824. Cf. Letter 1366, p. 1190, n. 4.

[2] According to *TDR* V, 194, n. 3, this letter, a copy of which was found in Thayer's papers, was addressed to Karl. Nohl I, no. 331, maintains that it was addressed to Beethoven's brother. On internal evidence it was probably intended for Schindler, with whom Beethoven seems to have lived for a short period.

[3] Taken from *TDR* V, 194, n. 3.

[4] As Beethoven did not move to Baden until May 7th, there must be some mistake in the first transcription from the autograph, which was published in *Signale für die musikalische Welt*, 1857.

the one in the kitchen ; the two will cost 2 gulden, 12 kreuzer —
The key must not be paid for, since we found no key there.
Instead of being locked, the door was nailed up or bunged
up when we moved in ; and it remained in that condition
until I left. There never was a key there, since none was used
either by us or by the person who occupied the rooms before
us — Perhaps a collection will be arranged for. If so, I will
put my hand in my pocket.

LUDWIG VAN BEETHOVEN

(1368) *To Bernhard Schotts Söhne, Mainz*

[*Autograph in the Stadtbibliothek, Mainz*]

GENTLEMEN !   VIENNA, *May* 7, 1825

I am about to go into the country [1] and am just con-
valescing from an inflammation of my intestines. Hence I
am sending you only a few lines — Look at the passage in the
Opferlied, second verse, which runs :

I should like this passage to appear *exactly* as I am writing
it down here, namely :

NB. You must see too whether Tutti i Violoncelli is
indicated *in the chorus* of the Opferlied in the cello part as well.
If not, this must be done [4] —

By now you will have received the quartet.[5] It is the very
one I promised you. I could have had a fee of 60 ducats for
it from several publishers in Vienna, but I preferred to keep
my promise to you —

[1] See Letter 1370, where Beethoven says that he left for Baden on May 7th.
[2] The bass clef and the first sharp of the key-signature are missing.
[3] A correction to bar 44 (bar 7 of the second verse) of Op. 121b. But the key-signature should be four sharps. See *KHV*. 357.
[4] In the autograph this reminder appears at the top of the first page above the date.   [5] Op. 127, published by Schott in the spring of 1826.

Somebody has written an excellent German text for my Mass in C, quite different from the Leipzig one.[1] Would you like to do a new edition of this Mass with the new text ? —

Of minor works I could let you have four marches written for special occasions and all in the style of Turkish music, and also a Gratulationsmenuett.[2] For these my fee would be 25 gold ducats — — In regard to the publication of my collected works I now have the papers in front of me and will soon be able to put the necessary conditions before you, provided *that you are still interested in this project* — As for Henning's tricks I hope that you don't distrust me. But if you do, I will send you his letter in which he dissociates himself from everything connected with the overture. The arrangement was made here in writing with Bethmann who, as everyone knows, has quarrelled with the Society [3] —

(1369) *To Karl van Beethoven, Vienna*

[Autograph in the Deutsche Staatsbibliothek, Berlin] [4]

DEAR SON !   BADEN, *[shortly before May* 14, 1825]
I have just received your letter. I still feel very weak, and I am *alone* — And do just read this horrible letter from that person — I am sending you 25 gulden for you to buy the books at once — and you may use the balance if you need it. You must bring me Herr von Reisser's [5] note again —

On Saturday, May 14th, I shall send a carriage from here

---

[1] This was Benedikt Scholz, Director of Music at Warmbrunn, whose free translation of the Latin text of Op. 86 strongly appealed to Beethoven. Cf. Letter 1188, p. 1044, n. 2.

[2] WoO 18, 19, 20 and 24 ; and WoO 3. Schott did not take these works.

[3] The autograph ends here, but possibly the remainder of the letter is missing. For Beethoven's quarrel with Henning and Bethmann cf. Letter 1343.

[4] Autograph not available. Text taken from *TDR* V, 523-524. According to Thayer, who copied the documents, these two letters to Karl, the second of which was to be shown to Reisser, form one letter. Yet all the editors of the German *Gesamtausgaben* reproduce them as separate letters. See *TDR* V, 523, n. 2.

[5] Dr. Franz de Paula Michael Reisser (1769–1835) was Professor of Commercial Geography and History at the University of Vienna and at the Polytechnic Institute, of which he was Deputy Director. He became in 1825 co-guardian of Beethoven's nephew. Beethoven frequently miscalls him Reissig, confusing his name with that of the poet C. L. Reissig, some of whose poems Beethoven had set to music. Cf. Letter 242, p. 255, n. 3.

into town in order to fetch you and drive you out here. Carriages are still cheap. The old woman will find out in the morning what time will best suit you. You need not leave until six o'clock in the evening, in case you should miss something. Perhaps I shall come in too and then we could *buy shirts* for you. *For this reason, therefore, it would be well* if you could get away as early as four o'clock. But if I don't come, which is quite possible, then drive straight out here at five or six in the evening — Thus you will not be so exhausted and you can leave here on Sunday or perhaps even on Monday, if you are not missing anything — You can take with you from here the money for the crammer — Do you realize, by the way, that this business with the crammer and your board and lodging amount to two thousand gulden a year? —

I can't write any more today — I can hardly move my pen —

Your faithful father.

You must show the following note to Reissig.[1]

All sorts of cordial good wishes to my most esteemed and worthy co-guardian Dr. von Reissig. I still feel too weak to write to him myself. I trust that H[err] v[on] R[eisser] will have no objection to your coming out here on Saturday evening. You know well that even when you were at Blöchlinger's I never *abused* this permission — And in any case I am confident that you will use it wisely when you have *such a mainstay*.

Your faithful father
BEETHOVEN

(1370) *To Ferdinand Piringer, Vienna* [2]

[*Autograph in the Beethovenhaus, Bonn, H. C. Bodmer collection*]

BADEN, *May* 13, 1825

My warmest thanks to you for your readiness to undertake to correct a copy of my Mass. But please let me know

[1] Here Beethoven is referring to Reisser, not to the poet Reissig. Cf. p. 1193, n. 5.
[2] The autograph bears no address. But it is endorsed by this recipient: and on internal evidence the letter must have been intended for him. Ferdinand

as soon as you have finished your task. For I shall then send
someone to you to fetch your copy. Please be so kind as to
hand him the Mass. — Please tell Böhm, that sound fiddler,
how sorry I am not to be able to let him have the quartet
again.¹ But on the very day of my departure for Baden (i.e.
on May 7th) I only got it back with great difficulty from Herr
Mayseder.² — The effects of the intestinal inflammation from
which I have been suffering are very severe, for I feel so weak
that as yet I can hardly walk properly, still less do any work —
May God help me ! — As always your friend and servant

BEETHOVEN

(1371) *To Dr. Anton Braunhofer, Vienna*

[*Autograph in the Gesellschaft der Musikfreunde, Vienna*] ³

ESTEEMED FRIEND !   [BADEN], *May* 13, 1825

D[*octor*] : How are you, my patient ?

Pat[*ient*] : We are rather poorly — we still feel very weak
and are belching and so forth. I am inclined to think that I
now require a stronger medicine, but it must not be consti-
pating — Surely I might be allowed to take white wine
diluted with water, for that poisonous beer is bound to make
me feel sick — my catarrhal condition is showing the following
symptoms, that is to say, I spit a good deal of blood, but
probably only from my windpipe. But I have frequent nose
bleedings, which I often had last winter as well. And there is
no doubt that my stomach has become dreadfully weak, and
so has, generally speaking, my whole constitution. Judging
by what I know of my own constitution, my strength will
hardly be restored unaided.

Piringer (1780–1829) was a senior Viennese official and an ardent lover of music•
He played the violin, had a good bass voice and occasionally conducted and
deputized for F. X. Gebauer at the Concert Spirituel. After the latter's death in
1822 Piringer became a director of the Concert Spirituel and shared with Johann
Baptist Coissler the organizing and conducting of the concerts. See *FRBH* II,
21-22. Beethoven composed for Piringer's album his Klavierstück in B minor,
dated February 18, 1821. It is listed in *KHV.* as WoO 61.

¹ The Eᵇ quartet, Op. 127, had been first performed by the Schuppanzigh
quartet on March 6, 1825, but not very successfully. A much better performance
of it was given by the Böhm quartet on March 23rd.

² Cf. Letter 504, p. 476, n. 1.

³ In the autograph this letter covers two pages of the sheet, the canon which
follows is written on the third page, and the fourth page contains the address.

D[octor] : I will help you, I will alternate Brown's [1] method with that of Stoll.[2]

Pat[ient] : I should like to be able to sit at my writing-desk again and feel a little stronger.[3] Do bear this in mind — *Finis.*

I will look you up as soon as I go into town. Just tell Karl at what time I can find you. But it would help me if you could inform Karl what other remedies I should use. The last medicine you prescribed I took only once and then lost it — With kindest regards and my gratitude,

Your friend
BEETHOVEN

Dok - tor sperrt das Tor dem Tod, No = te hilft auch aus der Noth Dok - tor sperrt das Tor dem Tod No = te hilft auch aus der Noth.

Written on May 11, 1825 at Baden, in the Helenenthal at the second Antons Brücke looking towards Siechenfeld —

BEETHOVEN.

[1] John Brown (1735–1788), a distinguished Scottish physician who founded the Brunonian system of medicine. In 1780 he published his *Elementa Medicinae* written in Latin, propounding the doctrine that morbid action, often the result of weakness, demands stimulating treatment.

[2] Max Stoll (1742–1787) of Würtemberg, settled in Vienna in 1777. His method of treatment was entirely the opposite of Brown's.

[3] During May, 1825, Beethoven composed the third movement of his A minor quartet, Op. 132, which he called 'Heiliger Dankgesang eines Genesenden an die Gottheit'.

[4] This four-part canon for Dr. Braunhofer, written on the third page of Beethoven's letter, is listed in *KHV.* as WoO 189.

(1372) *To Karl van Beethoven, Vienna*

[*Autograph in the Nationalbibliothek, Vienna*]

DEAR SON!   BADEN, *May* 17, [1825]
The weather here is horrible. Today is even colder than
yesterday, so that I can scarcely move my fingers to write ;
but this weather seems to be prevalent only in the mountains
here, and particularly at Baden — I forgot the chocolate
today. I am sorry to have to give you this trouble. Doubtless
all these difficulties will soon cease. I am sending two gulden ;
please add the 15 kreuzer. If possible, send the chocolate
by the afternoon mail coach, for, if not, I shall have none the
day after tomorrow. No doubt the people in the house will
help you over this.
God be with you. I am beginning to compose a fair
amount again. But in this extremely gloomy, cold weather
it is almost impossible to do anything —
Ever your good and faithful father.

(1373) *To Karl van Beethoven, Vienna*

[*Autograph in the Deutsche Staatsbibliothek, Berlin*] [1]

[BADEN, *May* 18, 1825]
DEAR SON!   About 1 p.m.
This is just to inform you that the old woman has not
yet arrived, why, I don't know. Enquire at once at the
joiner's in the Kothgasse whether the Viennese joiner who
lives here has left for Baden? It is really very hard for me to
have to depend on such people, so much so that if I had
nothing higher to enjoy, I should find my life quite unbear-
able — You will have received my letter of yesterday with the
two gulden for chocolate. Tomorrow no doubt I shall have
to drink coffee. Who knows, perhaps it may be better for
me than chocolate. For the prescriptions of that B[raunhofer]
have been a failure before now. And on the whole he strikes me
as very narrow-minded and, therefore, a bit of a fool. He must

---
[1] Autograph not available. Text taken from *TDR* V, 524.

have known about the asparagus — After the meal at the inn I am suffering a good deal today from diarrhœa — The white wine has given out, so I have to get it from the inn and have now paid three gulden for it — The day before yesterday the old woman wrote down that she wanted to die in hospital. Perhaps she doesn't want to come here any more. God knows that she will always be a wicked old woman. In that case she must make arrangements with the person she knows. She wrote down for me 'that the people refused to hand over the bell-rope', a very different story from what she told you on Sunday; and how is one to know whether she has not some interest in it? — She went into town yesterday at six o'clock and I implored her to be sure to be here again this morning. If she does turn up, I shall probably have to go into town the day after tomorrow. Leave word (in writing) at what time I can find you —

Send me a few lines at once. How grieved I am that I must trouble you. But you see that I can't help it —

What a distressing state of affairs it is that I *have to be here and in such circumstances* ! !

Your faithful father

(1374) *To Karl van Beethoven, Vienna*

[*Autograph in the Deutsche Staatsbibliothek, Berlin*] [1]

The letter of May 17th   [BADEN], *Wednesday, May* 18, [1825]
written today was given
a wrong date.[2] It should
be May 18th.

DEAR SON!

The old woman has just turned up. So don't worry, work hard at your books and get up early in the morning. By doing so you could even manage to do several things for me which might crop up — It is certainly very desirable for a youth who is almost nineteen to combine the duties pertaining to his own education and advancement with those

---

[1] Autograph not available. Text taken from *TDR* V, 525.
[2] Cf. Letters 1372 and 1373.

he owes to his benefactor and supporter — Why, I certainly fulfilled in every way my duties to my parents —

In great haste,

your faithful father

The old bell-rope
has arrived here.

(1375) *To Karl van Beethoven, Vienna*

[*Autograph in the Deutsche Staatsbibliothek, Berlin*] ¹

[BADEN, *May* 18, 1825]

At last — do at least give the chocolate to the old woman — Ramler, if his time is not yet taken up, would perhaps attend to the old woman — I am getting thinner and thinner and feel more ailing than well and I have no doctor, not even a sympathetic soul at hand — If you can manage to come on Sundays, do come. But I don't want to interfere with your plans in any way, if only I were certain that your Sundays away from me were well spent. Indeed I must learn to give up everything ; and I will gladly do so to obtain this benefit, namely, to know that my very great sacrifices are going to bear good fruit —

Oh, where have I not been wounded, nay more, cut to the heart ? ! —

Your faithful father

(1376) *To Karl van Beethoven, Vienna*

[*Autograph in the Deutsche Staatsbibliothek, Berlin*] ²

[BADEN], *May* 19, [1825]

Landstrasse, Ungargasse, apartment no. 345, near the brewery, consisting of four rooms and a kitchen — with a view over the surrounding gardens. Particulars to be obtained from the caretaker. In the Hauptstrasse too there are supposed to be several — give *one gulden* to the caretaker in the Ungargasse so that he may reserve the apartment until Saturday

---

¹ Autograph not available. Text taken from *TDR* V, 526.
² Autograph not available. Text taken from *TDR* V, 526-527.

when I will certainly fetch you unless the weather is too bad —
It will depend on what we decide tomorrow — whether it
should be taken from Michaelmas or now — If I should go
into town on Saturday, do arrange for me to be able to find
you [1] —

Your faithful [2]

(1377) *To Karl van Beethoven, Vienna*

[Autograph in the Deutsche Staatsbibliothek, Berlin] [3]

BADEN, *May* 22, [1825]

So far only suppositions, though indeed someone assures
me that you and your mother have again been associating in
secret — Am I to experience once more the most horrible ingratitude? No, if the bond is to be broken, so be it. But you
will be detested by all impartial people who hear of this
ingratitude — my worthy brother's remarks, and moreover,
what he has heard from Dr. Reisser, as he says, and your
remark yesterday about Dr. Sonnleithner, which of course
must grieve me, in view of the fact that the Landrechte did
precisely the opposite *of what he demanded*, well, am I to mix
myself up again in these vulgarities? No, never again —
For God's sake, if the pact oppresses you — I hand you over
to Divine Providence. I have done my share and can therefore appear before the Supreme Judge of all judges. Don't
be afraid to come to me tomorrow. So far I am only guessing.
May God grant that *nothing of all this* is true. For indeed, if
it were, there would be no end to your unhappiness, however
lightheartedly my rascally brother and perhaps even your —
mother may consider your action —

I am expecting you for certain — with the old woman.

[1] Beethoven was writing on Thursday.
[2] According to *TDR* V, 527, the autograph breaks off here.
[3] Autograph not available. Text taken from *TDR* V, 527. Facsimile of
first page of autograph in Stephan Ley, *Beethoven* (Berlin, 1939), p. 343.

(1378) *To Charles Neate, London*

[*MS in the Beethovenhaus, Bonn, H. C. Bodmer collection*] [1]

MON AMI !   VIENNA, *May* 25, 1825

Je crois nécessaire de vous écrire encore une fois. Je vois dans la lettre que vous m'avez écrite il y a deux ans que l'honoraire des Quatuors est £100 sterling. Je suis content de cette offre, mais il est nécessaire de vous avertir, que le premier Quatuor est si cherché par les plus célèbres artistes de Vienne que je l'ai accordé a quelques uns d'eux pour leur bénéfice. Je crois tromper votre amitié en ne vous avertissant point de cette circonstance, parceque vous pouvez aussi en faire usage à Londres. Or si vous me répondez que vous êtes content des propositions que je vous ai faites dans ma lettre dernière, je vous enverrai aussitôt le 1er Quatuor ; cependant je vous prie d'accélérer votre résolution, puisque les éditeurs désirent vivement de le posséder. Cependant vous n'avez point de remettre l'honoraire qu'après avoir reçu l'assurance de ma part, que les deux autres Quatuors sont achevés. Seulement je vous prie d'ajouter à votre lettre l'assurance de votre contentement en ce qui concerne mes offres. Voilà ce que j'ai cru devoir vous dire. Je crois vous avoir fait une complaisance, et je suis certain que vous ferez le même envers moi. Conservez votre amitié pour moi. Je suis, avec la plus grande estime, votre ami sincère

LOUIS VAN BEETHOVEN

(1379) *To Karl van Beethoven, Vienna*

[*Autograph in the Deutsche Staatsbibliothek, Berlin*] [2]

DEAR SON !   BADEN, *May* 31, 1825

I intend to go into town on Saturday and to return here on Sunday evening or Monday morning [3] — Please enquire therefore at Dr. Bach's at what time he can generally be seen ;

---

[1] Written by another hand and signed by Beethoven.
[2] Autograph not available. Text taken from *TDR* V, 528-529.
[3] Beethoven was writing on Tuesday.

and get the key too from our worthy brother the baker [1] in order to see whether in the room owned by my worthy un-brotherly brother there is enough furniture to enable me to spend the night there, whether the linen is clean, and so forth. Since Thursday is a holiday [2] and you will hardly come to Baden, nor do I ask you to do so, you could surely undertake these few errands; and when I come in on Saturday you can give me a report about everything — I am not sending you any money, for, if you need some, you can borrow a gulden in the house. Economy is necessary for young people, and to this you do not seem to have given sufficient attention, seeing that you got some money *without my knowing it or even knowing where it came from*? — Fine goings-on! It is not advisable for you to visit the theatre *now* on account of its too great distraction; at any rate that is what I think — Meanwhile the five gulden obtained from Dr. Reisser [3] I will pay back punctually every month — and thus basta — Spoilt as you are it would not do you any harm to cultivate *at last simplicity and truth*. For my heart has suffered too much from your deceitful behaviour to me; and it is hard to forget it. Even if I were willing to pull the whole burden like a yoked ox and without murmuring, yet your behaviour, if it is directed against others in the same way, can never attract to you people who will love you — God is my witness that my sole dream is to get away completely from you and from that wretched brother and that horrible family who have been thrust upon me. May God grant my wishes. For I *can* no longer trust *you* —

Unfortunately your father

or, better still, not your father.

[1] Leopold Obermayr, whose sister Therese was married to Johann van Beethoven in 1812. Cf. Letter 1078, p. 946, n. 2.
[2] I.e. Corpus Christi.
[3] Cf. Letter 1369, p. 1193, n. 5.

(1380) *To Matthias Schlemmer, Vienna* [1]

[*Autograph in the Germanisches Nationalmuseum, Nuremberg*]

SIR!   [BADEN, *May*, 1825]

I find it very strange that it is almost impossible to make
Karl go into pleasant company where at this time he could
be enjoying himself in the most desirable fashion. Indeed
one might be led to suspect that perhaps he really is enjoying
himself in the evening or even at night in some company which
is certainly not so desirable — I request you to pay attention
to this and not to let Karl leave your house at night under
any pretext whatever, unless you have received something in
writing from me through Karl — He went once to Hofrat
Breuning's, but I knew about that — I do urge you to take
up this question which cannot be a matter of indifference
either to you or to me; and once more I recommend you to
pay the greatest attention to it — I am, Sir, your most devoted
                                    BEETHOVEN

(1381) *To Anton Felix Schindler, Vienna*

[*Autograph in the Deutsche Staatsbibliothek, Berlin*]

[BADEN, *May*, 1825]

As my note did not catch you today, *Friday*, I shall expect
you to dinner *tomorrow* for certain — for it so happens that
I must have a word with you. You may even come earlier
and take a walk in the fresh air, which would do you good —
                        In great haste.
                                    BEETHOVEN

[1] Matthias Schlemmer, a Viennese official with whose family Beethoven's
nephew lived from Easter, 1825, until the end of July, 1826. Schlemmer's family
occupied the first floor of Alleegasse No. 72, near the Karlskirche and the Polytechnic Institute, where Karl was pursuing his studies.

(1382) *To Anton Felix Schindler, Vienna*

[Autograph in the Deutsche Staatsbibliothek, Berlin]

[BADEN, *May*, 1825]

Please let us have the corrected and attested copies, together with the originals, for they are to be sent to St. Petersburg today —

I earnestly beg you to enquire from Smetana when his consulting hour is now and whether he is in Vienna. My stomach is not yet in order. Let me know whether you can come to dinner today —

Vale.

(1383) *To Dr. Anton Braunhofer, Vienna*

[Autograph in the Beethovenhaus, Bonn]

[BADEN, *May*, 1825]

MOST EXCELLENT AND AMAZINGLY INTELLIGENT SIR,

We thank you for *the advice which was well given and well followed* by means of the *wheels* of your inventive genius; and we inform you that in consequence we now feel very well.

Our heart and soul are inclined to overflow and might therefore cause you, Sir, some inconvenience. Hence we are observing a reverent silence.

BEETHOVEN

(1384) *To Joseph Henikstein & Co., Vienna*

[Autograph in the Stadtbibliothek, Vienna]

[BADEN, *May*, 1825]

P.P.

I do most urgently request you to tell my Karl what happened at the time to Prince Galitzin's bill of exchange and whether you were able to give only 215 gulden instead of 225 for it. For I am not always satisfied with what my brother does; and it would grieve me if you should have been shabbily treated in that transaction. — Further, I should like to know whether you received a letter dated April 29th from Prince Galitzin to *yourself* or whether you have never received any communication from him. For he wrote to me *that he had written to you as well.*[1] Finally, please be so kind as to forward to St. Petersburg for me a parcel which is too large to be sent by letter post — Further, I am having my quartet copied for the Prince; the quicker this is done, the better will it please His Excellency to receive it.[2] But I find it somewhat too bulky to send by letter post — I await your kind replies about these matters and remain with all due respect your most devoted

BEETHOVEN

(1385) *To Dr. Anton Braunhofer*

[Autograph in the collection of the late Ernest Horch]

[VIENNA], June 4, [1825]

In the evening of June 4th when I did not find my esteemed friend Braunhofer at home —

BEETHOVEN

(1386) *To Karl van Beethoven, Vienna*

[Autograph not traced] [4]

BADEN, June 9, 1825

I hope at any rate that you are coming here on Saturday.[5] I ask in vain for an answer — God be with me and with you.

As always, your faithful father

I have written to Herr von Reisser telling him to ask you to come here on Saturday. The carriage leaves Vienna at six

---

[1] For Galitzin's letter to Beethoven of April 29, 1825, see *TDR* V, 564.
[2] Beethoven is obviously referring to the second Galitzin quartet, Op. 132, which was not dispatched, however, until February, 1826.
[3] This two-part canon is listed in *KHV*. as WoO 190.
[4] Text taken from *TDR* V, 529-530.
[5] Beethoven was writing on Thursday.

o'clock and, I should add, *from the Kugel auf der Wieden.*[1] So if you will only work or study a little more before then, you will not be losing any time. I am sorry to have to cause you this annoyance—You will drive back to Vienna in the same carriage at five o'clock in the afternoon. The carriage has been paid for in advance. So that you may arrive there in time, you can shave here in the morning and you will find a neckcloth and a shirt here too. — All good wishes. Even though I am cross with you, it is not without good cause ; and indeed I should not like to have disbursed so much in order to send *a vulgar man* into the world — I hope to see you for certain — By the way, *if the intrigues have already matured,* let me know this frankly and naturally ; and you will find someone who is always the same, always anxious to further a good cause.

The rooms were advertised again in Tuesday's newspaper. Why could you not do something, at least through somebody else, or ask someone to write, if you were perhaps indisposed ? — I should prefer *not to have to suspect anything else* — You know how I am living here, and, moreover, in this cold weather. To be constantly alone makes me only weaker, for in fact my weakness often takes the form of faintness. Oh, don't hurt me any more. In any case Death with his scythe will not spare me very much longer.

If good rooms could be found for me in the Alleegasse, I would decide to take them.[2]

(1387) *To Joseph Karl Bernard, Vienna*

[*Autograph in the Beethovenhaus, Bonn, H. C. Bodmer collection*]

DEAR FRIEND !   BADEN, *June* 10, [1825]
It would be a good thing if you were to see Karl occasionally. His address is Alleegasse, No. 72. It is the last house in the street. It would be a good thing too if you could supervise his reading, a matter which I myself will discuss with you sometime. His manners are greatly deteriorating. His treatment of me is extremely offensive and is also having a bad effect on my health. — He really ought to have written to me before

[1] An inn 'Zur goldenen Kugel' in the Wiedener Hauptstrasse 249.
[2] Cf. Letter 1380, p. 1203, n. 1.

Sunday. I have now written three letters, all to no purpose; no reply. Because I had to correct him on Sunday (and he absolutely refuses to be corrected) I had to face a behaviour on his part such as I have only experienced in the case of his deceased father, an uncouth fellow, on whom, nevertheless, I showered benefits — I suspect that that monster of a mother is again involved in this little game and that it is partly an intrigue of that gentleman, my brainless and heartless brother, who is already planning to do business with him and who is always out to censure and instruct me (as the sow does to Minerva in Demosthenes [1]) because I refuse to have anything to do with his overfed whore and bastard,[2] and, still less, to live with people who are so very much my inferiors — What is more, it was on his account that I chose Reisser, Deputy Director of the Polytechnic School, to be co-guardian with me, and that too solely *in writing*. As Peters is so rarely in Vienna, I thought that this would be suitable for Karl.[3] But I fear that there is trouble ahead, for I know nothing about Reisser, seeing that I have never met him. That much I have been able to extract from my ass of a brother, apart from his and Herr von R[eisser]'s anxiety that Karl should no longer be with me. How very clever of them! Yet I am still obliged to disburse the money. — I wrote to R[eisser] from Baden only a few days ago, for I was *so* weak that I could hardly attend to anything; and how lovingly I was cared for, all that I shall tell you when we meet. That awful fourth floor, O God, *without a wife*, and what an existence; one is a prey to every stranger — Since you live in the neighbourhood, please go to R[eisser] as well and give him particulars of my qualifications as a guardian, which I enclose below. Tell him that Blöchlinger absolutely refused to have her at his house, that on that account Dr. B[ach] and I had to send for and obtain help from the police and that for the same reason

[1] A Greek saying equivalent to 'teaching your grandmother to suck eggs'. The anecdote connected with Demosthenes is to be found in Plutarch, *Demosthenes*, II, and also in his *Moralia*, 803 D. It was the orator Demades who exclaimed that Demosthenes putting him right was like the sow correcting Athena.

[2] Before her marriage to Johann in 1812 his wife had an illegitimate daughter, Amalie, born in 1807.

[3] Hofrat Karl Peters had been appointed co-guardian on April 8, 1820. But when Karl entered the Polytechnic Institute after Easter, 1825, Reisser, the Deputy Director, replaced Peters as co-guardian.

she is still under police supervision — In this matter I shall remain true to my principles until I die. But if Karl associates with her again in secret or if anyone helps him to do so, people little know how I shall act, for I am now worn out by encountering the most shameful ingratitude for so many sacrifices and for my magnanimous conduct — Do not worry about the oratorio. I shall not fail to let you know when I need your help — Perhaps you and your wife could come out with Karl to Baden one Sunday and dine with me. One can now hire carriages from here to Vienna at reasonable prices — R[eisser] can be seen any time after four o'clock in the afternoon and also after nine o'clock in the morning, but at the latter time, I believe, only at the Polytechnic School and before the classes begin.[1]

(1388) *To Tobias Haslinger, Vienna*

[*Autograph in the Deutsche Staatsbibliothek, Berlin*]

MOST EXCELLENT FELLOW!   BADEN, *June* 12, [1825]

We have patched up something for you, do your best with it; and then you can be sure of a small tip together with a refund of your expenses — In regard to the march with the chorus [2] — you must send me the last proof of this — and also a proof of the overture in $E\flat$ [3] — Out with the trio, the elegy, the cantata, the opera,[4] or I shall play havoc with them, since your rights have already lapsed. It is due entirely to my magnanimity that I am giving you a larger fee for the work than you are giving me — I need the score of the cantata for a few days, because I should like to compose a kind of overture to it.[5] My score is so scattered about that I cannot put it together and should have to have it copied from the parts — Has the Leipziger Musikalische Messzeit[ung] not yet retracted its lying statements about the medal awarded to me by His

---

[1] This letter is not signed.
[2] Op. 114.   [3] Op. 117.
[4] Op. 116, 118, 136 and 'Fidelio'. With the exception of Beethoven's opera all the above works were first published by Steiner or, after Steiner's retirement in July, 1826, by Haslinger.
[5] The cantata 'Der glorreiche Augenblick', Op. 136. There is no evidence that Beethoven carried out his intention.

late Majesty the King of France? [1] For it will certainly be
shabby enough not to send me any more copies. If it does not
retract its statements, I will have the editor and his consump-
tive deputy *harpooned* amongst the whales in Northern waters.—
Why, even Baden, that centre of barbarism, is becoming
enlightened. Instead of writing Guttenbrunn, as they used
to, people now write *Gutenbrun.* But what are the P[ater]
N[ostergasse] people doing? They still write Grosse instead
of Grosze.[2] Well, I remain with *all due* respect, that is to say,
I have no respect whatever for the barbarous P[ater] N[oster-
gasse] people.

Your more devoted (in the comparative)

B———N

Like Mephistopheles P[ater]n[oster]gässl[er] Primus will
again shoot flames of fire out of his jaws —

(1389) To Karl van Beethoven, Vienna

[Autograph in the Deutsche Staatsbibliothek, Berlin] [3]

DEAR SON!   *Tuesday morning,* [BADEN, *June* 14, 1825]
    A little more or less than 21 gulden seems to me the best
amount. Perhaps the landlord can give you better advice —

Trousers   58

$4\frac{1}{2}$

You are receiving herewith 62 gulden 30 kreuzer V.C.
    Let me have an exact account of this sum. It was hard
work to raise it — But indeed for the sake of *one* gulden per
ell it is not worth while not to take the best cloth. Choose,
or perhaps get someone to choose for you, the best of the two
costing about 21 gulden — similarly the best material for the

---

[1] Louis XVIII, who died on September 16, 1824, had subscribed to the
'Missa Solemnis' and had sent Beethoven in February, 1824, a handsome gold
medal, which is now in the Gesellschaft der Musikfreunde, Vienna. The Leipzig
Allgemeine Musikalische Zeitung of November 11, 1824, had, however, denied this.

[2] As usual, Beethoven is making fun of Haslinger's peculiar pronunciation.
The first form with a short o is incorrect, the second with a long o followed by sz is
the correct form of pronunciation and spelling.

[3] Autograph not available. Text taken from *TDR* V, 530.

trousers too — By the way, do not wear your good clothes indoors. Whoever may call, one need not be fully dressed at home. As soon as you come home take off your coat at once and make yourself comfortable in clothes intended for that purpose —

Meanwhile all good wishes — your faithful father

BEN

Postscript

The wench went off yesterday and has not returned. You will see in due course how things are going to turn out. The old beast was very anxious that the wench should leave, because she had no peace with that wild animal devoid of purpose and reason. God have mercy upon me. Yesterday indeed the dance began with the cooking —

(1390) *To Karl van Beethoven, Vienna*

[*Autograph in the Deutsche Staatsbibliothek, Berlin*] [1]

MY DEAR SON !   BADEN, *June* 15, [1825]

I trust that you have received the 62 gulden, 30 kreuzer V.C. — you could also have another pair of trousers made of the same cloth. Do so. I hope that you have chosen the best cloth at about 21 gulden. On such occasions one must not deny oneself the best for the sake of a few gulden. From the grey cloth for trousers you could have two pairs made. In your calculation you may add what the additional tailoring and so forth costs and I will meet the extra expense — the left hand should not know what the right hand is doing — That is how noble-minded people act. Unfortunately you yourself are to blame if you have to be reminded of this — Don't forget to go to Fries [2] — Aurora must not only wake you, but also lend wings to your activity — Now for the daily domestic matters. The damsel did come, but she is not going to stay. Meanwhile I have talked to the old woman *like an old man* and *said as much* as one can say to such people —

---

[1] Autograph not available. Text taken from *TDR* V, 530.

[2] The forms of this name vary in the German editions. Nohl and Thayer have 'Riess'. This is not impossible, because Ferdinand Ries had a brother, F. J. Ries, living in Vienna, who was musical and is frequently mentioned in Smart's journals. Prelinger has 'Reisser'. Kalischer has 'Fries'.

Away with that damned nonsense —
My brother Asinaccio [1] has written to me — What I find
most trying of all is to be alone at table.   And really it is to
be wondered at that I can compose here *even tolerably well* —
Perhaps I shall come into town on Saturday, and then *perhaps*
at six o'clock you could drive back with me to Baden? —
Now all good wishes, son of my heart, but deserve the designation.   Take what you need.   Whatever else you need, I will
buy for you when I go into Vienna — I embrace you.   Be
my good, hardworking, noble son as I am always
                                        Your faithful father —

I should just like to know that the money has arrived
safely.   Has the crammer turned up?

(1391) *To Karl van Beethoven, Vienna*

[Autograph in the Deutsche Staatsbibliothek, Berlin] [2]

DEAR SON!   BADEN, *June* 28, [1825]
   Since you perhaps like to bathe in this heat, I am sending
you another two gulden.   But I insist that everything be put
down in writing both conto as well as by those who have
received something from you.[3]   For proofs of the mistakes you
made are the blue cloth and the three gulden for the mirror.
You are already a Viennese although I hope that you will not
become a sport of Viennese currency.   Nevertheless it does
you no harm at your age to have to give a full account of
the money you receive, since you do not reach your majority
until you are 24 and since you yourself, if you had money of
your own, would at your age have to give a full account of it
to your guardians — Do not make me recall incidents of long
ago, which would be easy to do but only painful for me ; and
in the end you would just say as usual 'after all you are a very
good guardian' or something similar.   If only you had some
depth of character, you would always act quite differently —
Well, to turn to this contemptible tribe of domestics.   The

[1] Wretched ass.   See Letter 1441.
[2] Autograph not available.   Text taken from *TDR* V, 532.
[3] Beethoven evidently means that Karl himself should keep an account of the
sums he disburses as well as the recipients of the sums.

kitchen-maid disappeared yesterday but returned later. What it is all about is very difficult to fathom in the case of such an old witch, who is now all smiles again and refuses to admit that *she was the loser when the accounts were made up*. What do you say to that? [1]

(1392) *To Karl van Beethoven, Vienna*

[*Autograph in the Deutsche Staatsbibliothek, Berlin*] [2]

DEAR SON!   [BADEN, *June*, 1825]
    Here are the 90 gulden. See that you get a receipt of a few lines for this amount. Then it is not so necessary for the housewife, although it is customary everywhere in the case of those who are in the care of a guardian — My wafers have come to an end — Could you not send me a small box of them here in some way? Let me know at once when you have received this letter — God be with you; and do all that is possible so that I may be delivered from this old devil —
    Don't let yourself be drawn into secret intrigues with my worthy brother — and in general don't do anything secretly against me, against your most faithful father

BEN
Good night [3]

All good wishes, all good
wishes — from the little old witch
and Satanas and me?!
You have only to enter
the sum in the receipt;
that is all you have
to do. H.[4] is receiving
his instructions herewith.

---

[1] The remaining portion of this letter was written on two pages of a sheet, half of which has been torn off. Hence what is left is quite unintelligible. The mutilated passages are quoted, however, in Kal. no. 1087.
    [2] Autograph not available. Text taken from *TDR* V, 531-532.
    [3] According to *TDR* V, 532, these two words are written at the side of the last page.
    [4] Probably Henikstein.

(1393) *To Karl van Beethoven, Vienna*

[*Autograph in the Deutsche Staatsbibliothek, Berlin*] ¹

[BADEN, *early July*, 1825]

I am delighted, my dear son, that you are happy in your present surroundings and, seeing that this is so, that you are also actively seizing upon everything that is necessary — I did not recognise your handwriting.   I am only enquiring, it is true, about the *sense* and the *meaning*, for you must now achieve the fine external appearance — If it is far too difficult for you to come here, then do not bother — but if it is at all possible for you to do so, well then, in my solitude I shall look forward to having a human heart beside me — Should you be able to come, the housekeeper will help you to leave Vienna at five o'clock, so that you may still save some time for your studies —

With all my heart I embrace you,

Your faithful father.

Don't forget to bring the morning paper and Ries's letter ² —

(1394) *To Karl van Beethoven, Vienna*

[*Autograph in the Deutsche Staatsbibliothek, Berlin*] ³

DEAR SON — DEAR BOY —   [BADEN, *July* 10, 1825]

The point about Bonheur ⁴ should be mentioned, for in the case of Lichnowsky (the late Prince) I have already experienced that these so-called great lords do not like to see *an artist* who in any case is already *their* equal, in affluent circumstances as well — Voila le même cas ⁵ — Votre Altesse !   In the

¹ Autograph not available.   Text taken from *TDR* V, 539.

² According to *TDR* V, 539, this remark is written in pencil beside the address. It probably refers to a letter from Ries to Beethoven of June 9, 1825, describing a performance of the ninth symphony at Aix-la-Chapelle.   Cf. Letter 1351, p. 1178, n. 2, and *TDR* V, 168-169.

³ Autograph not available.   Text taken from *TDR* V, 533-535.

⁴ Here Beethoven is referring to a remark in Prince Galitzin's latest letter to him of June 21, 1825, quoted in *TDR* V, 566.   Galitzin says in this letter: 'J'ambitionne le bonheur de faire personnellement votre connaissance'.

⁵ According to *TDR* V, 533, there are two words deleted and illegible before 'Votre Altesse'.

text of the letter use occasionally V.A. — on the cover of the letter A son Altesse Monseigneur Le Prince etc. — it is impossible to know whether he has not the same weakness — I am enclosing a sheet which I have already signed — By the way, you might add that he must not be annoyed by newspaper gossip which, if I desired, would loudly blow my trumpet. Say that the quartet was admittedly a failure the first time, because it was performed by Schuppanzigh, who owing to his stoutness now requires more time than he did formerly to master a work quickly; and add that many other circumstances contributed to its failure and that I warned him that it would be a failure.[1] For although Schuppanzigh and two others draw pensions from persons of princely rank, yet the quartet is no longer the same as it was when all the players were constantly together.[2] On the other hand the quartet has been splendidly performed six times by other artists and received with the greatest applause. On one evening it was played twice in succession and *again* after supper; and a violinist called Böhm performed this work at his benefit concert — And even now I still have to give it to other musicians.

In the letter to Peters at Leipzig call it a '*grand quartet*' — make haste so that he too may reply quickly — these wretched business dealings are necessary, because we must get on our high horses —

Close this letter to my brother and give it to the post — Tell the tailor in the Kärntnerstrasse to fetch the Sanclotin for a pair of trousers for me and to make them long, but without a strap, cashmere and cloth trousers. It can also be fetched at Wolfmayer's after — —[3] —

The cobbler has his shop in town in the Spiegelgasse almost immediately after one enters it from the Graben. He is called Magnus Senn bei der Stadt Paris No. 1093[4] — Go to Henikstein and *be frank*. Then we may *find out how that wretched fellow has acted*. It would be advisable to be fully informed before we write the letter to Galitzin — I can well believe that people are trying to get something else for you

---

[1] Op. 127, when it was first performed by the Schuppanzigh quartet on March 6, 1825.   [2] I.e. when it was the Razumovsky quartet.
[3] According to *TDR* V, 534, there is here an illegible word. For Wolfmayer cf. Letter 487, p. 464, n. 2.   [4] Not identified.

for the winter — We shall discuss this — Before you come here on Saturday ask about knives *in the Naglergasse.* These you could deliver first. The old woman has made a mess of things —

When driving out here yesterday I met Clement, Holz, Linke and Pechatschek at Neudorf.[1] They had all been to visit me while I was in town — They wanted to have the first quartet again. Holz even drove back here again from Neudorf and dined with me in the evening. Whereupon I gave him the quartet to take back —

The attachment of first-rate artists is not to be despised and indeed affords one pleasure —

Write to me as soon as you have spoken to Henikstein — To the overture in C you should add the dedication to Galitzin.[2] If the g[entlemen] undertake to dispatch it, give it to them, but preferably in a closed parcel.

God be with you. Well, I expect a letter from you for certain, my dear son. God be with you and me.

Things will soon be over with your faithful father.

All good wishes, little rascal.

NB. In connexion with the overture remember to say in your letter to Galitzin that an announcement has already been made to the effect that it is to be engraved and published and dedicated to him — [3]

(1395) *To ?* [4]

[Autograph in the Beethovenhaus, Bonn, H. C. Bodmer collection]

DEAR AND ESTEEMED SIR ! BADEN, *Monday, July* 11, 1825

I am coming into town to-morrow and I must see you. Please inform the bearer of this letter at what hour I may

---

[1] This was on Saturday, July 9th. For a note on Holz see Letter 1409, p. 1230, n. 2. Franz Pechatschek (1793–1840), born in Vienna, the son of a popular Bohemian composer of light music, became a famous violinist. In 1820 he was appointed leader of the Stuttgart orchestra and after many successful tours settled at Karlsruhe as leader of the local orchestra. [2] Op. 124.

[3] According to *TDR* V, 535, this NB. is added at the side of the page.

[4] The autograph is not addressed. The note, which may have been intended for Dr. Anton Braunhofer or Johann Baptist Bach, was first published with a facsimile by the present editor in an article on 'The text of Beethoven's letters' in *Music and Letters*, vol. xxxiv, no. 3 (July, 1953), pp. 212–223.

come to you, for eight o'clock in the evening would be too late for me. I shall be in Vienna at about ten o'clock and I am only awaiting your command *when to present myself to you* after that hour?

Your admirer and friend
BEETHOVEN

(1396) *To Karl van Beethoven, Vienna*

[*Autograph in the Deutsche Staatsbibliothek, Berlin*] [1]

Come soon! [BADEN, *shortly after July* 11, 1825]
Come soon!
Come soon!

MY DEAR SON!

All right — Bring G[alitzin]'s letter with you again.[2] I myself have hardly read it — The day before yesterday I had a visit from my Signor Fratello [3] with his worthy brother-in-law [4] — What a *miserable fellow* — The old witch, who yesterday had another *shocking* lapse of memory, is bringing you his reply about his *brother-in-law's book*. If you find in his reply no guarantee about it, send this letter at once to the miserable fellow — If Cato shouted to Caesar *this man* and *we*, what is one to do against such a person? [5]

I am not closing this letter — The day after tomorrow will be time enough — It is getting too late —

I am pressing my loving seal on your dear loyalty to and affection for me — If you delay, then stay where you are — As always your loving father who cares for you.

[1] Autograph not available. Text taken from a facsimile in the Beethovenarchiv, Bonn.
[2] Prince Galitzin's letter dated June 21st, quoted in *TDR* V, 566.
[3] I.e. Mr. Brother.
[4] Leopold Obermayr. Cf. Letter 1078, p. 946, n. 3.
[5] The context of this saying has not been traced.

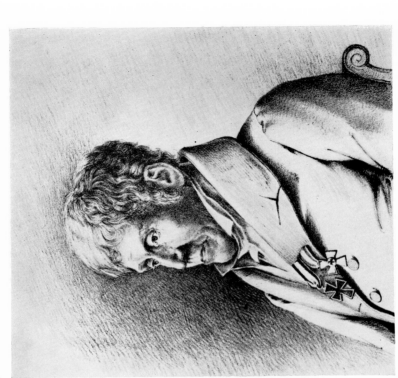

FRANZ GERHARD WEGELER (1765–1848)
From an engraving by an unknown artist
(*Bildarchiv der Oesterreichischen Nationalbibliothek, Vienna*)

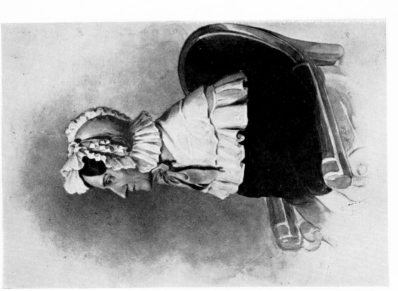

FRAU NANETTE STREICHER (1769–1833)
From a water-colour drawing by an unknown artist
(*Historisches Museum der Stadt Wien*)

(1397) *To Karl van Beethoven, Vienna*

[*Autograph in the Deutsche Staatsbibliothek, Berlin*] [1]

[BADEN, *July* 13, 1825]

Send off the enclosed letter at once to my pseudo-brother [2]
— Add a few lines.   It is impossible to let this state of affairs
go on any longer.   Today there was no soup, no beef, not
even an egg — finally I got *a small cut off a joint* from the
inn — The other day when *Holz* stayed on,[3] we had hardly
anything to eat in the evening.   Her impudent, indecent
behaviour as well as her incompetence — I told her today
that I would put up with her until the end of this month at
most —

That is all for today.   All that we have to do about the
Magistrat is for me to write a note stating that you are authorized to draw the money.   By the way, it would be a good
thing if you would enquire at the same time what should be
done so that these bank shares could be exchanged for Rothschild lottery tickets [4] — I am merely adding today that I
shall always regard you as my son who is dear to me and who
deserves my affection —

However little I may need to be *fully* fed with the lower
type of food, as you know, yet all this is really too bad ; and,
what is more, every moment of the day to run the risk of being
poisoned —

All good wishes.   Take care of your health in this heat.
Dear son, do keep your good health.   Avoid everything that
can enfeeble and impair your youthful strength.   All good
wishes.   Dear God, how much better it would be to talk to
one another —

Ever your faithful father who presses you to his heart.

[1] Autograph not available.   Text taken from *TDR* V, 535-536.
[2] Letter 1398.
[3] This was on July 9th, after the meeting at Neudorf.   Cf. Letter 1394, p. 1215,
n. 1.
[4] See Letter 1423, p. 1243.

(1398) *To Johann van Beethoven, Gneixendorf*

[Autograph in the Royal College of Music]

DEAREST BROTHER!   BADEN, *July* 13, 1825

Since you obtained the *book* for me so successfully, I now request you to see that it is returned to its *owner in Vienna* — Another very pretty kettle of fish — As for your desire that I should visit you, I already expressed my opinion long ago. I beg you never to mention the subject again, for in this you will find me, as always, adamant. Spare me further details, since I dislike to have to repeat unpleasant statements. *You* are happy, and that is certainly what I desire — so let it be, for each of us is happiest in *his own sphere*. I used your rooms only once; but the stove almost made me ill, and that is why I stayed there only once — And as I now have taken rooms of my own, I shall hardly ever use the other room which you offer me — When you write, do *at least seal* the letters and address them to Karl in Vienna, for a letter from your home to Baden is too expensive — Once more I urgently request you to return the book which belongs to the art mechanic in the Graben. Indeed such slackness is almost inconceivable and I am not a little embarrassed — Therefore the book, the book! Send it to Karl in Vienna quickly and speedily —

All good wishes, my dear and worthy brother.[1] God be with you.

Yours
LUDWIG

(1399) *To Karl van Beethoven, Vienna*

[Autograph in the Deutsche Staatsbibliothek, Berlin] [2]

[BADEN, *shortly after July* 13, 1825]

The old goose is following you with this note — She did give you the quills and so you have lied to me again — Alas! alas! — All good wishes. I am merely awaiting your report

---

[1] In this last sentence Beethoven abandons the Du-form and says 'Leben Sie wohl, mein werter Herr Bruder', using a rather stiff form of address.
[2] Autograph not available. Text taken from *TDR* V, 538.

about the book — She is going to Kathel today, so she won't have much time to play foolish tricks —

Surely God will set me free, Libera me Domine de illis etc.¹ —

(1400) *To Karl van Beethoven, Vienna*

[Autograph in the Deutsche Staatsbibliothek, Berlin] ²

DEAR SON!   [BADEN, *c. July* 14, 1825]
    You will understand everything if you read the enclosures — Write this letter to Schlesinger

To Schlesinger
in
Berlin

to be delivered
at Schlesinger's
art and bookshop.³

Word several passages more suitably. I believe that we could probably count on getting 80 — *If necessary*, keep back the letter to Galitzin, but send off the one to Schlesinger on Saturday ⁴ — You have doubtless received the parcel. Please bring some *shaving soap* for me and at least two *razors*. The knife-grinder has six. Here are also two gulden in case you have anything to pay for. But do be economical, for you are always being given too much money —

    Well, there is nothing to be done about it, a Viennese will always be a Viennese. I was glad when I could help my poor parents. What a difference compared with you, in the matter of your behaviour to me — Thoughtless fellow. All good wishes.

Your faithful father

Bring the newspaper stuff with you again —

¹ Lord, deliver me from them etc. Possibly Beethoven adapted to his own context the opening phrase of the Responsory of the Absolution which follows the Requiem Mass 'Libera me, Domine, de morte'.
² Autograph not available. Text taken from *TDR* V, 536.
³ See Letter 1403.
⁴ For Beethoven's draft of the letter to Prince Galitzin see Letter 1405.
    The letter to A. M. Schlesinger, Berlin, drafted by Beethoven, was sent off by Karl on July 19th. Saturday, the day which Beethoven suggests, was July 16th.

This time you have a good deal to do, but you will surely write before Sunday. Be sure not to flatter that Miserablatzin ¹ — He is a weak customer etc.

I embrace etc.

No better!

(1401) *To Karl van Beethoven, Vienna*

[*Autograph in the Deutsche Staatsbibliothek, Berlin*] ²

DEAR SON!   BADEN, *July* 15, [1825]

When writing to Schlesinger you should enquire too whether Prince Radziwill is in Berlin ³ — About the 80 ducats you may add that these need only be paid in A.C. gulden, that is to say, reckoning the ducat as equal to 4 gulden 30 kreuzer. However, I leave that to you. In any case it is not too much for *him*, seeing that he has England and France as well — You must also express yourself clearly about the draft for four months — Mayseder gets 50 ducats from Artaria for violin variations — In any case you must always make these people see that my ill health etc. and other circumstances now compel me to consider my own interests more than I used to do. I find it difficult to haggle, but I must do so — How depressed I am when I again feel so lonely among all these people! Do forward the letter to my brother so that the book may be returned.⁴ What a low trick. Moreover I should like to do as much as possible to improve my hearing. And at Baden I should have time to do so. What unfortunate circumstances, and to have such a brother! — Alas, alas! — All good wishes. I embrace you with all my heart.

Your faithful father

Don't neglect anything. You must make things easier for yourself by getting up early in the morning — If you can't manage to do so, don't come on Sunday.⁵ But in that case you must write. At the moment it is not worth your while

¹ I.e. Galitzin. See Letter 1405.
² Autograph not available. Text taken from *TDR* V, 537.
³ See Letter 1403, p. 1223, n. 1.
⁴ Cf. Letter 1398.
⁵ Beethoven was writing on Friday.

to write, since we can discuss everything, that is to say, if you are able to come here on Sunday. —

(1402) *To Karl van Beethoven, Vienna*

[Autograph in the Deutsche Staatsbibliothek, Berlin] ¹

DEAR SON !   BADEN, *Monday, July* 18, [1825]
You will see from this letter what can easily be deduced — If only you would *observe moderation.* Success is crowning my efforts. Do not by adopting false opinions lay the foundations of your own unhappiness. Be truthful and accurate too in the lists of your expenses. Let the theatre go for the time being — Follow your guide and father, follow him whose one thought is always for your moral welfare, and who is also not quite useless to you for your *ordinary* material existence — This Herr Thal will call on you.² He will be with Henikstein too. If you think it advisable you can give him the overture as well.³ He is staying here for three weeks. You may suggest that he might dine here some time, on a Sunday, of course, when a certain little rascal will be with us too, and of course very early. He could drive out here in a carriage which I would send for him. Be on your most mannerly behaviour in the company of this man. For the best and noblest people are united through art and science ; and your future career does not exclude you from such a society — I should like you to take a carriage and drive to Rampel, if you have the time. In regard to the copying of the quartet you may tell him that I write quite differently now, much more legibly than during my illness and that this quartet would have to be copied twice and immediately.⁴ I would then send it into town. Somebody here has offered to copy it too. But I don't know what his work is like. At first indeed

---

¹ Autograph not available. Text taken from *TDR* V, 537-538.
² According to Prince Galitzin's letter of June 21st (see *TDR* V, 566), Thal, who delivered the Prince's letter by hand, was the son of a prominent business man in St. Petersburg.
³ Op. 124.
⁴ No doubt Beethoven is referring to the second Galitzin quartet, Op. 132, which Rampel copied in August, 1825. See *KHV.* 401. This quartet was first published in score by Moritz Schlesinger, Paris, in September, 1827.

I was not inclined to entrust too much to the *wood of Christ* or to the chip of the *wood of Christ* ¹ —
Write at once. The old goose will go into Vienna perhaps the day after tomorrow — All good wishes. Follow my precepts.
Your faithful father who warmly embraces you.

Perhaps you will go to Henikstein with this Herr Thal. But you must not ask about the money too insistently ² —

(1403) *To Adolf Martin Schlesinger, Berlin*

[MS in the Beethovenhaus, Bonn, H. C. Bodmer collection] ³

SIR !   BADEN, *July* 15-19, 1825
    I have received with great pleasure your communication of June 24th together with the Allgemeine Berliner Musikalische Zeitung. Please arrange for it to be sent to me regularly in future. When turning over its pages I noticed a few articles which I immediately recognized as the products of that gifted Herr Marx.⁴ I hope that he will continue to reveal more and more what is noble and true in the sphere of art. And surely that ought gradually to throw discredit upon the mere *counting of syllables.*
    Since you ask me, I am letting you know that I could let you have two grand new violin quartets ; my fee would be 80 ducats (*for each work*).⁵ I must add that for some time now people everywhere have been clamouring for my works. Thus for each of these quartets I have already been offered the sum of 80 ducats. So if you would like to have them at this price,

¹ I.e. Karl Holz. For a note on Holz see Letter 1409, p. 1230, n. 2.
² Evidently the fees to be paid by Galitzin.
³ There are two versions extant of this letter, one a draft in Beethoven's handwriting dated July 15th, the other the above letter, dated July 19th, written by Karl, signed by Beethoven and despatched to A. M. Schlesinger. Both versions are now in the H. C. Bodmer collection. Both versions are reproduced in Unger, nos. 113 and 114. Beethoven's draft is longer, rather confused and repetitive.
⁴ Adolph Bernhard Marx (1795–1866), an eminent composer and musicologist, had founded in 1824 the *Berliner Allgemeine Musikalische Zeitung* which he edited until its cessation in 1830. In the first numbers Marx had discussed Beethoven's symphonies and two of his late pianoforte sonatas, Op. 110 and 111. In 1859 Marx published his valuable study in two volumes of Beethoven's life and works.
⁵ Op. 132 and Op. 130. Both were published posthumously, the former by Moritz Schlesinger, Paris, the latter by Artaria, Vienna.

I will gladly give you the preference. This offer ought to be quite welcome to you particularly as you can send the quartets to Paris and London as well. Since my friend Ries is no longer in London, I myself send nothing more there, because the correspondence and the arrangements involved take up too much of my time.

Should you care to accept my offer, please let me know this very promptly, because this matter cannot be delayed. You could send me drafts on a good house in Vienna, payable in three or even four months. As soon as I receive them, I will send you the quartets without delay.

But in any case please do not be slow to reply. You need only address the letter to *Vienna*. I shall certainly receive it although I am staying at Baden for the sake of my health, which is impaired.

With kindest regards, I remain, Sir, your most devoted

PS.   LUDWIG VAN BEETHOVEN

    Is Prince Radziwill
      in Berlin ? [1]

(1404) *To Karl van Beethoven, Vienna*

[Autograph in the Deutsche Staatsbibliothek, Berlin] [2]

[BADEN, *July*, 1825]
Today is Friday,
tomorrow
Saturday.

Here comes Satanas — her seething wrath and her madness have abated a little today, but in the meantime — should she want to apply to you, refer her to me the day after tomorrow — the whole week I have had to suffer and to endure my sufferings like a saint — away with that beastly rabble. What a reproach it is to our civilization that we need the services of such people at all, that we have to have around us people whom we despise — Go with her to the Karolinentor tomorrow about the soda water, as you did before. If the *small tankards are just as pure* as the large ones you could take some of them. But I think that *the large ones ought to be safer*. Ce depend de

---

[1] This postscript is in Beethoven's handwriting. Cf. Letter 1401, p. 1220, n. 3.
[2] Autograph not available. Text taken from *TDR* V, 533.

votre esprit votre distinction etc. — Now all good wishes, dear son, see to it that we get the pure soda water, *not the artificially produced kind.* Do go with her or else I might be given who knows what — Well, all good wishes, most excellent little rascal. We are rather attached to you. We expect to see you the day after tomorrow at eight o'clock. You will certainly have breakfast: provided that it is not, as usual, *late breakfast* — Ah au diable avec ce grands coquins de Neveux — Alles vous en — Soyés mon fils mon fils bien aimé — Adieu — Je vous baise Votre père sincere Come toujours

(1405) *To Prince Nikolas Galitzin, St. Petersburg*

[*Autograph not traced*] [1]

VOTRE ALTESSE !   BADEN, [*late July*, 1825]

In regard to the contestation [2] Zeuner [3] a parfaitement raison — la viola a un ré♭ dans cet passage c'est à dire

 les motifs se trouvent deja dans le thême

d'ecrire ainsi, but, what is more, on account of the melody, which always deserves to have the preference over everything else. By the way, this passage is based on the chord of the $\frac{6}{4}$

 in spite of the in the first violin part,

which is nothing but a grace note *or* an ornament (anticipating the next chord), a device which every true musician will employ,[4] inasmuch as Nature is founded on Art and, again, Art is founded on Nature — But if I had written

---

[1] Taken from the facsimile in Sonneck, p. 40. The autograph, an untidily written and unsigned draft of a letter which may have been dispatched, was then in private ownership in America. It is Beethoven's rather confused reply to a lost letter from Galitzin dated *c.* June 13, 1825, in which he describes 'une contestation entre des musiciens de la capitale' about a particular passage in the Andante con moto movement of Op. 127. See *TDR* V, 566.

[2] Beethoven is referring to Galitzin's remark in his letter of June 21, 1825. See *TDR* V, 566.

[3] Karl Traugott Zeuner (1775–1841), born at Dresden, became a pianist and a composer. After prolonged travelling he settled in St. Petersburg, where he later became the teacher of Glinka. Zeuner had met Beethoven during his stay in Vienna.

[4] I.e. a perfectly normal musical procedure.

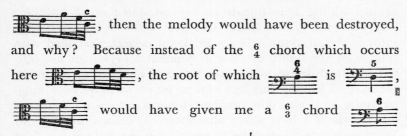

, then the melody would have been destroyed,
and why ? Because instead of the $\frac{6}{4}$ chord which occurs
here , the root of which is ,
would have given me a $\frac{6}{3}$ chord
based on the chord of F minor , which would have
been contrary to the whole trend of the melody and harmony
and altogether too startling. In short, Zeuner a parfaitement
raison ; and I am delighted that such a capable artist instantly
guessed my intentions — The new quartet in A minor is now
finished [1] and I am endeavouring to send it to Y.E. as quickly as
possible.[2] In my next letter I will deal with several matters
and I shall hope in this way to dispel some dark clouds which
I fancy are trying to form themselves against me in Y.E.'s
mind. Believe me when I say that my supreme aim is that
my art should be welcomed by the noblest and most cultured
people. Unfortunately we are dragged down from the super-
natural element in art only too rudely into the earthly and
human sides of life. Yet is it not precisely they who are
related to us ? And without really wanting or being able
to amass riches, we must see to it that they in general
shall bless our memory, seeing that, when all is said and done,
we are not great Princes who, as we know, merely leave the
welfare of their subjects to the future and to God [3] — Finally,
let me just add that I have heard what difficulties confront
me in the matter of roubles and ducats etc. Hence I beg
Y.E. not to make the slightest effort in this respect. I am
perfectly satisfied if the same arrangements are made as
hitherto, the more so as you are allowing me to publish these
quartets at once. In this connexion I have just availed
myself of Y.E.'s permission in respect of the first quartet and
have given it to a publisher [4] — Please do not be offended

[1] Op. 132 was finished in August, 1825.
[2] The second Galitzin quartet, Op. 132, was not sent to the Prince until
February, 1826.   [3] No doubt Beethoven is referring to his nephew.
[4] Op. 127 was published by Schott in 1826, the parts in March and the score
in June.

at my adding four ducats to my estimate; as I am very
conscientious, I must point out that I am still two gulden
short in my account. As I said, I am perfectly satisfied with
the fee for the quartets. For so eminent a personage as yourself has to disburse in all directions. Therefore give me the
pleasure of leaving this last sum to be decided by your magnanimity — I am now giving Hönigstein ¹ two overtures,²
one of which I have taken the liberty of dedicating to Your
Excellency; and I shall be extremely delighted if you consider
this dedication worthy of you — May Heaven bless you and
your family. Please count me among the most grateful of
your acquaintances; and thus I remain, Y.E., and so forth.
The third quartet too is almost finished.³

(1406) *To Karl van Beethoven, Vienna*

[*Autograph in the Deutsche Staatsbibliothek, Berlin*] ⁴

DEAR SON!   [BADEN], *Tuesday, August 2*, [1825]
See that this enclosure catches the post at once, i.e.
tomorrow (Wednesday).⁵ On account of proof-reading *it is
still extremely necessary to hurry* as much as possible ⁶ — We
must have nothing more to do with this wicked old woman —
Hardly anything to eat, and at the same time the brazen
nature and the impertinence of that veritable old witch — and
paying her as much as I do — I fancy that I shall have to let
the pseudo-brother come and that I probably ought to take
on again the one who looked after us that winter in the Kothgasse and who really was a *good* cook —
Write me a few words — send them to me tomorrow.
Here is another florin. Don't forget to bathe — Keep well.
Take care of yourself so that you do not *fall ill* — and only
spend your money in *the right way* — Be my dear son. What

¹ Joseph Henikstein, the Viennese wholesale merchant and banker. Cf. Letter
984, p. 858, n. 2.
² Op. 124, dedicated to Prince Galitzin, and probably Op. 115.
³ The third Galitzin quartet, Op. 130, was not sent to the Prince until the
spring of 1826.
⁴ Autograph not available. Text taken from *TDR* V, 540.
⁵ I.e. Beethoven's letter to Schott of the same date (Letter 1407).
⁶ I.e. with the copying of the A minor quartet, Op. 132.

unheard of dissonance there would be if you were *false* to me, in the way some people indeed declare that you really are —
   God be with you.

Your faithful father —

NB. Be sure to
deliver the letter
tomorrow (Wednesday) —
I too know nothing about
the *knives*. Moreover I am
beginning to run short of
cut quills also —

(1407) *To Bernhard Schotts Söhne, Mainz*

[Autograph in the Fürstlich Fürstenbergische Hofbibliothek, Donaueschingen]

GENTLEMEN !   BADEN, *August* 2, 1825

   You must see *whether* in the Mass a few passages here and there are *exactly* as I have written them out here

Bar 39

1) In the Kyrie $\frac{3}{2}$

After the Christe where the Kyrie comes in again

2) a rest of half a bar is missing in the clarinets

Bar 87

3) In the Gloria at bar 10, the second flute part, instead of

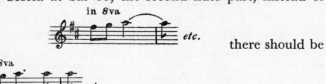

there should be

 etc.

1227

4) In the same portion at bar 87 of Allegro ma non troppo

e ben marcato

N3 : Bassi con pedale

In the Credo at the Incarnatus at the very beginning the four upper vocal parts should be marked 'solo' and the four lower vocal parts 'coro'. In general this should be observed throughout the work —

I received only a fortnight ago the numbers of the Leipziger Musikalische Zeitung where I found your subscription terms of last April. Why you concealed them from me I cannot think. And indeed I fancy it would be better to insert notices of this kind in the general public newspapers, since musical periodicals reach too small a public — Moreover I ought to have been specially informed about this publication, for I have not yet *sent you the title of the Mass*. This shall now be done in a few days. Hence I should prefer you to postpone a little longer the dispatch of the copies. For provided I have time to do so, I will let you have the tempi with the metronome markings and so forth as well. The symphony is going to be dedicated to a great lord.[1] The same thing applies to the Mass, although indeed in this case everything has already been decided.[2] Such is not yet the case with the symphony — So far as I am concerned, not a note of what belongs to you will be given away. You know all about that. There was a danger that the overture might be stolen for the second time.[3] Fortunately I discovered this twelve days ago ; and, thank Heaven, the attempt was completely frustrated. Therefore just keep calm about this. I should not have mentioned it to you, did I not think that you might hear something and harbour unfounded suspicions about *me*. I

[1] Beethoven's first intention, according to Letter 1175, p. 1032, was to dedicate Op. 125 to Ries. Then he thought of the Austrian Emperor. In the end the symphony was dedicated to the King of Prussia.

[2] The 'Missa Solemnis' was dedicated to the Archduke Rudolph.

[3] Op. 124. For particulars of the first stealing cf. Letter 1343, p. 1165.

have never done anything of the kind.   And people will never find me anything but extremely honourable —

The day before yesterday I received your letter of July 19th through Frau von Streicher.

Apart from that one letter I have received *none* — and moreover, so far as the chief points are concerned, I shall never write anything more to you about them.   For your previous persistent invitations to me were the sole reason for my letters.   Compliments leave me quite cold.   Let me add that I shall soon commission my worthy brother at [Linz and] ¹ Herr Gottfried Weber ² to arraign Herr B[ernhard] Schott before a court of law, in the way I am accustomed to deal here with the people in the little Paternostergasse and other places — I have informed you of the title and the dedication of the overture and also of the dedication of the quartet ³ — All good, very good wishes.   I am curious to hear who will pounce on your letter to me of the — — —

Your most devoted

BEETHOVEN

(1408) *To Johann van Beethoven, Gneixendorf*

[*Autograph in the Stadtbibliothek, Vienna*]

BADEN, *August* 4, 1825

MOST EXCELLENT AND WORTHY BROTHER!

I request you, you, you ⁴ to come here as soon as possible, for I can't put up any longer with this old witch who 200 years ago would certainly have been burnt.   It would be too low for a man like myself to give all the reasons — why — It is easy to talk about taverns, but that solution lasts only as long as people are here — It will not solve the difficulty any

---

¹ In the autograph the paper is torn here.   The words in brackets have been supplied by the present editor.

² Gottfried Weber (1779–1839), by profession a lawyer, was also an amateur composer and writer on the theory of music.   Beethoven's brother had suggested in a letter to Schott, dated February 4, 1825, that Gottfried Weber, then living at Mainz, should undertake to correct the proofs of some of the composer's works, a suggestion which Weber turned down very rudely.   See Nohl II, no. 284, note, and *FRBH* II, 401.   Cf. Letter 1349, p. 1175, n. 4.

³ Op. 124 and 127.   Both these works, dedicated to Prince Galitzin, were published by Schott in December, 1825, and March and June, 1826, respectively.

⁴ The German original is 'Sie, euch, ihn'.

more than it did before — The evil nature of this female monster is the chief reason why she makes it impossible for herself to show the smallest signs of goodness — So I beg you to turn up in a few days. Otherwise I shall have again to take up with Herr Schindler who has already been here and kissed *my hand* — But I should like to say again, like the Viennese, 'I kiss my hand', to Mr. *Shitting* — True enough, you too are a rascal and a pseudo-brother — At the same time, if *I must have someone near me*, my brother still has the first claim — I am awaiting your arrival, so let me have a few lines to say when you are coming. In the greatest haste — your most faithful *Fratello*.

All good wishes
Live —
Do live —
May you live —

Adje !! [1]

(1409) *To Karl Holz, Vienna* [2]

[Autograph in the New York Public Library]

[BADEN], *August* 10, [1825]
On the 10th, I repeat, on August 10th

MOST EXCELLENT CHIP !

Most excellent wood of Christ !

Why are you dawdling ? — I blow the wind to Vienna in order to haul you hither in a gale — if only the quartet is here by Friday at least ; but if it is to take even longer, do see that *Karl* brings it out here on *Sunday*. That you will be most cordially welcome if you come yourself, that you know *per se* — Voilà quel home de langue en moi ! — I am astounded

---

[1] A very colloquial form of 'Adieu'.

[2] Karl Holz (1798–1858), who held a minor official appointment in Vienna, was a good amateur violinist who occasionally played in the Schuppanzigh and Böhm quartets. He also added to his income by giving violin lessons. Holz seems to have met Beethoven in 1824. In the summer of 1825 they became close friends; and for over a year Schindler, who strongly disapproved of Holz, made himself scarce and did not resume his association with his beloved master until the onset of the latter's fatal illness in December, 1826.

In a document dated August 30, 1826, Beethoven entrusted to Holz the writing of his biography. See Appendix I (7). For further particulars of Karl Holz see *FRBH* II, 224-226. The German word 'Holz' means 'wood'.

to hear that those blackguards at Mainz have dared to misuse my jest.[1] It is disgraceful. I can solemnly declare that such was not my intention. What I wanted was that Castelli [2] should write a poem based more or less on that sketch of mine, but just under the name of the musical Tobias, and with canons composed by me. Well, as it has been treated *in this way*, we must regard it as a dispensation of Providence; it forms a pendant to Goethe's Bahrdt [3] — *sans comparaison* with any writer whatever. But I fancy that Tobias himself has offended *them* in some way or other. — Et voila the revenge — In any case it's better than finding oneself in the jaws of some monster — I cannot shed tears over it, but must laugh like — If you come on Friday, you will get the best meal in my luxurious household — It is quite possible that I may be entertaining a *secret member of the little Paternostergasse firm* — Piringer will *growl*, he can't *yell*; he is in the same predicament, I fancy, as Schreyvogel, of whom someone said 'that he could neither yell nor rape' [4] — All good wishes, dear Holz, *write and come to me*, do both *at a suitable time* —
In the greatest haste, your friend
BEETHOVEN

(1410) *To Karl van Beethoven, Vienna*

[*Autograph in the Deutsche Staatsbibliothek, Berlin*] [5]

DEAR SON!   BADEN, *August* 11, [1825]

I am in a mortal fright about the quartet.[6] For Holz has taken away the third, fourth, fifth and sixth movements. But the first bars of the third movement are still here, that is to say, thirteen bars of it — *I have heard nothing from Holz* — I wrote to him yesterday. He usually writes. What a terrible

[1] Cf. Letter 1345, p. 1169.
[2] Cf. Letter 423, p. 417, n. 3.
[3] Evidently a reference to Goethe's three-page satire, *Prolog zu den neuesten Offenbarungen Gottes verdeutscht durch Dr. Karl Friedrich Bahrdt* (Giessen, 1774). Bahrdt was a rationalistic professor of theology who seemed to Goethe shallow and pretentious. In this skit the four evangelists appear to Bahrdt in their rude strength and he reminds them that they must be polished up for modern readers.
[4] Beethoven uses the verbs 'schreien' and 'vögeln', which have these meanings. See Letter 1412, p. 1234.
[5] Autograph not available. Text taken from *TDR* V, 542.
[6] The second Galitzin quartet, in A minor, Op. 132.

misfortune if he has lost the manuscript. *Between ourselves, he is a hard drinker.* Make my mind easy as quickly as possible — At Haslinger's you can find out where *Linke* lives. Haslinger was here today. He was very friendly and brought with him the periodicals and other papers of the same kind. He begged me very hard for the new quartets. By the way, never indulge in gossip, for that eventually leads to vulgar wrangles — For God's sake do make my mind easy about the quartet, for that would be a terrible loss. The ideas for it are only jotted down on small scraps of paper ; and I shall never be able to compose the whole quartet again in the same way.

Your faithful father.

Further, I must remind you that next *Sunday and Monday* are both holidays.[1] So you can make your arrangements accordingly. On this occasion you could perhaps drive out with me on *Saturday* if I go into town. Then you would have the whole morning to yourself.[2]

(1411) *To Bernhard Schotts Söhne, Mainz*

[*MS in the Stadtbibliothek, Mainz*] [3]

SIR !   VIENNA, *August* 13, 1825

I am amazed to see that in the seventh number of 'Caecilia', P. 205, together with the canons inserted [4] you have also published a jest sent to you as a friend, a jest which may easily be regarded as a biting insult, though indeed such was not at all my intention, seeing that it has always been alien to my character to hurt anybody's feelings.

In regard to my attitude as an artist, no one has ever found me reacting to anything written about me in connexion with my art. But in regard to my attitude as a man, there I am touched in quite a different way.

It should have been obvious to you when you first perused

---

[1] Monday, August 15th, was the Feast of the Assumption.
[2] According to *TDR* V, 542, this postscript is added at the top of the page, at the side.
[3] Written and signed in another hand. The MS has an endorsement suggesting that Holz wrote and signed the letter for Beethoven.
[4] WoO 180 and WoO 187.

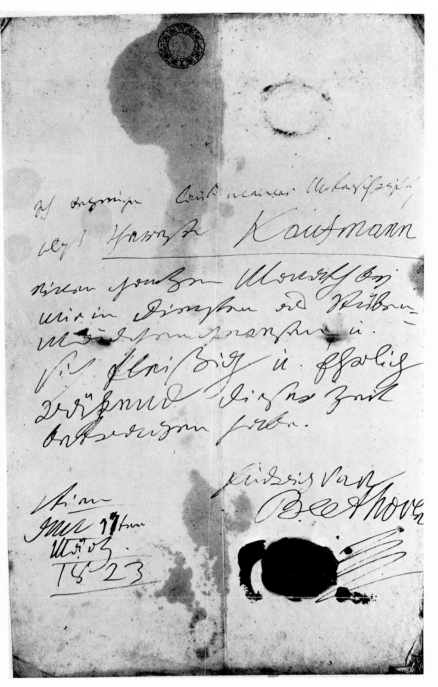

TESTIMONIAL FOR THERESE KAUFMANN (March 17, 1823)
(*Autograph in the possession of Dr. Richard Sterba*)

LETTER TO HIS NEPHEW (August 31, 1825)
(*Autograph in the Library of Congress*)

it that the whole sketch of a biography of my respected friend Herr Tobias Haslinger was only a *jest* and, moreover, was never intended to be anything else. For, as my letter stated, in order to enliven the jest, I wanted, on the strength of an invitation from yourself, to request his consent to the publication of his biography.[1] Well, it seems that it was my sketchy and often illegible handwriting which gave rise to a misunderstanding.

You would have completely fulfilled my purpose to send you contributions which you yourself have been asking for, if you had just inserted the two canons, the titles of which already sufficiently prove that they cannot be easily connected with a biography of Haslinger. But I should never have dreamt that you would misuse a private correspondence and display a jest of that kind to the public, who must fail to understand the absurdities which, moreover, you have been pleased to interpolate (for instance, line 2, 'canons, which I *contributed* as *supplements*, etc.').

The word '*geleert*' which belongs to the whole body of the humorous sketch, might pass in a circle of people who are talking and jesting. But it would never have occurred to me to use it in public instead of '*gelehrt*'.[2]

That would be pushing a joke too far!

In future I will certainly make a point of ensuring that my writing shall not give rise to fresh misunderstandings.

I expect you therefore to insert this in the 'Caecilia' without delay, without reservations and without any omissions. For the matter is exactly as I have described it here and must on no account be interpreted in any other way.

L. VAN BEETHOVEN

I am most certainly counting on this statement being inserted in the 'Caecilia' immediately —

Your devoted

BEETHOVEN [3]

[1] Cf. Letter 1345, p. 1169.   [2] Cf. p. 1169, n. 5.
[3] The postscript sentence and the second signature are in Beethoven's handwriting.
The *Caecilia* did not publish Beethoven's *amende honorable*.

(1412) *To Tobias Haslinger, Vienna*

[Autograph in the Beethovenhaus, Bonn, H. C. Bodmer collection]

[BADEN, *shortly after August* 13, 1825]

I hope, my dear fellow, that *Holz* has shown you my letter to those people at Mainz, or, rather, has given it to you to be forwarded at once.[1] You will see clearly from this letter that I would have died rather than countenance such an abuse of what was really only a jest. So dispatch it to Berlin and Leipzig by the next post. — I have never revenged myself, not even on my fiercest enemies, as is proved by my treatment of Karl's mother to whom I do a good turn whenever I can. The whole story was merely a jest, which even excuses the word '*geleert*' instead of '*gelehrt*', with which I intended to make a pun, not to be taken literally. Further, those scoundrels have added something which was not there at all, for I wrote 'geleerter *Gesellschaften*'.[2] But as the latter is quite untrue, it is far less offensive in a jest such as mine; and indeed that was all it was intended to be. — I never dreamt *that it would be published* —

I request you to have the receipt which Karl will bring you signed either by his mother or by the judge on her behalf.[3] *I insist that both shall not sign, but only one.* Further, don't hand over the money until the *document has been signed*, and don't accept any signature but mine *in my own handwriting.* — All good wishes, dear Tobias — you will soon be avenged, *all wickedness has its own revenge* — *Those people* are as stupid as they are *wicked* — Give my greetings to the growling Director-General S[chreyvogel], for, as you know, he can neither yell nor rape [4] — I hope that we shall certainly meet here; but I must be informed beforehand, because, if the weather is fine, I usually take long walks [5] —

Your amicus

BEETHOVEN

---

[1] Letter 1411.

[2] This is not so. In his letter to Schott, which included his humorous biography of Haslinger (cf. Letter 1345, p. 1169), Beethoven wrote 'geleerte Vereine'; and the *Caecilia* quoted these words.

[3] Since the beginning of 1824 Beethoven had exempted his sister-in-law Johanna from contributing to the cost of her son's education.

[4] Cf. Letter 1409, p. 1231, n. 4.

[5] The word in the original is 'Ausflüchte', possibly a mistake for 'Ausflüge' (excursions). But, of course, Beethoven may have purposely used this expression,

(1413) To [*Karl van Beethoven, Vienna*] ¹

[*Autograph in the Beethovenhaus, Bonn, H. C. Bodmer collection*]

[BADEN, c. *August* 20, 1825]

It is understood, of course, that on the receipt for the Archduke you must alter the name to His Imperial Highness the most excellent Archduke Rudolph, Cardinal and Eminence and so forth. The money can already be drawn on the 25th or after that date (that is immaterial). But you will have to use my small seal, as I have no sealing-wax here —

(1414) To Karl van Beethoven, Vienna

[*Autograph in a private collection*]

BADEN, *August* 22, [1825] ²

Well then, dear son, if you think it advisable, we might even ask Peters to give 80 ducats for one quartet and 70 for the other.³ If you get no reply from Holz — take your letter to the post on Wednesday.⁴ I don't think that H[olz] is going to arrange anything. I should like to have my mind easy about this matter by September, and I shall compose something pleasant too in your company. My good fellows! You again took the bill away with you yesterday. Do send it back to me —

Let me know too on what kind of stamped paper the receipt for the pension must *now* be written. Do enquire, for I don't know this —

Volti subito.⁵

NB. In the letter to Peters, alter what you consider unsuitable.

You can hardly conceive how depressed and sad I felt yesterday after you had all gone. It is too bad to be left alone

which can mean 'flights' and, in an abstract sense, 'evasions'. See also Letter 1529, p. 1310.
¹ This note is neither addressed nor signed; but it was evidently intended for Karl.
² In the autograph the date (without the year) is entered above the NB.
³ Doubtless Op. 127 and 132, neither of which was published by Peters.
⁴ Beethoven was writing on Monday.
⁵ P.T.O., at the foot of the first page of the autograph.

again with this evil rabble who will never be reformed —
Well, it is extremely necessary to consider and think carefully
about Stein, the pianoforte tuner and mechanic. I will tell
you more about that tomorrow — *Remember* that the letter to
Peters must be written in my name.[1] Hence I am enclosing
the sheet of paper for it, as I have done *on previous occasions also*.
And perhaps this very fact may cause the *unnecessary delay*.
Don't dawdle, but give the letter to the post on Wednesday —
Be good, be kind, and call me niggardly if I exhort you to
treat your clothes *with greater care*. Away with all secrecy
and *cunning* —

In the greatest haste, your faithful father

(1415) *To Karl Holz, Vienna*

[*Autograph in the Koch collection*]

BADEN, *August* 24, [1825]

MOST EXCELLENT PIECE OF MAHOGANY!

We have no quills available, so you will have to put up
with this [2] — Your letter made me laugh. Yes indeed, *Tobias*
will always be a T[obias], but we will make him even more
of a Tobias — Castelli must lend a hand, and our story will
be printed and engraved for the benefit of all poor Tobiases —
I am writing this moment to Karl telling him to postpone
sending the letters to Peters and Schlesinger, which means
that I am awaiting a reply from Herr A[rtaria] at Mannheim.

On the other hand it is all the same to me what hellhound
licks or gnaws away my brain, since admittedly it must be
so ; but let us hope the answer will not be delayed for too
long. That hellhound at L[eipzig] [3] can wait and in the
meantime enjoy in Auerbach's cellar the company of Mephistopheles (the editor of the L[eipziger] Musikal[ische] Zeitung).[4]
Beelzebub, chief of the devils, will shortly seize the latter by
the ears —

---

[1] There is no trace of this letter, unless it was the revised and dispatched
version of Beethoven's draft (see Letter 1420).

[2] Beethoven is apologizing for his rather illegible scrawl.

[3] Obviously a reference to C. F. Peters.

[4] Breitkopf & Härtel, Leipzig, had founded in 1798 the *Allgemeine Musikalische
Zeitung*, which they continued to publish until 1848. From 1798 until 1818 it was
edited by J. F. Rochlitz, who continued to supervise its publication until 1835.

My dear fellow, the last quartet too is to have six movements ; and I hope to complete them by the end of the month.¹
— If only somebody could give me something for my sick
stomach — My worthy brother has again been to the P.N.G.²
Heigho ! But, my dear fellow, we must see to it that all these
newly invented words and expressions will survive into the
third and fourth generations of our posterity ³ — Come on
Friday or Sunday — Come on Friday when Satan's performances in the kitchen are most tolerable — My best wishes —
A thousand thanks for your devotion to me and for your
affection. I trust that you will not be punished for it.

In love and friendship, your

BEETHOVEN

Yes, yes ! The little Paternostergasse and our *Director*
are implicated quite nicely. It is a good thing to know all
this even if one doesn't gain anything by it.⁴

Do write to me again, but it would be even better if you
would come ! ! ⁵

N'oubliès pas de rendre visite à mon cher Benjamin.⁶

(1416) *To Karl van Beethoven, Vienna*

[*Autograph in the Beethovenhaus, Bonn*]

DEAR LITTLE RASCAL !   BADEN, *August* 24, [1825]

Just look at our piece of mahogany, how active it is.⁷
I have already made up my mind. We will give this quartet
to Art[aria] and the last one to Peters ⁸ —

Well, have I too not learnt something ? I now see that

¹ Beethoven had begun to compose the B♭ quartet, the third of the Galitzin
quartets, Op. 130. He had finished the second one, Op. 132, in July.
² Paternostergasse, i.e. Steiner's firm.
³ A reference to Castelli's endeavours to restore the purity of the German
language and to invent new expressions.
⁴ This postscript is written at the top of the first page.
⁵ This sentence is written at the left side of the second page.
⁶ I.e. Karl. The remark, written in French so that the bearer of the letter
should not understand it, is added on the fourth page below the address to Karl
Holz, who was then living 'im Bergenstammischen Hause, Mölkerbastei 96'.
⁷ I.e. Holz.
⁸ In the end Op. 132, the second Galitzin quartet, was published by Moritz
Schlesinger, Paris; and Op. 130, the third Galitzin quartet, was published by
Artaria. Both were published after Beethoven's death.

for your sake I had been acting the *business man* in advance — so that you might find *the path prepared* for you — My stomach is in a very bad state and I have no doctor — I need sharpened *quills*, so do send some in a letter ¹ — And don't write to Peters, not even on Saturday, for we will just wait a bit; and in that way *we pretend and make him feel* that it is a matter of indifference to us —

Since yesterday I have eaten nothing but soup and a couple of eggs and have drunk only water; my tongue is quite yellow; and without bowel motions and tonics my stomach will never, whatever the Cornö etc. Doktor ² may say, never be cured — The third quartet too will have six movements and will really be quite finished in ten or, at most, twelve days ³ — Be fond of me, my dear fellow, and remember that when I pain you, I am not doing so to hurt you, but in order to do you good *for the future* — Well now, I am closing this letter once more — I embrace you with all my heart. Provided you are kind, good, hard-working and sincere, that is all I need for my happiness — Do write, my dear son. I am sorry that you have to run about so much for me. Things will be easier later on — *Holz* seems likely to become a friend of ours ⁴ — I am expecting a letter from my Benjamin very soon.⁵

Your loving father

(1417) *To Karl van Beethoven, Vienna*

[Autograph in the British Museum]

BADEN, *August* 25, [1825]

Although this day deserves to be taken notice of as little by you as by me, yet I hoped to have at least *a letter from you* —

¹ Cf. Letter 1415, p. 1236, n. 2.

² Possibly Beethoven is referring to some oculist who treated him for conjunctivitis in 1823. This is suggested by Max Unger in his monograph, *Beethovens Handschrift* (Bonn, 1926), p. 21.

³ According to *KHV.* 392, the third quartet, Op. 130, was not finished until November, 1825.

⁴ Beethoven's acquaintanceship with Holz, which led in the summer of 1825 to an intimate friendship, seems to have been made in 1824.

⁵ I.e. a letter for Beethoven's name-day, August 25th. See Letter 1417.

but in vain — By the way, you need not write to Peters yet, not on Saturday — and assuming that you want to come here on Sunday, then come early or not at all.

Your faithful father

(1418) *To Tobias Haslinger, Vienna*

[*Autograph in the Gesellschaft der Musikfreunde, Vienna*]

DEAR FELLOW!   B[ADEN], *August* 26, [1825]
Send the parts of the overture ¹ to Karl. Then I shall receive them at once and you too will have them returned quickly — You may again give something to Holz for me and he will deliver it — Let me have more particulars about the Mariabrunner wine, for I must not drink red wine *only*, but *white wine with water* as well — In any case drop your Director out of the window by a rope tomorrow at 4 a.m. and bring him here again. You can have plenty of *Vöslauer*.² It will all be paid for in foreign money. You are not giving me anything worth mentioning —

(1419) *To Karl van Beethoven, Vienna*

[*Autograph in the Library of Congress*]

[BADEN], *Wednesday, August* 31, [1825]
Here, dear son, is what Czerny left today, when I was locked in. So it does not seem to be so after all — The best arrangement is for you to invite Schlesinger ³ to come out here with you on Sunday. We can rehearse the quartet some other day later on — Besides in this way we could make many other arrangements. I shall expect a letter from you tomorrow evening at latest — Alas for this separation where all these questions are concerned —

Your faithful father

Should you perhaps not find him, then leave a message to say that you will call again.

¹ Probably Op. 115, which Steiner had published in score in April, 1825.
² A well-known red wine produced at Bad Vöslau near Vienna.
³ Moritz Schlesinger, who had founded his own music publishing firm in Paris in 1821, was on a visit to Vienna.

(1420) *To Carl Friedrich Peters, Leipzig*

[*Autograph in a private collection*] ¹

For Peters   [BADEN, *August*, 1825]
I wrote to tell you that a quartet (and, what is more, a grand one) was lying ready for you.² Therefore, as soon as you let me know that you will take it for 360 gulden A.C. or 80 ducats, it will be sent to you at once. My compositions are now being paid for at higher rates than ever. But indeed you yourself are to blame for all that has happened. *Your letters* indicate what you originally asked for; and what I sent was *what you were entitled to* (the many pirated editions prove the truth of my statement); ³ and indeed the quartet will convince you that I do not revenge myself *on you*, but that I give you as good a work as I could give to my best friend —

Please make haste so that I may have a reply by the next post. For if I don't hear from you, I shall have to return to you the 360 gulden A.C. In any case I shall be embarrassed, for someone wants to have both this quartet and another one and also a new one I have just finished.⁴ At the moment he is not keen on having only one. Such objections are raised in all quarters. It is really out of consideration for the long time you have been waiting and for which you alone are to blame, that at this moment I am detaching this quartet from its successor which is already finished (do you think that we should offer the latest one to someone in Vienna?). (Of course it would have to be done astutely, very astutely) je vous laisse come Marchand coquin.

Well now, do not distrust me and do not think that I am sending you something in order to have my revenge. No, I

---

¹ This is evidently an autograph draft of a letter with asides to Karl, who was to write it. The letter, if it was ever written and dispatched to Peters, has disappeared. See Nohl II, p. 278, n., where a letter from Karl to Peters, dated July 19, 1825, is quoted in full. In Karl's letter the A minor quartet, Op. 132, is offered to Peters with the reminder, quoted verbally from a draft sent to him by his uncle, then living at Schloss Gutenbrunn, Baden, 'that I am offering Peters the best work I have at the moment *and that I have forgotten the past*'.

² Op. 132. See *KHV*. 403. The bracketed clause was deleted by Beethoven.

³ The bracketed clause is added at the foot of the first page.

⁴ Op. 132 and 130, and possibly Op. 131, on which Beethoven had just begun to work. He is referring, of course, to Moritz Schlesinger of Paris, who was then in Vienna.

assure you on my honour as an artist that you may denounce me and treat me as the most abominable of human beings, if you find that it is not fully worthy of me as a work of art —

(1421) *To Karl Holz, Vienna*

[Autograph in the Beethovenhaus, Bonn, H. C. Bodmer collection] [1]

MOST EXCELLENT SECOND VIOLIN!   [BADEN, *August*, 1825]
    The passage in the 1st violin part of the first Allegro is as follows:

So make it exactly like that.
    And in the first Allegro as well you must add in the four parts these expression marks

All the notes are correct — but do read me correctly — Volti Subito.[2] Well, now for your copy, my dear fellow.
    Obbligatissimo — but the marks p ◄══ ►══ etc. etc. have been horribly neglected and frequently, very frequently, inserted in the wrong place. No doubt, haste is responsible for this. For God's sake please impress on Rampel to copy everything exactly as it stands. If you will just have a look now at what I have corrected, you will find everything

---

[1] Holz, who first published this letter with annotations in F. S. Gassner's *Zeitschrift für Deutschlands Musikvereine und Dilettanten*, 1845, IV, no. 24, added the following introductory remarks, which are not quite accurate: 'When Beethoven had finished in May, 1825, his A minor quartet dedicated to Prince Galitzin, he moved to a summer residence at Gutenbrunn, near Baden. He left the quartet with me, for I promised to have it copied quickly and to make provisional corrections which I would send to Baden. But I retained the original score because the copyist, Rampel by name, had to copy the parts. A few days later Beethoven's nephew on his way back from a visit to Baden brought me the following letter.' See Letter 1424.
    [2] P.T.O. In the autograph this indication is at the foot of the first page.

that you have to tell him. Where there is a dot above the note a dash must not be put instead and vice versa — and are not identical).[1] Sometimes the are inserted intentionally after the notes. For instance,

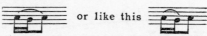

The slurs should be exactly as they are now. It is not all the same whether it is like this

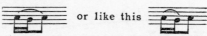 or like this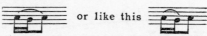

In the Adagio it is predominantly thus

Pay attention to what those who know better are telling you — Why, I have spent no less than the whole of this morning and the whole afternoon of the day before yesterday correcting these two movements and I am quite hoarse from cursing and stamping my feet — In great haste, your   BEETHOVEN

You must please excuse me for not writing more today. It is almost two o'clock and Karl leaves at four. We have had a very happy time together [2] —

(1422) *To [Karl Holz, Vienna ?]*

[*Autograph in the Beethovenhaus, Bonn, H. C. Bodmer collection*]

[BADEN, *August*, 1825]

Keep one and if you find somebody send the other one. Today it is impossible to do anything from here even if it costs money — Moreover on account of the investigation haste is necessary —

Since yesterday I have had a fresh and rather violent attack of my abdominal trouble.

We shall meet at dinner —

In great haste, yours [3]

[1] This bracketed remark is added at the top of the third page.
[2] This postscript is written at the side of the second page with an opening bracket. There is no closing bracket.
[3] This note bears no address, date or signature.

(1423) To Karl van Beethoven, Vienna

[Autograph in the Deutsche Staatsbibliothek, Berlin] [1]

MY DEAR LITTLE RASCAL !　　　　BADEN, *[August,* 1825]
This very evening I have received your letter, but how
heartily I had to laugh — It is very wrong of those Mainz
people to have done such a thing. But since it has now been
done, it doesn't matter. Our age needs powerful minds to
castigate these petty, deceitful, miserable wretches of human
hearts — however much my heart refuses to give pain to anyone. Besides, it was merely a jest and I never intended that
such a story should be printed.[2]

Ask at once at the Magistrat's for the form for transferring
the bank shares into Rothschild lotteries so as to be able to
apply for this to the Magistrat (supreme guardian back-
biters) [3] — Be good, be kind, here you have an example of
how the whole world rejoices when people of that type are
honoured as they should be — Be my dear son, my only son,
and imitate my virtues, but not my *faults.* But since a man
must have faults, do not have worse faults than I, your sincere
and faithful father who embraces you.

Write to me too about the interview on Sunday ; *it is
about court — court stuff —* against which one must be on
one's guard — *Holz* did not come today. Sometimes I wonder
whether he is to be trusted.

(1424) To Karl Holz, Vienna

[Autograph in the Library of Congress] [4]

DEAR ? ! HOLZ !　　　　　　[BADEN, *August,* 1825]
Why, nobody doubts that wood is a neuter noun. So
what a contradiction is the masculine form, and what other
consequences may be drawn from *personified wood?* — As for

---

[1] Autograph not available. Text taken from *TDR* V, 541.
[2] Cf. Letters 1411 and 1412.
[3] Cf. Letter 1397.
[4] Holz noted on the autograph ; 'I received this letter from Baden in August,
1825, when I was seeing to the copying of the A minor quartet which Beethoven
had just finished. He had entrusted to me the score written in his own hand.'

our affair, please do not let anyone see or hear the quartet [1] —
Friday is the only day on which the old witch, who two hundred
years ago would certainly have been burnt to death, cooks
tolerably well, for on that day the devil has no power over
her [2] — So come or let me have a reply in writing — That is
all for today — Your friend

BEETHOVEN

(1425) *To Karl Holz, Vienna*

[*Autograph in a private collection*] [3]

DEAR HOLZ !   [BADEN, *Summer*, 1825]
    Well, all right, come tomorrow a few hours before dinner.
In this way you won't miss so much — My income from the
Archduke should now be drawn. I know nothing about
stamped forms — The sooner, the faster, the better — so that
a small reserve fund may still remain — Do come tomorrow.
Everything will be arranged — The doctor too must testify,
and after him the parson. Do all you can in this matter —You
need not go to the parson —
    Vale et fave [4]

Your friend

BEETHOVEN

(1426) *To Moritz Schlesinger, Vienna*

[*Autograph in the Beethovenhaus, Bonn, H. C. Bodmer collection*]

MY DEAR S[CHLESINGER] !   BADEN, *September* 1, [1825]
    I am greatly delighted to have my Karl's assurance that
you will come out here with him on Sunday — Your visit to
me the other day was too much of a surprise for me to behave
to you in a really calm and collected manner, the more so as
I happened to be busy composing and immediately afterwards
had some business matters to deal with, an experience similar
to that of being suddenly whisked from Etna to the glaciers
of Switzerland. — You still have something to deliver to me

[1] The A minor quartet, Op. 132. In his comment Holz calls it Op. 129.
[2] The words from 'for on' to 'over her' are added at the foot of the
page.
[3] This letter is written in pencil.
[4] All good wishes and be fond of me.

and I have many questions to put to you! It is hardly necessary for me to tell you how pleasant it is to enjoy the company of a very cultured man, the kind of company which formerly I was always accustomed to; but — among the Phaeacians [1] I rarely meet a person of this kind. Hence I shall enjoy your company all the more — Your most devoted

BEETHOVEN

(1427) *To Friedrich Kuhlau, Vienna* [2]

[*MS not traced*] [3]

BADEN, *September* 3, 1825

Kühl nicht lau nicht lau Kühl nicht lau Kuhl-au nicht

lau Kühl nicht lau Kühl nicht lau nicht

in 8va Basso

lau Kühl nicht lau Kühl nicht lau Kühl nicht lau

I must confess that in my case also the champagne went too much to my head and that again I had to experience the fact that such indulgence hampers rather than promotes my ability to work. For though I am usually well able to reply on the spot, yet I haven't the faintest recollection of what I wrote yesterday —

Remember now and then your most devoted

BEETHOVEN

[1] Beethoven's favourite description of the Viennese. Cf. Letter 483, p. 457, n. 5.

[2] Friedrich Kuhlau (1786–1832), born in Hanover, became a popular composer of operas and easy pianoforte pieces. In 1810 he settled at Copenhagen where he soon filled various musical appointments at the Danish Court. When on a visit to Vienna in 1825 he met Beethoven.

[3] Taken from Seyfried, *Beethovens Studien*, Anhang 5, no. 23.

[4] This three-part canon is listed in *KHV.* as WoO 191.

(1428) *To Karl Holz, Vienna*

[Autograph in the possession of Vizekonsul Fritz Hunziker]

MOST EXCELLENT FELLOW !   [BADEN], *September* 3, [1825]

Hardly had I got home when it occurred to me what stuff and nonsense I may have scribbled down yesterday — Deliver this to Kuhlau [1] — You know all the rest — Write very soon or come out here on Thursday — or Friday, but write beforehand — Enquire whether the cook knows too how to serve up game, so that she may know her way about my hunting ground —

As for Karl it would be even better to *threaten him at atrappe,*[2] and to let me know — Make haste with everything prestissimo — Only where our friendship is concerned, always look upon me as a cantus firmus. All good wishes. Cordially your friend

BEETHOVEN

(1429) *To Karl van Beethoven, Vienna*

[Autograph in the Beethovenhaus, Bonn, H. C. Bodmer collection]

DEAR SON !   [BADEN], *September* 6, 1825

I quite see how inconvenient it is for everyone to come out here. So we could ask them all to meet at Schlesinger's on Friday morning; and I shall come into town.[3] For I really ought to be present in case something goes wrong. That is the best arrangement; and thus the question will be settled. — He was here again yesterday and said that he would pay for the quartet immediately, i.e. as soon as you delivered it to him.[4] Entre nous il est pourtant juif —

It will be enough if they perform only the *new* quartet.

---

[1] Letter 1427, which was probably written at midnight on Friday, September 2nd. On the verso of Letter 1428 are the date (but not the year) and the words 'The recovered gulden'.

[2] I.e. when you catch him in the very act.

[3] Beethoven is referring to a rehearsal of the A minor quartet, Op. 132, by the Schuppanzigh quartet, which Moritz Schlesinger desired to hear. Rehearsals took place on Friday, September 9th and Sunday, September 11th and performances were given on November 6th and 20th. See *KHV.* 401.

[4] Moritz Schlesinger, who published Op. 132 in score in September, 1827.

No doubt you will see what is the best arrangement to make. If they want to play on Thursday, I will come in on that day too [1] — But make sure that the question is settled as quickly as possible so that a money draft can be sent to Peters at L[eipzig]. And you must not mention him on any account — Schlesinger fancies that he will no longer be in Vienna on Sunday. Hence we must act with all speed. By the way, the ducats should be gold ones, for any others are interchangeable —

Write to me today at once and send your letter by the old woman, — that reminds me, all I require is a specimen of the corrections. Don't dawdle, pull yourself together and make sure that the old woman gets here in time — Probably the best arrangement would be for you to fix up everything for Friday in town. Then I will certainly come in. Has Schles[inger] brought you the quartet (the first one?).[2] I trust he has not made a fuss. I can see that it is difficult to get him to pay —

Your letter has just reached me. So Holz is not coming until Thursday, and that is not even certain?

Your letter has now altered everything, since *Friday has now been decided on*; whether the meeting is to be here or in Vienna Holz no doubt will tell me. But if he doesn't come out here, well then I will come into town on Friday [3] — Our chief concern is to come to an arrangement with Schles[inger], for we cannot wait any longer — If he is waiting to hear a rehearsal first, then I shall not let him have the quartet. He said again yesterday that he would certainly not publish the quartets in Vienna. I said that that was a matter of indifference to me — The Lord bless you and keep you and your loving father —

I am sending off the above scrawl only because it is about Schlesinger.[4]

[1] Beethoven was writing on Tuesday.

[2] Op. 127. Both the score and the parts of this quartet were published in 1826 by the Paris branch of Schott.

[3] The rehearsal did take place in Vienna on Friday, September 9th; and according to Smart's journal the A minor quartet was played twice and each time lasted for 45 minutes.

[4] This remark is added at the side of the page.

(1430) *To Karl van Beethoven, Vienna*

[*Autograph in the Deutsche Staatsbibliothek, Berlin*] [1]

DEAR SON,   [BADEN, *shortly before September* 14, 1825]
 Don't forget to give Tobias the receipt as well as the money — The worthy instruc[tor] should have come sooner — in view of the *present state* of the affair, you must *do what he says.*
 I too do not want you to come to me on September 14th. It would be better for you to finish those studies — God has never forsaken me. No doubt someone will be found to close my eyes — On the whole there seems to me to be some pre-concerted plan in everything that has been going on; and I fancy that my worthy brother (pseudo) has a hand in it — I know that later on you too will not want to live with me; of course not, my manner of life is a bit too *pure* — Last Sunday you again borrowed 1 gulden, 15 kreuzer from the house-keeper, that vulgar old skivvy — I had long ago forbidden you to do this — Everywhere it is the same story. I would have managed for two years with the one frock-coat. Admittedly I have the bad habit of putting on a worn out coat at home. But that gentleman Karl, faugh, the shame of it, and why should he do it? Well, because Herr L. v. B[eethove]n's money-bag is there solely for that purpose — You need not come this Sunday either, for owing to your behaviour there can never be true harmony and concord between us — And why this hypocrisy? Only when you cease to pretend will you became a better man. You need not dissemble or lie; and in the end your moral character would undoubtedly improve — You see, *your wickedness finds its reflection* in me. For what avail the most loving reprimands?! And, more-over, you get angry — However, don't be anxious, I shall always provide *for you*, as I am doing now continually. But you provoke me to make *such scenes* — for instance, when I again found that sum of 1 gulden, 15 kreuzer on the house-keeper's bill.
 Do not write on such thin sheets in future, for the house-keeper can read them by holding them against the light. I have this moment received this letter from Leipzig. But I

[1] Autograph not available. Text taken from *TDR* V, 545-546.

BEETHOVEN'S NEPHEW,
KARL VAN BEETHOVEN
(1806–1858)
From an unsigned miniature done
on ivory (*c.* 1827)
(*Historisches Museum der Stadt Wien*)

KARL HOLZ (1798–1858)
From a miniature on ivory by
Betty Fröhlich (1824)
(*Historisches Museum der Stadt Wien*)

don't think that as a *reply* we should send them the quartet
just yet. We can discuss this on Sunday. — Formerly, that
is to say three years ago, I asked only 40 ducats for a quartet.
So now we must find out *what sort of letter you* actually wrote —
    All good wishes. He who, although he did not beget you,
has certainly provided for you and, what is more important
than anything else, has seen to the cultivation of your mind
as a father, yes, even more than a father, most earnestly begs
you to be sure to follow the only true path leading to all that
is good and right — All good wishes.

Your kind and faithful father

Bring the letter again on Sunday.[1]

(1431) *To Karl van Beethoven, Vienna*

[Autograph in the Beethovenhaus, Bonn, H. C. Bodmer collection]

DEAR SON !   BADEN, *in the evening of September* 14, [1825]
    It will either rain tomorrow, and perhaps heavily, or
not at all ; both kinds of weather are bad for my health, the
horrible dust and the rain — I am sorry to think that you
have to be with that old devil for so long — do keep away
from her — You should write a letter for her in my name to the
Administrator of the Hospital, stating that she did not come
on the 1st, partly because she was not well and partly because
several people came out here to see me —
    Basta così —
    Here are the 40 gulden for your crammer. Get a written
receipt for this amount. How many mistakes one avoids by
doing this ; and everyone who pays a bill for somebody else
does it. You will remember that *Holz*, without being asked
to do so, brought the receipt from Rampel ; and do not others
do likewise ? — You must take the white waistcoat and have
the other one made *for me* — You could bring the metronome
with you, nothing can be done with it — Bring your sheets
and two blankets — *That reminds me, you could surely bring* some
pencils and quills as well, but buy the former only at the Brand-
statt. And now farewell, dear son, come to my arms tomorrow

---

[1] According to *TDR* V, 546, this sentence is added at the side of the page.

and try not to come too late; perhaps it will rain.[1] Ever your most loving father.

The only arrangement I could make is to send for you and the old woman the coach which, when everything is included, costs 8 gulden, 36 kreuzer, — Don't forget anything, and be sure to be mindful of your health.

(1432) *To Tobias Haslinger* [2]

[*Autograph in the Deutsche Staatsbibliothek, Berlin*]

[VIENNA, *September* 20, 1825][3]

MOST EXCELLENT AND WORTHY NORTH AMERICAN
DEALER IN NOTES
AND, WHAT IS MORE, A RETAILER!

As I am here for only half a day, I am asking you *what is the cost of Clementi's School of Pianoforte Playing translated into German.*[4]

Please be so kind as to let me have particulars about it at once and to inform me whether you have it in stock or, if not, *where else* I could find it? —

Most excellent Sir, Hm, Hm, Hm! Have a thoroughly good time in your newly decorated working room. See to it that what was formerly a nest shall now become an ale-house, since all beer drinkers are good musicians and must also call *to see you* —

Your most devoted

BEETHOVEN

[1] Beethoven was writing on Wednesday. Sir George Smart visited him on Friday, September 16th, at Baden, where he spent most of the day. In his journal Smart gives a lively description of this visit.

[2] The address on the verso runs as follows :—

An des Herrn
Tobias Hasslinger
Wohlgebohrn
ehemaliger B[ie]rw[ir]t
nunmehriger
Kunstfabrikant

[3] The autograph is endorsed 'Vienna, September 20, 1826', but on internal evidence the year must be 1825. See *TDR* V, 257, n. 3.

[4] Beethoven was ordering a copy of this work for Stephan von Breuning's young son Gerhard, then aged 13, who first met the composer in August, 1825. See Gerhard von Breuning, *Aus dem Schwarzspanierhause* (Vienna, 1874), pp. 1-3. See also Letter 1473.

(1433) *To Moritz Schlesinger*

[*Autograph not traced*] [1]

VIENNA, *September* 26, 1825

Si non per portas   per muros   per muros per muros

I wish you the most lovely bride, my dear fellow; and on this occasion I request you to give my compliments to Herr Marx in Berlin and ask him not to be too hard on me and to let me slip out occasionally through the back door.

Yours

BEETHOVEN

(1434) *To Sigmund Anton Steiner, Vienna*

[*Autograph in the possession of the Mayeda Ikutoku Foundation, Tokyo*]

LITTLE PATERNOSTERGASSE!   [BADEN, *September*, 1825]

Be so kind as to hand this letter to Karl if he calls for it; and if the pillory money [3] has arrived, let me have that too.

BEETHOVEN

(1435) *To Karl van Beethoven, Vienna*

[*Autograph not traced*] [4]

[BADEN, *September*, 1825]

As you have not yet got the money from the Archduke, which is annoying, well then the 100 gulden A.C. which I

---

[1] From the facsimile in A. B. Marx, *Beethoven*, 2nd edition (Berlin, 1863), Vol. II, Appendix C.   [2] This two-part canon is listed in *KHV*. as WoO 194.
[3] In the original the word is 'Prangergeld'. Beethoven is probably referring to money due to him for works the composing and correcting of which had been anything but enjoyable, literally, money earned by being tortured on the rack.
[4] Taken from *TDR* V, 251. According to *TDR* V, 250, one side of this leaf, then in the Artaria collection, consisted of a statement drafted by Beethoven and to be signed by Moritz Schlesinger, declaring that he had received two quartets, for one of which (presumably Op. 132 which Schlesinger published in September, 1827) he would pay Beethoven 80 gold ducats. The verso of the leaf contained this note, obviously addressed to Karl. The other quartet which Schlesinger received was Op. 135.

am enclosing must be used for the purchase of necessities;
and you must see that whatever sum is over is duly returned to
me — Unfortunately you must take it to the *tailor* on account
of the bill — If you need money, take two gulden out of it——

ADE [1]

(1436) *To ?* [2]

[Autograph in the Beethovenhaus, Bonn, H. C. Bodmer collection]

[BADEN, *September*, 1825]

P.P.

I hope, and I remind you [of my invitation], to see you
at dinner at my place. Should you arrive here beforehand
and wish to visit Karl, then it would be helpful to learn from
what date the chocolate should be paid for. Moreover I understand
that in his case a fresh circumstance has arisen —

In great haste, your

BEETHOVEN

(1437) *To Moritz Schlesinger, Vienna*

[Autograph in the Beethovenhaus, Bonn, H. C. Bodmer collection]

[BADEN, *September*, 1825]

Karl is authorized to discuss the business side of the arrangement with you. Afterwards I shall be delighted to see you
once more here at Baden.

Your most devoted

BEETHOVEN

(1438) *To Karl van Beethoven, Vienna*

[Autograph in the Deutsche Staatsbibliothek, Berlin] [3]

DEAR SON! BADEN, *October* 4, [1825]

Like the cunning Ulysses I too know how to help myself.
You need not fear that if you come on Saturday [4] you will

---

[1] A colloquial form of 'Adieu'.
[2] The autograph is not addressed. It may have been written to Karl Holz,
but the internal evidence for this is admittedly slender.
[3] Autograph not available. Text taken from *TDR* V, 547.
[4] Beethoven was writing on Tuesday.

find it too cold. A portion of the old window-shutters are here and with these we can make ourselves more or less comfortable — I am hoping too to shake off my cold and catarrh while I am still here. But on the whole it is not very safe for me to be at Baden now with this catarrh. The winds or, rather, the hurricanes still persist. — As for Biedermann,[1] ask him whether S[chlesinger] gave him a commission. For we can still write to Peters at once, if Biedermann has not received any order from Schlesing[er] —

I had no letter from you today, but no doubt it was hardly possible for you to write to me so soon. Tomorrow, however, I hope to have a letter from you and to see you for certain on Saturday. I hope that you will never have to feel ashamed of your callous behaviour to me. I hope and trust that all the reasons you put forward here to explain your return to Vienna had their foundation in truth —

Rest assured that at all times you need only expect from me whatever is good and kind. But can I hope to receive the same treatment from you? — Even when you see me in a towering rage,[2] do ascribe it to my great anxiety about you, seeing that dangers can so easily threaten you — I hope to have a letter from you tomorrow at any rate. Don't make me anxious. Oh, just think of my sufferings. On that account I should rightly have no cares whatever. Yet how much have I already endured?! As always your most faithful father

Remember that I am
stuck here and may
easily fall ill.

N'oublies pas de demander des quittances e donnes moi aussi vite que possible des nouvelles.[3]

[1] Not identified. He was probably the agent in Vienna of A. M. Schlesinger, Berlin or, more probably, of Moritz Schlesinger, Paris.
[2] Beethoven uses the word 'stürmisch'.
[3] According to Kal., no. 1116, this reminder in French is added on the verso of the autograph and is written upside down beside the address.

(1439) *To Karl van Beethoven, Vienna*

[*Autograph in the Deutsche Staatsbibliothek, Berlin*] ¹

DEAR AND BELOVED SON !   [BADEN], *October* 5, [1825]
I have this moment received your letter. Before it came
I was full of anxiety and had already decided to hasten to
Vienna today — Thank God, that is not necessary. Only
obey me, and love and inner harmony coupled with human
happiness will be our portion ; and you will unite an intensely
spiritual life to your external existence ; it is better, however,
that precedence be given to the *former* over the *latter* — Il
fait trop froid — Well, I shall see you on Saturday.² Just
write whether you are coming in the morning or in the evening
and I will hasten to meet you —
    I embrace and kiss you a thousand times, not as my *prodigal
son, but as my newly born son* — I have written to Schlemmer.³
Don't be annoyed with me. I am still too full of anxiety ⁴ —
— — and my cares for you who have been found again will
only prove to you how loving is your father.

Ayes la bonté, de m'envoyer an *inflammable bottle* ⁵ with *matches*
from Rospini ⁶ ou en portes avec vous puisque de celle de
Kärtnerthor on ne peut pas faire usage ⁷ —

(1440) *To Karl van Beethoven, Vienna*

[*Autograph in a private collection*]

DEAR SON !   BADEN, *Wednesday, October* 12, [1825]
    Yesterday I received a letter from you without *a date or
even mention of the day* — The chief thing is the pianoforte, for just
now the weather is very fine and dry — The Stein pianoforte

¹ Autograph not available. Text taken from *TDR* V, 548.
² Beethoven was writing on Wednesday.
³ Cf. Letter 1380, p. 1203, n. 1.
⁴ According to *TDR* V, 548, a portion of the autograph has been torn off here.
⁵ Probably some kind of spirit lamp.
⁶ Possibly Joseph Rospini, who had a shop at the Stephansplatz. See Schünemann II, 54, and III, 315, where, however, the particulars differ.
⁷ According to *TDR* V, 548, this sentence is added under the address to Karl.

can be attended to later.   As soon as I am in Vienna I will have it seen to and will gladly pay him for it, since otherwise it will be completely ruined.   I trust that the carpenter found you today and is going to bring the trunk here ; and he wants to make the shutters.   Probably it will not be possible to come in before Saturday in order to have everything brought into our new rooms from my brother's.[1]   It wouldn't do to let the old woman undertake this on her own — If I don't come in, however, come out on Sunday in the carriage in which Holz came out here with you —

It is my wish that *your selfish behaviour to me shall* cease once and for all.   *It does me as little good as it sets you on the right and most honourable path.*   Well, go on and persist in your behaviour, but you will regret it.   This does not mean that perhaps I may die all the sooner, although that may be what you want. But as long as I live I shall cut myself off from you completely without forsaking you, of course, or failing to support you — Find, if you can, a fool who has made so many sacrifices and who has been and is *daily being rewarded by you in such a way.* What distresses me most of all is the thought of the consequences which *you will suffer* as a result of your behaviour. Who will believe you or trust you who has heard what has happened and how you have mortally wounded and are daily wounding me ? — Make arrangements for me to be able to find you.   I am coming and I may turn up at any time — If I come on Saturday, you can come back here with me in the evening.   (It is still particularly lovely outside Baden.   I am taking long walks.   Yesterday, however, I was in danger.[2] *But* — although my nephew could be here, he thinks that he is not wasting his time at billiards —

Don't become Rameau's nephew, I implore you [3] —

Your faithful father.

[1] On Saturday, October 15th, Beethoven moved into his rooms in the Schwarzspanierhaus, which was his last residence.   See Letter 1444.

[2] As is frequently the case in Beethoven's letters, the closing bracket is missing.

[3] Beethoven is referring to Diderot's famous imaginary dialogue between himself and the nephew of the French composer Rameau.   Rameau's nephew was a parasite and a cynic.   The dialogue written in 1760, shortly before the death of Rameau, was first published in 1805 in a German translation by Goethe, to whom Schiller had lent the MS.   The MS then disappeared until 1891 when it was recovered and published.   Meanwhile in 1821 a French translation of Goethe's German translation was published by Delauney, Paris.

I spend every morning with the Muses — and on my walks they make me happy.[1]

Both the old woman and the young one continue to behave disgracefully. On my return to Vienna I shall dismiss them both at once [2] —

(1441) *To Karl van Beethoven, Vienna*

[*Autograph in the Deutsche Staatsbibliothek, Berlin*] [3]

DEAR SON !   [BADEN, *before October* 15, 1825]

Well then, to the carpenter today with the old — witch — Don't forget the paintings in Asinaccio's [4] apartments and what was brought in during the summer. Do look after things a bit — perhaps I shall come on Saturday after all — if not, you will come on Sunday.

Dear son, may God enlighten you. Your father.

I can't write much.

Do write me a few words.

I am coming to the usual place at three o'clock; s'il vous plait.[5]

(1442) *To Karl van Beethoven, Vienna*

[*Autograph in the possession of Frau Tilla Götz*]

DEAR SON !   [BADEN, *October* 14, 1825] [6]

I am letting you know with all speed that if *it is not raining* tomorrow, I shall most certainly be in Vienna and will fetch you before lunch — Don't be afraid. You will be received in a fatherly way by your faithful father.

Baden, on Friday.

[1] This sentence is added at the foot of the first page.
[2] These two sentences are added at the right side of the first page.
[3] Autograph not available. Text taken from *TDR* V, 550.
[4] 'Asinaccio' (wretched ass) was one of Beethoven's descriptions of his brother. Cf. Letter 1390, p. 1211.
[5] According to *TDR* V, 550, this sentence was added under the address, written in pencil and then deleted.
[6] This note was written on the same day as the letter which follows (Letter 1443) and which is dated October 14th. In 1825 October 14th fell on a Friday.

(1443) *To Karl van Beethoven, Vienna*

[*Autograph in the Deutsche Staatsbibliothek, Berlin*] ¹

BADEN, *October* 14, [1825]

I am letting you know in a great hurry that even if it is raining I will certainly come in tomorrow morning. So be sure to let me find you — — — I am looking forward to seeing you again; and even if you still see lowering clouds, don't put it down to deliberate nastiness; they will be completely dispelled by the better efforts you have promised me to make for your true and pure happiness founded on strenuous activity. When writing my last letter I was haunted by something which, though it was not *quite* real, plunged me into a black humour. After all we have gone through, such a thing is quite possible. Yet who would not rejoice when the erring one returns to the right path; and indeed I hope to experience this joy — I was extremely hurt that on Sunday you came so late and rushed off again so early. I am coming tomorrow with the carpenter. The tribe of witches must leave; it is too bad. Before the other housekeeper arrives,² I can make use of the carpenter — I have a lot to tell you, and you will admit that I am right — Expect me therefore tomorrow for certain in spite of rain etc. — Your loving father who presses you to his heart.³

(1444) *To [Karl Holz?]*

[*Autograph in the possession of Alfred Cortot*]

SCHWARZSPANIERHAUS [VIENNA], *October* 17, [1825]

Like a shipwrecked mariner I arrived here the day before yesterday in the evening.⁴ I tried to find you yesterday, but

---

¹ Autograph not available. Text taken from *TDR* V, 550-551.

² Probably Rosalie (Sali), the housekeeper who remained in Beethoven's service until the end.

³ According to *TDR* V, 551, the autograph has this reminder written under the address to Karl: 'The quickest delivery of this letter is requested'. Beethoven returned to Vienna for good on the following day, October 15th.

⁴ On Saturday, October 15th. This pencilled note is written in a trembling hand.

everything was silent — It would help me very greatly if you could come and see me before you go to your meeting —
In great haste, your friend

BEETHOVEN

(1445) *To Karl van Beethoven*

[*Autograph in the Deutsche Staatsbibliothek, Berlin*] [1]

MY BELOVED SON !   [VIENNA, *after October* 17, 1825] [2]
Stop, no further — Only come to my arms, you won't hear a single hard word. For God's sake, do not abandon yourself to misery. You will be welcomed here as affectionately as ever. We will lovingly discuss what has to be considered and what must be done for the future. On my word of honour you will hear no reproaches, since in any case they would no longer do any good. All that you may expect from me is the most loving care and help — But do come — come to the faithful heart of

your father

BEETHOVEN

Volti sub[ito] [3]

Come home as soon as you receive this note.
Si vous ne viendres pas
vous me tûerès surement
lisés la lettre et restés
a la maison chez vous, venes
de m'embrasser votre pere
vous vraiment adonné soyes
assurés, que tout cela resterà
entre nous.[4]

For God's sake, do come home again today. If not, who knows what danger may confront you ? Hurry, hurry.[5]

[1] Autograph not available. Text taken from *TDR* V, 549. For a facsimile of the recto of the sheet see Stephan Ley: *Beethovens Leben in authentischen Bildern und Texten* (Berlin, 1925), p. 121.
[2] According to *TDR* V, 549, and on internal evidence, this letter must have been written after Beethoven's return to Vienna on October 15th. Possibly Karl had gone to his mother again.   [3] P.T.O.
[4] According to *TDR* V, 549, this passage in French is written outside under the address to Karl.
[5] According to *TDR* V, 549 the last three sentences are written on top of the first page.

(1446) *To Karl Holz*

[*Autograph in the Beethovenhaus, Bonn, H. C. Bodmer collection*]

[VIENNA, *October*, 1825]
The new housekeep[er] has not yet turned up ; has she been told to come ?

In great haste, yours
BEETHOVEN

Please come at once yourself; I am still in the hands of this rabble.[1]

(1447) *To Karl van Beethoven*

[*Autograph in the Library of Congress*]

[VIENNA, *Autumn*, 1825]
Fr[au] Schlemm[er][2] is to receive, or has received, her money from our housekeeper. A few letters must be written tomorrow; let me know when you can most easily spare the time ? —

Your uncle.
I have left my handkerchief behind me.[3]

(1448) *To Joseph Linke*

[*Autograph in the Beethovenhaus, Bonn*]

DEAR LEFT AND RIGHT ![4]   [VIENNA, *Autumn*, 1825]
As I have heard many favourable things about Herr von Bocklet, I think that the best thing would be to request him to be so kind as to play the trio at your concert.[5] I do not

[1] I.e. the two servants Beethoven had taken to Baden and now wanted to get rid of. This note is written in pencil.
[2] Karl was then lodging with the family of a Viennese official called Schlemmer. Cf. Letter 1380, p. 1203, n. 1.
[3] This sentence is written on the verso of the note beside the address.
[4] Beethoven is here playing on the surname 'Linke', which means 'left'.
[5] In his note to this letter in vol. I, p. 279, Nohl, who copied the autograph then in the possession of Carl Maria von Bocklet (cf. Letter 774, p. 677, n. 4), states that the latter declared that he had rehearsed the trio with Holz, violinist, and Linke, cellist, at Beethoven's rooms in 1825 or 1826. But see *TDR* V, 259, where it is stated that the concert was held on November 6, 1825, and that the A minor quartet, Op. 132, and the pianoforte trio in B♭, Op. 97, were performed.

know him personally or I would have interceded with Herr
v[on] B[ocklet] on your behalf. Always count on me whenever I can serve you.

Your friend
BEETHOVEN

(1449) *To Karl Holz*

[Autograph not traced] ¹

DEAR FELLOW!   [VIENNA, *early November*, 1825]
    Why, I told you yesterday that I had already discovered
that she did not cook food tastefully or in a way beneficial
to one's health. It was plain to see that when I rebuked her
she behaved quite impudently. But I reminded her as gently
as possible that she must pay more attention to her cooking —
I left the servants alone yesterday and went out for a walk in
the evening. When I returned she was not to be found and
had left me the enclosed letter. As she has run away, it will
be best to inform the police who will see that she returns —
Please let me have your support. If you could come for a
moment, it would be very pleasant. —

Yours
BEETHOVEN

(1450) *To [Karl Holz?]*

[Autograph in the Bibliothèque de l'Opéra, Paris]

[VIENNA, *shortly before November* 6, 1825]

AMAZINGLY DEAR FELLOW!
    Here is the letter to The Deputy Director Reisser ² —
Please have a talk with him about K[arl], but very gently
and with great reserve. I am doing my share *in accordance
with my views and in my own way*; and I am convinced that
eventually we shall achieve a desirable result. As yet we have
nothing to prove that *those who err* would be led back to the
right path by fresh errors and wrong treatment on our part —
Furthermore, please be so kind as to enquire from R[eisser]

---

¹ Taken from Nohl, *Mosaik* (Leipzig, 1882), p. 333. Nohl transcribed the
autograph then in private ownership.
² Beethoven wrote 'Reissig or', which he then deleted.

whether he finds it a nuisance to discuss these matters with me in writing, because, if so, I would then go to see him sometime in person —

Haslinger knew yesterday about the housekeeper having run away. It is not my fault. In any case such a thing is not unheard of. If it were, there would not be the police regulation that an occurrence of this kind must be reported to them immediately so that another housekeeper may be provided on the spot. Admittedly it is I who have to bear the brunt, for I am certainly not of a phlegmatic temperament; and in the *Criminal Court* the causes have first to be investigated, and these may bring all kinds of things to light where a person is concerned. Well, thank God, things have not yet come to that pass. You say, however, that I act too hot-headedly.[1] To be sure, I don't stand at the river's edge looking on until someone is drowned. Well, in the case of the housekeeper, we shall again have a bit of Viennese *fun*; and no doubt we shall experience the same thing in the case of Fr[au] v[on] Vivenot.[2] For you are all quite heartless. What has happened would suit Castelli and his *bears*.[3] I most humbly request you if you happen to be passing the office of the Verein, to get me two tickets for Sunday.[4] I am not, it is true, one of the *seeds* of the Verein, but, after all, I am fertilizing the musical soil *in a way* that is evoking the gratitude of several people — Well, all good wishes, I trust that veritas *non* odium parit — Let those of you whom the cap fits wear it — Please inform me soon at any rate of the result of your interview, for in accordance with my letter to R[eisser], as you will see, it is necessary for me to know about it. And until I have found someone here with a Diogenes lantern, please do express some sympathy for me —

As always your

BEETHOVEN

[1] The German original has 'feurig'.
[2] Probably the wife of Dominik Vivenot, a medical consultant in Vienna.
[3] The term used by Castelli to describe his collection of anecdotes and *obiter dicta*, published in twelve parts during the years 1825 to 1832, which occasionally bordered on vulgarity.
[4] For the concert held in the hall of the Gesellschaft der Musikfreunde, which was then housed in the building 'Zum roten Igel' in the street Unter den Tuchlauben. Linke organized this concert at which Beethoven's pianoforte trio, Op. 97, and A minor string quartet, Op. 132, were performed.

Postscript
It is impossible to conceal everything about K[arl], but
I do hope that R[eisser] has not heard about his playing
billiards — try to find out — very cunningly — whether he
really has five hours of lectures — Urge H[err] v[on] R[eisser]
to observe the greatest secrecy on account of Schlemmer.   I
have *good reasons of my own* to ask this — Indeed you will
think our worthy Vice-Director an absolute vice; — All I
want him to tell you is whether it is really necessary to apply
to a Professor to find out some place for Karl? On no account
must you leave the Mass in his hands, that Viennese fellow —
What a plight I am in.   Oh God, if only I could get right
away from here! — to suffer — persistently — the great distance.[1]   Vale etc., fave.
You may take the maid with you too, to carry the Mass ad
libitum —
I will send for it tomorrow morning ad libitum —
Read my letter to R[eisser].[2]   Three months from November to the end of January have been paid in advance.   But I
am quite willing to cut this loss [3] —

(1451) *To Carl Friedrich Peters, Leipzig*

[*MS in the Beethovenhaus, Bonn, H. C. Bodmer collection*] [4]

SIR!   VIENNA, *November* 25, 1825
When I offered you the quartet, your partner's reply
was not definite and clear.[5]   And your last two letters are
just as vague.   As soon as you state clearly the sum, i.e. 360
gulden A.C. which I have now received from you, and assure
me that for this fee you will take *the quartet*, then you can have
one very soon.   Had you done this at once, you could have

---

[1] Here about 12 words are faded and illegible.
[2] This letter has not been traced.
[3] These two sentences are added at the side of the page.
[4] Written by Karl and signed by Beethoven.
[5] On July 19, 1825, Karl had written to C. F. Peters on behalf of his uncle,
offering him the A minor quartet, Op. 132, for the 360 gulden which Beethoven
had already received from the firm in August, 1822.

had two new quartets, but you can't expect me to be the loser. If I wished to tighten the strings still more, I could demand an even greater sum for a quartet.

As soon as you let me know, therefore, I will make you the owner of a new quartet as quickly as possible. But if you prefer to have your money back, well then, you can have it back immediately, for it has been lying there untouched for a long time. Let me add that I send nothing on approval [1] — I am expecting an early reply about this.

Your devoted

L. v. Beethoven

(1452) *To Bernhard Schotts Söhne, Mainz*

[*MS in the Stadtbibliothek, Mainz*] [2]

Sir!   Vienna, *November* 25, 1825

The tempo markings according to Maelzel's metronome will soon follow. I am now sending you the title of the Mass.

Missa
composita, et

Serenissimo ac Eminentissimo Domino Domino Rodolpho Joanni Caesareo Principi et Archiduci Austriae, S.R.E. tit. s. Petri in monte aureo Cardinali et Archiepiscopo Olomucensi

profundissima cum veneratione [3]
dedicata
a
Ludovico van Beethoven

[1] C. F. Peters replied at once on November 30, 1825 (see Nohl II, p. 279), asking for the return of the 360 gulden, which Beethoven, according to Peters's receipt dated December 7, must have refunded without delay. So far as is known, Peters did not publish any of Beethoven's compositions, although his predecessors Hoffmeister & Co. and Ambros Kühnel had done so.

[2] The letter and the statement were written by Karl. Only the two signatures are in Beethoven's handwriting.

[3] Inside the autograph of Letter 1154, now on deposit in Tübingen University Library, there is a copy of this dedication in which Beethoven has scratched out 'profundissima', written 'massima' above it and scrawled underneath 'profund ist Barbarismus', all done in pencil.

In the engraved copies the list of subscribers is to precede the dedication.

1. The Emperor of Russia
2. The King of Prussia
3. The King of France
4. The King of Denmark
5. The Elector of Saxony
6. The Grand Duke of Darmstadt
7. The Grand Duke of Tuscany
8. Prince Galitzin
9. Prince Radziwill
10. The Caecilia Association of Frankfurt

Please delay a little longer the dedication of the symphony, as I am still undecided about this. And I request you on the whole to postpone the publication of these works for about another three months. You will oblige me very much if you do this. What is missing will be supplied as quickly as possible.

I again request you to be so kind as to send me a copy of the corrected bassoon parts.

Perhaps you have not yet received an assurance of your ownership of the E♭ quartet. So I herewith add this assurance.[1]

Your devoted

L. v. BEETHOVEN

I herewith confirm by my signature that Herren B[ernhard] Schotts Söhne have received from me a quartet in E♭ for two violins, viola and violoncello and that this quartet is *entirely their property.*

Vienna, November 25, 1825

LUDWIG VAN BEETHOVEN

(1453) *To [Karl Holz?]*

[Autograph not traced] [2]

MY DEAR FELLOW!   [VIENNA, *November,* 1825]

Forgive me for your not having found K[arl] and me. I thought that today was Friday, whereas it is Saturday; and

[1] This statement is on a separate sheet. Op. 127 was published by Schott in March and June, 1826.   [2] Taken from *TDR* V, 258-259.

BEETHOVEN GOING FOR A WALK

A posthumous drawing by Johann Peter Lyser (1833)

(From a photograph in the British Museum)

BEETHOVEN

From the bust by Anton Dietrich (1821)

(Historisches Museum der Stadt Wien)

a long time ago we were invited to Hofrat Breuning's for today.
I beg you not to put any wrong construction on this. We hope
therefore that you will dine with us tomorrow, Sunday, for
certain —

Your friend
BEETHOVEN

Rest assured that all this is due to my having made this
mistake.

(1454) *To* [*Karl Friedrich Müller?*] [1]

[*Autograph not traced*] [2]

SIR !   [VIENNA, 1825]
Owing to my housekeeper's stupidity your mother was
turned away the other day and I was not told a word about
her having called. I have reprimanded my housekeeper for
her improper conduct, the more so as she did not even bring
your mother into my room. Everyone knows of *the boorishness
and rudeness of these people* whom I am so unfortunate as to have
about me. So I beg you to forgive me.

Your most obedient servant
L. v. BEETHOVEN

(1455) *To* ?

[*MS in the Deutsche Staatsbibliothek, Berlin*] [3]

SIR !   [VIENNA, 1825]
I am unwell ; and if this were not the case, I should
not find it too troublesome to go to you in person. Please
be so kind as to inform the bearer of this letter, H[err] v[on]

---

[1] There is a remote possibility that the addressee was the Viennese actor Karl
Friedrich Müller who, having been prevented through illness from following his
profession, published at his own risk three collections of dances, the work of several
composers whom he petitioned to assist him. Out of compassion for Müller
Beethoven contributed WoO 84, 85 and 86. See Nohl I, no. 325, n. and *KHV*.
537-540.
[2] Taken from Nohl I, no. 325.
[3] MS not available. Text taken from *TDR* V, 156, n. 1. According to
this source this draft in Karl's hand is in a Conversation Book for November,
1825.

Holz, who is also an Imperial and Royal official, why you desire to speak to me. In regard to the arrears of class tax still unpaid I must state that these are in no wise due to any unawareness of what I owe. Even if it were burdensome for me, I should always be ready to discharge to the Government any debt which I had undertaken to pay. These principles of mine are shown by my former behaviour, seeing that long ago when I was in better circumstances I offered to pay higher taxes. But when this arrangement later became too burdensome for me I came to an agreement with our Government about a rebate of this sum. Whereupon I was placed in my *present* category of contributors.

The present delay is due in part to an excess of work and business. Moreover my domestic arrangements are not such as I really ought to have; and also I am not only defraying the entire cost of my nephew's education, but am even supporting his mother.

It is not a matter of indifference to me to be treated in such a way. And most certainly no other government would do this, for I enjoy the respect of the highest ranks in all Europe. —

(1456) *To Johann Baptist Jenger, Graz* ¹

[Autograph in the Beethovenhaus, Bonn, H. C. Bodmer collection]

MY ESTEEMED FRIEND,   [VIENNA, 1825]

I shall be truly delighted to send you during the next few days the score of Matthisson's Opferlied.² All my compositions, published or unpublished, are always at your service. Why do my circumstances not allow me to let you have at once the greater works I have composed, even before they have been heard elsewhere? Unfortunately I am bound to observe my present procedure. Yet it may well be that later on such an occasion may present itself; and, if so, I shall be glad to comply with your wishes.

¹ Johann Baptist Jenger (1792–1856), a Viennese official, who was an excellent pianist. He had a close friendship with Schubert and was also acquainted with Beethoven. His official duties kept him at Graz during the years 1819–1825, but later he was settled in Vienna. See *FRBH* I, 241-242.

² Op. 121b had been published by Schott in July, 1825.

The enclosed letter is for Hofrat von Kiesewetter.[1] Please be so kind as to deliver it to him, the more so as the letter concerns you, just as much as the worthy Hofrat —

With my very special regards, your most devoted friend

BEETHOVEN

(1457) *To Tobias Haslinger*

[*Autograph in the Central State Archives, Moscow*][2]

[VIENNA, 1825]

YOU ABSOLUTELY MOST AMAZING FELLOW! AMAZING FELLOW! You have had the impudence to send me word that you do not consider me worthy of having my hair cut by you, and that you are really sending me a personal barber —

Ach To bi as To bi as

Ha! That is too annoying; and for that I impose a fine of one and a half ducats; and a third will also impose an additional half ducat. Hence one ducat becomes two and there will be a salade brilliant — It will be splendid if you come to early breakfast tomorrow, but not to *late breakfast* [4] —

Consider the miserabilia of life — And that is not nearly everything —

Well now, as early as poss[ible], I will wait until you come, without paying up the half ducat fine —

Your amicus fidelis [5]

BEETHO[VEN]

[1] There is no trace of this letter. Raphael Georg Kiesewetter, Edler von Wiesenbrunn (1773–1850), a Viennese official who was created a Hofrat in 1803, was an accomplished musician and an enthusiastic musicologist. In 1828 and 1834 he published books on the music of various countries. He collected the scores of old composers. His house at Vienna was a meeting place for musicians.

[2] This letter is reproduced in facsimile in an article in *Sovetskaya Muzika*, May, 1953, pp. 76-78.

[3] This musical setting is not listed in *KHV*. Only the notes and indications which are certain are quoted here.

[4] Beethoven liked to use the terms 'Frühstück' and 'Spätstück', when reminding his nephew and his familiar friends to be punctual. He often invited them to breakfast.

[5] I.e. faithful friend.

(1458) *To Karl Holz*

[Autograph in the Deutsche Staatsbibliothek, Berlin]

[VIENNA, 1825]

Piringer has been dealt with as he deserved to be — The witches' cavern in the P[ater]n[oster]g[asse] is being set on fire — If you can do so, send the tailor today — and, if it is not out of your way, bring some matches too — It is absolutely impossible for me to go out, nay rather, I ought to go into Eternal Salvation.

In the greatest haste, your

BETN —

(1459) *To Karl Holz*

[Autograph in the Beethovenhaus, Bonn, H. C. Bodmer collection] [1]

[VIENNA, 1825]

I have come home because the proof-reading etc. were finished by half past eleven — I hope to see you at dinner for certain.

In great haste, yours

BEETHOVEN

(1460) *To Karl Holz*

[Autograph in the Deutsche Staatsbibliothek, Berlin]

My greetings to you !   [VIENNA, 1825] [2]

And I inform you that I am not going out today. It would give me much pleasure if you could visit me perhaps this evening after your office hours —

In great haste, your friend

BEETHOVEN

I am not feeling well.

[1] The note is written in very faint pencil.
[2] Possibly owing to its rather formal tone this may be one of Beethoven's earliest notes to Karl Holz. But it was obviously written in Vienna and therefore probably after October 15, 1825. The autograph is now on deposit in Tübingen University Library.

(1461) *To Karl Holz*

[*Autograph not traced*] [1]

[VIENNA, 1825]

. . . I am running around to find a prima donna.

(1462) *To[Karl Holz?]* [2]

[*Autograph in the Benedictine Abbey, Göttweig*]

[VIENNA, 1825]

My greetings to you ! —
Please send me a statement of the sums you have disbursed
and forgive me if in every respect I must regard myself as your
debtor —

In haste, your friend
BEETHOVEN

(1463) *To Ferdinand Wolanek* [3]

[*Autograph in the Beethovenhaus, Bonn*]

Stupid, conceited ass of a fellow.[4]   [VIENNA, 1825]
And am I to exchange compliments with such a scoundrel
who filches my money ? Instead of that I ought to pull his
ass's ears.

[1] Taken from sale catalogue of J. A. Stargardt of December 3, 1889, no. 185,
where the letter is described as autograph and written in pencil.

[2] The autograph which is written in pencil is neither addressed nor dated.
The signature is in Latin script. Cf. Letter 1460, addressed to Karl Holz, which is
similar in tone.

[3] Ferdinand Wolanek, born *c.*1761 in Bohemia, was a copyist whom Beethoven
employed to copy portions of the 'Missa Solemnis'. See *FRBH* I, 293 and *FRBS*.
II, 3-19. Wolanek's inferior work was the occasion for frequent quarrels with the
composer ; and in the end this copyist returned the MSS without finishing his task.
When doing so he wrote a covering letter thanking Beethoven for having allowed
him to have some share in the work, alluding to Beethoven's emotional temperament which had led to 'dissonances', but consoling himself with the thought
that if Mozart and Haydn had copied for Beethoven, the latter would have
abused them in precisely the same manner.

[4] These six words are scrawled over Wolanek's letter, which consists of one
page. For the letter see *TDR* V, pp. 175-176. The remainder of Beethoven's
outburst is written under Wolanek's letter.

Slovenly copyist!
Stupid fellow!
Correct the mistakes you have made through your ignorance, arrogance, conceit and stupidity. That is more fitting than to want to teach me. For to do so is exactly as if the *sow* should want to teach Minerva.[1]

BEETHOVEN

I beg you to do Mozart and Haydn *the honour* of not mentioning *their names.*[2]
Indeed yesterday and even before then it was decided *not to employ you any more* to copy for me.[3]

(1464) *To Ignaz Schuppanzigh*

[*Autograph not traced*][4]

DEAR FRIEND,   [VIENNA, 1825]
I am heartily delighted to be able to serve you; and thus my desire is fulfilled — If the composition has some merit, yet thanks to his performance Schuppanzigh's merit is even greater — As often as you all need the quartet, I shall be delighted to place it at your disposal. Nobody else is to have it — I trust that the financial side also has turned out well.— Unfortunately I can do nothing about that — I embrace you, most excellent and honoured Mylord, and shall gladly receive you tomorrow —

Your friend
BEETHOVEN

[1] Cf. Letter 1387, p. 1207, n. 1.
[2] Added at the right side of the page.
[3] Added at the left side of the page.
[4] Taken from an article by Hans Holländer in the *Daily Telegraph* of June 10, 1939.

1826

1826

(1465) To Karl van Beethoven

[*Autograph not traced*] ¹

[VIENNA], *January* 4, [1826]

I shall be with you this evening —

B

e je porte avec moi aussi l'argent pour votre maître.

(1466) To Bernhard Schotts Söhne, Mainz

[*MS in the Stadtbibliothek, Mainz*] ²

GENTLEMEN! VIENNA, *January* 28, 1826

In reply to your latest communication I inform you that you will soon receive the metronome markings for all the works. Please do not forget that the first quartet is dedicated to Prince Galitzin.³ — So far as I know, Matth[ias] Artaria has already received from you two copies of the overture.⁴ I too should very much like to receive several copies of this work and also of the quartet. If I have not yet thanked you for the previous copies, well, that was really due to my forgetfulness. By the way, you may rest assured that I never sell nor act as agent for the sale of a single copy. Only a few artists whom I really esteem are to receive copies; and that will not injure you, seeing that in any case they could not afford to buy these works.

Well, there is something else I should like to hear and that is whether Prince Galitzin when he sent you particulars of the title for the dedication asked you at the same time for the number of copies of the quartet and the overture which he required. For, if not, I must send them to him from here.

---

¹ According to an entry in a sale catalogue of Albert Cohn (1896), no. 209, lot 19, this short note is autograph and beside the address on the verso 'Pour M. Charles de Beethoven' are the following pencilled words in German: 'and also the umbrella and the frock-coat'.
² Written by Karl and signed by Beethoven, who also added the musical phrase at the end of the letter. ³ Op. 127.
⁴ Op. 124, published by Schott in December, 1825.

By the way, I request you to arrange for your deliveries to me to be made in future through Matth[ias] Artaria and no longer through Steiner, because I hope to receive everything more quickly through the former.

In the Mass the list of subscribers should be printed first and then followed by the dedication to the Archduke worded exactly as I have sent it to you.

I will soon let you have particulars about the dedication of the symphony. It was to have been dedicated to the Emperor Alexander.[1] The delay has been caused by the events which have taken place.

You would again like to have some works of mine? Excellent fellows ! !

You have grossly insulted me !

You have played several wrong notes !

Therefore you must first purge yourselves before my judgment seat here in Vienna. As soon as the ice has thawed Mainz must betake itself hither. The reviewing Councillor of the Supreme Court of Appeal must turn up here in order to answer for his actions. And now I send you all good wishes !

We are far from being particularly attached to you !

Handed in on the heights of Schwarzspanien without handing anything.

BEETHOVEN

il / Posaun 16 füssig — trillo / minacciando

---

[1] Alexander I of Russia had died on December 1, 1825.

(1467) *To* [*Joseph Karl Bernard?*]

[*Autograph in the Beethovenhaus, Bonn*]

[VIENNA, *February* 3, 1826]

Just read this. And I am also enclosing the reply which is quite suitable for that shameless woman — You need only deliver the letter without having anything to do with her —

Please see that you are chucked out tomorrow and then come and have dinner with me — Today all that remains to be done is to find out *Schlesinger's correct address* ¹ — All good wishes to both of you — I hope to have some news of you both.

(1468) *To the Abbé Maximilian Stadler* ²

[*Autograph in the National and University Library, Prague*]

[VIENNA], *February* 6, 1826

MY ESTEEMED AND MOST WORTHY SIR!

You have really performed a very good deed by rendering justice to the shades of Mozart in your truly masterly work, which is such a penetrating study of the subject.³ Both lay and profane people and all who are at all musical or can even be accounted such ⁴ must feel indebted to you —

Either no talent whatever or a very great one is required to produce what H[err] W[eber] has produced. Let us bear in mind too that, so far as I remember, this person has written

¹ Probably the address of Moritz Schlesinger in Paris.
² Maximilian Stadler (1748–1833), born at Melk, became a priest and in 1789 was Abbot of Kremsmünster. From 1796 to 1803 he was in Vienna, devoting most of his time to the study of music; and in 1815 Vienna became his permanent home. An ardent admirer of Mozart's compositions, Stadler had little understanding of Beethoven's style. See *FRBH* II, 241-242.
³ Gottfried Weber had recently published in *Caecilia*, III, 205 ff. an article casting doubts on the genuineness of certain obviously genuine passages in Mozart's 'Requiem'. Stadler immediately defended Mozart in a monograph published in Vienna, 1826, and sent a copy of it to Beethoven. Furthermore, Stadler first published this letter from Beethoven in his monograph: *Zweiter und letzter Nachtrag zur Vertheidigung der Echtheit des Mozartschen Requiems* (Vienna, 1827), pp. 46-47.
⁴ The words from 'or can' to 'such' are added at the foot of the page.

a book on composition and yet tries to attribute to Mozart passages like

And if we add an example of W[eber]'s own clumsy work, such as

then when appreciating H[err] W[eber]'s extraordinary knowledge of harmony and melody, we are reminded of the former old Imperial composers Sterkel,[1] Haueisen [2] Kalkbrenner (I mean the father),[3] André (but by no means the other one) [4] and so forth.

Requiescant in pace — But I am particularly grateful to you, my esteemed friend, for the pleasure you have given me by sending me your treatise. For I have always counted

[1] Abt Johann Franz Xaver Sterkel (1750–1817), born at Würzburg, after travelling widely was appointed court chaplain and organist at Mainz in 1778. He wrote a considerable number of works for the pianoforte.

[2] I am indebted to Professor J. Schmidt-Görg for deciphering this illegible name and for providing the following information : W. N. Haueisen, who was an organist at Frankfurt am Main, founded a music publishing firm there in 1773. He published his own works and those of other composers, notably those of Sterkel.

[3] Christian Kalkbrenner (1763–1806) after a varied musical career settled in Paris where he became in 1799 producer and choirmaster at the Opera. His own operas, however, met with little success. He is better known for his writings on the theory of music and as the father of his more famous son Friedrich Kalkbrenner. Cf. Letter 1268, p. 1112, n. 2.

[4] Johann André (1741–1799), composer of songs and operas, founded in 1784 at Offenbach the music publishing firm which was carried on after his death by his more famous third son Johann Anton André (1775–1842). Here Beethoven is playing on the usual meaning 'andre', i.e. other.

myself amongst the greatest admirers of Mozart and shall remain so until my last breath —

Reverend sir, *I will very soon ask you for your blessing* —

With sincere regards, most worthy sir, I remain yours faithfully

BEETHOVEN

(1469) *To Dr. Anton Braunhofer*

[Autograph in the Beethovenhaus, Bonn, H. C. Bodmer collection]

ESTEEMED FRIEND !   [VIENNA, *February* 23, 1826]

I am extremely obliged to you for your attentive care for my health. So far as it has been at all possible, I have kept to your prescriptions; of wine, coffee and everything else I have drunk only the amounts you ordered. It is difficult to judge at once the extent of the effect of your treatment after only a few days. The pain in my back is not severe, I admit, but it shows that the trouble is still there. So I believe that I am right in using the medicines you sent me today (but I don't know how much they cost) — Don't neglect your own welfare when attending to the health of other people. I am extremely sorry not to be able to prescribe something for you in return and must just leave you to your own devices — I hope to see you as soon as possible —

With kindest regards, your grateful

BEETHOVEN

(1470) *To Karl van Beethoven*

[Autograph in a private collection]

DEAR SON !   [VIENNA, *February* 24, 1826]

This receipt must be cashed at Court tomorrow morning, February 25th. You do not bind yourself in any way in the formal wording when you fill in as well: from September 1, 1825 until the last day of February, 1826 — Give less time to sleep and all will go well. At noon tomorrow you will hand me over the money — Chiefly on my own account I am [sorry]

1277

to have to trouble you.   Who knows but that Fate may soon free you completely from all this.[1] —

Your faithful father

In the context the wording should be: to His Imperial Highness the Archduke Rudolph, Eminence and Cardinal.[2]

(1471) *To Dr. Anton Braunhofer*

[*Autograph in the Beethovenhaus, Bonn, H. C. Bodmer collection*] [3]

SIR!   [VIENNA, *February*, 1826]

Please do visit me, for I have been plagued for some time with rheumatism or gout.   I am well aware that I am still in your debt, but I shall not be so for very much longer — I am always at home.   Indeed this weather makes us bar our doors.

I hope that I shall see you for certain, whenever you can come, and tomorrow at any rate —

With kindest regards, your friend

BEETHOVEN

(1472) *To Bernhard Schotts Söhne, Mainz*

[*Autograph in a private collection*] [4]

GENTLEMEN!   VIENNA, *March* 28, 1826

I have been informed today through the Prussian Envoy in Vienna [5] that His Royal Majesty graciously permits me to dedicate to His Supreme Person the D minor symphony with choruses [6] — So you may now think out the title-page and you may consider and arrange for the allegorical indication

[1] Beethoven is referring to the possibility of his death.
[2] This additional sentence is written on a separate sheet.
[3] Page 3 of this autograph note has the following addition:

Meine Wohnung
Schwarzspanier
2[ter] Stock.
No. 201 Links.

[4] The autograph consists of four untidily written and partly illegible pages, the fourth of which bears the address in Beethoven's hand and the firm's endorsement.
[5] Prince Hatzfeld.   See Letter 1508, which owing to an oversight has been misplaced.
[6] Op. 125, published by Schott at the end of August, 1826.

and expression and execution of the other emblems of the Royal
Prussian attributes, so that there may be no infringement of
etiquette but rather a well set-out title-page —
    You will soon receive the metronome markings not only of
the Mass but also of the symphony and the quartet.[1] Ars longa
vita brevis — [For Paris?] I should perhaps be able to produce
a new quartet. Although I certainly do not compose merely
for the sake of the fee, yet my circumstances demand that I give
some consideration *to this matter.* But what am I to do when I
am still awaiting a reply to my letter in which I asked 60
ducats for a quartet?!! And yet the very great competition
has raised the fee even higher!! — All I need *add* [three words
illegible] is that now I receive *for a quartet of this kind* at least 80
gold ducats — My deepest thanks for the money you have sent
me and for the translations — The sons of Apollo are rather
difficult to propitiate, as Homer has already described in the
Iliad. By way of atonement you must send me three large casks
of Johannesberger; and on each cask there must be a Bacchante.
                    Your most devoted
                                        BEETHOVEN

(1473) *To Stephan von Breuning*

[*Autograph in the Beethovenhaus, Bonn, H. C. Bodmer collection*]

[VIENNA, *Spring,* 1826]
    You, my esteemed friend, are up to the eyes in work and
so am I. And, what is more, I am not yet quite well —
I would have invited you to dinner before, but even now I
still need the assistance of several people, of whom the gifted
leading spirit is the cook. Their intellectual works are *not
indeed* to be found *in their own cellar,* for they pry into kitchens
and cellars and their company would serve you ill. But
things will soon be changed — Don't use Czerny's Klavierschule.[2] During the next few days I shall receive fuller particulars about another one [3] —
    Here is the fashion journal [4] which I promised your wife,

---

[1] Op. 123, 125 and 127.
[2] This work was published by Haslinger in 1826.   [3] Cf. Letter 1432.
[4] Probably the *Wiener Zeitschrift für Kunst, Literatur, Theater und Mode,* familiarly
called the *Wiener Modenzeitung,* which was edited by Johann Schickh (cf. Letter
955, p. 823, n. 1) and published by Anton Strauss.

and here is something for your children. If you like, I can continue to provide you with the fashion journal. And indeed you have only to order from me anything else that I possess and that you would like to have —

With love and deep regard, your friend

BEETHOVEN

I hope that *we* shall soon meet again.

(1474) *To Karl van Beethoven*

[Autograph in the Beethovenhaus, Bonn, H. C. Bodmer collection] ¹

[VIENNA, Spring, 1826]

I shall be very glad to know when you want to or can come to me? — You know that we must pay that call. And then we can go and dine wherever you like —

Your loving uncle

Not later than half past twelve or one o'clock at the latest [2] —

(1475) *To Sigmund Anton Steiner*

[Autograph in the possession of Paul Wittgenstein]

[VIENNA, Spring, 1826]

If you are willing to give a certain Grünbaum's Fidelio [3] to be copied, then do so, or leave it so — At the theatre it would take too long to obtain it from the people who are really taking over the management. [4]

BEETHOVEN

[1] A pencilled note written in a bold, clear hand.
[2] The postscript is written on the right side of the note.
[3] Possibly a copy belonging to the tenor Johann Christoph Grünbaum (1787–1870) or to his wife Therese (1791–1876), a daughter of Wenzel Müller, who became an operatic singer.
[4] This was Louis Antoine Duport, who was again in charge of the Kärntnertor Theatre, from 1825 to 1828. Cf. Letter 429, p. 424, n. 3.

(1476) *To Karl Holz*

[*Autograph not traced*] [1]

[VIENNA, *Spring*, 1826]

Cito, Citissime.[2] Schindler is not coming. Come to lunch. In any case we must meet. Yours

BEETHOVEN

(1477) *To [Antonio Diabelli ?]*

[*Autograph in the Nationalbibliothek, Vienna*]

[VIENNA], *April* 3, 1826

Holz assures me that you also want to have the copperplate engraving representing Handel's monument in St. Peter's Church in London enlarged and engraved and published.[3] This affords me infinite pleasure, apart altogether from the fact that I have been the cause of your undertaking.

Please accept my thanks in advance —

Your most devoted servant

BEETHOVEN

(1478) *To Karl Holz*

[*Autograph in the Beethovenhaus, Bonn, H. C. Bodmer collection*]

MOST EXCELLENT WOOD ! — [VIENNA, *early April*, 1826]

Don't be — wood — en. Our beloved Government wants to interview me today at 10 o'clock. So I beg you *to go there*

---

[1] Taken from *TDR* V, 188, n. 1. [2] Quickly, very quickly.
[3] Beethoven is referring to the marble monument to Handel in Westminster Abbey, completed in 1760 by Louis François Roubiliac. Westminster Abbey is officially termed the Collegiate Church of St. Peter's. Probably the allusion is to the drawing of this monument by Edward Francis Burney, the talented nephew of Dr. Charles Burney, which appeared as Plate 2, engraved by J. M. Delattre, in Burney's *Commemoration of Handel*, London, 1785. A German translation of this volume by Johann Joachim Eschenburg was published in the same year. It is in two volumes, the first of which has a rather poor reproduction of Delattre's engraving. Beethoven's library contained a copy of Dr. Burney's *History of Music*, and he may well have come across the latter's Handel Commemoration volume either in the original or in the German translation. But according to Professor O. E. Deutsch this engraving was never enlarged and published in Vienna, although Antonio Diabelli, suggested as the possible recipient of this letter, published *c.* 1825 a folio print of Haydn's monument in the Gumpendorf cemetery, Vienna. This would explain the introduction of 'also'.

instead of me. But please come to me *first*, and you may do so whenever it is most convenient for you. Further, I have already written a letter *to our high and mighty Government*, which you can take with you. I am sorry to have to trouble you again. But I cannot go myself; and yet the matter must be settled.

Your friend
BEETHOVEN

(1479) *To the Censorship Authorities*

[*Autograph in the Benedictine Abbey, Göttweig*]

[VIENNA, *shortly before April* 9, 1826]

MOST WORSHIPFUL CENSORSHIP !

There is a threat to publish several works of mine, in which owing to a spirit of revenge against me the mistakes I have indicated are not to be corrected. The titles are worded so barbarously that their publication would be a disgrace to Vienna.[1] Hence I request our Worshipful Censorship not to allow these works to be announced until I can assure the public by my signature that they are appearing in a present-able condition.[2]

(1480) *To Tobias Haslinger*

[*MS not traced*] [3]

VIENNA, *April* 9, 1826

I inform you that neither the overture [4] nor the 'Elegischer Gesang' [5] requires any further proof-reading and that the titles too are correct. In regard to the march with chorus [6] and the vocal trio,[7] however, the previously wrong notes have now been corrected, I admit, but again the titles are not exactly

---

[1] Op. 114, 116, 117 and 118, published by Steiner's firm in 1826. See Letter 1480.

[2] The autograph is not signed.

[3] Taken from Unger no. 94. The letter was written by Karl and signed by Beethoven.

[4] Op. 117, published by Haslinger in July 1826.

[5] Op. 118, published by Haslinger in July, 1826.

[6] Op. 114, published by Steiner in April, 1826.

[7] Op. 116, published by Steiner in February, 1826.

as I gave them to you. Seeing that this business has now dragged on for six weeks and that moreover I have already had several experiences of my failure to overcome your obstinacy, I have handed over to the Worshipful Censorship both titles in their proper form; and I am informing you that I have done so.[1]

LUDWIG VAN BEETHOVEN

I have desired to communicate the above information to you out of kindness, so that you may take steps accordingly. For I will *never* allow these works to be published with the titles which you have prefixed to them.

(1481) *To Moritz Schlesinger, Paris*

[*MS not traced*] [2]

DEAR FRIEND!   VIENNA, *April 22, 1826*
I have just received your letter of April 13th and am answering it with all speed, so that our relations which suffered a rupture may now be restored.

I inform you that another new quartet will be finished in two or three weeks at latest.[3] Please arrange therefore that the sum of 80 Imperial and Royal gold ducats be paid to me immediately. And let there be no delay, for quartets are now in demand everywhere; and it really seems that our age is taking a step forward.

I see from your letter that you misunderstood what I wrote, for I gave the quartet not to my brother but to Matthias Artaria.[4] My brother, however, was also in touch with Biedermann. So you will realize that nothing more can be done about this quartet. As to the other quartets and quintets you would like to have, I will try to finish them as quickly as possible.

With all my heart I thank you for your friendly sentiments. As to the trip to London I will explain my views on this at the next opportunity.

[1] Cf. Letter 1479.
[2] Taken from Chantavoine, *Le Ménestrel*, no. 86 (1924), p. 138.
[3] Op. 135.   [4] Op. 130.

Please hasten to transmit the fee and at the same time to let me know where I am to collect it after the delivery of the new quartet. I will leave at the same place too the score of the A minor quartet ¹ which I would have sent you long ago, had I but received some news from you.

I wish you all that is good and beautiful and I remain, as always, in friendship and devotion

yours sincerely,

BEETHOVEN

I, too, who have written this letter, send you heartfelt thanks for remembering me. And I hope that you will keep your promise to pay us a visit in Vienna very soon.

KARL

(1482) *To Karl Holz*

[MS not traced] ²

BELOVED FRIEND!   VIENNA, *April* 26, 1826

You may rest assured that I have completely forgotten the recent incident and that it will never alter my feelings of gratitude to you. Please, therefore, do not show anything of this in your behaviour. You will always be welcome to me.

I hope that next Sunday you will not despise my dinner table. I have too much to do this week and shall have no peace till everything is finished. And moreover in such cases it is impossible to fix the dinner hour in my household; and in general I have always been accustomed since my thirteenth year to dine very late. I have been encouraged in this habit by respectable business men *in Vienna*; and it is difficult now to give it up completely. Do not treat this remark ironically. Remember that I am dependent on the Muses; and then you will certainly admit that I am right. For a very long time I have been thinking of some means of proving my gratitude to you; and as soon as possible I will set things

¹ Op. 132.
² Taken from Nohl II, no. 296. According to Nohl who transcribed the letter then in private ownership, it was written by Karl and only the last four words, including the signature, were written by Beethoven.

going. If you have time to visit me this week I shall be delighted if you will do so. You will find me quite unchanged, the same as usual. I shall expect you on Sunday for certain.

Ever your friend

BEETHOVEN

(1483) *To Karl Holz*

[Autograph in the Beethovenhaus, Bonn, H. C. Bodmer collection] [1]

[VIENNA], Thursday, May 4, [1826]

With all haste and speed.

I did not think the day before yesterday that you would come so *early*; and, moreover, I was detained somewhere, which accounts for my arriving so late — Please bring the pension form with you today, for yesterday in fact somebody was sent to me about the pension.

Vale etc., fave.[2] Don't forget to turn up today for our feast.

B——N

(1484) *To Karl August, Freiherr von Klein* [3]

[MS not traced] [4]

VIENNA, May 10, 1826

Through Hofrat von Mosel [5] I received a letter from you which, as I have been very busy, I could not answer at once. You desire to dedicate a work to me. However little I can claim such a favour, yet I shall be delighted to accept the dedication of your fine work. But you want me to play at the same time the part of a critic. You forget, however, that I myself have to submit to criticism! Still I hold with Voltaire 'that a few midge-bites cannot hold up a lively horse in his canter'.[6] Please follow me in this respect. But so that I may

---

[1] This letter was first published in the *Beethoven-Jahrbuch*, 1953/54, p. 37.

[2] Cf. Letter 1425, p. 1244, n. 4.

[3] Little is known about this recipient who was born at Mannheim in 1794 and was evidently a composer. [4] Taken from *TDR* V, 340, and Kal., no. 1141.

[5] Cf. Letter 845, p. 727, n. 1.

[6] A quotation from Voltaire's tale *L'Ingénu*, chapter 11, where the hero, after perusing some periodicals containing defamatory statements by literary critics, exclaims : 'Je les compare à certains moucherons qui vont déposer leurs œufs dans le derrière des plus beaux chevaux : cela ne les empêche pas de courir'.

meet you not surreptitiously, but in a way which is open and frank, as I always am, let me just tell you that in future works of this kind you might pay more attention to the individuality of the voices.

I shall always regard it as an honour if I can serve you anywhere in any way whatsoever. I commend myself to your friendly sentiments for me and I remain, Sir, with the most cordial regards,

your most devoted

BEETHOVEN

(1485) *To Bernhard Schotts Söhne, Mainz*

[MS in the Stadtbibliothek, Mainz] [1]

VIENNA, May 20, 1826

Overwhelmed with business affairs and constantly dogged by ill health I have been unable to reply sooner to your esteemed communication of April 6th. Moreover at that time the quartet which is now finished was not yet ready.[2] You may well believe that I am unwilling to reduce my fee of 80 ducats offered and paid to me for each of the two earlier quartets which immediately followed yours. But as you have already agreed to pay me this fee I will gladly accede to your proposal to have it paid to me in two instalments. Therefore be so kind as to send me two bills of exchange, one for 40 ducats *a vista* and the other for the same amount payable after two months. As no doubt you have heard of the misfortune which has befallen the House of Fries, I should prefer you to make out the bills of exchange to Arnstein & Eskeles.[3]

You will receive the metronome markings by post this day week. Everything has been slowed down because my health has to be considered. I have not yet received from you anything of the E♭ quartet,[4] nor indeed the Minerva [5] — I must

---

[1] Written by Karl and signed by Beethoven.
[2] The C sharp minor quartet, Op. 131.
[3] This famous banking house was directed by Baron Nathan Adam von Arnstein and Baron Eskeles who had married two sisters, daughters of the Berlin banker Itzig. The Baroness Fanny Arnstein had a salon in Vienna.
[4] Op. 127. Schott had published the parts in March, 1826. It was published in score in June, 1826.
[5] No doubt Beethoven means Schott's music review *Caecilia*.

again ask you not to think that I want to sell a work twice. You yourself know what happened in the case of the overture — I could not possibly have replied to you about the accusation of having sold your quartet over again to Schlesinger. For such an accusation was really far too despicable for me to desire to defend myself against it. Something like that cannot be washed out even by the best Rhine wine. For that you must make in addition some Liguorian expiations such as we go in for here.[1]

Your most devoted
L. v. BEETHOVEN

NB.   I request you to answer this letter with all speed.

(1486) *To Karl van Beethoven*

[*Autograph not traced*] [2]

[VIENNA, *end of May*, 1826]

Faites comme vous croyez de cette lettre à S[chlesinger], de donner ou que non, ce dépend tout à fait de votre intention.

(1487) *To Adolf Martin Schlesinger, Berlin*

[*MS in the Conservatoire de Paris*] [3]

SIR !   VIENNA, *May* 31, 1826

In reply to your esteemed letter of April 15th I inform you that Count Brühl, although he expressed himself quite favourably on the whole about the poem Melusine by Herr Grillparzer, would like me to make another choice, because

---

[1] A reference to Alfonso Maria de Liguori (1696–1787), who was born at Marianella near Naples. In 1732 he founded, with the permission of Pope Benedict XIV, the Congregation of the Most Holy Redeemer whose members vowed to serve the destitute and unfortunate. De Liguori was consecrated Bishop in 1762 and canonized in 1839. His outstanding contribution to theology is his *Theologia Moralis* in eight volumes. The order founded by de Liguori was established in Austria in 1820.

[2] Taken from Kal., no. 1149. Possibly this sentence was written on the cover of a letter which has disappeared.

[3] Written by Karl and signed by Beethoven.

the aforesaid opera has some similarity with Undine by Baron de la Motte Fouqué.[1] Well, as soon as I have dealt with this matter and have finished the composition too, I shall give you the preference over all other publishers — My best greetings to Herr Marx. I will soon let him have something — For a very long time now I have been awaiting some news from your son about my latest quartet.[2] His accident may have been the cause of the delay.[3] But I believe that father and son are at any rate the same. Seeing that relying on him I have already refused several other publishers, you yourself might take on the quartet. You know that the fee is 80 gold ducats.

The following trifles are ready: serenade or Gratulationsmenuett[4] and an entr'acte,[5] both for full orchestra. I could let you have both for 20 gold ducats.

But I must beg you to reply as quickly as possible. In regard to the works, please choose some place in Vienna where I can deliver them in exchange for the sum in gulden.

Let me add that it will afford me much pleasure to make your personal acquaintance very soon.

Your most devoted
BEETHOVEN

(1488) *To Heinrich Albert Probst, Leipzig*

[*MS in the Deutsche Staatsbibliothek, Berlin*][6]

SIR !   VIENNA, *June* 3, 1826

I always consider myself to some extent under an obligation to offer you works composed by me, should I be in a position to do so. I am now more free than I used to be, i.e. when I was obliged to give to those who took greater

---

[1] Count Karl Friedrich Moritz Paul von Brühl (1772–1837) had been appointed in 1815 General Intendant of the Royal Theatre in Berlin. In July, 1816 E. T. A. Hoffmann's last opera 'Undine', based on the story by Friedrich de la Motte Fouqué, was produced at that theatre.

[2] Op. 132, which was not published by Moritz Schlesinger, Paris, until September, 1827.

[3] The building which housed Moritz Schlesinger's firm in Paris had been destroyed by fire. Cf. Letter 1267, p. 1111, n. 2.

[4] WoO3. Cf. Letter 1105, p. 975, n. 6.

[5] WoO 2b, entr'acte music for Christoph Kuffner's tragedy 'Tarpeja'. Cf. Letter 272, p. 288, n. 4.

[6] Written by Karl and signed by Beethoven.

works from me some smaller ones as well, without which they refused to take the greater ones. But so far as I remember, you did not want to be bothered with greater works. In this connexion I am offering you an absolutely new quartet for two violins, viola and violoncello.[1] But you must not be surprised if for this I ask a fee of eighty gold ducats. I can assure you on my honour that this sum has already been paid to me for several quartets. Meanwhile I must ask you to write to me very quickly about this matter. Should you accept my offer, then I request you to remit the sum to a banking house in Vienna, where I can draw it after delivering the work. But if you decline my offer, in that event also I expect a speedy reply, for other publishers have already made offers to me. I have also the following trifles ready and these I could let you have: a serenade-Gratulations-menuett and an entr'acte, both for full orchestra; the two works for 20 gold ducats.[2]

Awaiting an early reply I remain, Sir, your devoted

BEETHOVEN

(1489) *To Karl van Beethoven*

[*Autograph in the Beethovenhaus, Bonn, H. C. Bodmer collection*] [3]

[VIENNA, *June*, 1826]

If only because at any rate you have obeyed me, all is forgiven and forgotten. I will tell you more when I see you. I am quite calm today — Do not think that I have anything else in mind but your welfare; and judge my actions by this. — Do not take any step which would make *you* unhappy and put an early end to *my* life — I did not get to sleep until about three o'clock, for I was coughing the whole night — I embrace you with all my heart and feel convinced that soon you will no longer *misjudge* me. For to that I ascribe your action yesterday — I expect you without fail at one o'clock today; but do not cause me any more sorrow and anxiety — Meanwhile all good wishes.

Your sincere and loving father —

---

[1] Probably the C sharp minor quartet, Op. 131. It was published posthumously by Schott in June, 1827.

[2] Listed in *KHV.* as WoO 3 and WoO 2b respectively. Cf. Letter 1487.

[3] The whole letter is written in pencil, in a bold, clear hand.

We shall be alone, for I am not letting H[olz] come, the more so as I should not like anything of what happened yesterday to leak out. Do come — don't let my poor heart *bleed any longer*.

(1490) *To Karl Holz*

[*Autograph not traced*] [1]

[VIENNA, *June*, 1826]

Please come as soon as possible, so that we may arrange all that is necessary. It is no easy task, for he wanted to go off again early this morning.[2]

In the greatest haste.

Your
BEETHOVEN

(1491) *To Bernhard Schotts Söhne, Mainz*

[*MS in the Stadtbibliothek, Mainz*] [3]

VIENNA, *July* 12, 1826

Referring to your esteemed communication, the last one, in which you inform me that you have now sent to Herr Frank [4] in Vienna a draft, to be collected immediately, for the first half of the fee for my latest quartet, I must tell you that the above-mentioned work is finished and ready for delivery. Hence all that remains to be done is that you should be so kind as to send me a draft for the second half, to be collected in two months and amounting to 40 ducats. As soon as I receive it I shall not delay to deliver the work to Herr Frank.

I should have paid no attention whatever to this circumstance which I attribute purely to some slight forgetfulness on your part, did I not intend soon to undertake a short trip for the sake of my health; and for this I still need a sum of money which I can easily raise with the help of such a draft.

[1] Taken from *TDR* V, 352.
[2] Evidently a reference to Karl.
[3] Written by Karl and signed by Beethoven.
[4] Franck (not Frank) & Co. were wholesale dealers and bankers in Vienna.

I close with the request to send me this draft by return of post as I shall be here only for a very short time.

With kindest regards, I remain your most devoted

L. v. BEETHOVEN

(1492) *To Bernhard Schotts Söhne, Mainz*

[*MS in the Stadtbibliothek, Mainz*]

VIENNA, *July* 26, 1826

From the postscript to your esteemed communication of July 8th I gather that you want to send two copies of the symphony to the King of Prussia. Please postpone doing so for the time being, for I intend to send a manuscript copy of this work to the King by a courier from here; and this can be arranged quite safely in that way. The only request I have to make of you is that you postpone the publication until I inform you that the King has received the copy. You realize that when a work is published the copy ceases to have any value. For the copies intended for the King I request you to use fine paper specially chosen for that purpose.

In my last letter of July 12th,[2] which you have doubtless received, I told you that on account of my uncertain health I had decided to take a short trip. For this purpose I am still awaiting your draft on Messrs. Frank in Vienna, on receipt of which I will immediately carry out my intention.

So I beg you to be so kind as to hasten your reply. With kindest regards, your most devoted

BEETHOVEN

Postscript [3]

The present Tobias Primus, formerly Secundus,[4] complains that he has had many enquiries for the E♭ quartet and that *two months ago* he wrote to you for *an additional supply*, but has not received any copies [5] — This belongs to the

---

[1] Written by Karl and signed by Beethoven who also wrote the postscript.

[2] Letter 1491.

[3] This postscript is in Beethoven's hand.

[4] On Steiner's retirement in July, 1826, Haslinger had become sole manager of the firm.

[5] Op. 127.

numbers emanating *from Schwarz-Spanien*, which are due to appear very soon [1] —

(1493) *To Karl van Beethoven*

[*Autograph not traced*] [2]

[VIENNA, *Summer*, 1826]
On account of the letters you must kindly write and let me know when you will and can come to me. Your postponement may be genuine — I am awaiting your kind decision.

B

A une heure je vous attend surement.[3]

(1494) *To Bernhard Schotts Söhne, Mainz*

[*MS in the Stadtbibliothek, Mainz*] [4]

VIENNA, *July* 29, 1826
I hasten to tell you of the safe arrival of your esteemed communication of July 19th.

At the same time I inform you that in a few days I shall deliver to Herr Frank the quartet and your letter as well. This I would have done sooner, if my anxiety to send you the work absolutely correct and ready for engraving had not decided me to check it again most carefully.

With all my heart I thank you for sending me the bill of exchange and I beg you once more not to treat this request of mine as indicating my distrust of your esteemed firm.

You will shortly receive the metronome markings.

However much I should like to write to you about a matter of equal importance to you and to me, yet I am so overwhelmed with business affairs that it is impossible for me to do so today. Hence I am postponing the full statement until next post-day and I remain your most devoted

BEETHOVEN

[1] Beethoven is referring to his latest residence in the Schwarzspanierhaus and possibly to his work on more string quartets.
[2] Taken from Kal., no. 1147.
[3] According to Kalischer this sentence is written on the cover.
[4] Written by Karl and signed by Beethoven.

(1495) *To Dr. von Smetana* [1]

[Autograph in the Beethovenhaus, Bonn]

[VIENNA, *July* 30, 1826]

MOST HONOURED HERR VON SMETANA,

A great misfortune has happened, a misfortune which *Karl* has accidentally brought upon himself.[2] I hope that it is still possible to save him, but my hope depends particularly on you, provided you can come soon. Karl has a *bullet* in his head. How this has happened you will learn in due course [3] — But come quickly, for God's sake, quickly.

Yours respectfully,

BEETHOVEN

As help had to be provided quickly, he had to be taken to his mother's where he now is. I enclose her address.[4]

(1496) *To Professor Wilhelm Ehlers, Mannheim* [5]

[Autograph not traced] [6]

MY DEAR EHLERS!   [VIENNA], *August* 1, 1826

As I have been overwhelmed with work — my reply is arriving rather late — I agree to everything you are arranging about the 'Ruinen von Athen'. But do not forget to restore *the truth* which has greatly suffered in Meissner's adaptation.

[1] Karl von Smetana, the surgeon who had operated on Karl for hernia. Cf. Letter 657, p. 599, n. 2.
[2] On Sunday, July 30th, after pawning his watch on the previous day in order to buy a pair of pistols, Karl drove out to Baden and tried to commit suicide in the nearby Helenental.
[3] For further details of this event see *TDR* V, 354-358.
[4] Johanna was then living at Innere Stadt 717. See *TDR* V, 359.
[5] Wilhelm Ehlers, born at Hanover in 1774, became a famous singer and teacher of singing. He came to Vienna in 1809, in 1821 was singing at Pest, in 1822 at Pressburg and from 1824 to 1826 was Regisseur at the Königstadt Theatre in Berlin. In 1826 he settled at Mannheim as Regisseur of the Court Theatre and teacher of singing.
[6] Taken from a seemingly careful transcript in the British Museum. The transcriber states that the letter is in Beethoven's hand, as also the long address on the verso. See *TDR* V, 367. Cf. also L. Nohl, *Mosaik* (Leipzig, 1882), p. 334, where the version given is a transcript of the letter then in private ownership.

And, of course, this truth can *only* be found in Kotzebue's original text — If you can make something of it,[1] you have my full approval. But do see that everything is right. For there was another overture in G minor[2] to the '*Ruinen von Athen*' and there was a further one for Meissner's adaptation for the Josephstadt, which has been engraved by Schott at Mainz.[3] Hence it depends upon the manner in which the most recent adaptation has been made. If you require the latter in C major, I would, as soon as you let me know, refer you at once to Schott about *this one*. For the Kapellmeister of the Königstadt Theatre has made a disgraceful pianoforte arrangement of the overture in C; and presumably he has committed offences against the score as well.[4] He probably thought that he would be at Königsberg and that at Königsberg *he would be able to apply to it Kant's Criticism of Pure Reason* —

I am delighted to let you have any profits you may make out of this work with which you have taken so much trouble. And I will accept nothing from you but a small present as a remembrance. I will write to Schott to let you have *the Opferlied* as well, should you write for it. For the original and *true draft* of it was found only later. It will afford me pleasure if you will just let me know soon about this matter — I warmly embrace you — Your friend

BEETHOVEN

(1497) *To Karl Holz*

[Autograph not traced] [5]

[VIENNA, *probably August* 8, 1826]

Kindly leave the name of the Police Inspector whom we saw. What a pretty mess! Yesterday Karl was taken away after all by the police and in a very objectionable way [6] —

---

[1] Beethoven has deleted here 'and come to some arrangement with those people in Berlin'.

[2] 'In G minor' has been added at the foot of the page.

[3] Op. 124, the overture 'Die Weihe des Hauses', Beethoven's free adaptation of Op. 113, had been published by Schott in December, 1825. In this letter Beethoven confuses Professor A. G. Meissner (cf. Letter 85) with Karl Meisl (cf. p. 1123, n. 2). [4] Karl Wilhelm Henning. Cf. Letter 1343.

[5] Taken from Nohl II, no. 307.

[6] On August 7th Karl was removed by the police from his mother's house to the General Hospital.

They are not satisfied.   I am now running around to find someone to help me.

(1498) *To Bernhard Schotts Söhne, Mainz*

[*Autograph in the possession of the Historical Society of Pennsylvania*]

GENTLEMEN!   [VIENNA], *Saturday, August* 19, 1826
    This is just to inform you that the quartet [1] was delivered to Frank a week ago. You said in your letter that it should be an original quartet. I felt rather hurt; so as a joke I wrote beside the address that it was a bit of patchwork.[2] But it is really *brand new* — The metronome markings (the deuce take everything mechanical) will follow — follow — follow — I have had a great misfortune. But with God's help all will perhaps turn out well — With friendly greetings, your most devoted

BEETHOVEN

    My dear adopted son, who frequently wrote my letters to you, nearly killed himself. But it is still possible to save him.[3]

(1499) *To Johann van Beethoven, Gneixendorf*

[*Autograph in the Stadtbibliothek, Trier*]

VIENNA, *August* 28, 1826

I am not coming —
            Your brother ? ? ? ? ? ? ! ! ! !
                                LUDWIG

    [1] The C sharp minor quartet, Op. 131, which Beethoven began to compose late in 1825 after finishing the third Galitzin quartet, Op. 130. It was published posthumously by Schott in June, 1827.
    [2] On the copy sent to Schott Beethoven wrote: 'Fourth [crossing out fifth] quartet [of the latest] for two violins, viola and cello, by L. v. Beethoven. NB. patched together from pieces filched here and there.'
    [3] After his attempted suicide Karl was first taken to his mother's house, then removed by the police to the General Hospital on Monday, August 7th, and finally discharged from hospital on September 25th.

(1500) *To Karl Holz*

[*Autograph in the Peabody Institute Library, Baltimore*]

[VIENNA, *August*, 1826]

MOST EXCELLENT WOOD OF CHRIST!

Here is the pianoforte arrangement for four hands [1] — for H[err] Matthias, and may God decide him to take it [2] — The latter will realize that it was impossible for me to waste so much time to no purpose. Besides, it has now become a separate work of my own; and yet I am asking not more than 12 gold ducats. Supposing that I had immediately consented to make the p[ianoforte] a[rrangement] myself, no one could have offered me a lower fee than 25 or 30 ducats. But in view of the fact that A[rtaria] too has lost 100 gulden V.C., I shall be satisfied with the amount I have quoted above. You know that in this transaction I am not *a winner but rather a heavy loser*. Furthermore, in fairness the *penalty* already agreed upon could still be paid, seeing that our very dear H[err] Matthias has grossly insulted me in connexion with the quartet which he wanted to take and then refused — Besides Herr M[atthias] knows in any case that we do gladly assist, and will frequently assist, him without payment — But the present service which I am rendering him with the p[ianoforte] arrangement is too slavish for me not to insist on being compensated — I now appoint you my executor in this affair and request you, worthy Sir, to be the receiving party. Your

BEETHOVEN

[1] Op. 134, Beethoven's own arrangement for pianoforte duet of the Grosse Fuge, Op. 133. The composer had first entrusted this task to Anton Halm (cf. Letter 623, p. 570, n. 3) who gave him his arrangement on April 25, 1826. Beethoven did not like it and decided to do one himself, although Artaria had already paid Halm 40 gulden for his work. According to Artaria's account books (quoted by *KHV*. 406) Beethoven was paid twelve ducats for his arrangement on September 5, 1826.

[2] The meaning of this clause is obscure. In the original the words are 'Gott gebe am ersten'.

(1501) *To Karl Holz*

[*Autograph in the Fürstlich Fürstenbergische Hofbibliothek, Donaueschingen*]

DEAR FRIEND !   [VIENNA, *August*, 1826]

Well now, you will kindly go to Breuning and ask him whether he will take over the guardianship, whether you should perhaps go to the Magist[rat] for him and *when he intends* to go with me to Karl. Entreat him particularly to make haste about the last point; and kindly inform him that he can always rely on *good wood* —

I am sending to your office later on for a reply about these points — Forgive me for being so troublesome. I shall make up for all this on your wedding day ¹ —

Yours
BEETHOVEN

Well, I shall see you at five o'clock this afternoon ² —

(1502) *To Ignaz von Czapka* ³

[*Autograph in the Gesellschaft der Musikfreunde, Vienna*]

SIR !   [VIENNA, *August*, 1826] ⁴

I urgently request you to arrange that my nephew, who will have recovered in a few days, shall not leave the hospital with anybody but *myself and Herr von Holz* — It is out of the question to allow him to be much in the company of his mother, that extremely depraved person. My anxieties and my request are warranted by her most evil, wicked and spiteful character, her enticement of Karl for the purpose of getting money out of me, the probability that she has spent sums of money with him, and that she too was intimate with Karl's

---

¹ Holz was married in September, 1826.
² This sentence is added on the verso.
³ Little is known about this recipient who was a Magistratsrat. See *FRBH* I, 101.
⁴ This undated letter may well have been written in September, 1826, seeing that Karl was not discharged from hospital until September 25th.

dissolute companion,[1] the sensation she has been causing with her daughter, *whose father is still being traced,* and, what is more, the likelihood that in his mother's home he would make the acquaintance of women who are anything but virtuous. Even the habit of being in the company of such a person cannot possibly lead a young man along the path of virtue — While asking you to give this matter your most serious consideration I send you my best regards. I merely add the remark that, although the occasion was a painful one, it has given me very great pleasure to have made the acquaintance of a man of such excellent intellectual and moral qualities —

I remain, Sir, with due respect, yours sincerely,

BEETHOVEN

(1503) *To Karl Holz*

[*Autograph in the collection of the late Sydney Courtauld*]

[VIENNA, *August,* 1826]

I am extremely short of money and have nothing more than these 100 gulden A.C., which I am sending you. If you could possibly let me have for the time being five gulden in bank notes, then use the remainder to suit your convenience — As for Castelli, don't stand on ceremony with that diplomat — that sublimated substance — All good wishes, hurriedly, I mean to say, in a hurry,

All good wishes, amice, amicus

BEETHOVEN

(1504) *To Karl Holz*

[*Autograph not traced*][2]

[VIENNA, *August,* 1826]

Don't forget about the money. I shall soon have none left. Karl is steadily recovering. Today the Queen of the Table is going to sing a song at my home.[3]

[1] Probably Niemetz. Cf. Letter 1315, p. 1146, n. 2.

[2] Taken from Nohl II, no. 306. According to Liepmannsohn's sale catalogue of March 9, 1891 this note was written in pencil.

[3] Possibly the famous operatic soprano Nanette Schechner (1806–1860), born at Munich, who first sang in Vienna on May 22, 1826.

(1505) *To Karl Holz*

[*Autograph in the Beethovenhaus, Bonn, H. C. Bodmer collection*]

[VIENNA, *August*, 1826] [1]
If possible, see — that only the doctor speaks. Take a cab — I shall see you at dinner tomorrow.

Yours

BEETHVN

(1506) *To Karl Holz*

[*Autograph not traced*] [2]

[VIENNA, *Summer*, 1826]
The [stick?] yesterday disbursed in advance the money it owed —

I think it would be much better if you could find somebody who would follow up the [trail?]. Perhaps [K?] could find something better than one is entitled to expect. And then, moreover, one would have to act against one's [conviction?]. I will gladly refund whatever it costs. But the business must be taken in hand very cunningly. I do earnestly beg you to ask your sister, to whom I send my kind regards, to buy two ells of flannel, the same as this pattern. You could bring it with you if you are coming to dinner today —

I am only sorry to have to trouble you with so many matters. In great haste, your

BEETHOVEN

(1507) *To Karl Holz*

[*Autograph in the British Museum, Royal College of Music collection*]

[VIENNA, *Summer*, 1826]
Hardly had you left when by chance I found the housekeeper's spoons, which were on the box. I happened to lay them on the table for her, because she was still busy. It then

[1] E. H. W. Meyerstein, who first published this undated note in *Music Survey*, Vol. I (1948), p. 132, suggested that it might have some connexion with Karl's attempted suicide.

[2] Taken from Kal., no. 1181. Kalischer transcribed the autograph then in private ownership. He has queried some apparently illegible words.

occurred to me to check once more the other spoons that are being used, and *again another one* was missing — So I immediately said that I would take back her spoons and keep them until she had produced mine. Well, God preserve us from wanting to steal things like *spoons* in our venerable old age — The best thing would be — to get rid of him — If it is not too inconvenient for them, they could both be let go the day after tomorrow and the other two could come. *That would be Sunday*, when we are entitled to look forward to a Sunday feast — You see that in regard to the spoon we are just as *far as we were the day before yesterday* — If it were possible for you to see me tomorrow morning for a moment in order to be able to discuss everything, that would be best — You could have *breakfast* — The best thing is to finish up the business as quickly as possible, otherwise something even worse might happen —

Friday evening — Yours Primus et Ultimus.[1]

(1508) *To Prince Franz Ludwig Hatzfeld* [2]

[*MS not traced*] [3]

YOUR E[XCELLENCY],   [VIENNA, *February or March*, 1826] [4]

I am about to publish the greatest symphony which I have so far composed. I would count it the highest honour and favour if I might be allowed to dedicate it to H.M. the King of Prussia. Hence I am taking the liberty of requesting Y.E. to be so gracious as to inform H.M. and to put my affair before him in a favourable manner. By so doing Y.E. will not bring any dishonour on yourself. Moreover I should like H.M. to know that I too am one of his Rhenish subjects and as such desire all the more to do him homage.

While [putting forward this request] [5] I do beg you to let me know as soon as possible whether Y.E. would be willing to grant me this favour.

[1] The autograph is not signed.
[2] Prince Franz Ludwig Hatzfeld (1756–1827) had been Prussian Envoy to the Imperial Court since 1822.
[3] Taken from Nohl I, p. 328, note. Nohl states that this unsigned draft, of which he copied the original, was written by Karl Holz.
[4] Owing to an oversight this letter has been wrongly placed. It should certainly precede Letter 1472 of March 28, 1826.
[5] The words in brackets have been added by the present editor.

(1509) *To Karl Holz*

[Autograph in the Beethovenhaus, Bonn, H. C. Bodmer collection] [1]

DEAR FELLOW! [VIENNA, *Summer*, 1826]

Come to dinner with us tomorrow after you have made sufficient Liguorian expiations.[2] I trust that you are not engaged and that if you have already been invited elsewhere you will not lack the strength to tear yourself away.

Optime amice, yours

BEETHOVEN

(1510) *To Karl Holz*

[Autograph in the Beethovenhaus, Bonn, H. C. Bodmer collection] [3]

[VIENNA, *Summer*, 1826]

Sf   Sf

Wood — bring some wood! — Tomorrow very early in the morning the *least dangerous* of all persons *may bring* the money for it — That s[coun]d[re]l of an agent — must it be? — It must be [4] — Do your share, as we do ours —

Amicus

BEETHOVEN

(1511) *To Karl Holz*

[Autograph in the Beethovenhaus, Bonn, H. C. Bodmer collection]

[VIENNA, *Summer*, 1826]

Dinner will be ready by one o'clock, when I shall certainly expect you. It grieves me to cause you so much inconvenience —

Your

B——N

[1] Written in pencil in another hand and signed by Beethoven.
[2] For this reference cf. Letter 1485, p. 1287, n. 1.
[3] The autograph is a single sheet, on one side of which the note is pencilled. On the verso is Holz's address in Beethoven's handwriting and then the following comment in Holz's handwriting; 'Dembscher refused to pay the sum of 50 gulden for the loan of Beethoven's B♭ quartet, Op. 130'. See *KHV*. 409 and 697. Ignaz Dembscher was a wealthy official attached to the Imperial Court, with the title of Hofkriegsagent.
[4] Beethoven was then composing his F major quartet, Op. 135, with the now famous setting of the words, 'Muss es sein?' (Must it be?) and 'Es muss sein!' (It must be!) under the heading 'Der schwer gefasste Entschluss' (the decision taken with difficulty).

(1512) *To Karl Holz*

[Autograph not traced] [1]

[VIENNA, *Summer*, 1826]

Most excellent Lignum Crucis! [2] We shall break through the ceiling in a quarter of an hour at latest and you will pick me up. Meanwhile have a rest.

B.

(1513) *To [Karl Holz]*

[Autograph in the possession of the Royal Philharmonic Society] [3]

[VIENNA, *Summer*, 1826]

Our chip of the wood of Christ must still correct the mistakes which *nobody* ever made — Moreover wood should be stirred up —

(1514) *To Karl Holz*

[Autograph not traced] [4]

[VIENNA, *Summer*, 1826]

On account of a special circumstance I request you to leave word when you go out where I can find you during the morning. In any case I shall see you at noon.

Yours

BEETHOVEN

(1515) *To [Karl Holz?]*

[Autograph not traced] [5]

[VIENNA, *Summer*, 1826]

Can't one have oneself shaved today?

BTVN

[1] Taken from Kal., no. 1174.
[2] Wood of the Cross. Beethoven is evidently quoting from 'Ecce lignum crucis', which is sung at the Veneration of the Cross on Good Friday.
[3] This pencilled note is neither signed nor addressed. But on internal evidence it was obviously intended for Holz.
[4] Taken from Kal., no. 1176.
[5] Taken from *NMZ*. no. 37 (1916), p. 380. According to Max Unger, the writer of the article, the autograph is not addressed.

(1516) *To Karl Holz*

[*Autograph not traced*] [1]

[VIENNA, *Summer*, 1826]

This is for the Magistrat — To be ill and at the mercy of such a woman and such a guttersnipe, what a fate indeed! The one who said she was coming has not come; and perhaps too she was purposely refused admittance. The best thing would be to arrange for these people to come when *you* are here. It would be a real piece of good fortune to find a competent woman at last! — Do bring a few sheets of fine notepaper and also some matches, such as one can find at Rospini's at the Stephansplatz.[2] Tormented Odoardo! [3]

This goose of a woman can't make porridge. All hail to this rabble! What a crowd they are! All good wishes until we dine together.

(1517) *To ?*

[*Autograph in the Beethovenhaus, Bonn*] [4]

[VIENNA, *Summer*, 1826]

. . . . where the procession will thence enter the Gärtnergasse — Meanwhile should there be such rain-drenching clouds as there are today, everything will be postponed until further notice.

Your and so forth
and so on.
Given without giving or having anything.

[1] Taken from Aloys Fuchs's transcript in Tübingen University Library.
[2] Cf. Letter 1439, p. 1254, n. 6.
[3] Probably a reference to Lessing's tragedy 'Emilia Galotti', in which Odoardo, the father of the heroine, finds himself deserted by all.
[4] This fragment, written in pencil, is neither addressed nor dated nor signed.

(1518) *To [Karl Holz?]* ¹

[Autograph in a private collection]

[VIENNA, *Summer*, 1826]

The sister's sister is going to see you today. Yesterday she handed me a testimonial 'non hai denaro'.² So please advance her the money and tell her at the same time that she is to have 100 gulden a year and also 36 kreuzer a week for bread. I forgot to say all that yesterday — Do bring with you the remaining portions of the B♭ quartet.³ —

Last night I dreamt that your parents were begetting you for this world and I saw in my dream how much sweat it cost them to bring to light such an amazing piece of work. I congratulate you on your *existence* — how, why?! and so forth, the riddles solve themselves —

I shall be delighted to see you here at dinner today —
Until then keep well. Yours

BEETHOVEN

(1519) *To Karl Holz*

[Autograph in the possession of Frau Tilla Götz] ⁴

[VIENNA, *Summer*, 1826]

Quite amazing, far from sulphuretted and most excellent fellow!

We shall certainly be at your rooms shortly after five o'clock.

BEETHOV ⁵ —

---

¹ The autograph is not addressed. The letter may have been written to Karl Holz.

² 'You have no money', evidently a hint from the servant that Beethoven should pay her wages.

³ The third of the Galitzin quartets, Op. 130. It was published posthumously in score by Artaria in May, 1827.

⁴ This note addressed on the verso is written in pencil.

⁵ The signature ends in a stroke.

(1520) *To Karl Holz*

[Autograph in the Deutsche Staatsbibliothek, Berlin] [1]

[VIENNA, *Summer*, 1826]

In this heat it is surely best for you to come to the inn we know of in the Rossau, exactly opposite the street in which Rampel lives. Come at half past one.

(1521) *To Karl Holz, Baden* [2]

[Autograph in the Stadtbibliothek, Vienna]

MY VERY DEAR FELLOW!　　　　[VIENNA], *September* 9, 1826

One can see how much good can be done by better and purer air and also by the good influence of women. For in less than three days your icy surface has wholly melted. I notice this in your letter written yesterday, whereas your letter of September 7th is *like a dried fish* — I received it only last night because I had gone off to Nussdorf yesterday to enjoy cooler and more pleasant air. I would join you at Baden too; and indeed *perhaps* I shall go tomorrow. That reminds me, I would like to look around for an apartment. But I must really hurry to finish the corrections for His Majesty [3] — K[arl] insists on joining the army. He has written about this; and I have discussed it with him too. Surely it would be better for him to go first to some military college, such as the one at Neustadt. If you and your friends happen to go to Neustadt, you might just enquire from *Colonel Faber* [4] there whether *the years* in Vienna would be counted *for that purpose*. I don't think so, for *one has to pay there*; and K[arl] could very likely *leave the college as an officer*. For I do not think that it would be a good thing for him to be a *cadet* for

---

[1] As this note is written on one side of a sheet beside the address to Holz, the sheet is probably the cover of a letter to Holz, either extant or missing.

[2] Karl Holz's address at Baden, written on the verso of the autograph, was 'Im Sauerhof, Tür 75'.

[3] I.e. corrections to the ninth symphony, dedicated to the King of Prussia.

[4] Philipp von Faber, then in charge of the military academy at Wiener-Neustadt, held the rank of Lieutenant-Field-Marshal. The Director-General was the Archduke Johann (1782–1859), an elder brother of the Archduke Rudolph.

long; and if we want him to become an officer *in that way*, we must ensure, first of all, that he receives his officer's pay and, in addition, provide a little extra to enable him to live. For he must certainly not be treated as a *convict*. On the whole I am *not at all* in favour of the army as a profession. Now that you are *there*, everything will surely go very quickly. I am worn out; and happiness will not be my portion again for a very long time. The terrible expenses which I now have to meet and shall have to meet in future are bound to worry me; all my hopes have vanished, all my hopes of having near me someone who would resemble me at least in my better qualities! — Enjoy yourself to the full out there, empty the cornucopias of all-enchanting Nature; and on Monday [1] I hope to see you again for certain and to embrace you.

Grateful as always I remain your

BEETHOVEN

(1522) *To Tobias Haslinger*

[*Autograph in the Deutsche Staatsbibliothek, Berlin*]

[VIENNA, *September* 12, 1826]

In accordance with my exclusive privilege the worthy bearer of this letter is to pull and wiggle etc., first of all, your right ear *cresc* : — — — — — — — — — — — — — — — — and then your left ear fortissimo — After this bracing operation he is to inform you that I desire the return *to me* of all those works which you have not yet engraved and published, for the same fee which you gave me *so shamelessly*, namely, for the same *disgracefully low fee* — Question? Answer! From the post of *steward* which it was intended that you should fill for a time you have now been promoted again to that of a manufacturer of bills of exchange — Look after yourself, formerly Tobias Juvenis and Secundus, henceforth Primum Caput Tobias Primus —

L. v. BEETHOVEN

---

[1] Beethoven was writing on Saturday.

(1523) *To* [*Stephan von Breuning*] [1]

[Autograph in the Beethovenhaus, Bonn]

[VIENNA, *c. September* 20, 1826]

In Karl's case three points should be borne in mind, I think. Firstly, he must not be treated like a convict, for such a treatment would not produce the result we desire, but precisely the opposite — secondly, if he is to be promoted to the higher ranks, he must not live too frugally and shabbily — thirdly, he would find it hard to face too great a restriction in eating and drinking — But I do not wish to forestall you.

(1524) *To* [*Karl Holz*] [2]

[Autograph in the Beethovenhaus, Bonn]

[VIENNA, *c. September* 20, 1826]

I wonder whether you have returned home today from the realm of love,[3] for I have written to you and to Breuning.[4] If not, then you could still take the letter to Breuning after leaving your office — But if — quel result? — I can't say anything more, for the copyist has turned up. Well, I hope to see you at about five o'clock this afternoon. Do take a cab; and always do so when you can strike a bargain with the driver. Indeed it grieves me to have to trouble you so much. But Heaven will help us! — Karl has only five days more to spend there [5] —

In great haste, your friend

BEETHOVEN

[1] This letter, which is very faintly pencilled, is neither addressed nor dated nor signed. But on internal evidence it must have been intended for Breuning who had been appointed Karl's guardian. Moreover, Beethoven here uses the Du-form which he used to very few friends.

[2] This letter, very faintly pencilled, is neither addressed nor dated. But on internal evidence it must have been sent to Holz.

[3] Beethoven is referring to Holz's stay at Baden. Cf. Letter 1521.

[4] Possibly the letter to Breuning, which is Letter 1523 in the present edition.

[5] According to *TDR* V, 359, where the documentary evidence is quoted, Karl left the hospital on September 25th.

(1525) *To Karl Holz*

[*MS not traced*] [1]

MR. ENAMOURED! [2]   [VIENNA, *c. September* 22, 1826]

I send you herewith the symphony. Give the bearer clear instructions how to find Haslinger's shop so that he may hand him the symphony to bind without vomiting.[3]

Could I have the copies of Clementi's *Klavierschule* fetched *at your rooms* this afternoon? If I am given one *gratis*, I will pay for *one*.[4] Unless one is given gratis I shall take only *one* and *duly pay for it*.

Karl would like you to bring him cigarros. Well, if all this and that could be in your hands this afternoon, it would be *pregnant with consequences*. — If you realize how necessary it is to go to the hospital with me once more, then we should do this at any rate the day after tomorrow in the morning. For we may still have something to face. My worthy *brother*, I think, will certainly not come. Thus you would be bringing at least a *quarter* of your *ego* from Döbling the day after tomorrow and you would haul it along to me at about seven o'clock — In the afternoon it would surely not be possible. Mr. Enamoured, I bow my knee before the almighty power of *love*.

Your most devoted

B——N

✝

Memento Mori

PS. It would be fine if you would ask T[obias] for the name of the bookbinder, so that it might be suitably bound and so that all the dirt might be removed.

E[n]a[mou]r[e]d

[1] Taken from *TDR* V, 375.
[2] See p. 1310, n. 1.
[3] Beethoven is punning on two meanings of 'übergeben', i.e. 'to hand' and 'to vomit'.
[4] Beethoven, who had ordered two copies of Clementi's work, means that he will pay for one copy, provided the other is a free gift.

(1526) *To Tobias Haslinger*

[*Autograph in the Beethovenhaus, Bonn, H. C. Bodmer collection*]

DEAR SIR! [VIENNA, *c. September* 22, 1826]

If you would be so kind as to have the score, which I am sending you herewith, as beautifully bound as befits *a king*, you would do me a great favour. But it must be done *as quickly as possible*. I shall pay the cost immediately either to you or to the bookbinder. You know far too much about *binding*, just as I do about letting go — I am counting absolutely on your kindness and merely add, most excellent Sir,

that I am your most excellent

HERR L. V. BEETHOVEN

NB.[1] I think that on the first page of the Allegro my name should be deleted and that a fresh sheet of fine writing paper, on which the title should then appear, should be pasted over this page.

(1527) *To Karl Holz*

[*Autograph in Harvard College Library, Amy Lowell collection*]

[VIENNA, *c. September* 23, 1826]

The two gentlemen have been here — but they are said to have been warned by both parties to observe the strictest silence about the order.[2] Haslinger declares that in this respect you are a son of the late Papageno — prénés garde — I told Karl today that it had been settled that he was to leave the hospital only with you or me [3] — I am dining at home tomorrow. So it will be pleasant for me if you come. As you *have no office* tomorrow, you may come later, if you like;

---

[1] The postscript is written on the verso of the autograph.
[2] Probably Dr. Spiker from Berlin and his companion. Cf. Letter 1021. The order referred to is no doubt the Order of the Red Eagle, second class, awarded to Beethoven by the King of Prussia. See Letter 1542, p. 1322.
[5] Karl was discharged from hospital on Monday, September 25th. He and his uncle went to Gneixendorf three days later, on Thursday, September 28th.

and that is really necessary — Portes vous bien, Monsieur terrible amoureux ¹ —

> your indeclinable friend

> B-E-E-T-HO-VEN

> BEETHOVEN

I am expecting a few lines from you to say that you are coming tomorrow for certain, because otherwise I shall not stay at home. By the way, have you anything to report about our m[anuscrip]t?

(1528) *To Tobias Haslinger*

[Autograph not traced] ²

[VIENNA, *September* 27, 1826] ³

I thank you — Please let me know how the dedication is to be arranged ⁴ — Can you send it to Dr. Spiker? — I am leaving here tomorrow ⁵ — and shall probably stay away so long that I shall miss meeting him — Have you not heard whether the Legation agrees to it? —

> Your most devoted

> BEETHOVEN

(1529) *To [Karl Holz]* ⁶

[Autograph in the Deutsche Staatsbibliothek, Berlin]

DEAR FRIEND,   [VIENNA, *c. September* 26, 1826]

At last I am fulfilling my desire to leave here the day after tomorrow for a short trip ⁷ and I shall be away for several

---

¹ Holz was about to get married.
² Taken from Nohl II, no. 309. Nohl transcribed the autograph then in private ownership.
³ According to Nohl the autograph was endorsed thus by the recipient.
⁴ The dedication of the ninth symphony, Op. 125, to King Frederick William III of Prussia. Cf. Letter 1472.
⁵ Beethoven, his brother and his nephew left Vienna on Thursday, September 28th, and arrived at Gneixendorf on Friday afternoon.
⁶ The autograph is neither dated nor addressed. But on internal evidence this letter must have been sent to Holz and, as Dr. Ivan Mahaim has pointed out, certainly before September 5th, when Artaria paid Beethoven the fee of 12 ducats (cf. p. 1296, n. 1). Hence this letter should probably be placed immediately before Letter 1500.
⁷ Beethoven again uses the word 'Ausflucht' instead of 'Ausflug'. Cf. Letter 1412, p. 1234, n. 5.

days. Hence I request you to tell Herr Matthias A[rtaria] that I do not wish in any way to compel him to take my pianoforte arrangement. Therefore I am sending you Halm's p[ianoforte] arr[angement] so that when mine is returned to you, you may immediately deliver Halm's to M[atthias] A[rtaria] ¹ —

But if Herr A[rtaria] wants to keep my pianoforte arrangement for the fee of 12 gold ducats, then all I ask is that I should have this from him in writing or that the fee should be paid to you — and for this purpose I am now enclosing the receipt.²

In no wise can the pianoforte arrangement be laid to my charge as a debt —

As always yours,

BEETHOVEN

You know how I am situated ! —

(1530) *To Tobias Haslinger*

[Autograph in the possession of Alfred Cortot]

[VIENNA, *September*, 1826]

P.P.

There are still a few mistakes including, as was to be expected, of course, a few little *Tobiassy ones* (i.e. of a certain Tobias who when he was a pupil of Fuchs and Albrechtsberger ran away and became a Kapellmeister among the little Paternostergasse people — see the humorous biography of Tobias published by Messrs. Schott & Sons at Mainz in 1825, Page 300) ³ — As soon as these mistakes which I have marked have been corrected, please return both the proof and the corrections. You will have them back immediately, i.e. provided I am convinced that in each case the correction

¹ According to Artaria's account book 40 gulden had already been paid to Anton Halm (cf. Letter 623, p. 570, n. 3) for his transcription ; and on September 5, 1826, 12 ducats were paid to Beethoven for his pianoforte arrangement of the Grosse Fuge (Op. 133), published in May, 1827 as Op. 134.

² The words from 'and' to 'receipt' are added at the foot of the third page of the autograph.

³ Beethoven's humorous biography of Haslinger appeared in Schott's review *Caecilia*, April, 1825, no. 7, p. 205, not p. 300.

has been made. Please also have these mistakes corrected in the parts and in the pianoforte arrangements — Further, I should like to add something to the title of the arrangement for pianoforte solo — Dixi — Well, if you would now make haste with this work, I should be delighted — All good wishes,

primus P[ATE]RN[OSTE]RG[ÄSSLE]R [1] —

Yours
Beethoven

(1531) *To Bernhard Schotts Söhne, Mainz*

[*MS in the Stadtbibliothek, Mainz*] [2]

Vienna, *September* 29, 1826

As I am just about to go off to the country, I inform you in great haste that you will soon receive the metronome markings of the symphony.

I hope that you have now received the C sharp minor quartet.[3] Don't be frightened at the four sharps. This work will shortly be performed in Vienna for the benefit of an artist.

Finally I must request you to hasten the necessary preliminaries connected with the publication of my collected works. I really cannot conceal from you the fact that if I did not keep my promises so honourably, you might easily find yourself at a disadvantage on account of proposals which other publishers have made to me on this subject.

Hoping to hear from you about this very soon, your devoted

Beethoven

PS. I must add the reminder that in the second movement of the symphony after the last bar of the Maggiore

the D.S. has been forgotten.

---

[1] Steiner had resigned and since the beginning of August Haslinger had been in charge of the firm.

[2] Written by Karl and signed by Beethoven. The date should be September 28th.   [3] Op. 131.

STEPHAN VON BREUNING (1774–1827)
From an engraving by an unknown artist
(*Historisches Museum der Stadt Wien*)

FIRST PAGE OF THE FIRST VIOLIN PART OF THE F MAJOR STRING QUARTET,
Op. 135, composed in 1826

(1532) To Stephan von Breuning

[Autograph in the Beethovenhaus, Bonn, H. C. Bodmer collection] ¹

MY DEAR FELLOW! [VIENNA, *late September*, 1826]
At last I can stop bragging. Here is Clementi's Klavierschule which I promised to send you for *Gerhard*. If he uses
it in the way I shall instruct him to do later on, it will certainly
produce good results —
I shall see you very soon. I embrace you most warmly.

Your
BEETHOVEN

(1533) To Ignaz von Czapka

[MS not traced] ²

SIR! [VIENNA, *late September*, 1826]
Hofrat von Breuning and I have carefully considered
what should be done and have quite decided that Karl will
have to spend a few days with me (before he leaves Vienna
to join the army). His statements are to be ascribed to the
outbursts of anger caused by the impression made on him by my
reprimands when he was thinking of taking his life. But even
after that time he behaved affectionately to me. Rest assured
that even in its fall humanity is always sacred to me. An
admonition from you would have a good effect. Moreover
it would do no harm to let him realize that during his stay
with me he is being watched unseen. —
Accept my very high regard for you and look upon me as
a warm-hearted philanthropist who only wants to do good
wherever he can.

Your most devoted
BEETHOVEN

¹ The autograph is sewn into a copy of Clementi's Klavierschule, on the last
empty page of which there is a pencilled note in Beethoven's handwriting; 'Für
H. Hofrath v. Breuning'. Cf. Letter 1432, p. 1250, n. 4. The copy has the
imprimatur: 'Tranquillo Mollo. Vienna. Plate 1407.' Mollo's German
edition entitled *Vollständige Klavierschule von Clementi* was advertised in the *Wiener
Zeitung* of January 31, 1807, at the price of 3 gulden.
² Taken from *TDR* V, 381.

(1534) *To Tobias Haslinger, Vienna*

[*MS not traced*] [1]

[GNEIXENDORF, *October* 2, 1826] [2]

Bester   To —————————————————————————

There is no time left today for the remaining consonantizings and vocalizings. But please deliver the enclosed letter at once.

I know you will forgive me for troubling you. But since you are now the proprietor of an art post office, well, naturally we cannot help making use of it.

You see that I am here at Gneixendorf. The name resembles to a certain extent a breaking axle. The air is healthy. As to everything else one must cross oneself and say Memento Mori.

By far the most amazing, the chief of all Tobiases, to the favour of the art shop and post office

we desire to commend ourselves.

BEETHOVEN

(1535) *To Bernhard Schotts Söhne, Mainz*

[*MS in the Stadtbibliothek, Mainz*] [4]

GNEIXENDORF, *October* 13, 1826

I am using what remains of the fine weather to take a holiday here in the country, since it was impossible for me to leave Vienna during the summer — Meanwhile I have worked

---

[1] Taken from Nohl I, no. 383. It is written in another hand, which according to Nohl, who transcribed the original then in private ownership, was probably Karl's, and signed by Beethoven, who also wrote the preceding five words.

[2] According to the sale catalogue of Joseph Baer, Frankfurt-am-Main, 1888, no. 210, this letter was dated 'Gneixendorf, October 2, 1826' and the musical setting was in Beethoven's hand.

[3] In *KHV*. this musical setting is listed as WoO 205[1].

[4] Written by Karl and signed by Beethoven.

out the metronome markings for the whole symphony and now add the tempi —

All°. ma non troppo	88 = ♪	Andante maestoso	72 = ♪
Molto vivace . .	116 = ♪·	Adagio divoto .	60 = ♪
Presto	116 = ♪·	All°. energico . .	84 = ♪·
Adagio, tempo 1ᵐᵒ	60 = ♪	All°. ma non tanto	120 = ♪
Andante moderato	63 = ♪	Prestissimo . .	132 = ♪
Finale presto . .	66 = ♪·¹	Maestoso . . .	60 = ♪
All°. ma non troppo	88 = ♪		
Allegro assai . .	80 = ♪		
Alla Marcia . .	84 = ♪·		

You may also have them engraved separately. Don't forget what I told you about the second movement.

I will soon let you have the metronome markings for the Mass as well.

I hope that you have now received the new quartet.

I should like to have your opinion about the publication of my collected works. I request you to let me have it as soon as possible. Had I not contrived with all my strength to prevent it, people would already have begun to publish some of my works, an event which would have been disastrous to my publishers and of little advantage to me.

The district where I am now staying reminds me to a certain extent of the Rhine country which I so ardently desire to revisit. For I left it long ago when I was young.

Write to me soon and send me some pleasant news. With kindest regards I remain ever your most devoted

BEETHOVEN

¹ For a different metronome marking for the Finale presto movement see Letter 1566.

(1536) *To Tobias Haslinger, Vienna*

[*MS in the Public State Library, Leningrad*] [1]

GNEIXENDORF, *October* 13, 1826

We are writing to you here from the Signor Fratello's castle.

I must again make myself a nuisance to you and politely request you to give the two letters enclosed to the post immediately.

As soon as I return to Vienna I will refund to you all the expenses to which I have put you, beginning with the Klavierschule.

The really lovely weather and the fact that I did not go into the country during the whole summer are the reason why I am staying on here a little longer.

The quartet for Schlesinger is now finished, but I do not yet know what is the safest way to send it to you, so that you could kindly deliver it to Tendler & Manstein and receive the money for it.

Schlesinger will probably not give a draft to be cashed in *gold*. But, as I have been paid in gold by all other publishers, you would greatly oblige me if you could arrange for me to receive the payment in gold.

Meanwhile, most excellent little Tobias, we need money,

---

[1] Written by Karl and signed by Beethoven who also wrote down the musical setting.

[2] This musical setting is listed in *KHV*. as WoO 205[k].

for it is not the same thing whether we have some money or none.[1]

If you catch a glimpse of Holz, then nail him to another piece of wood. The ecstasy of love has seized it badly, indeed it has almost caught fire, so that somebody has written in jest that Holz is a son of the late Papageno.

All good wishes, quite amazing, most admirable and quite unique representative of all the Tobiases. If it is not inconvenient, do write a few lines to me here. Is Dr. Spiker still in Vienna?

With the most respectful respect and sincerity

Yours

BEETHOVEN [2]

(1537) *To Tendler & Manstein, Vienna* [3]

[*MS in the Stadtbibliothek, Vienna*] [4]

SIR! GNEIXENDORF, *October* 30, 1826

I am sending you by my brother my latest violin quartet composed for Herr Schlesinger; [5] and I request you to hand to the former the fee of 80 ducats deposited with you for this purpose; and I herewith [acknowledge receipt] of this amount.

[With kindest regards

your most devoted

LUDWIG VAN BEETHOVEN]

---

[1] Beethoven is quoting the refrain of a song whose popularity persisted in Austria and Germany for over a century. It came from the two-act operetta 'Der lustige Fritz', words by Karl Meisl, music by Franz Volkert, produced at the Leopoldstadt Theatre on June 17, 1818. Ferdinand Raimund took the part of Fritz and the refrain of his song is :

'Uns ist's alles eins,
ob wir ein Geld haben oder keins'.

[2] The signature and the preceding word are in Beethoven's hand.

[3] A firm of booksellers housed in the Trattnerhof in the Graben.

[4] Written by Karl. Only the upper half of a quarto leaf has been preserved. The bracketed portions have been supplied from *TDR* V, 397, a copy made by Thayer from the original letter then in the possession of Karl's widow.

[5] Op. 135, published posthumously by Moritz Schlesinger, Paris, in September, 1827. Cf. Letter 1536.

(1538) *To Moritz Schlesinger, Paris*

[*MS not traced*] 1

[GNEIXENDORF, *c. October* 30, 1826]

Just see what an unfortunate fellow I am. First of all, it has been difficult to compose this, because I was thinking of a much greater work. I composed it solely because I had promised it to you and needed the money. That it was difficult for me to do so you can gather from the '*Es muss sein*'.2 But a further source of annoyance was that in order to have it quite accurate and easy to engrave I wanted to send it to you in parts; and in all Mödling 3 I could not find a copyist. So I had to copy it myself. Well, that was a gruelling piece of work, in truth! Ugh, it is finished. Amen!

(1538a) *To Moritz Schlesinger, Paris*

[*MS not traced*] 4

[GNEIXENDORF, *October*, 1826]

Here, my dear friend, is my last quartet. It will be the last; and indeed it has given me much trouble. For I could not bring myself to compose the last movement. But as your

¹ The letter was written down by Moritz Schlesinger from memory (his house having been destroyed by fire in 1826, probably with the loss of many letters from Beethoven) and sent to A. B. Marx on February 27, 1859, with his (Schlesinger's) interpretation of 'Es muss sein'. See A. B. Marx, *Ludwig van Beethoven*, 2nd edition, 1863, vol. II, p. 336. See also *KHV.* 409.

² The fourth movement of the F major string quartet, Op. 135, to which Beethoven gave the title 'Der schwer gefasste Entschluss'.

³ This is a slip of Schlesinger's memory. It should be Gneixendorf. The autograph of the parts is dated in Beethoven's hand 'Gneixendorf, October 30, 1826'.

⁴ The present editor is indebted to Dr. Ivan Mahaim for kindly providing another version of Letter 1538, the letter which Moritz Schlesinger drafted from memory in 1859. On June 19, 1867 Schlesinger, who since 1846 had been living in retirement at Baden-Baden, happened to hear a fine performance of Beethoven's F major quartet, Op. 135. This prompted him to publish the same letter in the *Badeblatt* of June 22nd, without stating, however, that in 1859 he had sent it to A. B. Marx. The discrepancies between the two versions are of some interest. This second version of Beethoven's letter to Moritz Schlesinger was discovered, republished and discussed in an article by Dr. Ivan Mahaim in the *Schweizerische Musikzeitung*, no. 9, pp. 316-321.

letters were reminding me of it, in the end I decided to compose it. And that is the reason why I have written the motto : *The decision taken with difficulty — Must it be? — It must be, it must be!* — —

— — I am an unfortunate fellow, for I have failed to find here a copyist who could write out the parts from the score. This seemed to me necessary for the printing, so I had to write it out myself. Hence I am sending it to you in parts copied in my own hand, and in the hope that the engraver will be able to read my scrawl, and with the request that the proofs, etc. —

(1539) *To Tobias Haslinger, Vienna*

[*MS in the Beethovenhaus, Bonn, H. C. Bodmer collection*] [1]

DEAR FRIEND! GNEIXENDORF, *November* 11, 1826

Since you did not reply to my first letter, I did not wish to trouble you any further. So I sent my brother off to Vienna with my latest quartet.[2]

Now I have one more request to make. A small parcel for Herr Matthias Artaria is being sent to your address. As soon as it arrives, please let him know that the parcel is with you. But you must give it to him only against a payment of 15 gold ducats.[3] Just say that you have certain payments to make for me out of this sum. I have written to him on the same lines adding that in any case I had something else to send him and that, therefore, in order to simplify matters, I had sent it to you at once in this parcel. These gentlemen always want to have a word with me in person in order to drive a hard bargain with me. So I am applying to you —

I hope that you are going to publish the works which you formerly set aside. If you suffered any inconvenience on that account, it was really partly your own fault. Holz told me

---

[1] Written by Karl. The last two words 'friend Beethoven' are in the composer's handwriting.

[2] Op. 135. Cf. Letters 1536 and 1537.

[3] The small parcel contained the new 'Finale' for Op. 130, the quartet published posthumously by Artaria in May, 1827. Artaria sent Haslinger the 15 ducats on November 25th. See *KHV.* 394.

that you were adding a bit more to the cantata and that you would have to pay an enormous price for this.¹ Do not worry about that. I shall act fairly and graciously in this, as in all other matters.

Your friend

BEETHOVEN

(1540) *To Tobias Haslinger, Vienna*

[MS in a private collection] ²

GNEIXENDORF, *November* 22, [1826]

I am sending you herewith, though a little later than I intended, the parcel about which I have already informed you.³ Please deliver it to H[err] Matthias Artaria who will pay you 15 ducats for it. Should I be in a position to return your kindness, I shall not fail to do so.

Your most devoted

BEETHOVEN

Please give the bearer a few lines stating that you have received the above-mentioned parcel.

(1541) *To Karl Holz*

[MS not traced] ⁴

YOUR OFFICIAL MAJESTY! [VIENNA, *c. December* 6, 1826]

I wrote to you immediately after my arrival which took place a few days ago.⁵ But the letter was mislaid. Then I fell ill, and so ill that I think it is wiser to stay in bed — Hence I shall be greatly delighted if you will visit me. It will be the

¹ Op. 136 was not published by Haslinger until 1837.

² Written by Karl and signed by Beethoven.

³ Mentioned in the preceding letter of November 11th. Cf. Letter 1539. The parcel contained the new final movement of the Bᵇ quartet, Op. 130, composed at Artaria's request to replace the original fugue. See *TDR* V, 405-406, and *KHV*. 394.

⁴ Taken from Nohl I, no. 385. According to Nohl, who transcribed the letter then in private ownership, it was written by another hand, but all the words from 'Finally' and also the musical setting are in Beethoven's handwriting.

⁵ Beethoven and his nephew left Gneixendorf on Friday, December 1st, and arrived in Vienna on Saturday, December 2nd.

less inconvenient to you to do so, since everybody has returned to town from Döbling —
  Finally I merely add the following

I

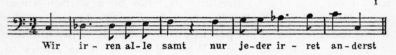

Wir   ir - ren al - le   samt   nur   je-der ir - ret   an-derst

Ever your friend
BEETHOVEN

(1542) *To Franz Gerhard Wegeler, Coblenz*

[*MS in the possession of Julius Wegeler*] [2]

My BELOVED OLD FRIEND !   VIENNA, *December* 7, 1826 [3]
  Words fail me to express the pleasure which your letter and Lorchen's have afforded me.[4]   And indeed an answer should have been sent off to you as swiftly as an arrow.   But on the whole I am rather slack about writing letters, for I believe that the best people know me well in any case.   Often I think out a reply in my head ; but when it comes to writing it down, I usually throw away my pen, simply because I am unable to write as I feel.   I remember all the love which you have always shown me, for instance, how you had my room whitewashed and thus gave me such a pleasant surprise, — and likewise all the kindnesses I have received from the Breuning family.   Our drifting apart was due to the changes in our circumstances.   Each of us had to pursue the purpose for which he was intended and endeavour to attain it.   Yet the eternally unshakeable and firm foundations of good principles continued to bind us strongly together. — Unfortunately I cannot write to you today as much as I should like to, for I have to stay in bed.   So I shall confine myself to answering a few points in your letter.   You say that I have been mentioned

---

[1] This musical setting of the words, which mean 'We all err, but each one errs in a different way', is listed in *KHV.* as WoO 198.   It is a two-part canon.
  [2] Written by Karl and signed by Beethoven.
  [3] In all the German editions of Beethoven's letters the month is given as October.   But it is undoubtedly December.   The autograph has 10^br and on internal evidence it must be that month.
  [4] Wegeler and his wife Eleonore had written to Beethoven on December 29, 1825.   These two letters are quoted in Ley, pp. 53-57 and Schmidt, pp. xxi-xxv.

somewhere as being the natural son of the late King of Prussia. Well, the same thing was said to me a long time ago. But I have adopted the principle of neither writing anything about myself nor replying to anything that has been written about me. Hence I gladly leave it to you to make known to the world the integrity of my parents, and especially of my mother. — You mention your son. Why, of course, if he comes to Vienna, I will be a friend and a father to him; and if I can be of any use to him or help him in any way, I shall be delighted to do so.

I still possess Lorchen's silhouette. So you see how precious to me even now are all the dear, beloved memories of my youth.

As for my diplomas I merely mention that I am an Honorary member of the Royal Scientific Society of Sweden and likewise of Amsterdam, and also an Honorary Citizen of Vienna. A short time ago a certain Dr. Spiker took with him to Berlin my latest grand symphony with choruses; it is dedicated to the King, and I had to write the dedication with my own hand. I had previously applied to the Legation for permission to dedicate this work to the King, which His Majesty then granted. At Dr. Spiker's instigation I myself had to give him the corrected manuscript with the alterations in my own handwriting to be delivered to the King, because the work is to be kept in the Royal Library. On that occasion something was said to me about the Order of the Red Eagle, Second Class. Whether anything will come of this, I don't know, for I have never striven after honours of that kind. Yet at the present time for many other reasons such an award would be rather welcome. — In any case my motto is always: Nulla dies sine linea;[1] and if I let my Muse go to sleep, it is only that she may be all the more active when she awakes. I still hope to create a few great works and then like an old child to finish my earthly course somewhere among kind people. — You will soon receive some music from the Gebrüder Schott at Mainz. — The portrait I am sending with this letter is certainly an artistic masterpiece, but it is not the latest one which has been done of me. — Speaking about my honours which I know you are pleased to hear of, I must add that the late King of France sent me a medal with the inscrip-

[1] Cf. Letter 1311, p. 1143, n. 3.

tion: Donné par le Roi à Monsieur Beethoven. It was accompanied by a very courteous letter from the Duc de Chartres, Premier Gentilhomme du Roi.

My beloved friend! You must be content with this letter for today. I need hardly tell you that I have been overcome by the remembrance of things past and that many tears have been shed while the letter was being written. Still we have now begun to correspond and you will soon have another letter from me. And the more often you write to me, the greater will be the pleasure you afford me. Our friendship is too intimate to need enquiries from either of us. And now I send you all good wishes. Please embrace and kiss your dear Lorchen and your children for me and when doing so think of me. God be with you all!

Ever your true and faithful friend who honours you,

BEETHOVEN

(1543) *To Tobias Haslinger*

[*MS in the Stadtbibliothek, Vienna*] [1]

MY VERY DEAR TOBIAS!   [VIENNA, *December* 7, 1826]

It is very necessary for me to have another copy of Clementi's Klavierschule. But I don't want to take it without paying for it, no more than I do the first copy I have received from you. I forgot, however, to enquire about the price or I should not have failed to send you the money. In no circumstances do I accept anything without paying for it. But I do earnestly beg you to procure this Klavierschule for me as soon as possible.

Your friend

BEETHOVEN

(1544) *To Bernhard Schotts Söhne, Mainz*

[*MS in the Stadtbibliothek, Mainz*] [2]

VIENNA, *December* 9, 1826

Your last letter of November 28th afforded me very great pleasure. Unfortunately an accident which befell me on my

[1] Written by Karl and signed by Beethoven. The letter was endorsed by Haslinger.   [2] Written by Karl.

way home from the country has made me very ill and forced me to remain in bed. — I have had the quartet parts written out and from them can draw the conclusion, but not with absolute certainty, that in your score also there are still a few mistakes. However, I have gone through them carefully. But one seldom treats one's own score so scrupulously. In order to be quite sure about this, I will inform you of the most important errors which I detect. You will receive as soon as possible the coat of arms of the Archduke Rudolph and also the metronome markings. You will have by the next post particulars of what should be done about the symphony.

Your postscript about the pirating of the quartet amazed me all the more as you yourself have a publishing house in Paris.[1] But I am not the slightest bit interested in this matter. If I may state my supposition about this, then I must admit that I should feel inclined to lay the blame on Schlesinger. You will remember that on one occasion he asked in writing for the quartet. At that time you yourself thought that I might be dishonourable enough to give him a work of that kind. Old Schlesinger of Berlin was here during the summer and he too wanted the Viennese publisher Matthias Artaria to give him one of my quartets. But it was refused. When I sent you an urgent warning relating to the publication of my works, well, it was definitely directed against Schlesinger. For he sent me a collection of my earlier works, up to the latest quartets, with the suggestion that he should publish them again. I gave him a flat refusal, because my honour does not allow me to comply with such an undertaking, and, still less, to affix my name to it. At the same time I advise you not to let anything be printed about this, for in such cases it is difficult to find absolute proofs — All good wishes, very good wishes. If I visit the Rhine, I will visit you as well. I trust that my health will soon improve.

Your devoted [2]

---

[1] Bernhard Schotts Söhne opened their branch firm in Paris on March 1, 1826.
[2] The letter is not signed.

(1545) *To Bernhard Schotts Söhne, Mainz*

[*MS in the Stadtbibliothek, Mainz*] [1]

[VIENNA, *c. December* 18, 1826]

I hasten to send you the coat of arms of His Imperial Highness the Archduke Rudolph. You could also add to the dedication the list of the other subscribers.

The metronome markings will be sent to you very soon. Do wait for them. In our century such indications are certainly necessary. Moreover I have received letters from Berlin informing me that the first performance of the symphony was received with enthusiastic applause, which I ascribe largely to the metronome markings. We can scarcely have *tempi ordinari* any longer, since one must fall into line with the ideas of unfettered genius.

You would do me a great favour if you would be so kind as to send the following works to one of my dearest friends, the Royal Prussian Regierungsrat, Franz von Wegeler at Coblenz, i.e. the Opferlied, the Bundeslied, the song 'Bei Chloe war ich ganz allein' and the bagatelles for pianoforte.[2] Please do me the favour to send him the first three works in score. I shall be delighted to refund you the expense.

In a few days you will also receive the dedication of the quartet.[3] I have now been in bed for about two weeks, but I trust that God will help me to get up again. While sending you my best remembrances I remain your most devoted

LUDWIG VAN BEETHOVEN

[1] Written by Karl and signed by Beethoven.
[2] Op. 121b, 122, 128 and 126.
[3] The C sharp minor quartet, Op. 131, originally intended for Johann Nepomuk Wolfmayer (cf. Letter 487, p. 464, n. 2), was dedicated to Baron Joseph von Stutterheim (1764–1831) who had facilitated Karl's joining the 'Erzherzog Ludwig' regiment stationed at Iglau in Moravia. See *KHV*. 399. To Wolfmayer Beethoven dedicated his quartet Op. 135.

(1546) *To Prince Franz Ludwig Hatzfeld, Berlin*

[*Autograph in the Deutsche Staatsbibliothek, Berlin*] [1]

SIR !   [VIENNA, *December*, 1826]
    I send you my warmest thanks for the letters you have
forwarded to me. But I must ask you to be so kind as to send
me the ring which H.M. the King of Prussia has decided
to give me — I am very sorry that an indisposition prevents
me from receiving in person this token (which is so precious
to me) of H.M's. love of art.   I should be very reluctant to
have it entrusted to the hands of a stranger — At the same
time I request you to inform me in a few lines whether the
worshipful Embassy would be so kind as to take charge of a
letter of thanks to H.M. the King and to arrange for him to
receive it —

    [1] This is the draft of a letter which may or may not have been dispatched.
Cf. Letter 1508, p. 1300, n. 2.

1827

1827

LETTER TO NIKOLAUS ZMESKALL VON DOMANOVECZ (February 18, 1827)

(Autograph in the Central Museum of Musical Culture, Moscow)

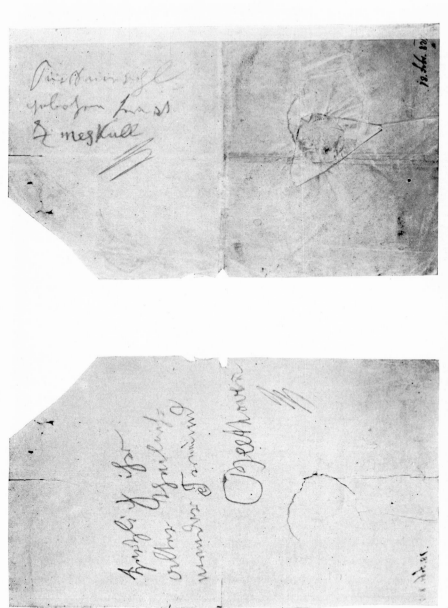

LETTER TO NIKOLAUS ZMESKALL VON DOMANOVECZ (February 18, 1827)—*cont.*

(1547) *To Johann Baptist Bach*

[*Autograph in the Deutsche Staatsbibliothek, Berlin*]

ESTEEMED FRIEND! VIENNA, *Wednesday, January* 3, 1827

Before my death I declare that Karl van Beethoven, my beloved nephew, is the sole heir to all my property, including, chiefly, seven bank shares and whatever cash may be available — Should the laws prescribe alterations pertaining to this bequest, then try to turn them so far as possible to my nephew's *advantage* — I appoint you *his trustee* and ask you together with his guardian, Hofrat von Breuning, to be a father to him — May God preserve you — A thousand thanks for the love and friendship you have shown me —

LUDWIG VAN BEETHOVEN [1]

(1548) *To Bernhard Schotts Söhne, Mainz*

[*MS in the Stadtbibliothek, Mainz*] [2]

GENTLEMEN! VIENNA, *January* 27, 1827

For the last two months I have been confined to bed and am suffering from dropsy — hence my silence.

You are now receiving the most essential corrections which have still to be made in the symphony. I can't understand why your people have not strictly adhered to my score. I request you, therefore, to make these corrections known every where.

The other additional mistakes were found in the E♭ quartet, both in the Paris and in the Mainz editions. In the score of the E♭ quartet, Page 30, line 2, there is a mistake in the 5th

[1] For the codicil to Beethoven's will see Letter 1568. Beethoven underwent his first operation on December 20, 1826. This was followed by three more, on January 8th, February 3rd and 27th.

Karl left Vienna on January 2nd to join his regiment at Iglau. Schindler then took his place as secretary to Beethoven.

[2] Written by Schindler and signed by Beethoven. The list of errata is written partly in ink and partly in pencil, with many alterations, erasions and corrections in the writing. Schindler has added in pencil the remark: 'If you wish, I will undertake the proof-reading'.

bar in the 2nd violin part, as I have already indicated.

If you have heard that this quartet has been published here, I declare that that is mere gossip.

Let me add that I remain, Gentlemen, with all due regard, your most devoted

LUDWIG VAN BEETHOVEN

PS. It will afford me much pleasure if you will send me your 'Caecilia' again soon to help me to recover my health.

NOTICE

of a few copying or printing errors in Beethoven's latest grand symphony in D minor and in his latest E♭ quartet.

I. In the D minor symphony, Page 65 of the score, there should be after the pause the following indication:

Dopo il Maggiore Presto si ricomincia dal segno 𝄋 il Minore ¾, e continuando si fa la seconda parte solamente una volta fin a questa fermata; poi si prende subito la Coda.

Page 73, after bar 8 there should be added: Da capo dal segno 𝄋

II. In the third movement of the quartet after the Presto ¾ time there is a passage a tempo ¾. In bar 17 of the latter in the second violin part instead of

there should be    (Page 30 of the score.)

In the second movement of the same quartet in the Adagio Molto Espressivo at bar 13 of the first violin part, instead of  there should be

(Page 5 of the first violin part, line 8, bar 4.)

In the Finale of the same quartet (Paris edition) in the first violin part, page 11, bar 33, there should be

[musical notation] instead of [musical notation]

In the first movement of the same quartet in the second violin part, page 2, in the Allegro

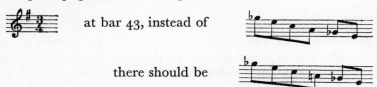   at bar 43, instead of

there should be

In the same movement and in the same part, page 3, line 8, bar 5, instead of

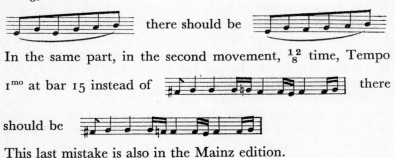

there should be

In the same part, in the second movement, $\frac{12}{8}$ time, Tempo 1mo at bar 15 instead of

there

should be

This last mistake is also in the Mainz edition.

(1549) *To Baron Johann Pasqualati*

[*Autograph in the Nationalbibliothek, Vienna*]

DEAR FRIEND !   [VIENNA, *January*, 1827]
  I am still confined to my room. Do please tell me or, rather, send me in writing the name of the valuation officer for this house and where he is to be found ? — If you have such a thing as a panacea, please provide me with it, for I am your poor Austrian musical drudge; and you are the local guarantor of the citizen.

L. v. BTHVN

(1550) *To Johann Andreas Stumpff, London*

[*MS not traced*] [1]

MY VERY DEAR FRIEND !   VIENNA, *February* 8, 1827

My pen is quite unable to describe the great pleasure afforded me by the volumes of Handel's works which you have sent me as a gift — to me a royal gift ! [2] — This present has even been mentioned in the Viennese papers, and I am sending you the notice.[3] Unfortunately since December 3rd I have been confined to bed with dropsy. You can imagine the situation to which this illness has reduced me. Usually I live entirely on the profits of my intellectual work and manage to earn everything for the support of myself and my Karl. But unfortunately for the last two and a half months I have not been able to write a single note.

My income only suffices to pay my half-yearly rent, leaving me a few hundred gulden V.C. Bear in mind too that the end of my illness is not by any means in sight. Nor do I know when it will be possible for me again to soar through the air on Pegasus in full flight ! Physician, surgeon, everything has to be paid for —

I well remember that several years ago the Philharmonic Society wanted to give a concert for my benefit. It would be fortunate for me if they would now decide to do so. Perhaps I might still be rescued from the poverty with which I am now faced. I am writing to Mr. S[mart] about this. And if you, dear friend, can contribute something to this object, do please come to an agreement with Mr. S[mart]. A letter about this is being written to Moscheles as well. And if all my friends combine I do believe that it will be possible to do something for me in this matter.

In regard to supplying Handel's works to His Imperial Highness the Archduke Rudolph I cannot say anything definite yet. But I will write to him in a few days and draw his attention to this suggestion.

[1] Taken from *TDR* V, 459-460. The letter was doubtless dictated to Schindler.
[2] Samuel Arnold's edition of Handel's works, published 1787-1797. See Appendix G (19).
[3] According to *TDR* V, 459, n. 3 this notice appeared in the Vienna *Modenzeitung* and a copy of it was among Stumpff's papers.

I thank you again for your splendid gift. Please make use of me and if I can serve you in any way in Vienna I shall be delighted to do so — Once more I appeal to your philanthropic feelings in regard to my situation which I have described to you in this letter. I send you my best and most cordial wishes and my warmest compliments.

With kindest regards, your

BEETHOVEN

(1551) *To Franz Gerhard Wegeler, Coblenz*

[MS in the possession of Julius Wegeler] [1]

MY WORTHY OLD FRIEND !   VIENNA, *February* 17, 1827

It was fortunate that I received from Breuning your second letter at any rate. I am still too weak to reply to it. But you can imagine how welcome and delightful to me are all your remarks. My recovery, if I may call it so, is still very slow. Presumably I must expect a fourth operation, although the doctors have not yet said anything about this. I cultivate patience and think : well, sometimes some good comes from all this evil. — But indeed I was surprised to read in your last letter that you had not yet received anything. — From the letter which you are now receiving you will see that I wrote to you as long ago as December 10th of last year.[2] The same remark applies to the portrait, for, when you receive it, you will verify this from the date inscribed on it. — Frau Stefan spoke [3] — In short, Stephan wanted to send you these things by some opportunity. But they were left lying about until today ; and indeed it was rather difficult to ask for their return until today. But you will now receive the portrait by post through Messrs. Schott who also sent you the music — There are many things I should still like to tell you today. But I am too weak ; and all I am able to do is to embrace you and your Lorchen in spirit.

[1] Written by Schindler and signed by Beethoven.
[2] Beethoven is evidently referring to Letter 1542, dated December 7th.
[3] A quotation from the first line of the second verse of the song 'Zu Steffen sprach im Traume' in Ignaz Umlauf's comic opera 'Das Irrlicht' on a text by C. F. Bretzner [1748–1807], produced at the Vienna Court Theatre in 1782.

With expressions of true friendship and affection for you and your family

your old and faithful friend

BEETHOVEN

(1552) *To Nikolaus Zmeskall von Domanovecz*

[*Autograph in the Central Museum for Musical Culture, Moscow*]

MY VERY DEAR FRIEND !   [VIENNA, *February* 18, 1827]

A thousand thanks for your sympathy. I do not despair. But what is most painful to me is the complete cessation of my activities. Yet there is no evil which has not something good in it as well — May Heaven grant you too an alleviation of your painful condition.[1] Perhaps we shall both be restored to health and then we shall meet and see one another again as friendly neighbours —

Heartfelt greetings from your old friend who sympathizes with you.

BEETHOVEN

(1553) *To Bernhard Schotts Söhne, Mainz*

[*MS in the Stadtbibliothek, Mainz*] [2]

GENTLEMEN !   VIENNA, *February* 22, 1827

I received your last letter through Kreutzer, the Kapellmeister.[3] For the moment I am replying only to the necessary points. The opus (the C sharp minor quartet) which you have is preceded by the one which Matthias Artaria has. Thus you can easily fix the number. The dedication is as follows: Dedicated to my friend Johann Nepomuk Wolfmayer.[4]

Now I have a very important request to make — My

[1] For some time Zmeskall had been suffering from gout.
[2] Written by Schindler and signed by Beethoven.
[3] Konradin Kreutzer (1780–1849), in his day a well-known German conductor and operatic composer, came to Vienna in 1804. After a period as Kapellmeister to the Royal Court of Würtemberg he returned to Vienna in 1822 and during various periods of three or four years conducted at the Kärntnertor Theatre. Cf. Letter 1260, p. 1104, n. 2.
[4] Op. 131 is preceded by Op. 130, the third Galitzin quartet. In the end it was dedicated to Baron von Stutterheim. Cf. Letter 1545, p. 1325, n. 3.

doctor has prescribed for me some very good old Rhine wine. Even if I were to offer an excessively large sum I could not obtain unadulterated Rhine wine in Vienna. So if I could have a small number of bottles I would show you my gratitude for the 'Caecilia.' I am inclined to think that something might be arranged for me at the Customs Office so that the cost of transport would not be too high — As soon as my health permits, you will receive the metronome markings of the Mass as well. But at the moment I am just about to undergo a fourth operation [1] — Hence the sooner I receive this Rhine wine or Moselle wine, the more beneficial it will be to me in my present condition ; — and with all my heart I do beg you to do me this kindness for which I shall be gratefully obliged to you.

With my kindest regards I remain, Sir, your most devoted

BEETHOVEN

(1554) *To Ignaz Moscheles, London*

[*MS in the possession of Julius Wegeler*] [2]

MY DEAR MOSCHELES !   VIENNA, *February 22*, 1827

I am convinced that you will not take it amiss if I trouble you with a request, and Sir Smart as well, to whom I enclose a letter.[3] Briefly the matter is as follows. A few years ago the Philharmonic Society in London made me the handsome offer to organize a concert for my benefit. At that time I was not, thank God, in such circumstances as to have to avail myself of this noble proposal. But now I am in a very different position, since for almost three months I have been confined to bed with an extremely trying illness. It is dropsy — Schindler will tell you more about it in a letter which he is enclosing.[4] You have known for a long time all about the kind of life I lead ; and you are aware too how and on what I live. For a considerable time now composing has been out

---

[1] The fourth operation was performed on February 27th.
[2] Written by Schindler and signed by Beethoven.
[3] Letter 1555.
[4] Schindler did this in a long letter to Moscheles reproduced in Ley, *op. cit.*, pp. 226-228. The three letters, i.e. Beethoven's to Moscheles and his letter to Smart and Schindler's letter to Moscheles, were sent off in one packet which arrived in London on March 8th.

of the question for me, and unfortunately I may find myself
faced with the prospect of being in want — You have not only
extensive acquaintanceships in London but also considerable
influence with the Philharmonic Society. So I beg you to
exert your influence to the utmost so that the Philharmonic
Society may now take up their noble decision again and carry
it out without delay. The enclosed letter to Sir Smart is on
the same lines; and I have already dispatched a similar one
to Herr Stumpff.[1] I merely ask you to deliver this letter to
Sir Smart and to join him and all my friends in London in
promoting this object.

I am so weak that I find it exhausting even to dictate a
letter. Please give my best regards to your amiable wife.
Rest assured that I shall ever be

your friend [2]

Do reply soon, so that I may know whether I have anything to hope for.

(1555) *To Sir George Smart, London*

[*MS in the Beethovenhaus, Bonn, H. C. Bodmer collection*] [3]

SIR !   VIENNA, *February* 22, 1827
Some time ago you were so kind as to give my nephew
Karl a very interesting present for which I am now rendering
you my heartfelt thanks — On this occasion too I wanted to
write to you in English as usual, but my nephew, who has
generally performed this task, is not with me at the moment.
So this time I must decide to write in German.

I remember that some years ago the Philharmonic Society
made me an offer to give a concert for my benefit. Referring
to this offer I now remind you, Sir, that if the Philharmonic
Society would now take this noble decision, this would be very

[1] Letter 1550, p. 1332, dated February 8, 1827.
[2] According to his own statement Moscheles cut off and gave away Beethoven's
signature.
[3] Written in German by Schindler and signed by Beethoven. Smart in his
Journals, p. 264, says: 'On March 1, 1827, I paid six shillings and eightpence for
the postage of a letter from Anton Schindler, which was signed by Beethoven a
few weeks only before the composer's death'. He then gives an English translation
of the above letter.

welcome to me in my present situation — For unfortunately
since as long ago as the beginning of December I have been
confined to bed with dropsy, an extremely trying disease;
and how long it will take me to recover no one can yet tell.
As no doubt you know already, I live entirely on what I
earn by my intellectual works; and at the moment I just
cannot think of composing. My income is so meagre that
with it I can hardly meet the half-yearly rent of my rooms
— So in the name of our friendship I do beg you to
use all your influence to promote this object; and judging
by your noble treatment of me I am convinced that you will
not take my petition amiss — I will write to Herr Moscheles
too on this subject; and I am convinced that he also will
willingly co-operate with you in furthering this plan — I have
written to Herr Stumpff as well about this — I am so weak
that I can't write any more, and even so I am only dictating
the letter — Give me the pleasure, dear Sir, of an early reply;
and let me know whether there is any hope that my request
will be fulfilled. Meanwhile accept the assurance of my
greatest esteem and admiration with which I shall ever remain,
Sir, your most devoted

BEETHOVEN

(1556) *To Karl Holz*

[*MS in the Beethovenhaus, Bonn, H. C. Bodmer collection*] [1]

DEAR HOLZ! VIENNA, *February* 25, 1827
    Please see whether my signature has been affixed to the
receipt for the Archduke.
    Further, please send your tailor to me as soon as possible.
If it were possible for you to come to me tomorrow morning
for a moment, it would be well, so that the money could also
be collected at the Archduke's. For I need it.

Ever your friend

BEETHOVEN

    [1] Written by Schindler and signed by Beethoven.

(1557) *To Anton Felix Schindler*

[*Autograph in the Deutsche Staatsbibliothek, Berlin*]

[VIENNA, *February*, 1827] [1]

As soon as we meet we can talk about the accident you
have unfortunately met with — I can communicate with
you through a third person without the least inconvenience.
Deal with the enclosed — here is something — Moscheles,
Cramer — although no doubt you have received another
letter from them.   There is a fresh reason to write on Wednesday
and to impress my request on them once more.   If by that
time you have not yet recovered, then one of my servants can
take the letter to the post and get a receipt for it —

Vale et fave [2] — I need not assure you of my sympathy
with you in your accident —

Do accept *this dish from me*, it all comes from my heart —
May Heaven give you help.

> Your sincere friend
> BEETHOVEN

(1558) *To Bernhard Schotts Söhne, Mainz*

[*MS in the Stadtbibliothek, Mainz*] [3]

GENTLEMEN !   VIENNA, *March* 1, 1827

I am about to make myself a nuisance to you again, a
thing which I am compelled to do.   For I shall be sending
you a parcel for the Royal Regierungsrat Wegeler at Coblenz.
Please be so kind as to forward it from Mainz to Coblenz.
You know, of course, that I am far too unselfish to ask you to
do all this for nothing.

I am again repeating a request I have already made you,
namely, *for some old white Rhine wine or Moselle wine*.[4]   It is extremely difficult to obtain that kind of wine here, in a genuine
and unadulterated condition, even for a large sum of money.

---

[1] On the autograph Schindler has noted February, 1827.
[2] Cf. Letter 1425, p. 1244, n. 4.
[3] Written by Schindler and signed by Beethoven.
[4] Cf. Letter 1553, p. 1335.

A few days ago, on February 27, I had my fourth operation. Even so I cannot yet hope for a complete recovery and cure. Pity your most devoted friend, who has the greatest regard for you.

BEETHOVEN

(1559) *To Sir George Smart, London*

[*MS in the Beethovenhaus, Bonn*] [1]

SIR !   VIENNA, *March* 6, 1827

No doubt, Sir, you have already received through Herr Moscheles my letter of February 22nd.[2] Nevertheless since I happen to have found your address among my papers, I do not hesitate to write to you direct and to urge you most insistently to fulfil my request.

Unfortunately as yet I cannot foresee the end of my dreadful illness. On the contrary, my sufferings and my anxieties coupled with them have only increased — On February 27th I was operated on for the fourth time ; and perhaps Fate may decide that I must expect this for a fifth time or even more often. If this is going to continue, my illness will certainly persist until the middle of the summer. And if so, what is to become of me ? What am I to live on until I have recovered my lost strength and can again earn my living by means of my pen ? — But I must be brief and not trouble you, Sir, with fresh complaints. I merely refer to my letter of February 22nd and beg you to exert all your influence to induce the Philharmonic Society to carry out now their former decision to give a concert for my benefit — My strength is not equal to saying anything more on this subject. Moreover I am too deeply convinced of your noble and friendly treatment of me to fear that I shall be misunderstood.

Accept the assurance of my highest esteem and be convinced that, while anxiously awaiting an early reply,

I shall ever remain, Sir, your most devoted

LUDWIG VAN BEETHOVEN

---

[1] Written by Schindler and signed by Beethoven.
[2] Letter 1555.

(1560) *To Baron Johann Pasqualati*

[*Autograph in the Nationalbibliothek, Vienna*] [1]

DEAR OLD FRIEND !   [VIENNA, *March* 6, 1827]
My heartfelt thanks for your present and for your wishes
for my good health. As soon as I have found the wine which
suits me best, I will let you know ; but indeed I shall abuse
your kindness as little as possible. I am looking forward to
the stewed fruit and will ask you for some quite often — Even
this note costs me an effort — Sapienti pauca [2] —
Your grateful friend
BEETHOVEN

(1561) *To Bernhard Schotts Söhne, Mainz*

[*MS in the Stadtbibliothek, Mainz*] [3]

GENTLEMEN !   VIENNA, *March* 10, 1827
According to my letter the quartet was to be dedicated to
someone whose name I had already sent you.[4] But something
has happened which has decided me to make an alteration in
this respect. The quartet must now be dedicated to the
Lieutenant Field-Marshal Baron von Stutterheim to whom I
am indebted for many kindnesses.[5] If you have perhaps
already engraved the first dedication, I beg you for Heaven's
sake to alter it, and I will gladly compensate you for the expense
of doing so. Do not treat my remarks as empty promises.
Indeed this matter is of such importance to me that I will
gladly and readily reimburse you to any extent whatsoever.
I enclose the title.
As for the parcel to my friend, the Royal Prussian Regierungsrat von Wegeler at Coblenz, I am delighted to be able

[1] This note was written and addressed in pencil. The recipient has dated it.
[2] Cf. Letter 953, p. 821, n. 1.
[3] Written by Schindler and signed by Beethoven.
[4] Johann Nepomuk Wolfmayer, a wealthy Viennese draper, who was an
enthusiastic lover of music and a fervent admirer of Beethoven's compositions.
He was to have received the dedication of Op. 131. But in the end Beethoven
dedicated this quartet to Baron von Stutterheim, and his last quartet, Op. 135, to
Wolfmayer. Cf. p. 464, n. 2.
[5] Cf. Letter 1545, p. 1325, n. 3.

to relieve you entirely of this commission. For an opportunity has been found to dispatch everything to him direct.

My health, which will not be restored for a very long time, demands that you should send me the wines I asked you for. They will certainly bring me refreshment, invigoration and good health.

I remain, Sir, with most sincere regards, your most devoted

LUDWIG VAN BEETHOVEN

(1562) *To Baron Johann Pasqualati*

[Autograph in the Nationalbibliothek, Vienna]

ESTEEMED FRIEND,   [VIENNA, *March* 14, 1827]

Many thanks for the dish of food you sent me yesterday; it will be quite sufficient for today as well — I am allowed to eat game; and the doctor has said that fieldfares are very wholesome for me — I am just letting you know this. Meanwhile you need not send me any game today — Forgive this stupid note, but I am worn out by sleepless nights. I embrace you and express my regard for you; and with my deepest respects I remain

your most devoted friend.[1]

(1563) *To Ignaz Moscheles, London*

[MS in the possession of Julius Wegeler] [2]

MY DEAR KIND MOSCHELES!   VIENNA, *March* 14, 1827

During the last few days I have heard through Herr Lewinger [3] that in a letter to him dated February 10th you enquired whether I was recovering from the illness about which people have been spreading such varying reports. Although I have not the slightest doubt that you have by now received my first letter of February 22nd [4] which will inform you about everything you want to know, yet I cannot

---

[1] Beethoven did not add his name. The note was written in ink and the handwriting is rather shaky. The recipient has dated it.
[2] Written by Schindler and signed by Beethoven.
[3] A bank clerk in Vienna.
[4] Letter 1554.

but thank you warmly for your sympathy with me in my sad misfortune and ask you once more to take a keen interest in my request which you will have read about in my first letter — Moreover, I feel almost assured in advance that by collaborating with Sir Smart, Mr. Stumpff, Mr. Neate and other friends of mine you will certainly succeed in obtaining a favourable result for me from the Philharmonic Society — Since my first letter I have written again to Sir Smart, as I happened to find his address, and once more urged him to deal with my request.

On February 27th I underwent a fourth operation; and already there are again visible signs that I must soon undergo a fifth. What is to be the end of it all? And what is to become of me, if my illness persists for some time? — Truly my lot is a very hard one! However, I am resigned to accept whatever Fate may bring; and I only continue to pray that God in His divine wisdom may so order events that as long as I have to endure this living death I may be protected from want. This would give me sufficient strength to bear my lot, however hard and terrible it may prove to be, with a feeling of submission to the will of the Almighty.

So, my dear Moscheles, I again ask you to deal with this matter which concerns me; and I remain with my most cordial regards ever

your friend [1]

Hummel is here and has already visited me a few times.[2]

(1564) *To Baron Johann Pasqualati*

[*Autograph in the Gesellschaft der Musikfreunde, Vienna*] [3]

ESTEEMED FRIEND!   [VIENNA, *March* 16, 1827]

I thank you for the dish of food which you sent me yesterday. An invalid craves like a child for something of that

---

[1] Moscheles gave away Beethoven's signature.

[2] On hearing of Beethoven's serious illness Hummel and his wife immediately repaired to Vienna where they remained until after the composer's death. The last quill used by Beethoven is still in the possession of Frau Margarete Hummel. Cf. Letter 466, p. 448, n. 2.

[3] This pencilled note written in a trembling hand is stuck into a handsome copy of Beethoven's 'Elegischer Gesang', Op. 118, dedicated to Baron Johann Pasqualati. The copy bears an inscription by Beethoven written in pencil.

kind. So I am asking you today for the stewed peaches. In regard to other dishes I must first consult the doctors — As for wine they consider Grinzinger suitable for me; but they prefer Krumpholz Kirchner [1] of an old vintage to all other kinds — I trust that what I say will not lead you to misjudge me in any way —

With cordial regards, your friend

BEETHOVEN

(1565) *To Anton Felix Schindler*

[*Autograph in the Deutsche Staatsbibliothek, Berlin*]

Truly a miracle ÷ ÷ [VIENNA, *March* 17, 1827] [2]
Those very learned gentlemen have both been beaten; and it is only thanks to Malfatti's skill that my life is being saved.[3] It is necessary that you should come to me this morning for a moment —

Yours

BEETHOVEN

(1566) *To Ignaz Moscheles, London*

[*MS in the possession of Julius Wegeler*] [4]

MY DEAR, KIND MOSCHELES! VIENNA, *March* 18, 1827
I cannot put into words the emotion with which I read your letter of March 1st. The Philharmonic Society's generosity in almost anticipating my appeal has touched my innermost soul.[5] — I request you, therefore, dear Moscheles, to be the spokesman through whom I send to the Philharmonic Society my warmest and most heartfelt thanks for their particular sympathy and support.

I found myself obliged to draw immediately the whole

---

[1] Gumpoldskirchner, a wine of Gumpoldskirchen, near Vienna.
[2] This date is noted on the autograph by Schindler who adds that this is the last note that Beethoven wrote to him.
[3] According to Schindler the 'very learned gentlemen' were the physician, Dr. Wawruch, and the surgeon, Dr. Seibert. Dr. Andreas Johann Wawruch (1772–1842) was a professor at Vienna University and Dr. Johann Seibert was one of the leading surgeons at the General Hospital in Vienna. For Dr. Malfatti cf. Letter 225, p. 243, n. 2.
[4] Written by Schindler and signed by Beethoven.
[5] Beethoven had just received a gift of £100 from the Philharmonic Society in London.

sum of 1000 gulden A.C., for I just happened to be in the unpleasant position of having to borrow money; and this would have caused me fresh embarrassment.

In regard to the concert which the Philharmonic Society has decided to give for my benefit, I do beg the Society not to give up this noble plan but to deduct from the proceeds of this concert the 1000 gulden A.C. which they have already advanced to me. And if the Society will be so kind as to let me have the remainder, I will undertake to return to the Society my warmest thanks by engaging to compose for it either a new symphony, sketches for which are already in my desk, or a new overture, or something else which the Society might like to have.

May Heaven but restore my health very soon and I shall prove to those magnanimous Englishmen how greatly I appreciate their sympathy for me in my sad fate.

But *your* noble behaviour I shall never forget; and I will shortly proceed to express my thanks particularly to Sir Smart and Herr Stumpff.

I wish you all happiness! With the most friendly sentiments I remain your friend who highly esteems you

LUDWIG VAN BEETHOVEN

My heartfelt greetings to your wife.

I am indebted to the Philharmonic Society and yourself for a new friend, namely, Herr Rau.[1] Please let the Philharmonic Society have the metronome tempi for the symphony. I send you the markings herewith.

Metronome markings of the tempi of Beethoven's last symphony, Op. 125,

Allegro ma non troppo	.	. 88 = ♩
Molto vivace	.	. 116 = ♩·
Presto .	.	. 116 = ♩·
Adagio tempo 1ᵐᵒ	.	. 60 = ♩
Andante moderato	.	. 63 = ♩
Finale presto	.	. 96 = ♩·[2]

[1] Rau was the steward of the house and property of the banker Baron Eskeles. Cf. Letter 1485, p. 1286, n. 3.

[2] For a different metronome marking for the Finale presto movement cf. Letter 1535.

BEETHOVEN ON HIS DEATHBED

Drawn by Joseph Danhauser on March 28, 1827

(From a photograph in the British Museum)

Allegro ma non troppo .	.	88 = ♩
Allegro assai .	.	80 = ♩
Alla Marcia . .	.	84 = ♩·
Andante maestoso .	.	72 = ♩
Adagio divoto .	.	60 = ♩
Allegro energico .	.	84 = ♩·
Allegro ma non tanto .	.	120 = ♩
Prestissimo . .	.	132 = ♩
Maestoso . .	.	60 = ♩

(1567) *To Stieglitz & Co.* [1]

[MS not traced] [2]

VIENNA, *March* 21, 1827

I had the honour of writing to you on January 10, 1827 to ask you to send me the sum of 125 ducats which according to the assurance given to me by His Excellency Prince Nikolas Galitzin he had lodged to my account with you.[3] But I have not yet had your receipt for this document. Therefore in case it should have been lost, I am setting forth in detail its contents and, moreover, am adding an extract from the letter in which Prince G[alitzin] informed me that he desired to lodge the aforesaid sum with you before his departure for Persia.[4] My request now amounts to this, i.e. that if this sum has really reached you, it be transferred to my account with Herren Arnstein & Eskeles in Vienna, so that this transaction may thus be wound up and I may be able to use this sum which I sorely need, particularly on account of my now very prolonged illness.

I render to you in advance my thanks for your kindness and have the honour, etc.

LUDWIG VAN BEETHOVEN

[1] This banking firm, of which Baron Ludwig Stieglitz was a director, were Prince Galitzin's bankers in Vienna.
[2] Taken from TDR V, 570-571.
[3] This letter from Beethoven to Galitzin's bankers has not been traced.
[4] For Galitzin's letter see *TDR* V, 569-570.

(1568) *Codicil to Beethoven's Will*

[*Autograph not traced*] ¹

VIENNA, *March* 23, 1827

My nephew Karl shall be my sole legatee, but the capital of my estate shall fall to his natural or testamentary heirs.

LUDWIG VAN BEETHOVEN

(1569) *To Baron Johann Pasqualati*

[*Autograph in the Nationalbibliothek, Vienna*]

ESTEEMED FRIEND!   [VIENNA, *March*, 1827]

Please send me some more stewed cherries today, but cooked quite simply, without any lemon. Further, a light pudding, almost like gruel, would give me great pleasure. My good cook is not yet competent to provide me with invalid diet. I am allowed to drink *champagne*; but please send me a champagne glass as well with your first delivery. — Now about wine. At first Malfatti said that it should be only Moselle. But he declared that there was no pure Moselle to be had in Vienna. So he himself gave me several bottles of Krumpholz Kirchner ² and declared that this was the best wine for my health, as it was impossible to obtain any genuine Moselle — Forgive me for giving you so much trouble; you must ascribe this in part to my helpless condition.

With kindest regards, your friend

BEETHOVEN

¹ From a photograph in the Stadtbibliothek, Vienna. The codicil is entirely autograph and the writing shows Beethoven's extreme weakness. Cf. Letters 1151 and 1547.

² Gumpoldskirchner. Cf. Letter 1564, p. 1343, n. 1.

(1570) *To Baron Johann Pasqualati*

[*Autograph not traced*] [1]

ESTEEMED FRIEND !   [VIENNA, *March*, 1827]

How can I thank you sufficiently for that excellent champagne which has so greatly refreshed me and will continue to do so ! I need nothing more for today and I thank you for everything — Please note down what further result you achieve in respect of the wines, for I would gladly compensate you as much as my strength allows. — I cannot write any more today. May Heaven bless you in every way and reward you for your affectionate sympathy with your respectful and suffering

BEETHOVEN

[1] Taken from Nohl II, no. 320. Nohl transcribed the letter which was then in private ownership.

Letters 1569 and 1570 may well have been written before Letter 1568, the autograph codicil to Beethoven's will.

APPENDIXES

APPENDICES

APPENDIX A

THE HEILIGENSTADT TESTAMENT

To Caspar Anton Carl and [Nikolaus Johann] van Beethoven

[*Autograph in the Stadtbibliothek, Hamburg*] ¹

HEILIGENSTADT, *October* 6, 1802

FOR MY BROTHERS CARL AND [JOHANN] BEETHOVEN ²

O my fellow men, who consider me, or describe me as, unfriendly, peevish or even misanthropic, how greatly do you wrong me. For you do not know the secret reason why I appear to you to be so. Ever since my childhood my heart and soul have been imbued with the tender feeling of goodwill; and I have always been ready to perform even great actions. But just think, for the last six years I have been afflicted with an incurable complaint which has been made worse by incompetent doctors. From year to year my hopes of being cured have gradually been shattered and finally I have been forced to accept the prospect of a *permanent infirmity* (the curing of which may perhaps take years or may even prove to be impossible). Though endowed with a passionate and lively temperament and even fond of the distractions offered by society I was soon obliged to seclude myself and live in solitude. If at times I decided just to ignore my infirmity, alas! how cruelly was I then driven back by the intensified sad experience of my poor hearing. Yet I could not bring myself to say to people: 'Speak up, shout, for I am deaf'. Alas! how could I possibly refer to the impairing *of a sense* which in me

---

¹ This famous document was found among Beethoven's papers after his death by Schindler, who sent copies of it to Rochlitz at Leipzig and Moscheles in London. Rochlitz published it in the Leipzig *Allgemeine Musikalische Zeitung* of October 17, 1827. After many wanderings the autograph was eventually sent to its present repository in 1888. It has been reproduced in facsimile many times, recently again in a monograph by Hedwig M. von Asow (Vienna and Wiesbaden, 1957).

² In the autograph the name of Beethoven's youngest brother, Johann, is omitted both in the letter and in the postscript dated October 10th.

should be more perfectly developed than in other people, a sense which at one time I possessed in the greatest perfection, even to a degree of perfection such as assuredly few in my profession possess or have ever possessed — Oh, I cannot do it; so forgive me, if you ever see me withdrawing from your company which I used to enjoy. Moreover my misfortune pains me doubly, inasmuch as it leads to my being misjudged. For me there can be no relaxation in human society, no refined conversations, no mutual confidences. I must live quite alone and may creep into society only as often as sheer necessity demands; I must live like an outcast. If I appear in company I am overcome by a burning anxiety, a fear that I am running the risk of letting people notice my condition — And that has been my experience during the last six months which I have spent in the country.[1] My sensible doctor by suggesting that I should spare my hearing as much as possible has more or less encouraged my present natural inclination, though indeed when carried away now and then by my instinctive desire for human society, I have let myself be tempted to seek it. But how humiliated I have felt if somebody standing beside me heard the sound of a flute in the distance and *I heard nothing*, or if somebody heard *a shepherd sing* and again I heard nothing [2] — Such experiences almost made me despair, and I was on the point of putting an end to my life — The only thing that held me back was *my art*. For indeed it seemed to me impossible to leave this world before I had produced all the works that I felt the urge to compose; and thus I have dragged on this miserable existence — a truly miserable existence, seeing that I have such a sensitive body that any fairly sudden change can plunge me from the best spirits into the worst of humours — *Patience* — that is the virtue, I am told, which I must now choose for my guide; and I now possess it — I hope that I shall persist in my resolve to endure to the end, until it pleases the inexorable Parcae to cut the thread; perhaps my condition will improve, perhaps not; at any rate I am now resigned — At the early

[1] Evidently Beethoven had moved to Heiligenstadt early in April. In his day it was a small village with sulphur springs. He stayed there also during the summers of 1807, 1808 and 1817.

[2] For Ferdinand Ries's moving account of Beethoven's gradual loss of hearing see *WRBN.* 117-118.

age of 28 I was obliged to become a philosopher, though this was not easy; for indeed this is more difficult for an artist than for anyone else — Almighty God, who look down into my innermost soul, you see into my heart and you know that it is filled with love for humanity and a desire to do good. Oh my fellow men, when some day you read this statement, remember that you have done me wrong; and let some unfortunate man derive comfort from the thought that he has found another equally unfortunate who, notwithstanding all the obstacles imposed by nature, yet did everything in his power to be raised to the rank of noble artists and human beings. — And you, my brothers Carl and [Johann], when I am dead, request on my behalf Professor Schmidt,¹ if he is still living, to describe my disease, and attach this written document to his record, so that after my death at any rate the world and I may be reconciled as far as possible — At the same time I herewith nominate you both heirs to my small property (if I may so describe it) — Divide it honestly, live in harmony and help one another. You know that you have long ago been forgiven for the harm you did me. I again thank you, my brother Carl, in particular, for the affection you have shown me of late years. My wish is that you should have a better and more carefree existence than I have had. Urge your children to be *virtuous*, for virtue alone can make a man happy. Money cannot do this. I speak from experience. It was virtue that sustained me in my misery. It was thanks to virtue and also to my art that I did not put an end to my life by suicide — Farewell and love one another — I thank all my friends, and especially *Prince Lichnowsky* ² and *Professor Schmidt*. I would like Prince L[ichnowsky]'s instruments to be preserved by one of you, provided this does not lead to a quarrel between you.³ But as soon as they can serve a more useful purpose, just sell them; and how glad I shall be if in my grave I can still be of some use to you both — Well, that is all — Joyfully I go to meet Death — should it come before I have had an opportunity of developing all my artistic gifts, then in spite of my hard

¹ Cf. Letter 54, p. 66, n. 4.   ² Cf. Letter 16, p. 23, n. 3.
³ The instruments given to Beethoven by Prince Karl Lichnowsky were a violin and a cello by Guarneri, an Amati violin, and a viola dated 1690. These are now in the Beethovenhaus, Bonn.

fate it would still come too soon, and no doubt I would like it to postpone its coming — Yet even so I should be content, for would it not free me from a condition of continual suffering? Come then, Death, *whenever* you like, and with courage I will go to meet you — Farewell; and when I am dead, do not wholly forget me. I deserve to be remembered by you, since during my lifetime I have often thought of you and tried to make you happy — Be happy —

LUDWIG VAN BEETHOVEN

For my brothers Carl and [Johann]
To be read and executed after my death [1] —
HEILIGENSTADT, October 10, 1802 — Thus I take leave of you — and, what is more, rather sadly — yes, the hope I cherished — the hope I brought with me here of being cured to a certain extent at any rate — that hope I must now abandon completely. As the autumn leaves fall and wither, likewise — that hope has faded for me. I am leaving here — almost in the same condition as I arrived — Even that high courage — which has often inspired me on fine summer days — has vanished — Oh Providence — do but grant me one day *of pure joy* — For so long now the inner echo of real joy has been unknown to me — Oh when — oh when, Almighty God — shall I be able to hear and feel this echo again in the temple of Nature and in contact with humanity — Never? — No! — Oh, that would be too hard.

[1] These two directions are added at the left side of the postscript, which is written on the fourth page of the autograph and dated four days later than the letter. Furthermore, in both cases Beethoven spells his country resort Heiglnstadt.

APPENDIX B

TWO LETTERS TO BETTINA VON ARNIM, NÉE BRENTANO, OF DOUBTFUL AUTHENTICITY

---

(1) *To Bettina Brentano, Berlin*

[*Autograph not traced*] [1]

DEAREST BETTINE,[2]   VIENNA, *August* 11, 1810

There has never been a more beautiful spring than this year's, that I do declare, and I feel it too, just because I have made your acquaintance. No doubt you yourself have noticed that in company I am like a fish out of water, wriggling and wriggling and unable to return to its element until some sympathetic Galatea puts it back into the rolling sea. Yes, I was indeed high and dry, most beloved Bettine, and you came upon me at a moment when peevishness had absolutely got the better of me. But, to tell the truth, it vanished at sight of you, and I shook it off completely. For I realized that you belonged to a different world, not to this absurd one to which with the best possible will one cannot really give a hearing. I am a wretched fellow and yet I complain about other people!! — Surely you will forgive me, you with your good heart, which can be seen in your eyes, you with your good sense, which can be found in your ears — at any rate your ears know how to flatter when you listen to others. Alas, unfortunately my ears are a partition through which it is not easy for me to have any friendly communication with

---

[1] Taken from *TDR* III, 227-228. Of the three letters supposed to have been written by Beethoven to Bettina Brentano only the second one, Letter 296 of February 10, 1811, is now accepted as genuine. But all three were published by Julius Merz in the *Athenäum für Wissenschaft, Kunst und Leben* (Nürnberg, 1839), and again by Bettina in her book *Ilius Pamphilius und die Ambrosia* (Berlin, 1857), vol. II. Doubtless the two spurious letters were based on reminiscences of conversations between Beethoven and Bettina and on certain events reported to her later. But until the autographs come to light the authenticity of these letters will remain a subject for speculation.

[2] Cf. Letter 296, where Beethoven addresses Bettina as Bettine.

1355

human beings. Otherwise! — perhaps! — I might have had more confidence in you. As it was, I could only understand the wide, intelligent look of your eyes, which has made such a strong impression on me that I shall never, never forget it — Dear Bettine, dearest girl! — Art! — Who understands it? — With whom can one talk about that great goddess! — How precious to me are those few days when we two were chattering or, rather, corresponding. I have kept all the little scraps of paper with your witty, dear, and charming answers.[1] Hence I have after all to thank my bad ears that the best part of those fleeting conversations has been jotted down. Since you left I have had melancholy hours, dark hours when I could do nothing. After your departure I strolled about the Schönbrunner Allee for fully three hours, but no angel met me there, no angel seized me in the same way as you, my angel — Dearest Bettine, forgive this abandonment of the usual key, but I must have intervals of this kind in order to relieve my heart. Well, no doubt you have written to Goethe about me? Indeed I would like to put my head in a bag where I should hear and see nothing of all that is happening in this world, chiefly because you, dearest angel, will hardly ever meet me there. But no doubt I shall have a letter from you? — This hope sustains me. Why, hope sustains half the world, and all my life hope has been beside me, and what should I have done without hope? — I am sending you a copy in my own hand of 'Kennst du das Land' as a remembrance of the hour when I met you.[2] I am sending you also the other song which I composed after I said goodbye to you, dear, dearest heart! —

> Oh my heart, what means this surging,
> This oppressive wearying stress?
> Whither are these feelings urging
> Me? I know not, I confess.[3]

[1] It was not until 1817 that Beethoven became so deaf that it was necessary for an interlocutor to write down questions and answers.

[2] Beethoven's setting of Goethe's poem was composed in 1809. It was published as the first of six songs, Op. 75, by Breitkopf & Härtel in October, 1810. See *KHV*, 199-205.

[3] So far as is known, Beethoven set Goethe's poem 'Herz, mein Herz, was soll das geben' to music twice. First, in 1798-1799, a setting published in 1808 by Simrock in a collection of German songs composed by Beethoven; and again, in

Yes, dearest Bettine, do reply to this letter. Let me know what is about to happen to me since my heart has become such a rebel. Write to your most faithful friend —

BEETHOVEN

(2) *To Bettina von Arnim, Berlin* [1]

[Autograph not traced] [2]

DEAR, KIND BETTINE!   TEPLITZ, *August,* 1812
Kings and princes are able, no doubt, to appoint professors, create Privy Councillors, award titles and affix order ribbons. But they cannot create great men or minds which rise above the rabble of this world; that they certainly need not try to do; and therefore great men of that type should be respected — When two such people as Goethe and I meet, the great lords should discern what is really great in men of our type. On our way home yesterday we met the entire Imperial family.[3] From a distance we saw them coming; and Goethe left me in order to stand aside; it was useless for me to protest, I could not make him move a step further. I pulled my hat down on my head, buttoned up my overcoat *and strode through the thickest crowd with my arms crossed*—Princes and flunkeys stood in line, the Archduke Rudolph took off his hat [4] and the Empress was the first to greet me — The courtiers know me — To my intense amusement I saw the procession file past Goethe — *who stood at the side with his hat off and making low bows* — Afterwards I blew him up thoroughly, gave him no quarter and reproached him for all his sins, and, most of all, for his sins against you, dearest Bettine! For we had just been talking about you. Dear God! Had I been able to spend

1809 as Op. 75, No. 2, published by Breitkopf & Härtel in October, 1810. The first and longer setting is listed in *KHV.* as WoO 127.
    In the Beethovenhaus, Bonn (H. C. Bodmer collection), there is a copy of nine bars of Op. 75, No. 2. The recto of this sheet is addressed in Beethoven's hand to 'Bettine von Brentano'; and under the copy on the verso the composer has written 'set to music by Beethoven'. See *KHV.* 201.
    [1] Bettina Brentano had married the poet Achim von Arnim in March, 1811.
    [2] Taken from *TDR* III, 328-329.
    [3] The 'entire Imperial family' were not at Teplitz in August, 1812. Nor was Beethoven. But the Grand Duke Karl August of Weimar and his secretary were there.
    [4] The Archduke Rudolph did not visit Teplitz in 1812.

as much time with you as that man did, believe me, I should
have produced far, far more works, and really great works.
For a musician is also a poet; he too by gazing into a pair
of eyes can suddenly feel himself transported into a lovelier
world where greater minds enjoy his company and set him
quite formidable tasks — All sorts of ideas occurred to me
after I made your acquaintance at the small observatory
during that delicious May shower which was quite stimulating for me as well. The most beautiful themes then found
their way from your eyes into my heart, themes which will
enchant the world some day when Beethoven will no longer
be there to conduct. If God spares me for a few more years,
then I really must see you again, my dear, dear Bettine;
for the voice which is always right where I am concerned,
tells me so insistently. Spirits too can love one another and
I shall always pay court to yours. Your praise is more precious
to me than that of the whole world. I have given Goethe
my opinion about how praise affects people like ourselves and
have told him that I want my kindred spirits to hear me with
the mind. To be emotionally stirred is only suitable for
women (forgive me for putting it in that way); *but the effect
of music on a man should be to fire his mind.* Ah, dearest child,
for how long a time now have we been of the same opinion
about everything!!! — There is nothing so soothing as to
possess a beautiful, kind soul, whom one recognizes in every
action and from whom one need not conceal anything. *One
must really be something if one wants to appear so.* The world
must recognize a man. For the world is not always unjust,
though indeed I pay little attention to it, because I aim at
something higher — I hope to find a letter from you in Vienna;
write soon, soon and very fully, for I shall be there in a week.
The court is leaving tomorrow; there is one more performance
today. He [1] has taught the Empress her part. He and his
Duke wanted me to produce some of my music. I refused
both of them. They are both infatuated with Chinese porce-
lain. It is necessary to be indulgent, because common sense
no longer guides them. But I will not fall in with their idiotic
whims. I refuse to participate in absurdities with princes at
public expense, seeing that those princes never discharge

[1] Presumably Goethe.

debts of that kind. Adieu, Adieu, most charming girl, your last letter lay on my heart for a whole night and refreshed me there. Musicians can take *every liberty.*

Dear God, how I love you!

Your most faithful friend and deaf brother

BEETHOVEN

APPENDIX C

DOCUMENTS RELATING TO BEETHOVEN'S LITIGATION ABOUT THE GUARDIANSHIP OF HIS NEPHEW

---

(1) *To the Imperial and Royal Landrechte of Lower Austria* [1]

[*MS in the Archiv der Stadt Wien*] [2]

VIENNA, *November* 28, 1815

MOST WORSHIPFUL IMPERIAL AND ROYAL LANDRECHTE OF LOWER AUSTRIA!

My beloved brother Carl van Beethoven died on the 15th of this month leaving a will and testament (Document A) [3] in which he appointed me guardian of his son aged between nine and ten years,[4] exactly as he had already nominated me his son's guardian on April 12, 1813 (Document B).[5] In accordance with Paragraph 196 of the Civil Code [6] I now have the chief claim to this guardianship. Moreover I hereby declare that I intend to undertake this guardianship without delay, because I cherished a deep affection for my brother, because his last charge is sacred to me and because he committed the welfare of his son to me several times by word of mouth. Thus in many respects I consider myself bound to discharge the duties of this guardianship in the most conscientious

---

[1] The Landrechte of Lower Austria was not merely a provincial court (Landgericht). It was the court for the privileged classes and institutions, such as the Landstände (estates of the county), the nobility, the clergy, etc., from 1783 until 1848. Beethoven, posing as a nobleman, applied first to the Landrechte.

[2] Written in another hand and signed by Beethoven. This document was first published by Professor O. E. Deutsch in an article entitled 'Drei neue Beethoven-Briefe' in the *Österreichische Musikzeitschrift*, 1953, nos. 3/4, pp. 79-82.

[3] For Document A (Carl's will dated November 14, 1815) see *TDR* III, 517-518.

[4] Karl van Beethoven, the son of Beethoven's younger brother, was born on September 4, 1806.

[5] Document B has not been recovered.

[6] The quotations are from the Allgemeines Civil (Bürgerliches) Gesetzbuch.

manner. In order that I may take up my duties as guardian in accordance with the rules set forth in Paragraph 204 of the Civil Code I beg

the most Worshipful Legal Authorities graciously
to make all the
necessary arrangements for this purpose.

LUDWIG VAN BEETHOVEN

(2) *To the Magistrat der Stadt Wien* [1]

[MS not traced] [2]

WORSHIPFUL MAGISTRAT!   VIENNA, *December* 15, 1815

In order to prevent the establishment of an illegal joint guardianship which would be detrimental to the interests of the ward, I, who am the testamentary guardian of my nephew Carl van Beethoven,[3] require proof of the sentence passed on his mother, Johanna v[an] Beethoven, who has been tried for embezzlement.[4]

Hence I beg that the Worshipful Magistrat will consent to supply me with a legally attested copy of the criminal accusations brought against her and of the relevant decision of the Supreme Court.[5]

LUDWIG VAN BEETHOVEN

[1] The Magistrat was the corporation of the City of Vienna. A member (Magistratsrat) was a paid official. This corporation had at that time three senates : (1) political, (2) civic court, and (3) criminal court. Until 1848 the last two dealt only with commoners, all other cases being dealt with by the Landrechte.

[2] From a contemporary official copy in the Archiv der Stadt Wien and first published by O. E. Deutsch in the article quoted in Appendix C (1), p. 1360, n. 2.

[3] Beethoven nearly always spelt his nephew's name with a K. But his nephew spelt it with a C; and it appears in this form in some official documents.

[4] In 1811.

[5] The Magistrat refused to supply the copy. But Beethoven obtained the necessary information from the Landrechte.

(3) *To the Imperial and Royal Landrechte of Lower Austria*

[*MS in the Beethovenhaus, Bonn*] [1]

VIENNA, *December* 20, 1815

MOST WORSHIPFUL IMPERIAL AND ROYAL LANDRECHTE OF LOWER AUSTRIA!

However reluctant the undersigned may be to reopen a wound, a deep wound that was inflicted on his family and especially on his unfortunate deceased brother and has but slowly healed, yet he feels that by reason of the legal regulation A and of the analogy of Paragraph 20 of the Civil Code it is his duty to draw the attention of the High Court to the fact that if the latter considers it compatible with the necessary care for the welfare of the nine to ten year old Karl van Beethoven to obtain official information about the earlier associations of his mother before entrusting her with the guardianship, the report B of the Worshipful Magistrat of Vienna will give the necessary particulars; and that honourable men holding distinguished appointments would be ready to give the most incontestable evidence about her behaviour before and after her marriage to my brother and until the time of his death, even if I refused to say anything about matters which I myself can prove up to the hilt. Moreover it must be borne in mind that a woman, even though she be equipped with moral and intellectual qualities, which unfortunately I am bound to confess is by no means the case with the widow of my deceased brother, can never be capable of supervising adequately the education of a boy as soon as he has passed the age of nine years. Admittedly his widow was nominated by my brother as joint guardian, but this was done in a codicil added when I was absent for an hour and a half, i.e. without my knowledge and behind my back.[2] Nevertheless it is obvious and can be quite easily proved that my brother made this later arrangement solely, as I know for

---

[1] This document, written in another hand and signed by Beethoven, was first published by L. Schiedermair in *Neues Beethoven-Jahrbuch*, 1938, pp. 62-64.

[2] For the text of this important codicil see *TDR* III, 518-519.

certain, because he was insistently urged to do so by his wife and was not in a condition to take an entirely free decision. For immediately afterwards he went back on this arrangement and sent the person who nursed him during his illness, Frau Anna Wildmann (a cutter, living at No. 53 in the Alservorstadt, on the ground floor), to Dr. Schönauer [1] to demand the return of the codicil. But the latter was not at home. When I happened to return to my brother, he repeatedly stated, expressing himself quite lucidly, that he was withdrawing the codicil extracted from him in my absence; and he urgently begged me to drive as quickly as possible with the aforesaid woman to H[err] Dr. Schönauer and retrieve it *because otherwise some great misunderstanding might arise therefrom*. Those were his very words.

Unfortunately we did not find Herr Dr. Schönauer at his home; and when we drove to his house a second time for the same purpose, he was again not to be found. In the meantime my poor brother died. The aforesaid Frau Anna Wildmann is willing to testify to these circumstances at any time. Moreover a comparison of the article in his will, by which I have been appointed sole guardian, with the codicil shows only too clearly that my brother was made to state quite different things from what he stated in his will, which expresses what he was wont to declare to me during his lifetime. Furthermore, it is as clear as daylight that, seeing that my brother's widow was excluded from the guardianship in his will, this circumstance is in no wise calculated to make one have confidence in her character.

Since, however, my unswerving and never abandoned aim is solely and entirely the future welfare of my nephew Karl and since my purpose is merely to provide him with an adequate and carefully planned education, I am disregarding those circumstances and I calmly hold to the comforting conviction that the Worshipful Landrechte of Lower Austria, in view of the events I have recounted, will proceed according to their own wise judgment, and consequently giving full consideration to my nephew's welfare, will entrust me alone and exclusively with the guardianship, or will do so by including my brother's widow, but that in the latter eventuality

[1] Cf. Letter 1009, p. 876, n. 3.

they will protect me by means of those measures which after previous consultation with the Worshipful Landrechte of Lower Austria I shall consider to be to my nephew's advantage and which most probably are bound to be frequently opposed by the narrow-minded views and judgment, and no less by the thoughtlessness, carelessness and excitability, but above all by the behaviour of the joint guardian, which is causing just concern — all this operating to the grievous detriment of the child.

At the same time I declare that I regard it as a sacred duty enjoined on my conscience not to abandon my rights to the guardianship under the will, and that in discharging this duty I shall make every effort to do whatever in my strongest conviction can contribute to and promote the true welfare and the moral and intellectual benefit of my nephew. I will do this without paying any attention to the terms of the codicil which, inasmuch as they are the instructions of a dying man and depend for their execution on circumstances which could not be foreseen, are in any case neither valid nor likely to serve as a pretext for obstructing suitable measures for the child's education, measures that have been adopted with pure and ingenuous intentions.

It has been my desire to present the above report and to leave all further arrangements to the superior judgment of the Worshipful Landrechte of Lower Austria.

LUDWIG VAN BEETHOVEN [1]

[1] The decision taken by the Landrechte was wholly in Beethoven's favour. It was dated January 9, 1816. See L. Schiedermair, *Neues Beethoven-Jahrbuch*, 1938, p. 64, where the Landrechte's reply, forwarded to Beethoven on January 17th, is given in full.

(4) To the Imperial and Royal Landrechte of Lower Austria

[*MS in the Beethovenhaus, Bonn, H. C. Bodmer collection*] [1]

VIENNA, *February* 15, 1816

MOST WORSHIPFUL IMPERIAL AND ROYAL LANDRECHTE OF LOWER AUSTRIA!

By virtue of the control as guardian of my nephew Karl van Beethoven entrusted to me in your decree of January 9, 1816,[2] I have considered it most conducive to his welfare that he should be removed from his mother's influence and begin his education at Herr Giannatasio del Rio's boarding school, which has been recommended to me most favourably from many quarters and where he has been living since the 2nd of this month, an arrangement which in this document I am duly reporting to the Most Worshipful Imperial and Royal Landrechte.

Since, however, the unpleasant case has arisen that the mother of my nephew Karl van Beethoven, by her thoughtless and unlawful desire to see the boy every day and to take him to her home whenever she likes, is threatening to disturb the course of instruction which has been introduced in the aforesaid boarding school (as is proved in Supplement A.) and since, moreover, owing to her ill-bred domestic behaviour she would have a very bad influence on the sensitive temperament of her child, whose reasoning powers are developing rapidly, my urgent request is that the Most Worshipful Imperial and Royal Landrechte of Lower Austria shall help me to ensure that this persistently harmful hindrance to the undisturbed education of my nephew Karl van Beethoven be removed, and that too the more drastically and speedily since the mother's manner of life is becoming daily more offensive, a fact which the accounts of her behaviour that I receive unfortunately confirm only too strongly.

LUDWIG VAN BEETHOVEN [3]

[1] Written by Häring and signed by Beethoven. This document, which is probably the petition mentioned in *TDR* III, 540, was first published by the present editor in *Notes*, September 1952, pp. 555-556.

[2] Cf. Appendix C (3), p. 1364, n. 1.

[3] In a reply dated February 20, 1816, the Landrechte again supported Beethoven's claim to be sole guardian.

(5) *To the Imperial and Royal Landrechte of Lower Austria*

[*MS not traced*] [1]

VIENNA, *March* 2, 1816

MOST WORSHIPFUL IMPERIAL AND ROYAL LANDRECHTE OF LOWER AUSTRIA!

When my late brother Karl van Beethoven was appointed cashier in the Imperial and Royal Bank (Head Office) he had to disburse a sum of 1000 gulden in addition to the security amounting to 1000 gulden that he had already deposited. Hence at the moment 2000 gulden are *in deposito aerari* in his name.

As this sum is part of his estate but is not entered in the inventory, I beg that the Supreme Court will agree to direct the Sperrskommissär [2] to cash the above sum of 2000 gulden and enter it in the inventory, and with a view to an arrangement about the obligations of the service security, to get in touch with the widow who should possess the necessary documents.

LUDWIG VAN BEETHOVEN [3]

(6) *Contract between Johanna van Beethoven and Ludwig van Beethoven* [4]

[*MS in the Beethovenhaus, Bonn, H. C. Bodmer collection*] [5]

VIENNA, *May* 10, 1817

1. The undersigned, Ludwig van Beethoven, as guardian of the minor Karl van Beethoven, agrees *salva ratificatione* to

---

[1] From a contemporary official copy in the Archiv der Stadt Wien and first published by Professor O. E. Deutsch in the article quoted in Appendix C (1), p. 1360, n. 2.

[2] An official of the Magistrat whose duty it was to block all accounts until an estate was wound up.

[3] This petition too was granted by the Landrechte.

[4] Possibly this contract should be included among the contracts in Appendix F. But as it forms an important addition to the documents bearing on Beethoven's prolonged litigation, the present editor decided to place it in Appendix C.

[5] Written in another hand and signed by Beethoven and his sister-in-law.

the transfer of Karl van Beethoven's estate to his widow Frau Johanna van Beethoven on the understanding

2. that she shall legally state her willingness to, and undertake to, make for the education and maintenance of her aforesaid minor son Karl a yearly contribution to whoever may be his guardian at the time, paid in quarterly instalments and always in advance; and that this yearly contribution must consist of at least half of the pension which the widow Frau Johanna van Beethoven is to receive *ab aerario* together with emoluments or any other nominal additions whatever that may be made to it —

3. that the widow Frau Johanna van Beethoven, as compensation for the estate bequeathed to her with certain encumbrances and profits and also for the payments already received from the house in the estate, shall forthwith make a legal contribution of 2000 gulden V.C. for her minor son Karl and shall transfer the usufruct to the aforenamed son for his better education and support —

4. that, finally, the payment of the contribution for his education and maintenance which the aforesaid widow has promised to make shall begin from the date of this agreement.

signed   LUDWIG VAN BEETHOVEN

signed   JOHANNA VAN BEETHOVEN

(7) *To the Imperial and Royal Landrechte of Lower Austria*

[*MS not traced*] [1]

VIENNA, *September* 25, 1818

MOST WORSHIPFUL IMPERIAL AND ROYAL LANDRECHTE OF LOWER AUSTRIA!

When the summons of the Imperial and Royal Landrechte of Lower Austria on the 22nd of this month was forwarded to Mödling where I am now staying, I happened to be in Vienna on business and therefore owing to this circumstance

---

[1] Taken from Nohl, *Mosaik*, 1882, pp. 320-322. According to Nohl, who transcribed the original document, this petition was written in another hand and signed by Beethoven.

could not obey it at the appointed time. Hence I am using the method of a written deposition which I herewith submit to the Imperial and Royal Landrechte of Lower Austria.

The mother of my ward, who on account of her moral disqualification has been wholly and rigidly excluded from his education by the Imperial and Royal Landrechte of Lower Austria, after several fruitless attempts to upset by her interference the educational plan I have worked out and followed, has again presumed to take a step to which I as the exclusively appointed guardian of my nephew Karl van Beethoven can by no means give my consent.

In order to achieve her purpose she resorts to methods which in themselves indicate a low mind. For she exploits, of course, my deafness, as she calls it, and my supposed ill health as a pretext in order to place my nephew's education in an unfavourable light.

In regard to the first point, everybody who is closely acquainted with me knows only too well that all verbal communications between me and my nephew and other people as well are carried on with the greatest ease and are by no means impeded by my indifferent hearing. Furthermore, my health has never been better; and from that point of view also there is no reason to fear that my nephew's education could suffer.

After having him educated for two years at Herr Giannatasio's boarding school entirely at my expense I have now taken him into my home in order to discover whether he has more taste for music than for the sciences.

Here under my very eyes he has had every opportunity to develop his talent for music, in which I myself have instructed him daily for two and a half hours, and also at the same time to continue his school work.

I have discovered that he shows greater inclination for scientific subjects. The certificates attached to Supplement A., which I ask to be returned to me, are sufficient proof that during the whole summer when he was with me in the country he pursued his studies as zealously as he did in Vienna.[1] As for the intention of my ward's mother to place him in a seminary I must state most definitely that I am opposed to this

[1] This file of documents is now in the Koch collection.

1368

plan, and for the following reasons :

I) The circumstances which led the court to decide to remove the mother not only from the guardianship but also from *all* influence over his education and from associating with the ward still persist.

II) If the ward were placed in a seminary, the court's precautions would be frustrated, because in a seminary the special limitations imposed on *this* mother would not be generally known and she could easily contrive to get hold of the child and take him home with her. Even in my home she has made attempts of this kind by bribing the servants and seducing the boy to indulge in lies and hypocrisy, although she has not been forbidden to see and speak to her son in my presence whenever she lets me know her desire to do so and whenever circumstances allow this to be arranged.

III) Supplements B. and C. sufficiently prove that the mother of my ward did make secret attempts of this kind even during his stay at the boarding school and that the head-master of the boarding school considered her association with the ward to be in the highest degree detrimental to the latter.

IV) Since the date when the Imperial and Royal Land-rechte entrusted me exclusively with the guardianship of my nephew,[1] I have not only defrayed all the expenses of his education (for in this connexion the mother's small contribution which she has only recently begun to make as a refund can hardly be taken into consideration) but have never ceased to take great trouble and care to have him taught as efficiently as possible everything necessary to enable him to become a good and useful citizen ; so much so that the most tenderly loving father could not be more particular about the welfare of his own child. When doing so I did not expect to be thanked by the mother ; but I trust that the Supreme Vormund-schaft will recognize what I have done.

V) The plan for the future higher education of my nephew was in fact drafted long ago and we have been working on these lines. Therefore a very harmful disturbance in the progress of his education would be caused if a different method based upon other ideas were suddenly to be adopted.

In any case with a view to choosing the most suitable

[1] In January, 1816. Cf. Appendix C (3), p. 1364, n. 1.

course in close co-operation with the Imperial and Royal Landrechte I will give due notice to that body of any change I propose to make in regard to my nephew. Thus in order to forestall any disturbance and obstruction, it will become more and more necessary to prevent the boy's mother from exercising *any* influence whatever over him. This is not only laid down in the particular case pertaining to her in Paragraph 191 of the Civil Code — certainly a very wise decision — but also because, as the boy grows older, she by reason of her intellectual and moral qualities will prove in general to be more and more unsuited to have any influence over his education and upbringing to manhood.

Yet that is the way in which Frau Johanna van Beethoven is behaving after the decision of the Court which declared her to be morally unfit and excluded her from the education of and all association with her child, and even after the subsequent decision of the Imperial and Royal Landrechte of Lower Austria, dated January 19, 1816,[1] which entrusted me as sole and exclusive guardian with the education of my nephew. I repeat, however, that her insolent attempt to appear as the guardian of her son, who is a minor, is to a certain extent understandable to me in view of her impudent behaviour on all other occasions.

LUDWIG VAN BEETHOVEN
who am the guardian of my nephew
Karl van Beethoven

(8) *To the Imperial and Royal Landrechte of Lower Austria*

[*MS not traced*] [2]

VIENNA, *December* 15, 1818

MOST WORSHIPFUL IMPERIAL AND ROYAL LANDRECHTE OF LOWER AUSTRIA!

At first it seemed to me unnecessary to give any more information to our Imperial and Royal Landrechte of Lower

---

[1] Obviously a mistake for January 9, 1816. Cf. Appendix C (3), p. 1364, n. 1.
[2] Taken from Nohl, *Mosaik*, 1882, pp. 323-326. The petition was written in another hand and signed by Beethoven.

Austria. But after the recent incidents which, I am becoming more and more convinced, are being provoked by intrigues woven for the purpose of separating my ward from me, I consider it advisable and necessary to describe in greater detail the attitude I have so far adopted. That the strictest truth predominates in all my statements is guaranteed by my well-known opinions and my publicly recognized moral character. In this connexion the following Appendixes will provide the most cogent proofs.

Supplement A. contains the school reports of my ward which have been asked for. They are sufficient proof of his progress and his moral behaviour. In a few scientific subjects they would perhaps be even more favourable, if the perpetual disturbances provoked by his mother had not placed obstacles in his way. At the moment the two letters of the servants cannot be found among my papers. Their contents are down-right stupid and, for the most part, exaggerated, vulgar gossip, such as, for instance, that my ward had nearly torn down the caretaker's bell, that he had wedged a capon between two pieces of wood where it was suffocated, that he had kept back 30 kreuzer from money given to him for shopping and had bought sweets, that he had abused the servants, etc. Since those letters were timed to reach me, so that I might tax my ward with his behaviour, exactly on the day on which it was arranged he should leave my house, it is obvious that they were written, perhaps even dictated, for the purpose of providing an excuse for his removal. And indeed how could servants take upon themselves to start a correspondence with persons of a superior social standing about the conduct of my ward?

Supplements B. quote the small contributions from his mother's pension to my ward's education, and also the expenses which I have defrayed for this purpose out of my own pocket. They clearly prove that it would have been impossible to provide him with a decent way of life and an adequate education, had I not voluntarily made such great sacrifices.

Supplement C. contains two letters to myself from the headmaster of the boarding school, Herr Giannatasio del Rio, who formerly had charge of my ward. They are sufficient proof that this headmaster was aware how harmful was the mother's interference in the arrangements for educating my ward. In view of the circumstances which are sufficiently well known, they require no further elucidation.

Apart from the very considerable disbursements for the boarding school I have also paid, as the supplements show, the lawyer and the solicitor employed in the affair of my ward, and that too out of my own pocket. I have undertaken at my expense a journey to Retz in his interest and I have made extra payments to the teachers for instruction in scientific subjects and in music. Furthermore, in addition to other unforeseen expenses, which it would be wearisome to enumerate, I have defrayed the considerable costs of an operation for hernia which was successfully performed on my nephew. On the other hand the amount of the contribution of half of the mother's pension is very meagre; and moreover I received it at first only after considerable delay; and now I have not received anything of it for the last six months.[1]

I have dealt with the economic aspect of my guardianship. In regard to the scientific and moral education of my ward I have endeavoured chiefly by word and by example to bring up a good man and a capable citizen and to enable him to acquire the necessary knowledge.

That is why I placed him at first at Herr Giannatasio del Rio's boarding school,[2] which, however, was subsequently not sufficiently advanced to enable me to achieve my object. So last summer I arranged for my ward to live with me under the supervision of an excellent teacher whom I paid; and as the time was approaching for a decision to be taken about his future career, I took him into the country in order to be able to ascertain to what extent his liking for music would develop under my guidance, but without allowing his school work to be neglected, as is proved by his certificates; for in the country too I employed a teacher.[3] Although he showed no small talent for music, yet his aptitude for scientific subjects was more marked; and so from that moment I decided to let him have the benefit of instruction at a public school. When we

[1] Since June, 1818.
[2] In February, 1816. Karl was removed from this boarding school on January 24, 1818.
[3] Johann Baptist Fröhlich, a clergyman at Mödling. Cf. Letter 904, p. 770, n. 1.

returned to town I immediately arranged for him to visit public schools and to have at home the necessary private tuition not only as a preparation for his school but so as to acquire proficiency in music, French and drawing. After the latest distressing interruption by his mother, I sent him for a time to Giannatasio's boarding school.[1]

At the moment, because he realizes his mistake, is sorry for it and only begs to be allowed to remain with me, he is again living with me under the guidance of myself and an experienced teacher who accompanies him to and from school and continually shares with me his instruction and his supervision. For all this I do not grudge paying the considerable sum of 600 gulden a year, not counting further extra payments for this teacher.

I should add that my nephew has been given the best recommendations to the professors and prefects and that the special supervision of him at school is very strict. The most conscientious father could not do more for his child.

Thus I shall continue to surmount all the obstacles which may yet be placed in my way. I shall have solely the welfare of my ward in view and be mindful of the prayers of my late brother and also of the duty enjoined on me in this difficult matter by the guardianship legally entrusted to me, by my relationship to my nephew and by my love of humanity. At the same time in pursuance of my honest endeavour and in virtue of the purity of my intentions and my desires I shall be willing at any moment to give the most satisfactory account of my actions to the Most Worshipful Imperial and Royal Landrechte of Lower Austria in charge of the Obervormundschaft.

LUDWIG VAN BEETHOVEN,
Guardian of my nephew Karl van Beethoven.

[1] After Beethoven's return to Vienna Karl, who in the meantime had passed his examination in August, was sent to the Akademisches Gymnasium. Early in December, 1818, however, he ran away to his mother and was brought back by Beethoven with the help of the police. He was then sent for a few days to Giannatasio del Rio.

(9) *To the Magistrat der Stadt Wien* [1]

[Autograph in the Archiv der Stadt Wien]

MOST WORSHIPFUL MAGISTRAT! VIENNA, *February* 1, 1819 [2]

Since I am to speak about the future education of my nephew, I consider it most appropriate to begin with the education he is already receiving; and it will be obvious that another change would only be *to his disadvantage.* It has already been reported that he has a tutor who will continue to instruct him. But in order that his zeal may be still further stimulated, I am letting my nephew pursue his studies in the company of his tutor with H[err] v[on] Kudlich, the head of an institution near my home in the Landstrasse.[3] He is being taught with only one other boy, the son of a Baron Lang, and is under constant supervision when he is there. Besides there is the additional advantage that Herr von Kudlich teaches entirely according to the thorough method followed at the University, or rather, practises it. It is a method which all experts, myself included, consider to be the best. But it is a method which every tutor does not follow and the lack of which therefore raises some difficulties for the pupil at examinations. Further, my nephew is having special lessons in French, drawing and music. He is thus not only usefully and pleasantly occupied the whole day but is also under *constant* supervision, which is *absolutely necessary.* In addition, I have found an excellent clergyman who gives him special instruction about his duties as a *Christian and a man.* For only on such a foundation can *genuine and honourable people* be reared and trained. Later on, when the summer comes, he will also take up the study of Greek. It is plain, therefore, that I am sparing no expense in order to achieve the fine purpose of giving to the state a useful and well-educated citizen. And the *present*

[1] On December 18, 1818, after discovering that Beethoven's 'van' was not a title of nobility and that the Beethoven family were commoners the Landrechte referred the whole question of Karl's guardianship to the Vienna Magistrat. On January 11, 1819, Beethoven and Karl, Karl's mother Johanna, and Jakob Hotschevar, a court secretary and a relative of Johanna's, had to give evidence before the Magistrat. Whereupon Beethoven drafted this 12-page report, setting forth his views on Karl's education.

[2] The autograph is dated 1818, but this is Beethoven's mistake, a not uncommon one. [3] Cf. Letter 950, p. 817, n. 1.

arrangement leaves nothing to be desired. Hence *no change* is necessary. But should I consider it necessary to make some change, I will *most conscientiously propose and arrange* for an even better scheme. — Every man who does not become an artisan, whatever other trade he may pursue, must have passed through at least five or six school classes. During that period it can then be ascertained what are his inclinations and talents. Whether he becomes a civil servant or a scholar, the foundation can be laid only *in this way*. My nephew's unusual gifts and partly, on the other hand, his peculiar traits of character demand, moreover, unusual methods. And never did I act more charitably and magnanimously than at the time when I took my nephew into my own home and attended to his education myself. Why (according to Plutarch), Philip of Macedon did not think it beneath his dignity to guide the education of his son Alexander and to give him the great Aristotle as a teacher, just because he did not consider the ordinary teachers to be suitable for that purpose. And if a Laudon [1] *himself* directed the education of his son, why should similar fine and sublime phenomena not be discerned in others of a later period as well ? My nephew's *father* during his lifetime had already entrusted his son *to me* ; and I confess that I myself feel that I am better fitted than anyone else to inspire my nephew *by my own example* with a desire *for virtue and zealous activity. Seminaries and boarding schools* do not provide enough supervision for him ; and all these learned men, including a Professor Stein [2] and a Professor Simerdinger,[3] whose subject is paedagogy, agree with me that *such institutions would be quite unsuitable for him.* Nay more, *they* even maintain that the majority of young people come out of them *completely ruined* and that several who enter them with *uncorrupted* characters leave them *utterly corrupted. Unfortunately* I must confirm the *experiences* and *opinions* of those men and also of *several parents* — If the mother could have repressed her wicked tendencies and allowed

[1] Ernst Gideon, Baron von Laudon (1717–1790), the renowned field-marshal, who together with Daun retrieved Maria Theresa's losses in 1757 and restored the prestige of the Austrian Empire.

[2] Probably Anton Joseph Stein (1759–1844), who was Professor of Classical Literature at Vienna University from 1806 to 1825. He wrote the text for Beethoven's Wedding Song, WoO 105. See *KHV.* 567.

[3] Possibly Wendelin Simmerdinger, who had a living at Hütteldorf near Vienna and was also adviser to the Archbishop's consistory in Vienna.

my plans to develop peacefully, then an entirely favourable
result would have been the outcome of the arrangements I
have so far adopted. But when *a mother of that type* tries to
initiate her child into the mysteries of her vulgar and even
perverse surroundings and in his tender years induces him
to dissimulate (what a plague such a mother can be for her
children ! ! !), to bribe my servants, *to tell lies*, inasmuch as
she *laughs at him* when he speaks the truth, nay more, even
gives him money in order to arouse lusts and desires which are
harmful to him [1] and which *I and other people* too consider
to be very *grave faults*, then this affair, which in itself is difficult, becomes even more complicated and dangerous. People
must not think, however, that she behaved differently when
my nephew was at a boarding school. But against *that too* a
new *dam* has been erected. In addition to the tutor a superior
woman is coming to my house to attend to the housekeeping ;
and she will in no wise allow herself to be bribed *by my* nephew's
mother.[2] Secret meetings between the son and the mother
always produce harmful results. But *that is all the mother wants*,
for she seems *to be most ill at ease* whenever she is with really
well-bred and *refined* people — Very many defamatory accusations have been levelled against me and, moreover, by *people
whom I really ought not to mention at all*, inasmuch as not only
has my moral character been recognized by the general
public but also excellent writers, such as Weissenbach [3] and
others, have considered it worth their while to write about it.
Only *prejudice can impute base motives* to me. Nevertheless I
consider it necessary to explain several points connected with
this question — In regard to my nephew's property, he has
7000 gulden V.C. as a mortgage on his mother's house which
has been sold, and the interest on which his mother enjoys.
Further, he has 2200 gulden V.C. in cash deposits, and half
of his mother's pension. In regard to the 2200 gulden, this
sum was originally 2000 gulden V.C., which I however com-
muted to 2200 gulden in cash at my expense (as I have reported to the Landrechte). Both the half of the pension and

---

[1] The following clause is added at the foot of the page : 'She tells *him* that
these are mere trifles'.

[2] The following clause is added at the foot of the page : 'and thus the supervision of my nephew is being still further intensified'.

[3] Cf. Letters 505 and 968.

the 2000 gulden are merely a compensation for the fourth share of the house which was sold and for the fourth share of the house rent, of which he never received anything as long as the mother had the house, which she owned *entirely for herself* from November, 1815 until 1818 and fully seven to eight months longer.[1] Yet her son was always entitled to a quarter of the house rent. — It is clear from the above particulars that the arrangement was not quite advantageous to him. And now should his mother die or marry again, he would forfeit his whole share of the pension. But nothing could be done with people whose dishonesty the Landrechte already discovered when the inventory was being taken ; and we had to be satisfied with having saved *even that much* for the child. In any case all I have ever had in view has been *the salvation of his soul*, that is to say, my object has been to remove him from his mother's influence. Material sources of happiness can be acquired. But *moral principles* must be *inculcated* at an early age (particularly if a child has already had the misfortune to imbibe *that kind of milk from his mother*, if he has spent several years under her care and been completely *perverted* and *even* made to help her *deceive* his own father). In any case he will inherit my property ; and even now I could leave him sufficient money to enable him, *living on that sum alone and without being in financial straits*, to pursue his studies until he is old enough to obtain an appointment. All that we need is *peace and no further interference by the mother*. And there is no doubt that I shall soon achieve *the fine purpose which I have set myself* — Since people have also been talking about what I have already received, it is better to state the amount ; and that is easily done. An agreement was concluded in May 1817 ; [2] and in October 1817 the arrears of the mother's pension were to be paid up. But she refused to pay and I had to force her to do so by bringing an action against her. The financial statement too can be found among the papers of the Landrechte ; and only a negligible amount was still left over. On May 19, 1818 I drew the first instalment of the pension ; and in February, 1818 the first instalment of the interest on the cash deposits ;

---

[1] Cf. Letter 897, dated March 29, 1818.
[2] Cf. Appendix C (6), the contract between Beethoven and his sister-in-law, dated May 10, 1817.

and now for the last six months I have not received a single farthing of her pension, because she has not drawn it, just as she formerly failed to do; and of course I cannot collect my nephew's share *until she has drawn her instalment.*[1] It is obvious that notwithstanding these difficulties my nephew *is not suffering in the least* so far as my arrangements for his education are concerned. It is evident too that many a count and baron would not feel ashamed of such educational advantages; and there are noblemen who neither would nor could meet such expenses. Besides I am by no means counting on that miserable contribution. My former intention was to pay her whole pension out of my own pocket. But her immorality and her atrocious behaviour *to her own child and to me* have made me realize that to do so would only provide her with more facilities *for her dissolute way of life* — The will of my poor brother who became so unhappy (thanks *to her conduct*) shows clearly how greatly he valued the benefits I bestowed on him and how grateful he was to me. Well — I have now transferred those benefits to his son. Immediately after my brother's death on November 15, 1815 I began to provide for his son while he was living with his mother, and even then at some considerable expense; and when he left her house for his boarding school and later on came to live with me, his education was paid for *entirely by me* until nearly 1818. What object could I possibly have in taking that miserable *contribution* which is mentioned above? And what selfish purpose can be imputed to me? Certainly none other than the object I pursued in the case of my brother, namely, *to do good* and to have the double satisfaction of having *acted honourably* and brought up a worthy citizen for the state! —Even after the *guardianship* was called in question, it was evident from the will also that in it my brother had appointed me *sole* guardian. The codicil — was extracted from him when he was already at death's door; and *my oath* and the *oath of a certain woman*[2] can confirm the truth of my statement that he sent *me several times* into town *to retrieve the codicil from Dr. Schönauer.*[3] Dr. Adlersburg,[4] whom the Landrechte proposed

---

[1] Cf. Beethoven's statement to the Landrechte, dated December 15, 1818 (Appendix C (8)), where he makes the same remark, i.e. that he had received nothing of Johanna's pension since June, 1818.

[2] Frau Anna Wildmann. Cf. Appendix C (3), p. 1363.

[3] Cf. Letter 1009, p. 876, n. 3.   [4] Cf. Letter 485, p. 459, n. 4.

as joint curator because they had *no confidence in the former*, never hesitated to attach to those circumstances, although the requisite number of witnesses was not available, full *legal credence and validity* and to quote them as *counter-evidence* in his written statement *attacking the codicil*. In any case *our laws in general exclude the mother from the guardianship* and in consequence she was excluded too by the Landrechte from *all influence on her son's education and associations*. If any alteration were to be made in this arrangement, a great danger would again threaten the boy and — *no further improvement can be expected in the case of the mother*, for *she* is *too* perverted. On the other hand that tender plant, my nephew, can certainly be nipped in the bud by the spraying of poison; and that man would shoulder no small responsibility who would place *my nephew* in *such* a position. I could be careless and, finally wearying of the whole business, let myself fall a prey to those many intrigues and defamatory statements. But this I will not do. I will prove that he who performs *good and noble* actions, *can also suffer* for their sake and that he *must never lose sight of the noble aim which he has set himself*. I have *sworn* to act *in the best interest of my nephew as long as I live*. Even if I had not acted in this spirit, yet from *my character* and *my opinions in general* one could *only expect what is most advantageous for my nephew in every respect*. Am I to discuss as well the intrigues *against me* of a worthy Court Secretary, named Hotschevar,[1] or talk about a *parson at Mödling*[2] who, despised by his congregation, has the reputation of *indulging in illicit intercourse*, has his pupils put on a bench to be flogged like soldiers, and can never forgive me for watching *him* and positively refusing to have my nephew bestially treated with thrashings? Am I to do this? No. Frau van Beethoven provides sufficient *evidence* against *both of them*; and moreover *only men of that type* could collaborate *with her against me*. — I here repeat that I will pursue without flinching the high aim I have set myself, namely, the *welfare of my nephew, intellectually, morally and physically*. At the same time there is nothing which demands *a peaceful procedure* so much as *education*. To obtain this it is necessary that Frau

---

[1] Jakob Hotschevar, who had married her step-sister, intrigued with Johanna to influence the Magistrat against Beethoven.

[2] Johann Baptist Fröhlich. Cf. Letter 904, p. 770, n. 1.

van Beethoven be *excluded once and for all*; and that was the purpose of the *last hearing by the Landrechte,* which I *myself* applied for and helped to arrange. But in order that I too may make some contribution to the promotion of this *desirable peace,* I *myself* will propose a *joint guardian whom* I would certainly have nominated today, were I not still *undecided whom to choose* — In regard to an *appeal, everyone,* of course, is entitled to make one ; *I* do not dread this at all. For as soon as the welfare *of my nephew,* which is most closely connected *with my own welfare,* is imperilled, I too will immediately lodge an appeal. *Nowhere* will any distinction be drawn between *a general law and its consequences.* — The complete rejection of Frau van Beethoven will still have *another favourable result.* For realizing that her intrigues *cannot destroy what is good* she will no longer despise *the magnanimity and the forbearance* which indeed *I have* so often endeavoured *to show her*; and this *unpleasant gloom might then be transformed into a day of sunshine* in so far as circumstances permit. May the result of all this be that, just as I have already been the benefactor of my nephew's father, I may deserve to be called an even *far greater benefactor of his son,* and indeed, with every right, *his father.* No self-interest, either secret or open, can be imputed to me in this task undertaken *solely for the sake of what is good.* Even the Landrechte themselves have realized this and have expressed to me their thanks for my fatherly care —

LUDWIG VAN BEETHOVEN

Guardian of my nephew Karl van Beethoven.

(10) *To the Magistrat der Stadt Wien*

[*MS in the Beethovenhaus, Bonn, H. C. Bodmer collection*] [1]

MOST WORSHIPFUL MAGISTRAT ! VIENNA, *July* 5, 1819

The Obervormundschaft authorities who deal with the affairs of my nephew Karl van Beethoven will recall that some time ago I handed over to H[err]Tuscher, the Magistratsrat,[2] the exclusive guardianship of my nephew to which I had been appointed by the last will and testament of my late brother and which had been recognized both by the Landrechte and

---

[1] Written in another hand and signed by Beethoven.
[2] Cf. Letter 941, p. 807, n. 1.

later too by the Magistrat. I did this in the hope of averting once and for all by an intermediary of this kind all further disturbances likely to be caused by the mother.

Unfortunately the result has proved only too deplorably that my intention set forth above, which at that time I made subservient to the wishes and opinions of the Obervormundschaft, has not only not been fulfilled but that the exact opposite has been the result. For the mother has contrived to use this new arrangement for her persistent counter-plots and with even more disastrous consequences.

This distressing experience and this depressing conviction have finally driven H[err] Tuscher, the Magistratsrat, who had been considered not only by myself but also by the Obervormundschaft themselves to be the most suitable intermediary in this very important and difficult business, to resign the guardianship in his turn.[1] For he realized that in the circumstances the purpose we had in view could not be achieved.

In accordance with the last will and testament of my late brother and the previous arrangements of the Landrechte and also of the present Obervormundschaft I immediately resumed the guardianship which I had handed over to H[err] Tuscher solely with the intention and on the assumption that the purpose set forth above would be achieved by his intervention and in his capacity of guardian; and in my official capacity I have now taken the necessary steps for the most careful higher education of my ward and nephew. For I am firmly convinced that only in that way can his welfare be promoted. Consequently I have placed him at the boarding school of Herr Blöchlinger, which is housed in Count Chotek's residence in the Josephstadt, in the Kaiserstrasse.[2] In the present circumstances this school is in every respect the most suitable educational institution for him.

While as guardian duly informing the Obervormundschaft of this step, I put forward at the same time the request that arrangements be made for my ward and nephew henceforth

[1] Tuscher was appointed Karl's guardian on March 29, 1819, but three months later, on July 5th, he applied to be relieved of this charge.
[2] Karl was at Blöchlinger's boarding school from June 22, 1819, until August 29, 1823. Before placing him at this school Beethoven had tried to persuade Giannatasio del Rio to take charge of his nephew again. But Giannatasio refused.

to remain undisturbed in his present surroundings. This is the primary requirement which must now be absolutely fulfilled in his case, so that he may again be brought to his senses and may be able adequately to acquire the scholastic qualifications for his future career.

I ask therefore that the necessary instructions be sent to H[err] Blöchlinger, the proprietor of this educational institution, so that he may be empowered to repel with due severity the mother's untimely and disturbing interruptions. Nothing else is required. Should the necessity arise for important alterations to be made in the future method of education of my ward I shall not fail to give due warning to the Obervormundschaft, as was, moreover, formerly done in the case of the Landrechte and as is everywhere the usual procedure in similar cases.

LUDWIG VAN BEETHOVEN

(11) To the Magistrat der Stadt Wien

[MS in the Deutsche Staatsbibliothek, Berlin] [1]

WORSHIPFUL MAGISTRAT!   [VIENNA, October 30, 1819] [2]

My brother Karl van Beethoven died in November 1815 and left an only boy Karl, who is now twelve years old.[3]

In his last will and testament A, Paragraph 5, he entrusted to me the guardianship of this boy; and in his codicil B he expressed the wish that his relict Johanna should also participate, adding that for the sake of his child's welfare he recommended her to comply with my wishes.[4]

Hence this clearly expressed desire of the father unquestionably entrusts to me, as does also the law dealing with the nearest relation, Paragraph 198, the guardianship of my nephew Karl van Beethoven; and the eminent Landrechte, by virtue of Decree E which deals with the particular circumstances in question, have entrusted this guardianship to me and, what is

---

[1] Written in another hand and signed by Beethoven.
[2] The document is wrongly dated 1818. But the endorsement has the correct year. And according to the endorsement Beethoven was then living 'im Blumenstöckl' near the office of the *Wiener Zeitung*.
[3] Karl, who was born on September 4, 1806, was then thirteen.
[4] For the text of this important codicil see *TDR* III, 518-519.

more, to the exclusion of the widow Johanna van Beethoven.

As I was absent for some time on a business trip I did not object to my place being taken for the time being by a legal guardian; and this was done by appointing the Stadtsequester Herr Nussböck.[1]

But as I have now returned to Vienna for good and as the welfare of this boy is close to my heart, my duty and my affection for him demand that I myself should again assume the guardianship, the duties of which I ought to be discharging, and indeed the more so as this talented boy is reaching the age when greater care and greater sums of money will have to be expended simultaneously on his education. His whole future depends upon this education, which cannot be left to a woman or to his mother alone, the more so as she has neither the will nor the strength of character to adopt those necessary measures demanded by the education suitable for a man.

I must again lay claim to this guardianship, especially as I have heard that for lack of funds to meet the expenses the boy is to be removed from his present boarding school which I selected and that the mother wants to keep him at home in order to use for herself the few dividends to which he is entitled and to keep for her own use the half of her pension which according to Regulation D she is supposed to expend on her son.

Until now I have cared for my nephew as a father; and in the same way I shall in future meet any deficit out of my own income. But the hopes of his late father and my expectations for this talented boy must be fulfilled; and he must become a useful man and citizen.

Having made these prefatory remarks I now request the Worshipful Magistrat to relieve the Stadtsequester Nussböck of the interim guardianship and to entrust to me without delay the guardianship of my nephew Karl van Beethoven.

LUDWIG VAN BEETHOVEN [2]

[1] Leopold Nussböck, who replaced Tuscher as Karl's guardian, was a municipal trustee or town clerk. See *FRBH* I, 463.

[2] The Magistrat's reply, sent on November 4, 1819, amounted to a rejection of Beethoven's application.

(12) *To the Magistrat der Stadt Wien*

[*MS in the Koch collection*] ¹

WORSHIPFUL MAGISTRAT!   VIENNA, *November* 20, 1819

On the basis of Document A drawn up and submitted I applied to be entrusted with the guardianship of my nephew Karl van Beethoven. But I was referred to an earlier decision.

Not only have the circumstances changed so that I have more time to resume this guardianship entrusted to me in the will of the father and by law, but also the present guardian, the Stadtsequester Herr Nussböck, has informed me that he is by no means opposed to this arrangement, seeing that, moreover, the contribution which I undertake to make in future to the cost of supporting and educating my nephew is urgently needed.

Hence in order to adopt the necessary measures I request the Worshipful Magistrat to condescend to fix the date for an immediate hearing.²

LUDWIG VAN BEETHOVEN

(13) *To ?*

[*Autograph in a private collection*] ³

[VIENNA, *December*, 1819]

In accordance with our agreement the Worshipful Landrechte sent to the Imperial and Royal General Financial Office the requisite order that the latter should remit to me as guardian half of Frau van Beethoven's yearly pension in quarterly instalments. In this agreement there is no mention of my having first to wait until Frau van Beethoven shall have drawn the half of her pension or anything of the kind, All that can be gathered from the drift of the Landrechte's order

¹ This application, drafted by J. B. Bach, Beethoven's friend and legal adviser, was written in another hand and signed by Beethoven.

² The result of this application was that Beethoven, Johanna and Nussböck were invited to give evidence during the following month. Beethoven's request was again rejected.

³ This fragmentary autograph is probably a draft of a formal application for payment of the pension instalments which Johanna had undertaken to pay as her contribution to the educational expenses of her son.

to the Imperial and Royal General Financial Office is that half of her *pension* is to be paid to me as guardian *in quarterly* instalments — Can this be done only by compelling Fr[au] v[an] Beethoven to draw her pension every quarter, seeing that such a procedure can only be ensured by employing a lawyer, a measure which will again cost me money? But I am inclined to think that this is not necessary and that the Imperial and Royal General Financial Office complying with the order of the Landrechte will remit to me the share of the pension in quarterly instalments. For Fr[au] v[an] Beethoven's death would be common knowledge as much as anyone else's; and thus there would be no breach of the law — But owing to the way in which the affair has taken its course I have already frequently been financially embarrassed, because for $1\frac{1}{2}$ years I have not received any contributions from this pension.[1] Whether this is compatible *with the care of an orphan* is a question which can be answered only in one way —

Although it is quite superfluous for me to do so, I add that if there were a breach of the law I am willing to refund everything. In any case the half of the pension amounts to only 13 gulden, 53 kreuzer A.C. per month.

(14) *To the Imperial and Royal Court of Appeal of Lower Austria*

[*MS in the Deutsche Staatsbibliothek, Berlin*] [2]

VIENNA, *January* 7, 1820

MOST WORSHIPFUL IMPERIAL AND ROYAL COURT OF APPEAL OF LOWER AUSTRIA!

In Document A I petitioned for the transfer to me of the guardianship of my nephew Karl van Beethoven, but was referred by the Worshipful Magistrat to an earlier decision.[3] And the same reply was given to the humble representations I made in Document B.[4]

I feel affronted, not merely because my rights are being

[1] I.e. since June, 1818. Cf. Appendix C (8).
[2] Written in another hand and signed by Beethoven. This is a preliminary version of Beethoven's famous draft memorandum. For this draft see Appendix C (15).   [3] Cf. Appendix C (9).   [4] Cf. Appendix C (11).

ignored, but because the very welfare of my nephew is receiving no consideration. Therefore I have found it necessary to take the case still further and to present to this High Court of Appeal my well founded petition; and I feel I am fully justified in asking that the guardianship of my nephew be again entrusted to me.

Firstly, I have been appointed to this guardianship not only by the will and testament of the father of my nephew, but also by law, seeing that the eminent Landrechte had granted it to me and, what is more, to the exclusion of the mother. When circumstances subsequently called me away from Vienna I complied with the arrangement that in my absence the Stadtsequester Nussböck should be appointed ad interim. But now that I am permanently domiciled in Vienna, the welfare of my nephew demands that I should resume this guardianship.

Secondly, my nephew is reaching the age when he ought to be given the advantages of a higher education. Neither the mother nor the present guardian are qualified to guide the boy towards this acquisition of knowledge. The former cannot do this because she is a woman and on documentary evidence has no recommendations or testimonials concerning her character; but about this I will not say anything more. Therefore the highly placed Landrechte too have wholly excluded her from the guardianship. I fail to understand why the Worshipful Magistrat could nevertheless summon her to appear. The latter, i.e. the present guardian, cannot do it because on the one hand as Stadtsequester his time is too much taken up with the administration of houses and grounds for him to be able adequately to discharge his duty as the guardian of a boy, and because on the other hand I cannot believe that he who was formerly a paper manufacturer could have the necessary knowledge and the requisite judgment for planning a scientific education.

Thirdly, what is dearest to my heart is solely the welfare of this nephew of mine. I myself am childless and have no nearer relation than this boy, who is extremely talented and, if suitably guided, is likely to justify the highest hopes. Well, I was told that he had already missed a whole year and was put back in his own class; I was told that there was even a likelihood of his being removed from his present boarding school on account of lack of funds and that the mother wanted to take him into her home. What a calamity that would be for this boy! He would undoubtedly be sacrificed to the extravagance of his mother, who would like to lavish on herself the portion of her pension which she ought to be spending on the education of her boy!

I therefore apprised the Worshipful Magistrat in a formal document that I would meet out of my own pocket the cost of his present boarding school and would myself provide the necessary funds to employ several teachers. Since I am a little hard of hearing, an infirmity which makes verbal communications difficult, I have asked for a co-guardian and have proposed Herr Peters,[1] legal adviser to Prince Lobkowitz,[2] in order that there should immediately be put in charge of the education and guidance of my nephew a man who by reason of his knowledge and of his moral character enjoys the respect of all and whose assistance will provide me and everyone who has the welfare of this boy at heart with the comforting assurance that the boy will be able to, and undoubtedly will, receive an education and a training worthy of his talents.

The sole object of my desire and endeavour is that the boy should be given the best possible education, inasmuch as his talents lead one to entertain the highest hopes of him, and in order that those expectations may be fulfilled which his late father founded on my brotherly love. The stem is still flexible. But if more time is allowed to elapse the plant will outgrow in some crooked way the guiding hand of the gardener who is tending it; and his upright bearing, his knowledge and his character will have vanished for ever. I know of no more sacred duty than that of supervising the education and training of a child. And the primary duty of the Obervormundschaft should consist in revering what is good and arranging what is suitable for that purpose. And only then will they have given full consideration to the welfare of their ward. But by obstructing what is good they will actually be neglecting their duty.

Furthermore, since my sole object is the welfare of the

---

[1] Cf. Letter 734, p. 651, n. 1.
[2] Prince Ferdinand Lobkowitz (1797–1868) had succeeded his father Franz Joseph Lobkowitz in December, 1816. Cf. Letter 734a.

boy, I am not opposed to some kind of co-guardianship being granted to his mother. This might take the form of her visiting the boy, seeing him and being informed of all the measures adopted for his education. But henceforth to entrust the guardianship to her alone, without appointing an efficient guardian to assist her, such a step would assuredly be tantamount to bringing about the ruin of the boy.

Hence on the basis of these crying needs I again lodge my well-founded petition and look forward to its rightful acceptance, the more so as in this case the welfare of my nephew alone is the reason for the steps I have taken.

LUDWIG VAN BEETHOVEN [1]

(15) *Draft of a Memorandum to the Court of Appeal, Vienna*

[*Autograph in the Beethovenhaus, Bonn, H. C. Bodmer collection*] [2]

VIENNA, *February* 18, 1820 [3]

Information about Fr[au] B[eethoven].
——————— —— the Obervormundschaft of my nephew
discharged by the Magistrat —
——————— —— my nephew and his school reports.
——————— —— what I have done for my nephew —
——————— —— his property.
Supplementary statement.[4]

---

[1] On January 10, 1820, the Court of Appeal asked the Vienna Magistrat for a full report, which the latter supplied on February 5, 1820.

[2] This draft of a memorandum to the Vienna Court of Appeal, the longest extant document in Beethoven's handwriting, was published in 1953 in a fine facsimile edition by the Beethovenhaus, Bonn. The facsimile itself is an exact reproduction of the original manuscript, which is bound in a thick blue paper cover. The document originally consisted of 48 pages, but pp. 7 and 8 are missing. This scholarly edition has been produced by Dr. Dagmar Weise with a most admirable introduction amounting to an exhaustive survey of the whole question of Beethoven's guardianship of his nephew.

As there is no documentary evidence to show that this memorandum was submitted or dispatched to the Court of Appeal, it is doubtful whether Beethoven's draft was ever rewritten.

[3] At the end of the memorandum, which is not signed but ends with a question mark followed by two paraphs, Beethoven has added this place and date, underlining the whole.

[4] This list of contents is entered on the inside of the front cover.

Information about Frau B[eethoven]. —

It is painful for a man like me to have to sully himself even to the smallest extent with a person like Fr[au] B[eethoven]. But since this is my last attempt to save my nephew, for his sake I am submitting to be so humiliated — *lite abstine, nam vincens, multum amiseris.*[1] I should very much prefer to follow this precept. But the welfare of a third person prevents me from doing so.[2]

Fr[au] B[eethoven] had no education whatever. Her parents, who were ordinary upholsterers by trade, left her more or less to her own devices. Hence in her early youth pernicious tendencies were already allowed to develop. When she was still living at her parents' home she had to appear before the police court for having accused her own *maid* of *perpetrating something* of which *she herself* was guilty; *and the maid was proved to be entirely innocent.* But the police out of compassion acquitted the culprit when she promised to mend her ways. In 1811 when she was already married and a mother, though indeed frivolous, of easy virtue, stubborn and malicious, having then partly lost her good name, she committed another more horrible crime, for which she had even to appear before the Criminal Court. Here too she *again looked on quite calmly* when *wholly innocent people were in-*

---

[1] The present editor is greatly indebted to Mr. D. M. Low for having traced three of the four Latin quotations in Beethoven's memorandum to the *Sententiae* of Janus Anysius : 'These consist of 641 separate gnomic lines in no particular order, as the author avows in the preliminary lines to Cardinal Mendoza. These, if not published before, were at any rate included in an edition of the *Distichs* of Cato and the *Sententiae* of Publilius Syrus issued at Zürich about 1529. It may be doubted whether they were reprinted as a whole during the next three centuries. But individual lines were included in at least one collection from various sources in the 17th century. The whole collection was re-issued, however, by J. Conrad Orelli at Leipzig in 1822, in a volume containing Publilius Syrus, the *Distichs* of Cato, and other collections of Renaissance writers, with commentaries. In his preface Orelli refers to the book issued *c.* 1529 and describes Anysius as unknown and the *c.* 1529 edition as very rare. It seems improbable, therefore, that there had been any other issue meanwhile. Hence it is likely that Beethoven possessed or had seen Orelli's book, especially as all three lines quoted in the memorandum come from the same source.' But Beethoven was writing in 1820 and must have found Anysius's lines in some other anthology, or have seen the 1529 volume.

The first quotation is the senarian iambic line no. 280 in the *Sententiae* of Janus Anysius. The meaning is : 'Refrain from litigation, for even if you win you will have lost a great deal'.

[2] The preceding three sentences beginning with the quotation from Anysius are written inside the front cover.

volved in her monstrous misdeed.[1] In the end she had to confess that *she was the sole perpetrator*; and it was only thanks to the greatest efforts on the part of her husband and of my friends that, though she was not unpunished, she was exempted from the most infamous form of punishment and again discharged — This dreadful event brought on my late brother a serious illness which compelled him to lead the life of a chronic invalid ; and it was only thanks to my charitable support that his life was still spared for a while. Some time before his death she drew *without his knowledge* a considerable sum of money. This made him want to divorce her. But Death the reaper *came and divorced him from* — *his life* on November 15, 1815. The day before his death, while thanking me in his will for having been his benefactor, he appointed me *sole guardian of his son*. *On that very day* I had scarcely left *my brother* for a few hours when on my return he told me that in my absence people had added something to the will, something which he had been induced to sign. (This was the codicil in which she had had herself nominated a guardian on the same footing as myself.) My brother begged me to recover *this document* from the lawyer immediately. But the lawyer could not be found that day, although *at my brother's urgent requests* I went several times to his house. My brother expired at five o'clock on the following morning — Yet only *one witness* was needed to prove that my brother wished to have *that codicil destroyed*, even though according to Paragraph 191 of the Civil Code it had ceased to be valid and seeing that the Worshipful Landrechte too seem to have *denied its legal validity*, inasmuch as they have confirmed my appointment as sole guardian. It is clear that in 1815 she had not yet taken any steps towards her moral improvement. For after what I have already recounted, her dishonourable treatment of her son was again displayed in the question of the inventory. I said nothing, for all I wanted to save was *the soul of my nephew*. Immediately after my brother's death she began to have intimate relations with a lover ; and her behaviour even shocked the modesty of her innocent son. She was to be seen in all the dance halls and at festivities, while her son was not even given the necessities of life and was

[1] The words from 'wholly' to 'misdeed' are added at the foot of the page, replacing two lines of the autograph which have been obliterated.

left to fend for himself in charge of some wretched maid of
hers. What would have become of him if I had not taken an
interest in him? And that, moreover, from 1815 to 1820 she
proved to be nothing but a depraved and extremely deceitful
woman, given in the highest degree to duplicity, is proved
by the following: whenever she could, wherever my nephew
happened to be, either in my home or at his boarding school,
she tried to teach him utterly wrong ideas, always to meet him
in secret and even to induce him herself to commit all kinds
of horribly deceitful actions of the same type and to tell lies.
She even tried to bribe him with money, and, what is more,
gave him money *to enable him to use other people for her evil pur-
poses.* A few times when he had behaved extremely badly,
she contrived to entice him into her own home and told
him that what he had done was of no consequence.[1] She
did her best by means of the most horrible intrigues, plots
and defamatory statements to disparage me, his benefactor,
mainstay and support, in short, his father in the true sense of
the word. She tried to infect everyone, even the most innocent people, with her moral poison — Finally, her hellish yet
stupid activities reached another climax under the worthy
Obervormundschaft of the Magistrat. For on the occasion
of the approaching Easter examination in 1819 she urged my
nephew to make sure that he would be placed in the second
or third class so that *he could not be sent away from Vienna.* In my
case she had always come up against a barrier which she tried
in vain to demolish. But as a guardian H[err] v[on] Tuscher
was rarely listened to or even treated with respect by the
guardianship authorities of the Magistrat. For the latter took
particular pleasure in enjoying a few devilish meals with that
charming woman. Hence *to her* my nephew must *ever return
thanks* for having wasted a whole year of his scholarly career
on account of the *attachment* which that respected Obervormundschaft formed for *his most loving mother.* As can be
imagined, that Worshipful Obervormundschaft promoted the
interests of their favourites as the latter deserved. Hence
from October, 1819 until this present month of February,
1820 we find her installed *as the guardian* of her son and we see
her disparaging in the *lowest and most vulgar way* the true and

[1] This sentence is added at the foot of the page.

1391

sole guardian, benefactor, mainstay and support of his deceased brother, the father of his nephew, and of my nephew himself —

However, we must now supply some information about the Obervormundschaft discharged by the Vienna Magistrat.

No more disastrous event nor one fraught with more evil consequences could have befallen my nephew than his having, owing unfortunately to his lack of a title of nobility, to be associated with *this Obervormundschaft*. The same can be said too of *myself, who am the guardian*, mainstay, support and promoter of all that is good in my nephew — The hypocritical character of Fr[au] B[eethoven] and her lying disposition seemed to have found a fair field in that quarter. ' Mendacio comites tenebrae '.[1]

The principles of the Worshipful Landrechte were forthwith set aside, namely, those which prohibited her not only from exercising any influence on his education, and according [2]

. . . .

was invited to give evidence against me and quite unabashedly to supply all information to my disadvantage ! ! It so happened too that during the period when the M[agistrat] was in control of the Obervormundschaft I once in anger pulled my nephew from his chair, just because he had done something very naughty. As he always had to wear a truss after his operation for hernia, performed two years previously,[3] my action caused him some pain *in the most sensitive spot* when he had to turn round quickly. So I immediately sent for Herr v[on] Smetana who declared at once that there was nothing wrong and that not the slightest harm had been done. Moreover the same thing had happened to my nephew when he was playing with other boys, on which occasion too H[err] v[on] Smetana had been called in. Nevertheless I made Smetana write down for me at once what the injury amounted to. Surely *a man of his stamp* would not tell a lie *to please me*. Still less would *his sense of duty* permit him to *say nothing about* an injury if it had really been caused. He laughed when I asked him for a certificate and said: ' Why, the injury is not worth mentioning '. But I knew perfectly well why I required a certificate,

[1] The context of this quotation, which is added at the foot of the page, has not been traced. It means : 'Darkness is companion to falsehood'.
[2] Pages 7 and 8 of the memorandum are missing.
[3] The preceding four words are added at the foot of the page.

and I sent it to the Obervormundschaft. That this precaution was necessary was proved by the papers which the Obervormundschaft subsequently handed in to the guardian whom I myself had chosen, namely H[err] v[on] Tuscher. Among these papers there was also *a letter from F[rau] B[eethoven] to the person who was then the Referent. In this letter she declared that I had done her son a physical injury on account of which he had had to remain in bed for three months.* One can realize what dreadful lies she was telling, for the boy always went out walking as usual, and Herr von Smetana's certificate was certainly genuine — From the foregoing it can easily be seen how this incident too may have been described by the Obervormundschaft authorities and how necessary it was to hear on all points the statements of myself and of my nephew — Among other things it so happened that when H[err] v[on] Tuscher was guardian F[rau] B[eethoven] accused me before the Obervormundschaft of having written a letter to my nephew *against* confession. H[err] v[on] Tuscher after reading this letter showed it of course to those gentlemen, whose eyes, as he said, filled with tears on reading the truly religious and fatherly admonitions about that solemn practice. But it will soon be realized that *even so that defamatory statement made by F[rau] B[eethoven] was not yet withdrawn,* although it was proved that on that very day (when he was no longer at my home) my nephew had *gone from the boarding school to her instead of to confession.* For that very reason *I myself took him later on to confess to the worthy holy Abbot of St. Michael* — Perhaps *that false* accusation will *again appear in the report* —

I consider that I should now make a few more brief historical statements about the Obervormundschaft authorities up to the present time —

Immediately after my case had been referred by the Landrechte to those M[agistrat] authorities *I, who according to the statements of the L[and]r[echt]e* was shielding my nephew as far as possible from the influence and evil propensities of Fr[au] B[eethoven], was *regarded as the cause of a family quarrel.* It appeared, in fact, that the matter was not being dealt with *a priori.* Meanwhile the mother's pernicious activities were intensified. Things became intolerable. She succeeded in enticing my nephew to her home for the second time. I chose Herr von Tuscher to be the guardian of my nephew; and, moreover, in the circumstances and in general I did not want to keep my nephew any longer in my home. For in view of what was going on my cares were too heavy. So in March, 1819 my nephew was sent to H[err] Kudlich's boarding school. Somehow or other I was not particularly keen on this arrangement and would rather have had my nephew at Giannatasio's. But it was well known how strongly the latter was *opposed* to the mother, because he considered that her removal from her son was a factor of the *very highest importance in the education* of my nephew. So it was thought *wiser to place him where* the mother would perhaps be accorded more favourable treatment. Although *I* was defraying the expenses of his education as I had done until then, nevertheless I was obliged to consent to this arrangement, for I was no longer the guardian — Meanwhile I had received an offer from the renowned and worthy scholar and clergyman J. M. Sailer [1] to take my nephew into his home at Landshut and to supervise his education.[2] The worthy Abbot of St. Michael described this as *the greatest stroke of luck* which could befall my nephew ; and other *enlightened people* expressed the *same opinion.* Even His Imperial Highness, the present Archbishop of Olmütz, endorsed this view and used his influence for this very purpose. H[err] v[on] Tuscher too was in favour of it, for he much preferred such an arrangement, inasmuch as the removal of my nephew from Vienna would entirely obviate *any further breaking of the commandment 'Honour thy father and thy mother '*, which he was always being directed to keep [3] and which in her company it was really impossible to observe. Although *the boy since his childhood has known full well what his mother is, yet the avoidance of all objectionable influences would certainly be more desirable and appropriate* ; and, moreover, *he would thus be entirely removed from disturbances caused by his mother.* This, however, could not be done without *the consent* of the Obervormundschaft. Hence an application was made to that body ; and just imagine with what result, what logic, what principles, what philosophy ! ! *The mother too was now invited to protest against it ! ! !* In short, the whole plan *fell through.* H[err]

[1] Cf. Letter 946, p. 810, n. 2.
[2] The words from 'and' to 'education' are added at the foot of the page.
[3] The words from 'which' to 'keep' have been added on a separate slip inserted between pages 14 and 15.

v[on] Tuscher was now regarded as *prejudiced*. Another Referent was attached to the Referent who had at last got to know perfectly well what sort of woman Fr[au] B[eethoven] was and who also regarded the removal of her son as the best arrangement.[1] But he too was accused of being prejudiced and therefore he resigned his appointment. During that period my nephew could leave the boarding school whenever he liked, the mother had free access to him and he became so *altered both outwardly and inwardly that he was no longer recognizable*. It was then that *the mother advised him* to make sure that *he would be placed in the second or third class, so that he could not be removed from Vienna*. *He has done this*, so he must now *remain another whole year in the same class* — One can easily imagine that the guardian who was by now suspected of being partial, *could not act with the necessary energy*. Nevertheless the boarding school received an order *whereby her association with my nephew was forbidden*. A few weeks later *another order arrived stating that on her name-day* [2] *my nephew was to show her his respect and spend that day with her*. The order appeared *to leave it to the discretion of the headmaster to comply with it or not*. The headmaster happened to be ill and did not dare to disobey it. He himself could not accompany my nephew. The teachers had no time to do so. Hence my nephew walked alone from the Landstrasse to his mother's home in the Tiefer Graben, where he spent the whole day and the following night, and stuffed himself with food and strong drink given to him by his mother *who is as stupid as she is depraved*. On the following morning when he could hardly move and was quite ill he had to walk back to his boarding school. The very same day I came in from the country to see how he was and found him lying in bed. The medicines he was taking seemed to me to be unsuitable for his condition, for she had sent him a quack of a doctor. So I immediately brought Dr. Hasenöhrl to him ; and the illness proved to be due to a haemorrhage. I made all arrangements for him to have the best possible care. Nevertheless she *stormed* into the boarding school *like a raging Medea*. *By making false allegations* she had *contrived to obtain permission to enter* ; and at the risk of his life and notwithstanding

---

[1] The words from 'who' to 'arrangement' are added at the foot of the page.
[2] May 30th.

Dr. H[asenöhrl]'s disapproval [1] she took her son home with her. She was afraid that *the real cause of his illness might be discovered*; and her evil disposition would gladly have induced her to put the blame on *me*. She had already tried to do this in the case of H[err] v[on] Tuscher; and who knows what may appear on this subject again in the M[agistrat]'s report? But such false trails are soon detected and ignored by *people of integrity*. My nephew then spent three weeks in bed. During that time H[err] v[on] Tuscher disclosed to me his decision to resign the guardianship. No honour could be gained from the appointment. He received little support from the Vormundschaft. Fr[au] B[eethoven] was daily becoming more arrogant. She lied to him and deceived him in every possible way [2] and *even threatened him* if he refused to fall in with her wishes. *Everything that was good suffered every moment a fresh defeat.* I myself saw that *he* could not possibly wade through that marshy waste, and that I could be a more efficient guide, if only because everything was being paid entirely out of my purse. So I accepted the offer and we came to an agreement. And on the same day that H[err] v[on] Tuscher forwarded to the Magistrat his resignation from the guardianship I wrote to the M[agistrat] stating that I had resumed it — My statement was accepted [3] — After an illness lasting three weeks my nephew was now recovered; and for very *good reasons* I took him on June 22, 1820 [4] to his present boarding school owned by H[err] Blöchlinger. Both the headmaster and I had adopted the arrangement that so far as my nephew was concerned a curtain should be drawn over all that had happened, so that he might forget it. And in any case *the memories of those catastrophes* were *not pleasant ones* for him. But my nephew was to be removed immediately *from Minerva's protection and again brought before a commission.* The headmaster wrote to me of his embarrassment at this suggestion. I wrote to him that he should *appeal to me as the guardian, that I did not consider such a move to be expedient for the time being, since my nephew was still partly to be treated as convalescent both in body and in soul,* but that *I was willing at any moment to betake myself*

---

[1] The preceding three words are added at the foot of the page.
[2] The words from 'she' to 'way' are added at the foot of the page.
[3] This sentence is added at the foot of the page.
[4] This should be 1819.

to the Obervormundschaft in order to report to it on all matters about which it might ask to be informed. This was considered sufficient. But as I was bound to suppose that a fresh summons might perhaps arrive, I wrote to one of my friends requesting him to inform me *thereof,* as *the letter in Supplement A.* will testify. Again, however, *there came a fresh summons for my nephew* to appear before a commission;[1] and I instructed my friend to put forward my reasons why at the moment both I and the headmaster considered it *wholly inadvisable* that my nephew should appear before a commission, since in any case, as has already been seen above, he had been wrongly used.[2] Whereupon this produced the letter *to me of August 20th, i.e. Supplement B.* The passages underlined should be noted. Thus the letter about confession, which H[err] v[on] Tuscher had already shown them, was again referred to. *But not one of the gentlemen* was then willing to *recall it.* Nor could I show them the letter, for I could no longer find it. In any case it is evident from Supplement B. that by reason of the *influence which Fr[au] B[eethoven]* exercised on the Magistrat, *her* gossip directed *against* me was constantly listened to. One can see that the Referent himself *wanted to get to know this person.* Yet on the other hand everything she said *against* me was *again to carry weight* — After receiving that letter I immediately sent my nephew to the Referent Herr P[iuk]. My friend informed me that the latter told my nephew ' *that in all matters he should be obedient to me, that he should be very grateful to me for all I had done and was doing for him, that it was only thanks to my support that he could acquire all that learning, etc.'.* In reply to the worthy Refer[ent]'s suggestion that I should again hand over the guardianship to someone else, I declared that *never again would I do that,* inasmuch as experience had proved that to do so was to the detriment of my nephew. Moreover I did not want to disburse such large sums merely to see a third person upsetting all my arrangements again. This statement was not in the very least directed against H[err] v[on] Tuscher. But in the case of such an Obervormundschaft *as the present one,* the guardian is merely a *cipher.* It has been seen that *notwithstanding H[err] v[on] Tuscher's voting in favour of the removal of the*

---

[1] The words from 'for' to 'commission' are added at the foot of the page.
[2] The words from 'since' to 'used' are added at the foot of the page.

boy from Vienna, the Obervormundschaft allowed the *mother to appear in order to lodge her protest — On the other hand* just compare the behaviour of the *Landrechte, where the guardian, who is after all the responsible person, can raise his voice against something he does not approve and is not only given a hearing but has the satisfaction of knowing that his opinion will decide the issue —* Well, in this particular case it so happens that *only one guardian, who at the same time has the means which I possess, can be of real benefit to his ward*; not to mention the fact that the guardianship of my nephew can never again be *rightfully* denied to me, who am *the nearest relative and the guardian appointed by my brother himself in his will*, and who have been the benefactor of father and son.[1] And what stranger is likely to care for his ward *in the same way* as the nearest relative? A hundred thousand people would regard it as a stroke of luck to be able to hand over their children to such an uncle and guardian! — Well, in the written communication I mentioned above I begged H[err] R[eferent] P[iuk] once more for peace and quiet for myself and my nephew. There is no doubt that by the highest authorities I had already been accepted as the guardian and was also *immediately regarded as such*. But the intrigues of Fr[au] B[eethoven] persisted without intermission; and then in Septemb[er] she wrote to H[err] Blöchlinger that she had been appointed *joint guardian with me*. Nothing was said and the whole affair was treated as one of her usual tricks devised in order to impress the headmaster. Finally Fr[au] B[eethoven] sent in October to Herr v[on] Blöchlinger a communication written in her own hand and signed by the M[agistrat] [2] ' *in which she described herself as the guardian and H[err] Nussböck as the co-guardian. It was stated in this communication that I was physically and morally unfit to carry out the duties of a guardian, that her son should never be allowed to leave the boarding school in my company, because I wanted to take him with me to Olmütz to be with the present Archbishop His Imperial Highness the Archduke Rudolph (another monstrous lie) and so forth.*' To this nonsense was added the statement that at the boarding school H[err] Nussböck had presented *her* to the headmaster H[err] v[on] Blöchlinger and to my nephew *as the guardian*!!! —

[1] The preceding ten words are added at the foot of the page.
[2] The words from 'Herr' to 'M[agistrat]' are added at the foot of the page.

Now compare the way in which Herr Refer[ent] P[iuk] expressed himself on the subject of Frau B[eethoven] in the above mentioned letter, Supplement B. The very person *to whom he had previously forbidden access to her son at the boarding school had now become the latter's guardian.* But let it not be believed that he was quite serious about it. For this H[err] Refer[ent] stated at H[err] Blöchlinger's *when he was quite alone with him,* that this nuisance would cease as soon as I should employ a lawyer. Yet in *the presence of Fr[au] B[eethoven]* at H[err] Blöchlinger's *he again sang a very different tune.* In short, he said exactly the *opposite* of what he had told him when they were alone. I have noticed in general that there is something *ingrained in the character* of those members of the M[agistrat] *which always prevents them from holding definite opinions. What is uppermost today will be lowest tomorrow, and vice versa.* One day someone said *that this was so.* The next day that opinion was demolished by a *diametrically opposite authority.* So I did not waste my time by talking to one of those worthy Refer[ents], because in any case I knew perfectly well that *even though my opinion might be accepted as the right one today, it would be regarded as the wrong one tomorrow.* God save us all from *authorities of that type —* Hardly had I come in from the country and had handed over *that business* to Dr. Bach when that worthy co-guardian Nussböck came to the boarding school and stated that in a few days he was to remove my nephew from that school and place him somewhere else. He said that ' it was thought that I would appeal, that he was exceedingly embarrassed, that he didn't know where he should take him, that he had no money and didn't know where to raise any '. He added that in any case he was only doing what H[err]Refer[ent] Piuk had told him to do. Behold the fatherly care of *that* Obervormunds[chaft] for its ward. What colossal barbarity displayed by that Oberv[ormund-schaft], first of all, *in respect of my removal from the guardianship,* what a bad example of ingratitude on the part of an authority *which by rights ought to be philanthropic and pedagogic* ; and, on the other hand, what thoughtlessness to be willing to abandon my nephew to chance or, worse still, to entrust him to his mother. *Who knows, perhaps that was really the intention?* ! ! ! It can easily be supposed that I immediately declared my absolute determination in no wise to allow my nephew to be removed from his present boarding school and that I continued to defray, as I had previously done, the whole amount of *his expenses* — Dr. Bach now appeared before the M[agistrat], and H[err] Refer[ent] P[iuk] again retailed the *well-worn complaints of Fr[au] B[eethoven] about me*, even adding ' *that I was supposed to be in love with her etc.*' and more rubbish of that kind. As Dr. Bach informed me that by reason of my deafness the law demanded that I should choose a co-guardian, this too was arranged. So Fr[au] B[eethoven] *was again invited* by the M[agistrat] *to give her consent to this move. What is to be said about that?* Nevertheless the M[agistrat] held another sitting, at *which I myself appeared with the co-guardian who had been selected*, namely, Herr Peters. On this occasion too there was talk of the *unnecessarily fine clothes* which I was giving my nephew etc. — such utter nonsense — Then another insignificant decision was taken — This completes my information about the Obervormundschaft of that M[agistrat].

Information about my nephew and his school reports —

The time has not yet come to ascribe a definite character to a boy of thirteen and, still less, to one of a tenderer age.[1] For those are the years when one cannot *attribute* fixed traits and, still less, deny their existence — Until his eighth year my nephew was nearly always in the company of his mother. His father had to attend to his business, and during his last years his chronic ill health prevented him from giving much attention to his son. From this fact alone one can gather that when he was with his mother he must have developed certain traits which could not be effaced immediately after he had left her. For she had already taught him to lie and dissemble; and altogether she had ruined his character.[2] Indeed this tendency to tell lies was noticed when he was at H[err] Giannatasio's. I discussed it several times with Herr v[on] G[iannatasio] who was inclined to think that it would probably take several years for my nephew to forget completely all his past impressions — Even at that boarding school com-

[1] The words from 'and' to 'age' are added at the foot of the page.
[2] This sentence is added at the foot of the page.

plaints were made occasionally about his behaviour. *Neither I nor anyone else blamed Herr v[on] G[iannatasio] for this.* But things were quite different when I took my nephew to live with me, which I really did on account of his great gift for music. And who knows what a fine musician he might have become under my tuition, *had it not been for the wicked intrigues* of his depraved mother? *But now the same behaviour* in which he had indulged at Herr v[on] G[iannatasio]'s was attributed solely *to me.* It can easily be imagined that everything was falsified and exaggerated by this permanent opposition party. In the information I have provided about her I have already shown how she herself beguiled him. Indeed she obviously exaggerated everything simply in order to be able to fix the blame for it upon me. You need only summon my nephew today and ask him whether I earnestly exhorted him to fear God and to practise his religion — At the boarding school too I always took an interest in his education; and when he lived with me he always had a tutor or a crammer; and the nature of his studies was always adapted to his temperament. At any moment I can provide the reasons for my proceeding in this way. Let me add that all these difficulties could only have arisen under a Vormundschaft with so little insight and such partiality and under a guardian who, because he had to deal with that kind of Vormundschaft, *could never really consider himself to be the guardian* — As to Herr v[on] Giannatasio's opinion that my nephew would need several years before the impressions formed during his childhood could be effaced, this opinion seems to be confirmed. Nature, moreover, seldom proceeds by leaps and bounds. Herr v[on] Blöchlinger is now well satisfied *with my nephew's diligence and conduct.* Why, a gardener is ever patient with his plants; he tends them, lets them grow at will and then ties them up again. And should a man not be patient with a young human plant?! But here too the stupidity [1] of that M[agistrat] was revealed. For the latter placed him in the most unfavourable surroundings with his unnatural mother and, moreover, condemned him in the *most perverse, harmful* and callous manner. The Magistrat even tried to detect definite tendencies of character *at that age.* Thank Heaven, I have now reached the point

[1] In the original the word is 'Obscurantismus'.

where there is only gratifying news to relate about him.

Information about what I have done for my nephew —

For five years now I have paid for my nephew's education, which has been chiefly at my expense, and I have cared for him as few fathers would have done. And in all circumstances I have never lost sight of my true purpose, i.e. to help my nephew to become a capable, intelligent and decent citizen. This aim I have pursued not only when I was his guardian but also when *I was not*; and even *now* when I am at law about this question I continue to pursue it and by doing so to ensure the future welfare of my nephew — For two years, i.e. from 1816 to 1818,[1] he was at Giannatasio's boarding school entirely at my expense. There he also had as an extra his own pianoforte teacher,[2] he underwent an operation for hernia, and a special legal trustee was engaged on his account both in Vienna and in Prague. Moreover, in connexion with his property I travelled to Retz, etc., etc. — The cost of those two years may well be calculated at 4000 gulden V.C. If necessary, accounts can easily be produced — Only then was some contribution made to these expenses, as will be seen in greater detail in the information about my nephew's property. During the time he lived with me and thereafter from March, 1819 when he entered Kudlich's boarding school until he left it he cost me at least 2000 gulden V.C. — Since June 22, 1820 [3] he has been educated at H[err] Blöchlinger's boarding school. As these happen to be the shortest accounts, I enclose them herewith — See Supplement C. — But I have not included in my calculations many other necessary expenses, such as clothes, illnesses, and so forth — You will find very few uncles and guardians in this kingdom who care for their dependents *so* generously and with such absolute unselfishness. At any rate my sole purpose is to regard myself as *the originator and promoter* of *something good* and to fashion a fine specimen of humanity —

Information about my nephew's property.

This consists of 7000 gulden V.C., of which the mother has the usufruct during her lifetime; for my nephew is the

---

[1] The preceding four words are added at the foot of the page.
[2] Carl Czerny. Cf. Letter 610.　　　　　[3] A mistake for 1819.

sole heir *of his grandmother*. Note that the latter was more sensible than the M[agistrat], inasmuch as she refused to give *her daughter full control* of this money. Nevertheless, the M[agistrat] acted even more senselessly *in giving her as guardian* even the control of my nephew's soul.

Furthermore, he has 2000 gulden V.C., which compensates him for the temporary surrender of his inheritance and for his education; and to this I have added a sum which raises it to 2200 gulden in two and a half per cent trustee stock [1] —

Half of Frau Beethoven's pension, i.e. 166 gulden A.C. a year which compensates him for the inheritance he has completely surrendered, can surely not be treated as his property, but simply as a contribution to the cost of his education, *for in the event of her death* he would forfeit this contribution.

The interest on the coupons of the 2200 gulden has provided some contribution to the expenses of his education; but it was not paid until February 1, 1818 — It amounts to $27\frac{1}{2}$ in silver every six months. Similarly the first contribution from her pension was not paid until the end of May, 1818 — The half of the pension and the interest on the coupons produce at the exchange rate of 250 approximately 450 gulden V.C. a year.[2] So far I have received in all about four quarterly payments, because *for the last* 13 *months I have not received a farthing of this pension. Observe her motherly solicitude, and the support my nephew is receiving from that Obervormundschaft*, who are mean enough *to have perhaps joined forces with her so that this sum belonging to him should not be paid to me!* —

Since before 1816, i.e. immediately after my brother's *death*, I have provided for my nephew's education entirely at my expense, it is easy to calculate what I have received. No contributions were paid in until 1818. And I have already mentioned that for the last 13 months I have not received any portion of the half of her pension — Provision has also been made for my nephew's future. 4000 gulden A.C. have been deposited by me in the Austrian National Bank *as a legacy* [3] *for him* — If to the interest on the 4000 gulden A.C. in the

[1] In the autograph this paragraph is enclosed between two lines heavily drawn across the page.

[2] The words from 'and' to 'year' are added at the foot of the page.

[3] The words '*as a legacy*' are added at the foot of the page.

Bank one adds the interest on the trustee stock, which amounts to at least 1058 gulden V.C., and probably a little more, there is now a fairly large sum in reserve for any eventuality — Supposing that his mother should die and he should inherit the usufruct of the 7000 gulden V.C., then the interest on his capital would amount to at least 1408 gulden V.C. —

Conclusion

In view of the dreadful gossip and tittle-tattle indulged in by that M[agistrat] and also of Fr[au] B[eethoven]'s persistent intrigues against me and defamatory statements about me, I considered that a deposition which should cover almost all sides of this guardianship story *would not be amiss.* In the Magist[rat]'s reports this deposition may serve *as a manual* for the lectures of a — *professor?!* — I must confess that I am utterly exhausted; and if a man *must suffer for the sake of what is right,* I fancy that in this respect I have done my full share. It is high time for the High Court of Appeal to put Fr[au] B[eethoven] in her place and make her realize that no cabals can now upset what has been fixed by the Worshipful L[and]-r[echte] and [1] *is going to remain so.* For at least four years indeed she has been cherishing this scheme *to have her son to live with her and to be his guardian.* Therefore it must be made *quite impossible for her to injure him.* Only then can *humane treatment and charitableness assert themselves,* though indeed *that was always the course* I pursued with respect to her, except whenever the welfare of my nephew demanded that her stubbornness should be crushed by legal methods. And yet she has *never* been willing to benefit by *considerate treatment or magnanimity or true kindness* — No one should credit what she declares, namely that I am actuated by personal hatred or a desire to revenge myself *on her.* It distresses me to have to discuss *her*; *and were it not for my nephew* I would never give *her* a thought, nor mention *her*, nor act against *her* — May the High Court of Appeal now grant my petition and decide whether *Fr[au] B[eethoven] and Nussböck, the Stadtsequester,* are to be entrusted with the guardianship of my nephew, or *I*, who am the guardian *appointed in the will*, (together with my co-guardian chosen by me, *Herr*

---

[1] The words from 'what' to 'and' are added at the foot of the page.

v[on] Peters, who is eminently congenial to me and useful to my nephew [1])
and who *for the last five years have been the benefactor, the mainstay
and the support of my nephew — The decision will mean happiness or
disaster* for my nephew; it will certainly be disastrous if a
decision *is not taken in my favour — For my nephew needs me though
I do not need him.* Not only would an unfavourable decision
injure him from the financial point of view, but his whole
moral existence would thereby undergo a harmful change.
In any case this affair has fallen into such bad hands that
*were it to remain in its present state I could no longer concern myself
with it and* [2] *should just have to leave my nephew to the protection of
Providence.* But if, on the contrary, his welfare is again entrusted
to me alone, as I hope it will be, I will continue to defray the
expenses of his education, as I have done hitherto and as in
any case I would always have done. It has now been made
clear to what extent I have provided for his future; and in
this respect even more might be done — And if, *being human,
I have erred now and then or if my poor hearing must be taken into
account, yet surely* a child is not taken away *from his father for
those two reasons.* And I have *always been a father to my nephew,*
just as I was a *benefactor to his father*! God bless my work,
for I am entrusting the welfare of an orphan to the heart and
the sovereign wisdom of the High Court of Appeal —
     Sapienti honestas lex est, libido lex est malis.[3]
              your most obedient

Supplementary Statement

     Since, as has already been made clear in the inform[ation]
supplied about Frau B[eethoven], even when she was still in
her parents' home she showed a tendency to father her own
misdeeds on *innocent persons,* just as in 1811 she accused *innocent
persons* of her crime, or at any rate knew that though *quite
innocent they were being implicated* without having had any part
in committing it; and since from the information about the
M[agistrat] it has also been made clear what false facts *she*

---

[1] The preceding four words are added at the foot of the page.
[2] The words from 'could' to 'and' are added at the foot of the page.
[3] Quoted from Anysius, *op. cit.* 249. The sentence should read 'Sapienti honestas lex, libido lex est malis'. The meaning is: 'Decency is a law to the wise, lust is a law to the wicked'.

has ascribed to me and how she has always *maligned* me, all that one can expect from this M[agistrat] is that in its reports it will serve up more statements of that kind which are directed against me and about which I know nothing. But from all the foregoing information one can judge what value should be attached to such statements — Since, moreover, the M[agistrat] may perhaps appear *against me* armed with the papers *supposed?* to have been supplied by the parson at Mödling, documents which *were already produced at the last commission of the Worshipful Landrechte,* an elucidation of this question will not be out of place — It was in May, 1818, that having removed my nephew from H[err v[on] Giannatasio's in February, 1818,[1] so that he might *live with me,* I also took him into the country with me. The tutor whom I was then employing could not accompany us because he was a student in Vienna. I was confident, however, that at Mödling too I should find the necessary time to develop my nephew's musical talent. The parson there was highly recommended to me as a capable teacher of boys. So I entrusted my nephew to him. Unfortunately I soon discovered that I had been very much mistaken in that parson. On a Monday that reverend gentleman had not yet slept off his Sunday carousing and still behaved like a wild beast. Yes, I felt ashamed for *our religion,* that *such* a parson should be described as *a preacher of the Gospel.* Nothing would induce my nephew to show him respect and obedience. Of course not, for that parson treated him most brutally and roughly about the smallest thing ; he made his pupils lie down on a bench like soldiers, and the toughest of them had to act as corporal and thrash the culprits with a cane. I absolutely forbade him to punish my nephew in this way, nor did I allow my nephew to go to church in the morning with the parson's pupils, for I had noticed their unseemly behaviour and did not wish my nephew to associate with that gang. It can easily be imagined that that in itself was *sufficient for people to accuse me* of having no religion and of failing to give my nephew a religious education. As I saw only too clearly how deceitful that fellow was, after a few weeks I no longer allowed my nephew to go to him, but engaged a teacher for him who came from town. That nothing was neglected is

[1] On January 24, 1818.

proved by my nephew's excellent report of August 26th, 1818, the last one issued under the Obervormundschaft of the Worshipful L[and]r[echte] and my guardianship,[1] a report which is even better than the previous one. It can easily be imagined that the removal of my nephew from the parson offended the latter's vanity. To this offence there were added the intrigues of Fr[au] B[eethoven], for His Reverence was known to be not entirely indifferent to the fair sex. In this connexion certain facts were reported about His R[everence] *which we poor but refined laymen would not only refrain from committing but even be ashamed of mentioning.* In general he was neither loved nor respected either by his congregation or by other clergymen. Indeed that man was not ashamed to become another tool in the hands of Fr[au] B[eethoven] to be used against me. To please her (so she said), he had written a report in which several false accusations were made against me and which, it seems, was given due consideration by the L[and]-r[echte] at the last commission, although the records must undoubtedly show that nothing was proved against me — It is conceivable that the M[agistrat] will not fail *to give due consideration to that kind of evidence again.* One can see clearly how since March, 1819, when my nephew was no longer living with me and *I was no longer his guardian, everything went wrong, how his habits deteriorated,* how his mother constantly dragged him about with her, *how he in turn ran away from the boarding school whenever he liked and how purely on that account a successful examination result was not to be expected.* Added to that, moreover, was Fr[au] B[eethoven]'s disgraceful advice that my nephew *should deliberately contrive to be placed in the second or third class ; and this did happen, as is shown in the certificate of the Easter Examinations in* 1819. Finally, *thanks to his mother* he even had a haemorrhage [2] — Seeing that since June, 1819, I have again regarded myself as the guardian and have acted *as such,* I suppose that the difference between what is better and what is worse will again be observed ; for with energy and dignity, as befits a man like me, I have opposed all further wrongdoing on the part of the M[agistrat] and have declared 'that once and for all I insist upon knowing that the money I disburse is being

[1] The words from 'the last' to 'guardianship' are added at the foot of the page.
[2] This sentence is added at the foot of the page.

spent on the object for which it is intended'. This statement, which I was finally compelled to make against an
authority which at all times stubbornly opposed all the good
which I had in view, provoked *its feelings of revenge against me*.
And those *vulgar fellows* quickly joined forces with that depraved Fr[au] B[eethoven] and through her became the means
of *again undermining the future welfare of my nephew and humiliating
me in every possible way, as they have always done*. But I put my
trust in *convitia hominum turpium, laudes puta*.[1] —

I appeal to the Almighty to be my witness. He who sees
into my innermost heart knows that I have acted and cared
for my nephew during more than five years and only in accordance with the best and soundest principles. Moreover, I have
always regarded it as my duty *never* to abandon my nephew.
But I have learned from the M[agistrat] that there is another
side to the question. Yet I hope that the High Court of Appeal
will endorse *my opinion* in the matter. Finally, I must add that
in my view it has by no means been proved whether or not I
should recognize the Magistrat as an authority competent to
deal with the question of the guardianship —

(16) *Protocol*

[*MS not traced*][2]

[VIENNA], *March* 29, 1820

Present: Councillor von Piuk, Councillor von Beranek,
Councillor von Bayer: Staudinger, who kept the minutes.
No. 13807. Result of appeal in connexion with the guardianship of van Beethoven. Ludwig van Beethoven and Joseph
Karl Bernard, Editor of the Wiener Zeitung, were present.[3]
After the most urgent representations were made to the former
in view of his great responsibility, he expressed himself as
follows: 1) that in accordance with the will and testament
of his brother and with the provisions of the law he demanded
to have the guardianship of his nephew and would not abandon

---

[1] Quoted from Anysius, *op. cit.* 58, where the text has 'convicia'. The meaning
is: 'Treat the abuse of odious men as praise'.

[2] Taken from *TDR* IV, 566.

[3] At the Court of Appeal's request Beethoven had again to give evidence before
the Vienna Magistrat.

his claim : 2) that he asked to have as joint guardian Hofrat von Peters, of the household of Prince Lobkowitz : 3) that he demanded that, as had been arranged by the Landrechte, Frau van Beethoven should be excluded from the guardianship : 4) that he referred to the statements [1] he had already made on a previous occasion to the Civil Senate of the Vienna Magistrat, i.e. that he was making ample provision for his nephew and that he would assuredly accept a joint guardian, but by no means a guardian, because he maintained his right to be entrusted with the guardianship and because he was convinced that experience had proved that any other guardian would not provide for the ward to the same extent as he, the worthy appellant, was providing.

LUDWIG VAN BEETHOVEN [2]

[1] J. B. Bach had helped Beethoven to formulate these statements.
[2] The result of Beethoven's appeal was the decision of April 8, 1820, which was wholly favourable to the appellant. Cf. Letter 1018.

APPENDIX D

DEDICATORY LETTERS

---

(1) *To Maximilian Friedrich, Elector of Cologne* [1]

[*MS not traced*] [2]

BONN, *October* 14, 1783

MOST ILLUSTRIOUS LORD!

In my fourth year music began to be the chief of my youthful occupations. Having become acquainted so early with the gracious Muse who tuned my soul to pure harmonies, I learnt to love her; and she, as it often seemed to me, began to love me too. I have now reached my eleventh year,[3] and since then my Muse in hours of sacred inspiration has often whispered to me: 'Make the attempt, just put down on paper the harmonies of your soul!' — Eleven years — I thought — and how could I look like a composer? And what would the experienced adults in this art say to this? I was almost too shy. But my Muse insisted — I obeyed and I composed.

And now may I dare, *Most Excellent Lord!* to lay the first-fruits of my youthful work on the steps of *your* throne? And may I hope that *you* will bestow upon them the gentle paternal look of *your* encouraging approval? — Oh, yes! For since time immemorial the arts and sciences have found in *you* their wise patron, their magnanimous promoter; and burgeoning talent has thrived under *your* gracious paternal care —

Filled with this heartening confidence I venture to approach

---

[1] Maximilian Friedrich (1708–1784) succeeded Clemens August as Elector of Cologne in 1761 and was succeeded by Maximilian Franz in 1784. Cf. Letter 3, p. 5, n. 6.

[2] Taken from Schiedermair, p. 170. This letter dedicating his three sonatas for the clavier to the Elector of Cologne appeared in the original edition published by Bossler at Speier in 1783. The work is listed in *KHV*. as WoO 47. See *KHV* 492-494.

[3] For many years Beethoven was unaware of his true age. He was then 13.

you with these youthful essays. Accept them as a pure sacrifice of childlike reverence and look upon them,

Most Illustrious Lord !

and their young composer with favour.

LUDWIG VAN BEETHOVEN

(2) *To ?*

[*Autograph not traced*] ¹

[VIENNA, 1795]

I have the honour to send you the quintet; ² and you will greatly oblige me if you will just regard it as a very trifling present from me. The only condition I must make in your case is that it shall not be given to anyone else—

(3) *To Count Johann Georg von Browne* ³

[*MS not traced*] ⁴

MONSIEUR ! [VIENNA, *July*, 1798]

L'auteur, vivement pénétré de Votre Munificence aussi délicate que libérale, se réjouit de pouvoir le dire au monde en Vous dédiant cette œuvre. Si les productions de l'art, que Vous honorez de Votre protection en connoisseur, dépendaient moins de l'inspiration du génie que de la bonne volonté de faire de son mieux, l'auteur aurait la satisfaction tant désirée, de présenter au premier Mécène de sa Muse la meilleure des ses œuvres.

¹ Taken from Nottebohm, *Zweite Beethoveniana* (Leipzig, 1887), p. 229. This short dedicatory note is written on a sketch for an early C major symphony which was never finished.

² Possibly the E♭ string quintet, Op. 4, published by Artaria in the spring of 1796. See *KHV*. 12–13. This quintet was an arrangement made by Beethoven of his octet for wind instruments, Op. 103, published posthumously in 1830 by Artaria. Cf. Letter 12, p. 19, n. 1.

³ Cf. Letter 50, p. 57, n. 1.

⁴ This dedicatory letter was printed with the three string trios, Op. 9, published by Johann Traeg in July, 1798. See *KHV*. 19–22.

(4) *To Karl Amenda* [1]

[*Autograph in the Beethovenhaus, Bonn*] [2]

DEAR AMENDA!   VIENNA, *June* 25, 1799

Accept this quartet as a small token of our friendship. As often as you play it to yourself remember the days we have spent together and at the same time how very fond of you was and ever will be

your sincere and warm-hearted friend

LUDWIG VAN BEETHOVEN

(5) *To Dr. Johann Adam Schmidt* [3]

[*MS not traced*] [4]

MONSIEUR!   [VIENNA, *January*, 1805]

Je sens parfaitement bien, que la Célébrité de Votre nom, ainsi que l'amitié dont Vous m'honorez exigeroient de moi la dédicace d'un bien plus important ouvrage. La seule chose, qui a pu me déterminer à Vous offrir celuici de préférence, c'est qu'il me paroit d'une exécution plus facile, et par là même plus propre à contribuer à la Satisfaction dont Vous jouissez dans l'aimable Cercle de Votre famille. — C'est surtout, lorsque les heureux talents d'une fille chérie se seront developpés devantage, que je me flatte de voir ce but atteint. Heureux si j'y ai réussi, et si dans cette foible marque de ma haute estime et de ma gratitude Vous reconnoissez toute la vivacité et la cordialité de mes sentiments.

LOUIS VAN BEETHOVEN

[1] Cf. Letter 32, p. 34, n. 1.

[2] This short note was written by Beethoven on the first violin part of a copy of the parts of his string quartet in F major, Op. 18, No. 1. Two years later all the six quartets of Op. 18, published by Tranquillo Mollo, were dedicated to Prince Lobkowitz.

[3] Cf. Letter 54, p. 66, n. 4.

[4] Taken from *TDR* II, 207. This dedicatory letter is engraved on the first page of the pianoforte part of Op. 38, Beethoven's arrangement for pianoforte trio of his septet, Op. 20. This pianoforte trio was published in January 1805, by the Bureau des Arts et d'Industrie. See *KHV*. 94-95.

(6) *To H.M. King Frederick William of Prussia* [1]

[*MS not traced*] [2]

Your Majesty!   [Vienna, *September*, 1826]

One of the great happinesses of my life is that Your Majesty has most graciously permitted me to dedicate the present work to you in all humility.

Your Majesty is not only the supreme father of your subjects but also the patron of arts and sciences. How much more, therefore, must your most gracious permission delight me, seeing that I too, since I am a native of Bonn, am fortunate enough to regard myself as one of your subjects.

I request Your Majesty most graciously to accept this work as a slight indication of the high regard I cherish for your supreme virtues — Your Majesty's most humble and most obedient

Ludwig van Beethoven

[1] Friedrich Wilhelm III (1770–1840) had succeeded to the throne of Prussia in 1797.

[2] Taken from *TDR* V, 368. This letter accompanied a manuscript copy of the ninth symphony, Op. 125, which Beethoven sent to Berlin shortly before his departure for Gneixendorf. Dr. Spiker (cf. Letter 1021, p. 892, n. 2), then in Vienna, delivered the copy and the letter. For the King's reply enclosing a diamond ring see *TDR* V, 369.

APPENDIX E

TESTIMONIALS AND LETTERS
OF INTRODUCTION

---

(1) *To Count György Festetich* [1]

[MS in the Helikon Library, Keszthély] [2]

VIENNA, *February* 2, 1795

The undersigned is pleased to certify that Herr Menzel possesses a considerable knowledge of music and plays with good technique.

LOUIS VAN BEETHOVEN

(2) *Testimonial for Carl Czerny*

[MS in the Gesellschaft der Musikfreunde, Vienna] [3]

VIENNA, *December* 7, 1805

We, the undersigned, cannot refuse to give to the young boy Carl Czerny a testimonial to the effect that he has made such extraordinary progress on the pianoforte, far exceeding what one would expect at his age of 14 years, that from this point of view as well as on account of his marvellous memory he should be considered worthy of all possible support, the more so as his parents have spent their private means on the training of their promising son.

LUDWIG VAN BEETHOVEN

[1] Not identified.

[2] This testimonial, found among papers belonging to the Festetich family, is neither written nor signed by Beethoven. It was first published in an article by Falvy Zoltán in *Új Zenei Szemle*, 1954, no. 10, p. 38. The writer of the article makes the sound suggestion that as this introductory letter is attached to a draft contract and a testimonial from Koželuch, both of which give the name Johann Maelzel, this letter from Beethoven was in reality a testimonial for Johann Nepomuk Maelzel (cf. Letter 436, p. 427, n. 4).

[3] Written in another hand and signed by Beethoven. Czerny gave this testimonial to the Gesellschaft der Musikfreunde. Cf. Letter 610, p. 560, n. 2.

(3) *Letter of Introduction for Herr von Kandler* [1]

[Autograph in the Nationalbibliothek, Vienna]

[VIENNA, 1817]

Admittedly it is the duty of every composer to know all the old and modern poets and to be able himself to select for singing what are the best and most suitable poems for his purpose. But as this is not the common practice, Herr von Kandeler's anthology will always be useful and to be recommended to those who desire to compose for the voice. Moreover it will act as an incentive to better poets to produce something for this purpose.

LUDWIG VAN BEETHOVEN

I entirely agree with H[err] v[an] Beethoven.

JOSEPH WEIGL [2]

(4) *Testimonial for Therese Kaufmann*

[Autograph in the possession of Dr. Richard Sterba]

VIENNA, *March* 17, 1823

By my signature I testify that *Therese Kaufmann* has been in my service as housemaid for a whole month and that during that time she has proved to be industrious and honest.

LUDWIG VAN BEETHOVEN

[1] Although in the autograph, which is not addressed, the surname is spelt Kandeler, this is doubtless a letter of introduction for Franz Sales Kandler (1792–1831) who, besides holding an official appointment in the Imperial War Council, was all his life engaged in literary work, chiefly about music. His official duties kept him in Italy (Venice, Naples and Milan) from 1817 to 1826. He translated and published through the interest of his chief, R. G. Kiesewetter (cf. Letter 1456, p. 1267, n. 1), portions of Baini's book on Palestrina and also translated into Italian the text of Beethoven's 'Christus am Ölberge', Op. 85, for the Italian edition published in 1828. See *KHV.* 230.

Nothing is known about Kandler's anthology. But before Kandler's departure for Italy in May, 1817, Beethoven wrote for his album the *a cappella* setting for male voices of the monks' song in Schiller's *Wilhelm Tell*, WoO 104.

[2] Cf. Letter, 155, p. 178, n. 2.

(5) *To Luigi Cherubini, Paris*

[*MS in the Deutsche Staatsbibliothek, Berlin*] [1]

MONSIEUR !   [VIENNA, *September*, 1825]
Le porteur de la présente lettre, Monsieur - - - - désire
ardemment vous rendre ses hommages. Je suis assez convaincu de l'estime, que vous marquez à des artistes dignes
de ce nom, pour lui faire espérer un acceuil favorable de
votre part. Acceptez en même l'assurance de la plus haute
considération avec laquelle j'ai l'honneur d'être, Monsieur,
votre très humble serviteur

L. v. B.

(6) *To Rodolphe Kreutzer, Paris* [2]

[*MS in the Deutsche Staatsbibliothek, Berlin*] [3]

MONSIEUR !   [VIENNA, *September*, 1825]
C'est dans l'espérance que vous vous souveniez encore
de votre ancien ami, que j'ose vous recommander le porteur
de cette lettre, Monsieur - - - un des artistes les plus distingués,
en vous priant de ne point lui refuser vos conseils ni votre - - - -
Je profite de cette occasion pour vous témoigner ma considération et mon amitié perpetuelle.
Je suis Monsieur votre très humble serviteur

L. v. B

[1] This is a draft in Karl's hand in a Conversation Book. It was first published
in *TDR* V, 245, n. 2, where it is stated that the bearer of this letter of introduction
and the following one was Johann Sedlaczek (1789–1866), born in Silesia, who
became an eminent flautist. He settled in 1810 in Vienna, where he had
resounding successes. In November, 1825, he left for Paris and for London,
where he settled for good in 1826. See Hanslick, p. 251.
[2] Cf. Letter 74, p. 91, n. 1.
[3] Cf. preceding letter of introduction to Cherubini.

APPENDIX F

CONTRACTS

---

(1) *Contract with Artaria & Co.*

[*MS in the Beethovenhaus, Bonn, H. C. Bodmer collection*] [1]

VIENNA, *May* 19, 1795

On today's date as affixed above the following agreement has been concluded between Herren Artaria & Co. and Herr Ludwig van Beethoven.

1) Herr van Beethoven hands over to Herr Artaria his three trios for pianoforte, violin and violoncello,[2] and in exchange Herr Artaria undertakes to make an advance payment of 212 gulden and to have these works engraved within six weeks at latest from the date quoted below and that too in fine copies provided with a decorative title-page.

2) Herr Artaria promises to deliver to him four hundred copies, each copy at the price of one gulden, and to arrange that counting from the day when the six weeks shall have expired 50 copies at least shall be printed off and delivered without fail until the fixed number of 400 has been reached. Nevertheless it is open to Herr van Beethoven to accept a smaller number.

3) After the fixed number of copies have been delivered Herr Artaria will take over the plates of the said three trios at the price of 90 gulden which he can also have deducted immediately from the aforesaid sum of 212 gulden.

4) Herr Artaria promises that counting from the day when the first copies shall have been delivered he will not sell a single copy in this city for two whole months. On the other hand he is free to sell copies abroad from that very day; and after the expiry of the two months he may sell in Vienna also copies of this work, which is his property by right.

---

[1] Written in another hand and signed by Beethoven and Artaria & Co.
[2] The three pianoforte trios, Op. 1, dedicated to Prince Karl Lichnowsky, were published by Artaria in July and August, 1795.

1417

5) At the same time if he thinks it advisable to do so Herr van Beethoven is entitled to sell any remaining copies after the expiry of the two months. But in that case he forfeits any claim to the further sale of his work. Moreover should he think it advisable not to accept up to that date the number of 400 copies, he will no longer be entitled to ask for copies on account of the said number.

6) The list of subscribers is to be delivered to Herr Artaria in a printed form, so that it may be attached to the copies intended for the subscribers.

In confirmation of this agreement the autograph signatures and the seals of the two contracting parties are appended.

LUDWIG VAN BEETHOVEN
ARTARIA & CO.

(2) *To Johann Traeg* [1]

[*MS not traced*] [2]

VIENNA, *March* 16, 1798

I, the undersigned, hereby declare that I have sold to Herr Johann Traeg, licensed art and music dealer, and wholly assigned to him as his property the three trios for violin, viola and violoncello, composed and dedicated by me to Count Browne, Brigadier in the service of His Imperial Majesty of all the Russians, the first of which is in G major, the second in D major and the third in C minor.[3] He can have them engraved on his own account and for his own advantage and can make use of them in any other way he may prefer. At the same time in return for the promise I have given him not to sell these trios to anyone else, and for the assurance I have given him that I have not yet sold them to anyone else, he is to pay me a fee of fifty ducats, a payment to which we have both agreed.

L. V. BEETHOVEN [4]

[1] Cf. Letter 12, p. 18, n. 2.

[2] Taken from *TDR* II, 84-85. Thayer, who copied the document then in private ownership, does not state whether it is autograph.

[3] Op. 9 was published by Traeg in July, 1798. For Count Browne cf. Letter 50, p. 57, n. 1.

[4] The document has the following additional agreement dated Vienna, June 5, 1823:

'By agreement with the composer I am handing over the above manuscript together with the copyright to S. A. Steiner & Co.

JOHANN TRAEG

I am delighted.

LUDWIG VON BEETHOVEN'

(3) *Contract between Muzio Clementi and Beethoven*

[*MS in the Deutsche Staatsbibliothek, Berlin*] [1]

VIENNA, *April* 20, 1807

La convention suivante a été faite entre Monsieur M. Clementi et Monsieur Louis v. Beethoven.

1. Monsieur Louis v. Beethoven cède à Monsieur M. Clementi les manuscrits de ses œuvres ci-après ensuivis, avec le droit de les publier dans les royaumes unis britanniques, en se réservant la liberté de faire publier ou de vendre pour faire publier ces mêmes ouvrages hors des dits royaumes :

    a. trois quatuors,[2]
    b. une symphonie
      N.B. la quatrième qu'il a composée,[3]
    c. une ouverture de Coriolan, tragédie de M. Collin,[4]
    d. un concert pour le piano
      N.B. le quatrieme qu'il a composé,[5]
    e. un concert pour le violon
      N.B. le premier qu'il a composé,[6]
    f. ce dernier concert arrangé pour le piano avec des notes additionnelles.[7]

2. Monsieur M. Clementi fera payer pour ces six ouvrages à Mr L. v. Beethoven la valeur de deux cents Liv. Sterl. au cours de Vienne par MM. Schuller et Comp.[8] aussitôt qu'on aura à Vienne la nouvelle de l'arrivée de ces ouvrages à Londres.

3. Si Monsieur L. v. Beethoven ne pouvait livrer ensemble ces six ouvrages, il ne serait payé par MM. Schuller et Comp. qu'à proportion des pièces livrées, p. ex. en livrant la moitié, il recevra la moitié, en livrant le tiers, il recevra le tiers de la somme convenue.

4. Monsieur L. v. Beethoven promet de ne vendre ces

---

[1] Written in another hand and signed by Clementi and Beethoven, Gleichenstein witnessing their signatures.
[2] Op. 59.   [3] Op. 60.   [4] Op. 62.   [5] Op. 58.   [6] Op. 61.
[7] This arrangement of Op. 61, made by Beethoven at Clementi's request, was published in August, 1807, by the Bureau des Arts et d'Industrie. The 'additional notes' are doubtless the additional keys on the keyboard, taking the work up to six octaves.   [8] Cf. Letter 44, p. 48, n. 2.

ouvrages soit en Allemagne, soit en France, soit ailleurs, qu'avec la condition de ne les publier que quatre mois après leur départ respectif pour l'Angleterre : pour le concert pour le violon et pour la symphonie et l'ouverture, qui viennent de partir pour l'Angleterre, Mons. L. v. Beethoven promet de ne les vendre qu'à condition de ne publier avant le 1. Sept. 1807.

5. On est convenu de plus que Mons. L. van Beethoven compose aux mêmes conditions dans un temps non determiné et à son aise, trois Sonates ou deux Sonates et une Fantaisie pour le piano avec ou sans accompagnement comme il voudra, et que Mons. M. Clementi lui fera payer de la même manière soixante Livres Sterl.

6. Mons. M. Clementi donnera à Mons. L. van Beethoven deux exemplaires de chacun de ces ouvrages.

Fait en double et signé a Vienne le 20 Avril 1807

MUZIO CLEMENTI   LOUIS VAN BEETHOVEN

Comme témoin I. GLEICHENSTEIN [1]

(4) *Draft Contract*

[*MS not traced*] [2]

[VIENNA, *February*, 1809]

The endeavour and the aim of every true artist should certainly be to win for himself a position in which he can devote himself entirely to the completion of great works and need not be debarred from this occupation by other avocations or by financial considerations. Therefore the most ardent wish of every composer should be to devote himself without interruption to the creation of really important works and then to be able to produce them in public. When doing so, however, he must not forget the future, i.e. his old age, and he must endeavour to acquire sufficient resources for his later days.

The King of Westphalia has offered Beethoven an income of 600 gold ducats for life and 150 ducats for travelling expenses

---

[1] Cf. Letter 95, p. 115, n. 1.

[2] Taken from *TDR* III, 123-124. Thayer suggests that Gleichenstein drafted these conditions which eventually led to the contract whereby the Princes Kinsky and Lobkowitz and the Archduke Rudolph guaranteed to Beethoven a permanent yearly income of 4000 gulden if he would remain in Vienna. For this contract, dated March 1, 1809, see *TDR* III, 125-126.

on the sole condition that he shall play for him occasionally and conduct his chamber music concerts, performances which are not frequent and all of which would be quite short. Certainly this offer is entirely to the advantage of the art and the artist.

At the same time Beethoven's preference to reside in this city is so great, he is so grateful for the many proofs of goodwill which he has received and he cherishes such patriotic feelings for his second fatherland that he will never cease to count himself among the number of Austrian artists and will never choose to live anywhere else, provided that the advantages listed below are granted to him to a certain extent.

As some highly placed and eminent persons have invited him to state the conditions on which he would be willing to remain in Vienna, he is complying with their request in the following way:

1) Beethoven would have to receive from some great lord the assurance of an income for life; or perhaps several highly placed persons might contribute individually to make up that income. In view of the present high cost of living this income could not be less than 4000 gulden a year. Beethoven would like the donors of this income to regard themselves as the joint originators of his new and greater works, inasmuch as they would be enabling him to devote himself to the composition of those works and ensuring that his time need not be taken up with the discharge of other duties.

2) Beethoven would have to retain his freedom to undertake journeys in the interest of his art, for only by so doing can he become very well known and acquire a small private fortune.

3) His greatest longing and his most ardent wish is to enter the Imperial service at some future time and by drawing the salary he would expect to enjoy from such an appointment to be in a position to resign the above income wholly or in part. For the time being, however, the title of Imperial Kapellmeister would make him very happy; and if this title could be obtained for him, his permanent residence in Vienna would become even more attractive.

Should this desire be fulfilled at some future time and were he to receive a salary from His Majesty, then Beethoven would forgo as much of the above yearly income of 4000 gulden as the Imperial salary would amount to; and were the latter to amount to 4000 gulden, then he would wholly renounce the above income of 4000 gulden.

4) Since Beethoven desires to produce his new and greater works now and then before a large public as well, he would like to receive from the Directors of the Court Theatres on their behalf and on behalf of their successors an assurance that on Palm Sunday of every year he would be granted the Theater an der Wien for a concert to be held for his own benefit. In return for this privilege Beethoven would undertake to organize and conduct every year a concert for the poor or, if this could not be arranged, to produce a new work to be performed at a concert for that purpose.

(5) *Contract between Beethoven and Breitkopf & Härtel*

[MS not traced] [1]

VIENNA, *July* 25, 1810

21. Mass set to music. Op. 86.
22. Lied aus der Ferne, with pianoforte accompaniment.
    (A present and furthermore the declared property of Herren Breitkopf & Härtel).
23. Andenken, by Matthisson, with pianoforte accompaniment
    (A present and likewise the declared property of Herren Breitkopf & Härtel).[2]

I certify that I have sold to Herren Breitkopf & Härtel and have granted them the unconditional publication rights of the works listed from 1 to 23 and that I have received from them the fee agreed upon for these rights

LUDWIG VAN BEETHOVEN

[1] Taken from the facsimile of the second page of this contract reproduced in GEMA (Munich), *Musik und Dichtung*, 1953, p. 65. Only the bracketed remarks under works 22 and 23 and the signature are in Beethoven's hand.
[2] The songs are WoO 137 and WoO 136, published in February, 1810 and March, 1810 respectively.

(6) *To Sigmund Anton Steiner & Co.*

[*MS not traced*] [1]

VIENNA, *April* 29, 1815

Particulars of the following original musical works which the undersigned has composed and handed over to Sigmund Anton Steiner, the licensed art dealer, as his property :—

1) Score of the opera Fidelio.
2) Score of the cantata Der glorreiche Augenblick.[2]
3) Score of a quartet for two violins, viola and cello.[3]
4) Score of a grand trio for voices together with the [4] pianoforte arrangement.
5) Score of the Schlacht bei Vittoria together with the pianoforte arrangement.
6) Pianoforte arrangement and score of a symphony in F major.
7) Pianoforte arrangement and score of a symphony in A major.
8) Grand trio for pianoforte, violin and cello in score.[5]
9) Grand sonata for pianoforte and violin in score.[6]
10) Score of a grand overture in E flat [7]
11)   Ditto   in C major [8]
12)   Ditto   in G major [9]
13) Twelve English songs with pianoforte accompaniment and German text.[10]—

For all these works which Herr Steiner is authorized to use as his property everywhere, with the sole exception of England, I have been compensated by him to my entire satisfaction.

[1] Taken from Unger, no. 3. This is an unsigned draft in another hand of Beethoven's first contract with Steiner, dated May 5, 1815.
[2] Op. 136 was not published until 1837, and by Haslinger.
[3] Op. 95.   [4] Op. 116.   [5] Op. 97.   [6] Op. 96.
[7] Op. 117.   [8] Op. 115.   [9] Op. 113.   [10] Possibly WoO 157.

(7) *To George Thomson, Edinburgh*

[MS not traced] [1]

[VIENNA, *November* 18, 1818]

I, Mr. Louis van Beethoven, composer of music residing in Vienna, acknowledge that I have received from Mr. George Thomson of the city of Edinburgh in Scotland by the hand of Mr. Fries and Co, Bankers in Vienna, per order of Mr. Thomas Coutts and Co., Bankers in London, one hundred and forty ducats in gold for composing Variations for the pianoforte upon twelve themes or national airs with an accompaniment for the flute, and also for composing ritornels, a symphony and accompaniment for the pianoforte, violin, flute and violoncello to eight Scottish airs, and for composing voice-part to the same for singing and trios.

And I formally declare and certify to all whom it may concern that the aforesaid twelve themes with variations and the sighs,[2] the harmonies as above are the sole and absolute property of the said George Thomson, his heirs and assignees, in perpetuity, without any reservation whatever.

And I further declare that all the ritornellos or symphonies and accompaniments which I have before at different times composed for Scottish, Irish and Welsh melodies, that is, for one hundred and eighteen of those melodies sent to me by the said George Thomson together with the additional voice part as harmony composed by me for those melodies are also the sole and absolute property of the said George Thomson, his heirs and assignees, in perpetuity without any reservation — And lastly I declare that the ritornels or symphonies and accompaniments which I composed for twenty five melodies of continental nations are likewise his sole and absolute property in perpetuity to the said George Thomson having through the aforesaid Messrs. Fries and Co. paid to me the full price which I demanded for the composition of those works for the pianoforte and as above. Given under my hand

---

[1] Taken from Frimmel, *Beethovenforschung*, 1911, no. 1, pp. 22-24. According to Frimmel, who copied the original document, it was written in English in another hand and signed by Beethoven.

[2] Meaning perhaps 'expression marks'; or a mistake in transcription.

at Vienna this eighteenth day of November one thousand eight
hundred and eighteen.

JOSEPH MÜLLER [1]
Witness
C. W. de BREVILLIER [2]
as witness
LOUIS VAN BEETHOVEN

(8) *To Sigmund Anton Steiner*

[*MS in the Beethovenhaus, Bonn*][3]

[VIENNA, *October 30, 1819*]

STATEMENT

Seeing that Herr S. A. Steiner has lent me today 750
gulden V.C. in cash, I undertake to repay in cash this amount,
together with interest at 6%, on December 30, 1819 to the
account of my creditor; and in exchange for this repay-
ment I shall have the present statement returned to me —

In confirmation of the above transaction I have written
and signed this statement with my own hand. —

LUDWIG VAN BEETHOVEN

[1] Not identified.   [2] Not identified.
[3] Written in another hand and signed by Beethoven.

APPENDIX G
RECEIPTS

———

(1) *To Nikolaus Simrock, Bonn*

[Autograph in the Beethovenhaus, Bonn, H. C. Bodmer collection]

VIENNA, *February* 3, 1804

I certify by my own signature that Herr Simrock at Bonn is entitled to regard as his exclusive property a sonata with a violin [1] in A minor, Op. 47, composed by me and consisting of three movements, the themes of which are added below,[2] and that for this work he has duly paid me the fee of 50 ducats.

LUDWIG VAN BEETHOVEN

(2) *To Count Franz Oppersdorff* [3]

[Autograph in the New England Conservatory, Boston]

[VIENNA], *February* 3, 1807

A receipt for 500 gulden received by me from Count Oppersdorff for a symphony which I have composed for him — I declare that this is my own handwriting —

LUDWIG VAN BEETHOVEN

[1] In the autograph Op. 47 is described as 'Sonate mit einer Violine'.
[2] The beginning bars of the three movements of Op. 47 are entered on the verso of the autograph, probably in the handwriting of Ferdinand Ries.
[3] Cf. Letter 166, p. 187, n. 3.

(3) *To Count Franz Oppersdorff*

[*Autograph not traced*] [1]

VIENNA, *March* 29, 1808

By my signature I certify that I received on March 29, 1808 from Count Oppersdorff bank notes amounting to 150 gulden.

LUDWIG VAN BEETHOVEN

Further, I received in June, 1807 200 gulden in cash. A sum has also been promised for the 5th symphony, but has not yet been received. November 25, 1808.

(4) *To Breitkopf & Härtel, Leipzig*

[*MS in the Beethovenhaus, Bonn, H. C. Bodmer collection*] [2]

VIENNA, *September* 14, 1808

I, the undersigned, hereby certify that I have sold to Herren Breitkopf und Härtel at Leipzig as their exclusive property (with the exception of England) the following five new works composed by me, i.e.

    1 symphony in C minor Opus — [3]
    1   ditto   in F major Opus — [4]
    2 trios for pianoforte etc., Op. —
    the first in D, the other in — [5]
    1 sonata for pianoforte with violoncello in A, Op — [6]

and that I have today safely received in cash the fee agreed upon for these works.

LUDWIG VAN BEETHOVEN

---

[1] Taken from *TDR* III, 12-13. According to Thayer, who copied this document, which bears two separate dates, the handwriting is that of Beethoven.
[2] Written by G. C. Härtel and signed by Beethoven.
[3] Op. 67.   [4] Op. 68.
[5] Op. 70. The second trio is in E♭.   [6] Op. 69.

(5) *To Breitkopf & Härtel, Leipzig*

[*MS in the Beethovenhaus, Bonn, H. C. Bodmer collection*] [1]

VIENNA, *September* 14, 1808

I hereby certify that I have received today from Herren Breitkopf und Härtel in Leipzig one hundred gold ducats in cash in payment of the fee agreed upon for five new works composed by me.

LUDWIG VAN BEETHOVEN

(6) *To Breitkopf & Härtel, Leipzig*

[*MS in the Beethovenhaus, Bonn, H. C. Bodmer collection*] [2]

VIENNA, *January*, 1810

I hereby certify that I have granted to Herren Breitkopf & Härtel the right to publish and to own the following works: i.e., 1) an oratorio : Christus am Ölberge   2) an opera Leonore, in two acts and   3) a Mass,[3] all of them in score, and that I have safely received for them the fee which was agreed upon.

LUDWIG VAN BEETHOVEN

(7) *To Robert Birchall, London*

[*MS not traced*] [4]

[VIENNA, *March* 9, 1816] [5]

Received March 1816 of Mr. Robert Birchall — Music Seller 133 New Bond Street, London — the sum of one hundred and thirty gold Dutch ducats, value in English currency sixty-five pounds, for all my copyright and interest, present and future, vested or contingent, or otherwise within the United

---

[1] Written by G. C. Härtel and signed by Beethoven. Cf. Appendix G (4).
[2] First published in the *Beethoven-Jahrbuch*, 1953/54, p. 26. Written in another hand and signed by Beethoven, who omitted to give the exact date.
[3] The Mass in C, published by Breitkopf & Härtel in October, 1812.
[4] Taken from *KFR*, no. 522.
[5] This document signed by Beethoven was listed in a catalogue of the American Art Association, January 5 and 6, 1927, item 62, where its date is quoted as March 9, 1816.

Kingdom of Great Britain and Ireland in the four following compositions or pieces of music composed or arranged by me, viz.

1st. A grand battle sinfonia, descriptive of the battle and victory at Vittoria, adapted for the pianoforte and dedicated to His Royal Highness the Prince Regent — 40 ducats.[1]

2nd. A grand symphony in the key of A, adapted to the pianoforte and dedicated to — [2]

3rd. A grand trio for the pianoforte, violin and violoncello in the key of B♭.[3]

4th. A sonata for the pianoforte with an accompaniment for the violin in the key of G dedicated to — [4]

And in consideration of such payment I hereby for myself, my executors and administrators promise and engage to execute a proper assignment thereof to him, his executors and administrators or assignees at his or their request and costs, as he or they shall direct — And I likewise promise and engage as above, that none of the above shall be published in any foreign country, before the time and day fixed and agreed on for such publication between R. Birchall and myself shall arrive.

L. VAN BEETHOVEN

(8) *To George Thomson, Edinburgh*

[Autograph not traced] [5]

[VIENNA, *c. August*, 1817]

For three Scottish songs, for a new accompaniment with violin and violoncello, for a letter from Mr. Thomson to me dated June 25, 1817, sent through the post, for which I paid 9 gulden V.C., for my manuscript — — total 12 gold ducats.

LUDWIG VAN BEETHOVEN

[1] Op. 91. (Birchall's Op. 81, incidentally the first edition of the pianoforte transcription.)

[2] Op. 92. There were three pianoforte transcriptions, the first of which was made by C. Czerny. All three were dedicated to the Empress of Russia. See *KHV.* 260. (Birchall's Op. 82.)

[3] Op. 97. (Birchall's Op. 86.)

[4] Op. 96 was dedicated to the Archduke Rudolph. (Birchall's Op. 85.)

[5] Taken from *KFR*, no. 681.

(9) *A Receipt in Beethoven's Handwriting, signed by Tobias Haslinger*

[Autograph in the Beethovenhaus, Bonn, H. C. Bodmer collection]

VIENNA, *January* 17, 1818

I Adjutant Tobias Haslinger, sinner and r[asca]l of the 88th class, hereby confess by virtue of my signature of my name that I have just received from Herr L. v. Beethoven in person for H[err] v. Steiner, L[ieutenan]t G[enera]l and *G[enera]l exploiter* of H[err] L. v. Beethoven, 25 gold ducats, which are to be handed to the highly born L[ieutenan]t G[enera]l v[on] Steiner for some wretched rag paper —

TOBIAS HASLINGER

(10) *To Artaria & Co.*

[MS in the Beethovenhaus, Bonn, H. C. Bodmer collection] [1]

VIENNA, *June* 8, 1819

I hereby confirm that I have received the 50 gold ducats (repeat fifty gold ducats) which have been paid to me and in exchange for which I hand over to you as your property on the continent my six variations on Scottish and Austrian themes with flute or violin accompaniment, Opera 105.

LUDWIG VAN BEETHOVEN

(11) *To Artaria & Co.*

[Autograph in the Beethovenhaus, Bonn, H. C. Bodmer collection] [2]

[VIENNA, *April* 4, 1820]

I hereby certify by my own signature that all the works listed here are the property of the H[erren] Artaria und Compagnie.

L. V. BEETHOVEN

---

[1] Written in another hand and signed by Beethoven. This receipt was first published in the *Beethoven-Jahrbuch*, 1953/54, p. 23.

[2] Enclosing a manuscript thematic catalogue of all the works composed by Beethoven which Artaria & Co. had published before 1820.

(12) *To Artaria & Co.*

[*Autograph in the Beethovenhaus, Bonn, H. C. Bodmer collection*]

VIENNA, *January* 28, 1821

I certify with gratitude that I have received from H[err] v[on] Artaria 150 gulden A.C. which I will soon repay; and for this act of kindness I have promised him some compositions.[1]

L. V. BEETHOVEN

(13) *To Henikstein & Co.*

[*MS not traced*] [2]

VIENNA, *October* 22, 1823

J'ai reçu de votre part pour compte de S.A. Monseigneur le Prince Nicolas Galitzin la somme de 50 ducats — je dis cinquante ducats en or effectifs, dont double quittances ne valent que pour une.[3]

LOUIS VAN BEETHOVEN

(14) *To Franz Christian Kirchhoffer*

[*MS in the British Museum*] [4]

VIENNA, *April* 27, 1824

This is to certify that I, the undersigned, have received today from Herr von Kirchhoffer 50 pounds sterling in full and in cash for the symphony delivered to him which I have composed for the Philharmonic Society in London.[5]

LUDWIG VAN BEETHOVEN

[1] Cf. Letter 1039, p. 907, n. 1.
[2] Taken from *TDR* V, 556.
[3] As payment for Prince Galitzin's manuscript copy of the 'Missa Solemnis.'
[4] Written in another hand and signed by Beethoven.
[5] The ninth symphony, Op. 125.

(15) *To Cappi & Co.*[1]

[Autograph in the Nationalbibliothek, Vienna]

VIENNA, *January* 30, 1825

I certify by my signature that Herren Cappi & Co. are the owners of the three trios for pianoforte, violin and violoncello — Op. I., which they are now publishing.[2]

L. v. BEETHOVEN

(16) *To Moritz Schlesinger*

[MS not traced] [3]

VIENNA, *September* 4, 1825

Je soussigné reconnais avoir vendu à Monsieur Maurice Schlesinger qui m'en a remis le montant convenu deux quatuors pour 2 violons, viola et violoncelle de ma composition, formant les œuvres (132 et 134) que je lui céde en toute propriété pour lui et ses héritiers.

Approuvé l'ecriture ci dessus

LOUIS VAN BEETHOVEN

(17) *To Moritz Schlesinger*

[MS not traced] [4]

VIENNA, *September* 10, 1825

I herewith certify that I have received from Herr Maurice Schlesinger eighty ducats as payment for handing over the manuscript and the ownership of my quartets for two violins,

[1] The autograph is not addressed.

[2] Op. 1 had been published by Artaria & Co. in July/August 1795 with a dedication to Prince Karl Lichnowsky. Cappi's edition in three numbers appeared in 1825.

[3] Taken from Unger, no. 116. The receipt was written by Moritz Schlesinger, who was then in Vienna. But the words from 'Approuvé' to the end, including the signature, are in Beethoven's hand. In the end, Schlesinger received the quartets Op. 132 and 135, which were published posthumously. See Appendix G (17). See also *KHV*. 403.

[4] Taken from Unger, no. 118. According to Unger, who transcribed the original document, this receipt was written and signed in another hand.

viola and violoncello op. 132 and 134, the 12th and 17th quartets.[1]

LUDWIG VAN BEETHOVEN

(18) *Receipt*

[*MS in the Romain Rolland collection*] [2]

VIENNA, *February* 24, 1826

I declare that I have received here today eight gold ducats in cash from N. Grünbaum [3] for the account of M. Herzfeld.[4]

LUDWIG VAN BEETHOVEN

(19) *To Johann Baptist Streicher* [5]

[*MS in the Beethovenhaus, Bonn, H. C. Bodmer collection*] [6]

VIENNA, *December* 14, 1826

TO HERR BAPTIST STREICHER in VIENNA.

I hereby confirm in duplicate (but valid only once) the safe receipt of the complete works of Handel in forty volumes,[7] which have been sent to me by Herr A. Stumpff in London through you; and also of Reichardt's Taschenbuch für Reisende [8] and of a letter from Herr George Smart.

LUDWIG VAN BEETHOVEN

[1] In the end Schlesinger received the quartets Op. 132 and 135. Cf. Appendix G (16).

[2] Written in another hand and signed by Beethoven.

[3] Not identified.

[4] Not identified.

[5] Johann Baptist, son of Johann Andreas and Nanette Streicher, took over their firm after the death of his father in 1833.

[6] Written in another hand and signed by Beethoven. An almost identical letter was sent to Johann Andreas Stumpff. See *TDR* V, 425.

[7] Samuel Arnold's fine edition of Handel's works, in 180 numbers, published from 1787 to 1797. At the auction held after Beethoven's death Haslinger purchased the set of 40 volumes for 102 gulden.

[8] Probably a copy of Heinrich A. O. Reichard: *Taschenbuch für Reisende durch Deutschland etc.*, the fourth edition of which appeared in 1835.

APPENDIX H

PRESS AND OTHER NOTICES

---

(1) *Notice in the ' Wiener Zeitung' of October* 20, 1802

I consider that I owe it to the public and to myself to state publicly that the two quintets in C major and E major, one of which (taken from one of my symphonies) was published by Herr Mollo in Vienna [1] and the other (taken from the well-known septet of mine, Op. 20) by Herr Hoffmeister at Leipzig,[2] are not original quintets, but merely transcriptions made by those worthy publishers — The making of transcriptions is on the whole a thing against which nowadays (in our prolific age of transcriptions) a composer would merely struggle in vain ; but at least he is entitled to demand that the publishers shall mention the fact on the title-page, so that his honour as a composer may not be infringed nor the public deceived — This is in order to prevent cases of this kind arising in future.

At the same time I am informing the public that a new and original quintet which I have composed in C major, Op. 29, will be published very soon by Breitkopf & Härtel at Leipzig.[3]

LUDWIG VAN BEETHOVEN

---

(2) *Notice in the ' Wiener Zeitung' of January* 22, 1803

TO LOVERS OF MUSIC

While informing the public that the original quintet in C major which I announced a long time ago has been published by Breitkopf & Härtel at Leipzig,[4] I also declare that I have nothing whatever to do with the edition of this quintet

---

[1] An arrangement for string quintet of Beethoven's first symphony, Op. 21. See *KHV*. 53.

[2] This quintet had been published in August, 1802. See *KHV*. 50.

[3] Op. 29 appeared in December, 1802.   [4] Op. 29.

produced at the same time by Herren Artaria and Mollo in Vienna.[1] Furthermore I am compelled to make this declaration particularly because the latter edition is extremely faulty, inaccurate and quite useless for the performer; whereas Herren Breitkopf & Härtel, the lawful owners of this quintet, have done their utmost to produce the work as handsomely as possible.

LUDWIG VAN BEETHOVEN

(3) *Notice in the ' Wiener Zeitung' of October* 22, 1803

WARNING

Herr Karl Zulehner, an engraver at Mainz, has announced an edition of my complete works for the pianoforte and stringed instruments. I consider it my duty publicly to inform all friends of music that I have nothing whatever to do with this edition. I would never have proceeded to make a collection of my works, an undertaking which in itself I regard as premature, before discussing the matter with the publishers of the individual works and arranging to ensure that accuracy which is lacking in the editions of the various separate compositions. Furthermore I must point out that such an edition of my works, undertaken illegally, can never be complete, inasmuch as several new ones are shortly to appear in Paris; and these Herr Zulehner, who is a French national, may not reprint. On some other occasion I will make a full statement about a collected edition to be prepared under my personal supervision and after a previous strict revision of my works.[2]

LUDWIG VAN BEETHOVEN

(4) *Notice in the ' Wiener Zeitung' of March* 31, 1804

After I, the undersigned, had had inserted in the Wiener Zeitung of January 22, 1803 a notice in which I publicly declared that the edition of my original quintet in C major produced by Herr Mollo had not been published under my

---

[1] Cf. Letter 63.   [2] See Appendix I (6).

supervision and was extremely faulty and useless for the performer, I hereby publicly withdraw that notice to the extent that Herr Mollo & Co. have nothing whatever to do with this edition; and I consider that in order to clear the good name of Herr Mollo & Co. I am in honour bound to inform the esteemed public.[1]

LUDWIG VAN BEETHOVEN

(5) *Notice in the ' Wiener Zeitung' of December* 17, 1808

On Thursday, December 22nd, Ludwig van Beethoven will have the honour of giving a concert in the Imperial and Royal Theater an der Wien. All the items are works of his own composition, are absolutely new and have not yet been heard in public. First half: 1. A symphony entitled: Memories of Country Life, in F major (No. 5).[2] 2. Aria.[3] 3. Hymn, with a Latin text, composed in the style of church music with chorus and solos.[4] 4. Pianoforte concerto with Beethoven as soloist.[5] Second half: 1. Grand symphony in C minor (No. 6).[6] 2. Sacred item with a Latin text, composed in the style of church music, with chorus and solos.[7] 3. Fantasia for pianoforte solo.[8] 4. Pianoforte fantasia, which gradually concludes with the participation of the whole orchestra and finally with the introduction of choruses.[9]

Boxes and reserved seats can be booked in the Krugerstrasse no. 1074, first floor — The performance begins at 6.30 P.M.

[1] Cf. Appendix H (2).
[2] Op. 68. This is the sixth symphony, known as the ' Pastoral '.
[3] Scena and Aria. 'Ah, perfido!' for soprano with orchestral accompaniment, published as Op. 65 by Hoffmeister & Kühnel in July, 1805.
[4] The Gloria of the C major Mass, Op. 86. [5] Op. 58.
[6] Op. 67. This is the fifth symphony.
[7] The Sanctus of the C major Mass, Op. 86. [8] Op. 77. [9] Op. 80.

(6) *Acknowledgment to be inserted in the 'Intelligenzblatt der Wiener Zeitung'* [1]

[Autograph in the Deutsche Staatsbibliothek, Berlin]

[VIENNA, *c. December* 15, 1813]

I consider it my duty to express my thanks to all the esteemed musicians who took part in the concerts given on December 8th and 12th for the benefit of the Imperial Austrian and Royal Bavarian soldiers wounded in the battle of Hanau, for the zeal they displayed for such a noble object. (It was an unusual assembly of eminent virtuosi, all of whom, inspired solely by the thought of being able by means of their gifts to contribute something for the benefit of our Fatherland, disregarding their rank and even occupying the lowest seats, played their part in an altogether excellent performance.) Not only did Herr *Schuppanzigh* lead the first violins and by his ardent and expressive performance sweep the orchestra along with him, but a certain Kapellmeister, *Salieri* by name, did not disdain to give the beat to the drums and cannonades. Herr *Spohr* and Herr *Mayseder*, each an artist worthy of being the leader, were content to play in the second and third places; and Herr Siboni and Herr Giuliani too were in the lowest seats — (The only reason why I conducted the whole concert was because the music had been composed by me. Had it been composed by anyone else, I would just as gladly have taken over the big drum, as Herr Hummel did, since we were all imbued solely with the pure feelings of patriotism and of delight at contributing what we could to those who have sacrificed so much for us.) (At the same time very special thanks should be accorded to Herr Maelzel, inasmuch as he first put forward the idea of giving this concert and subsequently was responsible for the most laborious part of the whole undertaking, which he duly introduced, planned and arranged.) Indeed I must express to him my very special thanks for giving me by this concert which he arranged, the opportunity of seeing in the composition of works written solely for that object of general benefit and presented to him free of charge,

---

[1] Beethoven's acknowledgment was never published.

1437

the fulfilment of an ardent desire which I had long cherished, i.e. the desire to be able to place some important work of mine on the altar of our Fatherland. Since, however, a notice with a list of all the persons who participated on that occasion and of the parts for which they were responsible will shortly appear in print, the public will be able to see for itself with what noble self-sacrifice an assembly of the greatest musicians collaborated for one fine purpose.

LUDWIG VAN BEETHOVEN

(7) *Notice in the ' Wiener Zeitung' of December* 31, 1813

CONCERT

Deferring to the wish of numerous friends of music whom I highly esteem, to hear once more my grand instrumental composition on Wellington's victory at Vittoria, I regard it as a pleasant duty herewith to inform the worthy public that on Sunday, January 2nd, I shall have the honour of producing with the help of the finest musicians in Vienna the said composition enlarged with new vocal numbers and choruses. The performance will take place in the Imperial and Royal Grosser Redoutensaal and will be for my benefit.

Tickets of admission can be obtained daily in the Kohlmarkt at the house of Baron von Haggenmüller [1] in the courtyard to the right on the ground floor, i.e. at the office of Baron von Pasqualati. The tickets cost two gulden V.C. for the stalls, and three gulden V.C. for the gallery.

LUDWIG VAN BEETHOVEN

(8) *Acknowledgment in the ' Wiener Zeitung' of January* 24, 1814

At the concert given by me on January 2nd I had the good fortune to be supported in the performance of my compositions by a large number of the most excellent and distinguished musicians of Vienna and to perceive that my works were being made known to the public in such brilliant

[1] Not identified.

fashion through the efforts of those eminent virtuosi. Even though these musicians may have felt that they rewarded themselves by their zeal for art and by the pleasure they afforded to the public by means of their talents, yet it is my duty to express publicly my warmest thanks for the friendship and ready support they have given me by so doing.

LUDWIG VAN BEETHOVEN

(9) *Notice in the ' Wiener Zeitung' of February* 24, 1814

CONCERT

Encouraged by the generous praise of the honourable public and by the express demand of several eminent lovers of music the undersigned will have the honour to produce next Sunday, February 27th, in the Grosser Redoutensaal his composition on Lord Wellington's victory in the Battle of Vittoria together with a new vocal trio that has not yet been heard. This performance will take place with the co-operation of the most excellent musicians in Vienna. The usual poster will inform the public of the necessary particulars.

LUDWIG VAN BEETHOVEN

(10) *Notice in the ' Wiener Zeitung' of June* 28, 1814

The undersigned, invited to do so by the Herren Artaria & Co., hereby declares that he has handed over the score of his opera Fidelio to the aforesaid firm of engravers who under his supervision will publish it in a complete pianoforte arrangement, as quartets or arranged for wind-instruments. The present musical setting is unquestionably different from any previous one, because hardly any number in it is exactly the same as formerly and more than half the opera is quite new. Scores, solely in authentic copies, together with the text in manuscript, can be obtained from me or from the reviser of the text, H[err] Fr[iedrich] Treitschke, Imperial and Royal Court Theatre Poet. Other copies obtained by illicit means will be seized by legal action.

LUDWIG VAN BEETHOVEN

(11) *Notice in the 'Wiener Zeitung' of July 15, 1814*

BEETHOVEN'S BENEFIT NIGHT

The Directors of the Imperial and Royal Court Theatres have granted to the undersigned a benefit performance of the opera 'Fidelio' composed by him. This performance will take place on Monday, July 18th, in the Court Theatre near the Kärntnertor, and the opera will have, in addition, two new numbers. Boxes and reserved seats can be booked on Saturday and Sunday at the undersigned's rooms in Baron Pasqualati's house on the Mölkerbastei, no. 94, first floor. But keys and tickets must be fetched at the Box Office of the Imperial and Royal Court Theatre, where, moreover, on the day of the performance applicants can obtain any boxes and reserved seats which by that time have not been sold. Those esteemed subscribers who desire to retain their boxes are requested to inform the Box Office of the Imperial and Royal Court Theatre by Sunday morning at latest.

LUDWIG VAN BEETHOVEN

(12) *Declaration and Invitation to Musicians in London*

[Autograph in the Deutsche Staatsbibliothek, Berlin]

VIENNA, *July* 25, 1814

Herr Maelzel, who is at present in London, on his journey thither produced at Munich my Siegessymphonie and Wellingtons Schlacht bei Vittoria, and according to report is also going to give concerts in London with these works, just as he intended to do at Frankfurt as well.[1] This impels me to make a public declaration that I have never nor in any wise handed over or transferred to Herr Maelzel the aforesaid works, that nobody possesses a copy of them and that I sent the only copy which I had made to His Royal Highness the Prince Regent. Therefore Herr Maelzel in producing these works is either deceiving the public, seeing that in accordance with my present statement he does not possess them, or if he pos-

[1] Cf. Letter 485.

1440

sesses them is encroaching on my rights, for he must have obtained them in some illegal way.

But even in the latter eventuality the public will be deceived. For the works entitled Wellingtons Schlacht bei Vittoria and Siegessymphonie which Herr Maelzel is inviting the public to hear, must obviously be false or mutilated compositions, because except for one single part which I lent him for a few days he never received from me any portions of those two works.

This suspicion becomes a certainty when I here add the assurance of certain Viennese composers, whose names I am authorized to make public, if necessary, that Herr Maelzel, when leaving Vienna, told them that he possessed these works and showed them some parts of them which, however, as I have already proved, can only be mutilated and not authentic.

We may ask whether Herr Maelzel is capable of such an infringement of my rights. The answer is provided by the circumstance that he has had himself described as the sole arranger of my concerts given in Vienna for the benefit of soldiers wounded in the war, concerts at which only my works were performed. He has had this announced in the public newspapers and without mentioning my name.

Hence I am asking the London musicians not to tolerate such an infringement of my rights, the rights of their colleague in music, by permitting a performance of the Schlacht bei Vittoria and the Siegessymphonie arranged by Herr Maelzel, and to prevent the London public from being deceived by him in the manner I have described and condemned.

(13) *Notice in the ' Wiener Allgemeine Musikalische Zeitung' of February* 14, 1818

Maelzel's metronome has arrived! The usefulness of his invention will be proved more and more. Moreover, all the composers of Germany, England and France have adopted it. But we have not considered it quite superfluous to voice our conviction and to recommend the metronome as a useful, nay, an indispensable aid to all beginners and pupils, whether in singing or for the pianoforte or any other instrument — By using it they will learn to judge and to apply in the easiest possible way the value of a note, and in the shortest time they will be enabled to perform without difficulty to any accompaniment and without becoming confused. For since the pupil observing the suitable method and directions provided by the teacher, must not in the latter's absence arbitrarily sing or play out of time, by means of the metronome his feeling for time and rhythm will quickly be so guided and corrected that he will soon have no further difficulties to encounter in this respect — We think that we should acclaim this invention of Maelzel's, which indeed is so useful from this point of view also, for it seems that for this particular advantage it has not yet been sufficiently appreciated.

LUDWIG VAN BEETHOVEN
ANTONIO SALIERI

(14) *An Invitation*

[Autograph in a private collection]

[VIENNA, *before April* 22, 1824]

The undersigned herewith most respectfully invites all amateur musicians to support him with their talents at his concert which is to take place on April 22nd in the Theater an der Wien. Those who kindly agree to take part are graciously requested to sign this invitation in their own handwriting.[1]

LUDWIG VAN BEETHOVEN

(15) *Notice in the ' Wiener Zeitschrift für Kunst, Literatur, Theater und Mode' of March 5, 1825*

I consider it my duty to warn the musical public against an entirely misleading pianoforte arrangement for four hands of my latest overture, an arrangement which, moreover, is not faithful to the original score. This arrangement has been

[1] Beethoven's autograph invitation is signed by 16 musicians, including Böhm and Karl Holz, who adds the remark that 'he will turn up'.

published by Trautwein in Berlin under the title 'Festival Overture by Ludwig van Beethoven'.[1] This warning is the more necessary as the pianoforte arrangements for two and four hands made by Herr Carl Czerny, which are absolutely faithful to the score, will shortly appear in the only authentic edition.[2]

LUDWIG VAN BEETHOVEN

[1] Cf. Letter 1343, p. 1165, n. 3.
[2] Cf. Letter 1317, p. 1148, n. 3. Czerny's transcriptions of Op. 124 for two and four hands were published by Schott in April and July, 1825 respectively.

APPENDIX I

MISCELLANEOUS

---

(1) *To the Directors of the Imperial and Royal Theatres in Vienna*

[*MS in the Beethovenhaus, Bonn, H. C. Bodmer collection*] [1]

[VIENNA, *December*, 1807]

WORSHIPFUL DIRECTORS OF THE IMPERIAL AND ROYAL COURT THEATRES! [2]

Admittedly the undersigned may flatter himself that so far during the period of his stay in Vienna he has won a certain amount of favour and appreciation not only from the distinguished aristocracy but also from the rest of the public, and that his works have been given an honourable reception both at home and abroad.

Nevertheless he has had to contend with all kinds of difficulties and as yet he has not been fortunate enough to establish himself here in a position compatible with his desire to live entirely for art, to develop his talents to an even higher degree of perfection, which must be the aim of every true artist, and to secure for an independent future the advantages which hitherto have been merely incidental.

Since on the whole the aim which he has ever pursued in his career has been much less to earn his daily bread than to raise the taste of the public and to let his genius soar to greater heights and even to perfection, the inevitable result has been that the undersigned has sacrificed to the Muse both material profit and his own advantage. Nevertheless works of this kind

---

[1] Written in another hand and signed by Beethoven.

[2] After the resignation of Baron Peter von Braun, who had been in charge of the Court Theatres from 1794 to 1806, a Directorate was formed consisting of the Princes Lobkowitz, Schwarzenberg and Esterházy and the Counts Franz Esterházy, Hieronymus Lodron, Ferdinand Pálffy, Stephan Zichy and Franz Nikolaus Esterházy. This Directorate, whose activities met with little success, was replaced in 1810 by one Director, Joseph Hartl von Luchsenstein, who had been financial adviser to this so-called 'consortium of cavaliers'.

have won him in distant countries a reputation which in several important centres guarantees to him the most favourable reception and a future suited to his talents and his knowledge.

Yet the undersigned must confess that the many years he has spent in Vienna, the favour and appreciation of high and low which he has enjoyed, his desire to see completely fulfilled the expectations which hitherto he has been so fortunate as to awaken and, he ventures to add, the patriotism of a German make his present place of residence more to be valued and desired than any other.

Hence before carrying out his decision to leave his present place of residence which he prefers, he feels compelled to take the hint so kindly given to him by His Excellency the reigning Prince von Lobkowitz, who has informed him that *the Worshipful Directors of the Theatres* would not be averse to engaging the undersigned on suitable conditions for the service of the *theatres* under their management and to securing his further residence by an appropriate *means of livelihood* more favourable to the exercise of his talents.

Since this statement accords perfectly with his wishes, the undersigned now takes the liberty of expressing his readiness to draw up a contract of this nature and of putting forward in seemly fashion the following conditions which the Worshipful Directors might be pleased to accept.

(1) He undertakes and binds himself to compose every year at least one grand opera, the subject to be chosen jointly by the *Worshipful Directors* and the undersigned; and for this he asks a fixed annual income of 2400 gulden as well as all the takings for his benefit at the third performance of each opera.

(2) He undertakes to provide gratis every year a little operetta or a *divertissement, choruses* or occasional compositions, according as the *Worshipful Directors* may demand and require; but he cherishes the hope that the Worshipful Directors will not object to granting him, if necessary, in return for special works of this kind, at least one day a year for a benefit concert to be given in one of the theatres.

If one considers what an expenditure of time and energy the making of an opera demands, inasmuch as it completely excludes every other mental exertion; furthermore, if one bears in mind that in other places where the composer and his family are entitled to a share in the takings at each performance, one single successful work establishes once and for all the whole reputation of a composer; furthermore, if one remembers what little advantage, owing to the unfavourable money currency and the high prices of all commodities, accrues to an artist living in Vienna who, moreover, can easily betake himself to some other country; then the above conditions can certainly not be regarded as exaggerated or excessively grasping.

In any case, however, whether the Worshipful Directors give consideration to and accept the present offer or not, the undersigned adds a request that he be granted a day for a concert in one of the theatrical buildings. For if his offer is accepted the undersigned would be compelled to devote all his time and his powers forthwith to the composition of the opera and could, therefore, not undertake any other work for financial profit. But if his present offer is not accepted, the undersigned, seeing that the concert which he was authorized to give last year never took place on account of several obstacles which happened to arise, would like to regard the immediate fulfilment of last year's promise as the very last token of the great favour he has so far enjoyed. He therefore begs that in the former eventuality he be granted the day of the Annunciation of the Virgin Mary and in the latter eventuality a day during the coming Christmas holidays.[1]

LUDWIG VAN BEETHOVEN

(2) *Draft Scheme for a Musical Constitution* [2]

[Autograph not traced] [3]

[VIENNA, *January*, 1809]

First of all, the King of Westphalia's offer will be set forth —
Beethoven cannot be bound by any obligations for the sake of this income, inasmuch as the chief object of his art, namely, the creation of new works, would thereby suffer.

[1] So far as is known, no reply was sent to Beethoven's petition. But his memorable concert of his own compositions was held on December 22, 1808, in the Theater an der Wien. Cf. Appendix H (5), p. 1436.

[2] According to Nohl II, no. 41, n., this is the title given by Beethoven himself to this autograph draft, evidently written during the negotiations which led to his contract of March 1, 1809, with the Princes Lobkowitz and Kinsky and the Archduke Rudolph.　　　　[3] Taken from *TDR* III, 122.

This remuneration must be assured to Beethoven until he voluntarily renounces it. To share, if possible, the Imperial title in turn — with Salieri and Eybler — the promise from the Court that he will very soon be able to enter its service — with some assistance, if it is feasible — A contract with the theatres, including the conferring of the title of member of a committee of the Directors of the Theatre — a fixed day to be granted perpetually for a concert, even if the Directors are changed, and in the theatre too, in return for which Beethoven would undertake to compose every year a new work for one of the charity concerts, for whichever one it may be considered most useful — or to conduct at two of these concerts — some place at a banker's or the like where Beethoven will draw the income granted to him — The income must also be paid by the heirs.

(3) *To* ?

[Autograph in the Stadtbibliothek, Vienna]

[VIENNA, 1809]

The historical *untruths* which have already appeared several times about me and everything connected with me in the Vienna *Musikzeitung* I must censure abroad. In short, one detects everywhere in this journal *the stinking Wien* — The *Sammler* had a much better and truer review of the symphony in F [1] and the other symphonies than the *Musikzeitung*.

(4) *To the Directors of the National Theatre, Stuttgart*

[MS in the Beethovenhaus, Bonn, H. C. Bodmer collection] [2]

VIENNA, *June* 24, 1814

The undersigned have the honour to offer to the Eminent Directors of the Royal National Theatre the libretto and

---

[1] Probably the sixth symphony, Op. 68.

[2] This letter, written by Treitschke and signed by him and Beethoven, is almost identical with that addressed to the Royal Theatre in Berlin on June 23, 1814, which has been reproduced in all the *Gesamtausgaben*. It was first published in the *Beethoven-Jahrbuch*, 1953/54, p. 38.

score of their opera Fidelio in an accurate and uniquely authentic copy for a fee of 12 gold ducats, to be used for their stage requirements, without, however, any further rights of communication or general and individual notification. This opera was produced a few weeks ago at the Imperial and Royal Court Opera Theatre in Vienna and had the good fortune to evoke more than the usual applause and to fill the house on each occasion. The libretto and the music must not be mistaken for the opera of the same name performed several years ago at the Imperial and Royal Theater an der Wien, of the score of which a few copies were stolen. The whole work has been revised in accordance with altered conceptions and has been rendered more in keeping with theatrical effects; and more than half of it is entirely new.

All the necessary precautions have been taken to safeguard this property. And in any case the Eminent Directors are herewith requested not to pay attention to any other offers but rather to be so kind as to notify the undersigned if any are put forward.

The Eminent Directors are requested to address their reply to the undersigned Friedrich Treitschke.

With best respects we sign ourselves

LUDWIG VAN BEETHOVEN
FRIEDRICH TREITSCHKE
Imperial and Royal Court Theatre Poet.

(5) *To the Imperial and Royal Landrechte, Prague*

[*MS not traced*] [1]

[VIENNA, 1814]

MOST WORSHIPFUL IMPERIAL AND ROYAL LANDRECHTE!

As I was totally unversed in legal matters and believed that all claims against an estate would have to be met, I sent to my legal friend at Prague the contract concluded with His Imperial Highness the Archduke Rudolph, His Excellency Prince von Lobkowitz and His Excellency Prince von Kinsky, by which these noble patrons did guarantee to me an annual sum of 4000 gulden. My persistent reminders to interest him-

---

[1] Taken from Nohl I, 116.

self in this matter and even, I must confess, the reproaches I made to him, accusing him of not having tackled the question properly because the protests he made to the guardianship authorities led to nothing, may have induced him to take legal action on my behalf —

Only he who knows of the great regard I cherished for the late Prince von Kinsky can understand to what extent this step runs counter to my feelings, i.e. my appearing as plaintiff against my benefactor.

In these circumstances I am choosing the shorter path, for I am convinced that the guardianship authorities of the noble princes will be likely not only to value art but also to uphold the actions of the late Prince von Kinsky.

According to the attached contract Supplement A. His Imperial Highness the Archduke Rudolph and Their Excellencies the Princes Lobkowitz and Kinsky joined forces to enable me to draw 4000 gulden until I should enjoy an income of the same amount. And, what is more, in the event of my being prevented by accidents or by reason of old age from exercising my art, these high contracting parties granted me this amount for life ; and in return I undertook not to leave Vienna.

Magnanimous was the promise and so was its fulfilment. For I was never confronted with any difficulty and quietly enjoyed my income until the high and mighty Finance Act came into force — In the case of H.I.H. the Archduke Rudolph this currency alteration made no difference, for I received his usual share in redemption bonds, i.e. bank notes without a fixed scale. For this very reason His Excellency the late Prince von Kinsky readily promised me to arrange to have his share of 1800 gulden paid to me in redemption bonds. As he omitted, however, to transmit the order to his exchequer, difficulties were raised in my case. Although my circumstances are not of the best, yet I would not dare to submit my claim to the Prince's trustees, if men of integrity had not themselves heard the late Prince give this assurance, i.e. that he would pay his contribution in Viennese currency both for the past year and for the current one, as indeed the supplementary documents B., C. and D. of my petition prove. In these circumstances I leave it to the Prince's trustees to judge whether I had not sufficient reason to disregard much sooner a feeling of delicacy and my conviction that I ought to be satisfied with the Prince's consent. Hence the worthy guardian's objection to the witnesses about their not being present when the Prince gave his consent must be regarded as extremely insulting to me. Therefore in order to extricate myself from the truly disagreeable position which has been forced upon me by this lawsuit, I venture to present to the Prince's trustees the offer and the assurance that I am prepared to content myself for the past and for the future with 1800 gulden in Viennese currency; and I flatter myself that they will most graciously take into consideration that I for my part also made no small sacrifice when solely out of regard for these most excellent Princes I chose Vienna as my permanent home at a time when the most advantageous offers were being made to me from abroad.

Hence I request the Imperial and Royal Worshipful Landrechte to present this petition to the trustees of the Prince von Kinsky for their consideration and to be so kind as to inform me of the result.

L. V. BEETHOVEN

(6) *Draft Statement about a Complete Edition of His Works* [1]

[*Autograph in the Beethovenhaus, Bonn*]

[VIENNA, *c.* 1822]

The law-books begin without more ado with a discussion of human rights which nevertheless the executors trample under foot; and in like manner the author commences his statement.

An author has the right to arrange for a revised edition of his works. But since there are so many greedy brain-pickers and lovers of that noble dish, since all kinds of preserves, ragouts and fricassés are made from it, which go to fill the pockets of the pastrycooks, and since the author would

---

[1] During his lifetime Beethoven often expressed his desire for an authentic edition of his collected works to be prepared and supervised by himself; and he even approached various publishers, Breitkopf & Härtel in 1810, Simrock in 1817 and 1820, C. F. Peters in 1822 and Schott in 1825 about this project.

be glad to have as many groschen as are sometimes disbursed for his work, the author is determined to show that the *human brain* cannot be sold either like coffee beans or like any form of cheese which, as everyone knows, must first be produced from *milk, urine* and so forth —

The human brain in itself is not a saleable commodity —

In short, a revised edition of all my works should be announced as a justifiable undertaking, seeing that so many inaccurate and forged editions are wandering about (anarchy) (between ourselves, although we are convinced republicans, yet there is something to be said for the oligarchical aristocracy), seeing that we owe it to the art of music to take stock of the progress of the artist and his art, seeing that each volume of each type of music will be paired with a new work of the same type, seeing that this is merely the notice that a complete edition of my works is being prepared, but that the time of publication of this great undertaking cannot yet be announced and that we are about to arrange for an entirely revised edition of the collected works.

(7) *To Karl Holz*

[*MS in the Beethovenhaus, Bonn, H. C. Bodmer collection*] [1]

VIENNA, *August* 30, 1826

It affords me much pleasure to make the declaration which my friend Karl Holz desires, i.e. that I consider him a suitable person to undertake later on the publication of my biography, on the assumption, of course, that such a work will be required. Further, I am fully confident that he will not hand down to posterity in a garbled form the information which I have given him for that purpose.

LUDWIG VAN BEETHOVEN

[1] Written by Karl Holz and signed by Beethoven. The document was originally written in pencil and then inked over. The second sheet, the third page, of the statement contains Holz's transfer of these rights to Ferdinand Simon Gassner (1798–1851), Director of Music at Karlsruhe, dated Vienna, November 4, 1843. For the wording of this transfer see Schindler, II, p. 326. Meanwhile Wegeler and Ries had published in 1838 their *Biographische Notizen*; and Schindler's first edition of his biography of Beethoven had already appeared in 1840.

(8) *To the Bundesversammlung, Frankfurt am Main* [1]

[*MS in the possession of Frau Margarete Hummel*] [2]

VIENNA, *after March* 8, 1827

The undersigned have joined forces to present to the Supreme Bundesversammlung in all obedience the following petition and their most humble proposal for the abolition of the positively disgraceful pirating of musical works in Germany. They do so in the flattering hope that the Supreme Bundesversammlung will deign to accede to this petition with a view to promoting German musical composition.

Furthermore, as Herr Ludwig van Beethoven, in particular, intends soon to arrange for an edition of his collected works by agreement with several publishers, he puts forward at the same time the request that the Supreme Bundesversammlung will condescend to take note of this and to protect both himself and the rightful publishers of his collected works against the very harmful pirating of them in Germany.

Herr Hummel, the Kapellmeister,[3] who represents the undersigned petitioners, will respectfully await the reply of the Supreme Bundesversammlung.

LUDWIG VAN BEETHOVEN

(9) *To Bernhard Schotts Söhne, Mainz*

[*MS in the Stadtbibliothek, Mainz*] [4]

VIENNA, *March* 20, 1827

DECLARATION

By virtue of this declaration I herewith transfer to the publishing firm Bernhard Schotts Söhne at Mainz the sole

---

[1] After the War of Liberation a Federal Assembly of all the German States and Austria was formed with Frankfurt am Main as its venue. It functioned from 1815 to 1848 and again from 1850 to 1866.

[2] This document was first published with a facsimile in Karl Benyovsky: *J. N. Hummel, der Mensch und Künstler* (Bratislava, 1934), p. 306.

[3] Early in March J. N. Hummel, then Kapellmeister at Weimar, on hearing of Beethoven's serious illness, hastened with his wife to Vienna and visited him on March 8th. According to the owner of the above document the last quill used by Beethoven was kept and treasured by Hummel and is now in her possession.

[4] Written by Schindler and signed by Beethoven, Breuning and Schindler.

ownership and also the sole copyright of my latest quartet in C sharp minor, Opus 131,[1] adding that, as it is their property, they are empowered to publish engraved copies of it both in Paris and at Mainz and also in all centres which the aforesaid publishing firm may consider advisable.

LUDWIG VAN BEETHOVEN

STEPHAN VON BREUNING
Imperial and Royal Court
Councillor,
as witness by request

ANTON SCHINDLER
Director of Music,
as witness by request

[1] Op. 131, which Beethoven dedicated to Baron Joseph von Stutterheim, was published in score by Schott in June, 1827.

INDEX OF PERSONS

*Where there are several entries under one name, the main
biographical note is indicated by* **heavier type**

Bonaparte, Joseph, 508 n. 2
Bonaparte, Louis, **411 n. 1,** 412
Bonoldi Bros., 1025 n. 1
Boosey, Thomas, 994
Botticelli, 1128 n. 6
Bouilly, J. N., 106 n. 1, 107 n. 1
Brahms, 871 n. 3
Brauchle, Joseph Xaver, 223 n. 2, **500,** 507, 518-520, 522-523, 527, 538, 579, 663
Braun, Baron Peter von, 51 n. 3, 107, 148, **149,** 168 n. 5, 353 n. 1, 1444 n. 2
Braun, Baroness Josephine von, **75 n. 1,** 149 n. 2
Braunhofer, Dr. Anton, 385 n. 2, 938, 1095, **1186,** 1195-1197, 1204-1205, 1215 n. 4, 1277-1278
Breitkopf & Härtel, 15 n. 3, 43 n. 7, **52,** 74, 76, 77, 80 n. 7, 83, 84 n. 1, 88, 90 n. 5, 93, 95, 97 n. 4, n. 6, 101, 115, 129, 132, 137, 150, 152, 156, 174 n. 1, 188, 190, 191, 195 n. 1, 211, 215 n. 2, 217, 220, 223 n. 2, 224, 230, 233, 236, 240, 241, 243, 244 n. 1, n. 2, 245, 248, 250, 259, 260, 275, 276, 283, 289, 293, 294, 295, 309, 311 n. 1, 314, 318, 319, 320, 322, 333 n. 4, 334, 336, 353, 359, 366, 372, 378, 381, 382, 383, 387, 388 n. 2, 444 n. 2, 500, 635 n. 5, 899 n. 2, 949 n. 1, 952 n. 1, 956, 973 n. 1, 1041, 1044 n. 6, 1088, 1236 n. 4, 1356 n. 2, 1422, 1427-1428, 1434-1435, 1450
Brentano, Antonia Josepha, *née* Birkenstock, 312, 328, **531,** 557, 568 n. 1, 600-601, 668, 872 n. 3, 931 n. 3, 932, 934, 944 n. 1, 965 n. 4, 983, 1026 n. 3, n. 6, 1064 n. 2, 1078, 1086, 1135 n. 4
Brentano, Bettina, 297 n. 4, 298 n. 1, **312,** 318, 340 n. 3, 531 n. 1, 568 n. 1, 1003, 1355-1359
Brentano, Clemens, **313 n. 3,** 531 n. 1, 568 n. 1
Brentano, Franz, 312 n. 2, 328 n. 2, 531 n. 1, 532, 558, **568,** 600-601, 667, 880 n. 5, 882, 889, 890, 894, 896, 899, 905, 906, 926, 931 n. 3, 932-934, 944-945, 969, 989, 1014, 1015, 1077, 1135 n. 4
Brentano, Maximiliane, 916, **931,** 934
Brentano, Peter, 568 n. 1
Bretzner, Christoph F., 1333 n. 3
Breuning, Christoph von, **61 n. 7,** 68
Breuning, Eleonore von, 5, **9,** 13, 21

n. 1, 27 n. 2, 60, 68, 602 n. 1, 1321-1323, 1333
Breuning, Hofrat E. J. von, 4 n. 3, 9 n. 4, 14 n. 3
Breuning, Gerhard von, 37 n. 1, **113 n. 2,** 118 n. 4, 1250 n. 4, 1313
Breuning, Frau Helene von, **13 n. 2,** 14, 62
Breuning, Johann Philipp von, 14 n. 3
Breuning, Lorenz von, 9 n. 4, **27,** 63 n. 1, 114 n. 1
Breuning, Stephan von, **4,** 37, 59 n. 3, 60, 61, 63 n. 1, 68, 111, 112, 113, 114, 115 n. 1, 147 n. 2, 148 n. 4, 186, 187 n. 2, 197, 198, 229, 270, 297, 315, 373 n. 4, 736, 844 n. 4, 1203, 1250 n. 4, 1265, 1279, 1297, 1307, 1313, 1321, 1329, 1333, 1452-1453
Bridgetower, George P., 90, **91,** 120 n. 5
Bridi, Dr. Antonio Giacomo, 755 n. 2
Bridi, Joseph Anton, **755 n. 2**
Broadwood, James, 755 n. 5
Broadwood, John, 755 n. 5
Broadwood, Thomas, **755,** 764 n. 2, 1145
Brown, John, **1196 n. 1**
Browne-Camus, Count Johann Georg von, 43 n. 6, **57 n. 1,** 76, 88, 95 n. 6, 782, 1411, 1418
Brühl, Count, 1287, 1288 n. 1
Brunsvik, Count Anatol, 117 n. 4, 130 n. 5, 168 n. 1
Brunsvik, Countess A. B. von, 117 n. 4
Brunsvik, Carolina (Charlotte), **118 n. 3,** 121 n. 4, 122, 311 n. 1
Brunsvik, Count Franz, 91 n. 6, 116 n. 4, 118, 167, **168,** 178, 226 n. 3, 233 n. 3, 285, 311 n. 1, 325, 329, 337 n. 2, 342, 343, 370, 408, 422, 420, 445
Brunsvik, Therese, 91 n. 6, 97 n. 5, 117 n. 4, 121 n. 3, 122 n. 3, 168 n. 1, 169, 175, 233 n. 4, 244 n. 2, 285, **311,** 373 n. 4
Bureau des Arts et d'Industrie, 16 n. 1, 59 n. 3, 64 n. 4, 75 n. 1, 76 n. 3, n. 5, 92 n. 4, 95 n. 5, n. 6, 97 n. 5, 106 n. 3, 116 n. 2, n. 3, n. 4, 121 n. 3, 130 n. 4, 135 n. 2, 150 n. 7, 152 n. 4, n. 6, 166 n. 4, n. 6, n. 10, 170, 171, **172,** 173, 189, 230, 263, 298 n. 4, 319, 320, 495 n. 1, 1184 n. 2, 1411 n. 4, 1419 n. 7
Bürger, Elise, **219 n. 4**
Bürger, Gottfried August, 219 n.

CLASSIFIED INDEX OF WORKS

*Unfinished or fragmentary compositions are marked ***
Where there are several entries under one work, the
main note(s) is (are) indicated by **heavier type.**
The year or years quoted as the time of composition
indicate the period when works, which may have been
sketched out several years earlier, were completed. For
instance, some of the bagatelles of Opus 119 may have
been written in 1804.

OPERA

Fidelio, originally *Leonore* (Opus 72, 1804–1805, 1806, 1814), 78 n. 3, 105 n. 4,
107, 131, 141, 142, 147-149, 150, 152, 204 n. 3, 225, 243, 246, 249, 250,
260, 286, 323, 443, 449-450, 454-455, 458, 463-468, 503, 511, 536, 549,
557 n. 3, 606, 618, 680, 1001, 1065, 1208, 1280, 1423

ORATORIO

Christus am Ölberge (Opus 85, 1803), 87 n. 3, 96 n. 5, **116 n. 1**, 133, 138, 150,
152, 225, 243, 246, 249-250, 260, 262, 286, 288, 297, 314, 334, 338-339,
345-346, 354, 357, 371, 380, 413, 422, 484 n. 1, 673 n. 2, 1105, 1178,
1415 n. 1

MASSES

Mass in C (Opus 86, 1807), **174 n. 1**, 175-176, 188-192, 205, 215 n. 2, 230,
234, 243, 246, 249, 260, 286, 297, 298, 309, 314, 340, 360, 378-379, 383,
385-387, 775, 791 n. 2, 899, **1044 n. 2**, 1176, 1193, 1422, 1436
Missa Solemnis in D (Opus 123, 1819–1823), 675 n. 3, 814, 832-833, 857, 872,
880, 916 n. 4, 932-934, 943-945, 963-964, 967-971, 987-990, 995-999,
1002, 1010, 1014-1017, 1020-1023, 1032-1033, 1037, 1039, 1043-1044,
1050-1051, 1057-1068, 1074-1077, 1089, 1092-1093, 1097, 1105-1107,
1111-1115, 1119 n. 1, 1120 n. 3, 1125-1129, 1132, 1134, 1137, 1140, 1154,
1168-1172, 1178, 1181, 1185, 1194-1195, 1209, 1213, 1227-1228, 1264,
1269 n. 3, 1274, 1279, 1335, 1431

CHORAL WORKS WITH ORCHESTRA

Fantasia for pianoforte, chorus and orchestra (Opus 80, 1808), **261 n. 2,** 277,
288, 314, 320-322, 338, 345-346, 1111, 1113-1114, 1436
March with chorus from 'Die Ruinen von Athen', arranged for 'Die Weihe
des Hauses' (Opus 114, 1811), **357 n. 4, 587 n. 5,** 966 n. 3, 973, 1166 n. 1,
1185
'Tremate, empi, tremate', trio for soprano, tenor and bass with orchestral
accompaniment (Opus 116, 1801–1814), **444 n. 3,** 446 n. 1, n. 3, 454,
510 n. 3, 1120 n. 3, 1128, 1130, 1149, 1185, 1208, 1282, 1423
'Der glorreiche Augenblick', cantata for four solo voices, chorus and
orchestra (Opus 136, 1814), **476 n. 4,** 477 n. 7, 479, 511, 606, 841 n. 1,
1208, 1320, 1423
Chorus with orchestra 'Die verbündeten Fürsten' (WoO 95, 1814), **451 n. 5**
'Meeresstille und Glückliche Fahrt', for chorus with orchestral accompaniment (Opus 112, 1814–1815), **524 n. 1,** 606, 941 n. 2, 997 n. 3

CLASSIFIED INDEX OF WORKS

ARIAS

ARIA FOR SOPRANO
Scena and aria, 'Ah perfido' (Opus 65, 1796), **1436 n. 3**
ARIAS FOR BASS
'Prüfung des Küssens' (WoO 89, 1790), 948
'Mit Mädeln sich vertragen' (WoO 90, 1790), 948

SONGS WITH PIANOFORTE ACCOMPANIMENT

'An Laura' (WoO 112, c. 1790), 41 n. 4
'Selbstgespräch' (WoO 114, 1792), 635 n. 5
'Adelaide' (Opus 46, 1795–1796), **41 n. 3**, 492 n. 6, 1061
'Opferlied' (WoO 126, c. 1796), 41 n. 4, **271 n. 1**
'Neue Liebe, neues Leben' (WoO 127, 1798–1799), **1356 n. 3**
Eight songs with pianoforte accompaniment (Opus 52, c. 1792–1803), **1184 n. 2**
'Der Wachtelschlag' (WoO 129, 1803), 95 n. 6
'Ich denke dein', song with six variations for pianoforte duet (WoO 74, 1799–1804), **97 n. 5**, 121 n. 3, 298 n. 4
'Gedenke mein' (WoO 130, 1804), 129 n. 3, 136 n. 4, 138
'An die Hoffnung' (Opus 32, 1805), **130 n. 4**
Arietta 'In questa tomba oscura' (WoO 133, 1807), **194 n. 5**
Six songs with pianoforte accompaniment (Opus 75, 1809), **233 n. 6**, 261 n. 8, **276 n. 3**, 285, 295 n. 2, 296, 298, 380, 383, 1356 n. 2, **1356 n. 3**
Four ariettas and a duet (Opus 82, c. 1796–1809), 192 n. 1, **261 n. 8**, 277, 293, 309, 314, 319, 320 n. 8
'Andenken' (WoO 136, 1809), 41 n. 4, **235 n. 2**, 236, 241 n. 2, 243, 1422
'Lied aus der Ferne' (WoO 137, 1809), **241 n. 2**, 261 n. 8, 262 n. 2, 263 n. 3, 295 n. 2, 298 n. 5, 1422
Three songs with pianoforte accompaniment (Opus 83, 1810), **277 n. 1**, 286, 293, 295 n. 5, 309, 319, 320 n. 8, 334, 355, 360, 366, 380
'An die Geliebte' (WoO 140, 1811), **244 n. 5**
'Des Kriegers Abschied' (WoO 143, 1814), 539 n. 3
'Merkenstein' (WoO 144, 1814), **477 n. 3**, 477 n. 4, 478, **521 n. 1**
'An die Hoffnung' (Opus 94, 1813–1815), 130 n. 4, **335 n. 3**, 346 n. 6, 573 n. 1, 575, 625, 663
'Merkenstein' (Opus 100, 1814–1815), **477 n. 3**, **521 n. 2**, 585 n. 2, 593, 662
'Das Geheimnis' (WoO 145, 1815), 943 n. 2, 979 n. 3
'Ruf vom Berge' (WoO 147, 1816), 707
Song cycle 'An die ferne Geliebte' (Opus 98, 1816), 442 n. 1, **572 n. 3**, **607 n. 2**, 608, 625, 651 n. 4, 652, 663
'Der Mann von Wort' (Opus 99, 1816), **614 n. 1**, 663
'So oder so' (WoO 148, 1817), 943 n. 2, 979 n. 3
'Resignation' (WoO 149, 1817), 979 n. 3
'Abendlied unterm gestirnten Himmel' (WoO 150, 1820), 979 n. 3, 1186 n. 1
Arietta 'Der Kuss' (Opus 128, 1822), **999 n. 3**, 1000, 1110, 1151, 1175, 1181, 1325

MISCELLANEOUS WORKS FOR VOICES

'Nei giorni tuoi felici', duet for soprano and tenor with orchestra (WoO 93, 1802–1803), **1185 n. 3**
'Elegischer Gesang', for four voices with string quartet accompaniment (Opus 118, 1814), 411 n. 2, 948, 1208, 1282, 1342 n. 3
'Germania', song for bass voice with chorus and orchestra for G. F. Treitschke's Singspiel 'Die gute Nachricht' (WoO 94, 1814), **323 n. 1**, **447 n. 1**, 449–452, 454, 456

SYMPHONIES

MISCELLANEOUS WORKS FOR ORCHESTRA

CLASSIFIED INDEX OF WORKS

CONCERTOS FOR PIANOFORTE AND ORCHESTRA

CONCERTOS FOR SOLO INSTRUMENTS AND ORCHESTRA

MISCELLANEOUS WORKS FOR VIOLIN AND ORCHESTRA

Romance for violin with orchestral accompaniment in F (Opus 50, *c.* 1798–1802), **76 n. 5**

Romance for violin with orchestral accompaniment in G (Opus 40, *c.* 1801–1802), **76 n. 5,** 97 n. 3

STRING QUARTETS

Six string quartets in F, G, D, C minor, A, B♭ (Opus 18, 1798–1800), **42 n. 3,** 52 n. 1, 54 n. 5, 62 n. 1, 74, 442 n. 1, **1412 n. 2**

Three string quartets in F, E minor and C, the 'Razumovsky' (Opus 59, 1806), 150 n. 8, **152 n. 4,** 153, 157, 166-169, 172, 1419

String quartet in E♭ (Opus 74, 1809), **233 n. 5,** 244 n. 1, 251, 261, 276, 278, 285-286, 294 n. 3, 296

String quartet in F minor (Opus 95, 1810), **417 n. 2,** 503, 510-511, 557 n. 3, 581, 584, 592-593, 606, 617, 619, 627, 643, 656, 1423

String quartet in E♭ (Opus 127, 1822–1825), xix n. 2, 949, 955, 988, 1065, 1114, 1126 n. 3, 1128, 1132, 1154-1155, 1171, **1173 n. 2,** 1177, 1179-1183, 1187 n. 2, 1192, 1195, 1201, 1214, 1224-1225, 1229, 1235, 1247, 1264, 1270, 1273, 1279, 1286, 1291, 1329-1331

String quartet in A minor (Opus 132, 1825), 1128, 1179, 1181, **1196 n. 3,** 1201, 1205, 1221-1222, 1225-1226, 1230-1231, 1235, **1237 n. 8,** 1240-1242, 1243 n. 4, 1244, 1246-1247, **1251 n. 4,** 1259 n. 6, 1261 n. 4, 1284, 1288, 1432-1433

String quartet in B♭, 'Grosse Fuge' (Opus 133, 1825), 137 n. 1, 1296 n. 1, 1311 n. 1

String quartet in B♭ (Opus 130, 1825–1826), 137 n. 1, 1128, 1179, 1201, 1222, 1226, **1237 n. 8,** 1238, 1240, 1283, 1295 n. 1, 1301 n. 3, 1304, 1319 n. 3, 1320 n. 3

String quartet in C♯ minor (Opus 131, 1825–1826), 464 n. 2, 1182 n. 1, 1240, 1286, 1289-1290, 1295 n. 1, 1312, 1324-1325, 1334, 1340 n. 4, **1453 n. 1**

String quartet in F (Opus 135, 1826), 464 n. 2, 1149 n. 2, **1251 n. 4,** 1283, 1301 n. 4, 1317-1319, 1340 n. 4, 1432

STRING QUINTETS

String quintet in E♭, an arrangement of the octet for wind-instruments, Op. 103 (Opus 4, 1795–1796), **19 n. 1, 1411 n. 2**

String quintet in C (Opus 29, 1800–1801), **43 n. 7, 78 n. 1,** 79 n. 1, n. 2, 137 n. 3, 672 n. 3, 1044 n. 6, 1434

String quintet in C minor, an arrangement of the pianoforte trio in C minor, Op. 1, No. 3 (Opus 104, 1817), **698 n. 1,** 709, 712, 762, 791, 793-796, 805-807, 815, 856

Fugue for string quintet in D (Opus 137, 1817), **726 n. 2**

MISCELLANEOUS CHAMBER MUSIC

Three trios for pianoforte, violin and cello in E♭, G and C minor (Opus 1, *c.* 1792–1794), **16 n. 2,** 23 n. 3, **25 n. 5,** 174 n. 1, 793 n. 1, 1417, 1432

Serenade for flute, violin and viola in D (Opus 25, *c.* 1795–1796), 97 n. 6

Serenade for violin, viola and cello in D (Opus 8, *c.* 1796–1797), 97 n. 6

Quintet for pianoforte and wind-instruments in E♭ (Opus 16, *c.* 1796–1797), **283 n. 2,** 560 n. 4

Duet for viola and cello in E♭ (WoO 32, 1795–1798), 32 n. 2

Three trios for violin, viola and cello in G, D and C minor (Opus 9, *c.* 1796–1798), 18 n. 2, **1411 n. 4,** 1418

PIANOFORTE SONATAS

CLASSIFIED INDEX OF WORKS

Pianoforte sonata in A♭ (Opus 110, 1821–1822), 902, 916, 918, 927, 944 n. 1, 954, 965, 983, 1003 n. 6, 1006, 1021, 1222 n. 4

Pianoforte sonata in C minor (Opus 111, 1821–1822), 902, 916, 927, 942-943, 944 n. 1, 954, 965, 983, **1003 n. 6**, 1006, 1021, 1026, 1031 n. 2, 1034, 1036-1037, 1043, 1045-1048, 1051-1054, 1222 n. 4

PIANOFORTE COMPOSITIONS FOR FOUR HANDS

Eight variations for pianoforte duet in C on a theme composed by Count von Waldstein (WoO 67, 1791–1792), **15 n. 4**, 17 n. 6

Three marches for pianoforte duet in C, E♭ and D (Opus 45, 1802–1803), 174 n. 1, **76 n. 3**, 96

Arrangement by Beethoven of Op. 133 for pianoforte duet (Opus 134, 1826), 1296 n. 1, 1311 n. 1, 1433

PIANOFORTE VARIATIONS

Thirteen variations in A on the arietta 'Es war einmal ein alter Mann' (WoO 66, 1792), **5 n. 1**, 16 n. 3, 19 n. 2

Nine variations in A on 'Quant' è più bello' (WoO 69, 1795), 23 n. 3, **335 n. 1**

Six variations in G on 'Nel cor non più mi sento' (WoO 70, 1795), **335 n. 1**

Twelve variations in A on the Russian dance in Paul Wranitzky's ballet 'Das Waldmädchen' (WoO 71, 1796), 867 n. 1

Ten variations in B♭ on 'La stessa, la stessissima' (WoO 73, 1799), 69 n. 3, 867 n. 1

Seven variations in F on 'Kind, willst du ruhig schlafen' (WoO 75, 1799), **195 n. 2**

Six variations in F (Opus 34, 1802), 69 n. 3, **76 n. 5**, 83 n. 6, 84 n. 1, 89, 96

Fifteen variations in E♭ with a fugue (Opus 35, 1802), **76 n. 5**, 83 n. 6, 84 n. 1, 89, 94 n. 1, n. 2, 96, 436 n. 1

Seven variations in C on 'God save the King' (WoO 78, 1803), **95 n. 5**, 99 n. 3

Five variations in D on 'Rule Britannia' (WoO 79, 1803), **95 n. 5**, 99 n. 3

Six variations in D (Opus 76, 1809), **216 n. 1**, 276, 293 n. 4, 297

Six themes with variations for pianoforte with flute or violin accompaniment ad libitum (Opus 105, 1817–1818), **627 n. 3, 846 n. 2**, 860, 867 n. 1, 888 n. 3, 1430

Six themes with variations for pianoforte with flute or violin accompaniment ad libitum (Opus 107, 1817–1818), **872 n. 2**, 880, 882, 885, 889, 891, 898, 915 n. 2

Thirty-three variations on a waltz by Antonio Diabelli (Opus 120, 1819–1823), 531 n. 1, 608 n. 5, 872 n. 3, 994 n. 1, 962 n. 1, 975, 1025-1026, 1030 n. 3, 1035, 1036, 1042, 1044, 1052-1054, 1064, 1076 n. 1, 1086

MISCELLANEOUS WORKS FOR PIANOFORTE SOLO

Rondo in C (WoO 48, 1783), 5 n. 2

Rondo in A (WoO 49, c. 1783–1784), 5 n. 2

Two preludes for pianoforte or organ (Opus 39, c. 1789–1803), 97 n. 3

Andante in F (WoO 57, 1803–1804), **135 n. 2**, 136

Fantasia in G minor (Opus 77, 1809), 168 n. 1, **233 n. 3**, 261, 276, 285, 1436

Bagatelle in A minor 'Für Elise' (WoO 59, 1810), **272 n. 2**

Polonaise in C (Opus 89, 1814), **492 n. 4**, 539 n. 3

* Short piece for the pianoforte in B minor (WoO 61, 1821), **1195 n. 1**

Eleven bagatelles for pianoforte solo (Opus 119, 1820–1822), 949, 955, 960, 962, 970, 976, 979, 999, 1006, 1008, 1025, 1035, 1048, 1064, 1154, 1160

Six bagatelles for pianoforte solo (Opus 126, 1823–1824), 1110, 1151, 1175, 1181, 1325

Waltz in E♭ (WoO 84, 1824), 1265 n. 1
Waltz in D (WoO 85, 1825), 1265 n. 1
Waltz in E♭ (WoO 86, 1825), 1265 n. 1
Short piece for the pianoforte in G (WoO 62, 1826), **1142 n. 3**

PIANOFORTE AND VIOLIN SONATAS

Three sonatas for pianoforte and violin in D, A and E♭ (Opus 12, *c.* 1797–1798), **36 n. 2**
Sonata for pianoforte and violin in A minor (Opus 23, 1800), 672 n. 3
Sonata for pianoforte and violin in F (Opus 24, 1800–1801), 97 n. 6, 672 n. 3
Sonata for pianoforte and violin in A, the 'Kreutzer' sonata (Opus 47, 1802–1803), 15 n. 1, **91 n. 1**, 92, 119, 120, 135 n. 3, 136 n. 6, 143, 373, 1426
Sonata for pianoforte and violin in G (Opus 96, 1812), **391 n. 5**, 401 n. 2, 510 n. 4, 511, 533-534, 536, 544, 551, 555, 559, 565, 571, 582, 585, 603, 618, 623, 625, 680, 1040, 1423, 1429

MISCELLANEOUS WORKS FOR PIANOFORTE AND SOLO INSTRUMENTS

Twelve variations for pianoforte and violin on 'Se vuol ballare' from Mozart's 'Nozze di Figaro' (WoO 40, 1792–1793), **7 n. 1**, 9 n. 4, 10 n. 2, 13 n. 3, 14 n. 5, 16 n. 5
Rondo for pianoforte and violin in G (WoO 41, 1793–1794), **14 n. 2**
Twelve variations for pianoforte and cello on a theme in Handel's 'Judas Maccabeus' (WoO 45, *c.* 1796), 33 n. 4
Sonata for pianoforte and horn in F (Opus 17, 1800), **49 n. 4**, 149 n. 2, 304
Serenade for pianoforte and flute in D, an arrangement of Op. 25 (Opus 41, *c.* 1802–1803), **97 n. 6**
Nocturne for pianoforte and viola in D, an arrangement of Op. 8 (Opus 42, *c.* 1802–1803), **97 n. 6**
Sonata for pianoforte and cello in A (Opus 69, 1807–1808), **115 n. 1**, 189, 190-193, 195 n. 1, 211, 216-217, 220, 221, 228 n. 1, 234, 236-240, 242, 373, 420-421, 561, 1427
Two sonatas for pianoforte and cello in C and D (Opus 102, 1815), 15 n. 1, 223 n. 2, 482 n. 2, 519-520, 557 n. 3, **575 n. 2**, 578 n. 6, 581, 584, 606, 620, 668, 680-681, 790, 815

MISCELLANEOUS WORKS FOR WIND-INSTRUMENTS ONLY

Octet for wind-instruments in E♭ (Opus 103, 1792), **19 n. 1, 1411 n. 2**
Sextet for wind-instruments in E♭ (Opus 71, *c.* 1796), **241 n. 3**, 242
Variations for two oboes and horn in C on 'Là ci darem' from Mozart's 'Don Giovanni' (WoO 28, 1796–1797), 949, 980, 1025

WORK FOR A MECHANICAL CLOCK

Five pieces for Count Deym's mechanical clock (WoO 33, 1799), 91 n. 6

CANONS

'Ta ta ta', four-part canon (WoO 162, 1812), **427 n. 4**
'Brauchle, Linke', three-part canon (WoO 167, *c.* 1815), **500 n. 1**
'Das Schweigen', 'Das Reden', two canons (WoO 168, 1815–1816), **554 n. 1**
'Ich küsse Sie', two-part canon (WoO 169, 1816), 550 n. 3
'Glück, Glück zum neuen Jahr', three-part canon (WoO 176, 1819), **860 n. 2**
'Hoffman, sei ja kein Hofmann', two-part canon (WoO 180, 1820), **884 n. 2, 1168 n. 2,** 1176, 1181, 1232

Three canons (WoO 181, 1819–1820), **1168 n. 3**
'Sankt Petrus war ein Fels', canon (WoO 175, 1821), 936
'O Tobias!', three-part canon (WoO 182, 1821), **923 n. 2**
'Bester Herr Graf', four-part canon (WoO 183, 1823), 436 n. 1
'Falstafferel', five-part canon (WoO 184, 1823), 1027-1028
'Edel sei der Mensch', six-part canon (WoO 185, 1823), **1033 n. 2**
'Te solo adoro', two-part canon (WoO 186, 1824), 1131
'Schwenke dich', four-part canon (WoO 187, 1824), **1168 n. 2**, 1176, 1181,
    1232
'Doktor, sperrt das Tor', four-part canon (WoO 189, 1825), 1186 n. 1, 1196
'Ich war hier, Doktor', two-part canon (WoO 190, 1825), 1186 n. 1, 1205
'Kühl, nicht lau', three-part canon (WoO 191, 1825), 1245-1246
'Si non per portas', canon (WoO 194, 1825), 1251
'Wir irren allesamt', two-part canon (WoO 198, 1826), **722 n. 1,** 1321

MUSICAL JOKES, QUIPS, MOTTOES AND THEMES

'Baron, Baron, Baron', musical quip (WoO 205^a, c. 1798), 31 n. 3
'Graf, Graf, liebster Schaf', musical joke (WoO 101, 1802), **81**
'Allein, allein, allein', musical quip (WoO 205^b, 1814), 471 n. 2
'O Adjutant', musical quip (WoO 205^c, 1817), 657
'Wo? Wo?', musical quip (WoO 205^d, 1817), 693 n. 1
Theme for variations, 'O Hoffnung' (WoO 200, 1818), **789 n. 3,** 807 n. 2,
    814, 833 n. 3, 848, 867 n. 3
'Ich bin bereit', set to music (WoO 201, 1818), 766-767
'Erfüllung, Erfüllung', set to music (WoO 205^e, 1819), 813
'Scheut euch nicht', set to music (WoO 205^f, c. 1821), 937 n. 2
'Das Schöne zum Guten', set to music (WoO 202, 1823), **708 n. 1**
'Tobias! Paternostergässler', set to music (WoO 205^g, 1824), 1144
'Das Schöne zu dem Guten', set to music (WoO 203, 1825), 1191
'Tobias, Tobias' musical setting (WoO 205^h, 1825), 1189
'Bester Tobias', musical setting (WoO 205^i, 1826), 1314
'Erster aller Tobiasse', musical setting (WoO 205^k, 1826), 1316

INDEX OF WORKS ARRANGED
ACCORDING TO THE KINSKY-HALM
THEMATIC CATALOGUE (1955)

*Unfinished or fragmentary compositions are marked ***
Where there are several entries under one work, the
main note(s) is (are) indicated by **heavier type.**
The year or years quoted as the time of composition
indicate the period when works, which may have been
sketched out several years earlier, were completed. For
instance, some of the bagatelles of Opus 119 may have
been written in 1804.

Opus 1 (Three trios for pianoforte, violin and cello in E♭, G and C minor, *c.* 1792–
 1794), **16 n. 2,** 23 n. 3, **25 n. 5,** 174 n. 1, 793 n. 1, 1417, 1432
Opus 4 (String quintet in E♭, an arrangement of the octet for wind-instruments,
 Op. 103, 1795–1796), **19 n. 1, 1411 n. 2**
Opus 7 (Pianoforte sonata in E♭, *c.* 1796–1797), 69 n. 3
Opus 8 (Serenade for violin, viola and cello in D, *c.* 1796–1797), 97 n. 6
Opus 9 (Three trios for violin, viola and cello in G, D and C minor, *c.* 1796–1798),
 18 n. 2, **1411 n. 4,** 1418
Opus 12 (Three sonatas for pianoforte and violin in D, A and E♭, *c.* 1797–1798),
 36 n. 2
Opus 13 (Pianoforte sonata in C minor, 'Sonate pathétique', *c.* 1798–1799), 23
 n. 3, 708
Opus 14 (Two pianoforte sonatas in E♭ and G, *c.* 1798–1799), **75 n. 1,** 149 n. 2
Opus 15 (Pianoforte concerto in C, *c.* 1795–1798), 43 n. 4, **43 n. 5,** 53, 69 n. 3
Opus 16 (Quintet for pianoforte and wind-instruments in E♭, *c.* 1796–1797), **283
 n. 2,** 560 n. 4
Opus 17 (Sonata for pianoforte and horn in F, 1800), **49 n. 4,** 149 n. 2, 304
Opus 18 (Six string quartets in F, G, D, C minor, A, B♭, 1798–1800), **42 n. 3,** 52
 n. 1, 54 n. 5, 65 n. 1, 74, 442 n. 1, **1412 n. 2**
Opus 19 (Pianoforte concerto in B♭, 1794–1795), **43 n. 4,** 47 n. 8, 50-51, 53, 55-56
Opus 20 (Septet for violin, viola, clarinet, horn, bassoon, cello and double bass in
 E♭, 1799–1800), **43 n. 1,** 43 n. 2, 47 n. 6, 51, 55-56, 66 n. 4, 69, 73 n. 4, 75,
 1412 n. 4, 1434
Opus 21 (Symphony No. 1 in C, 1799–1800), **43 n. 3,** 47 n. 7, 51, 55-56, 1434
Opus 22 (Pianoforte sonata in B♭, 1799–1800), **43 n. 6,** 47 n. 9, 51, 55, 57, 73 n. 3
Opus 23 (Sonata for pianoforte and violin in A minor, 1800), 672 n. 3
Opus 24 (Sonata for pianoforte and violin in F, 1800–1801), 97 n. 6, 672 n. 3
Opus 25 (Serenade for flute, violin and viola in D, *c.* 1795–1796), 97 n. 6
Opus 26 (Pianoforte sonata in A♭, 1800–1801), 23 n. 3
Opus 27, No. 1 (Pianoforte sonata in E♭, 'Sonata quasi una fantasia', 1800–1801),
 140 n. 2
Opus 27, No. 2 (Pianoforte sonata in C♯ minor, 'Sonata quasi una fantasia', 1801),
 67 n. 4, 140 n. 2
Opus 29 (String quintet in C, 1800–1801), **43 n. 7, 78 n. 1,** 79 n. 1, n. 2, 137 n. 3,
 672 n. 3, 1044 n. 6, 1434
Opus 31 (Three pianoforte sonatas in G, D minor and E♭, 1801–1802), **92 n. 2,**
 92 n. 6, n. 7, 93 n. 2, n. 5, 118 n. 1, 700 n. 1

PRINTED BY R. & R. CLARK, LTD., EDINBURGH